Arenas of Power

Arenas of Power

Theodore J. Lowi

Edited and Introduced by
Norman K. Nicholson

Paradigm Publishers
Boulder • London

green
press
INITIATIVE

Paradigm Publishers is committed to preserving ancient forests and natural resources. We elected to print this title on 30% post consumer recycled paper, processed chlorine free. As a result, for this printing, we have saved:

7 Trees (40' tall and 6-8" diameter)
2,642 Gallons of Wastewater
5 million BTU's of Total Energy
339 Pounds of Solid Waste
637 Pounds of Greenhouse Gases

Paradigm Publishers made this paper choice because our printer, Thomson-Shore, Inc., is a member of Green Press Initiative, a nonprofit program dedicated to supporting authors, publishers, and suppliers in their efforts to reduce their use of fiber obtained from endangered forests.

For more information, visit www.greenpressinitiative.org

Environmental impact estimates were made using the Environmental Defense Paper Calculator. For more information visit: www.papercalculator.org.

Copyright © 2009 Paradigm Publishers

Published in the United States by Paradigm Publishers, 3360 Mitchell Lane, Suite E, Boulder, CO 80301 USA.

Paradigm Publishers is the trade name of Birkenkamp & Company, LLC, Dean Birkenkamp, President and Publisher.

Library of Congress Cataloging-in-Publication Data

Lowi, Theodore J.
  Arenas of power / Theodore J. Lowi.
    p. cm.
  ISBN 978-1-59451-330-5 (hardcover : alk. paper)
  1. Policy sciences. 2. Power (Social sciences) 3. United States—Politics and government.
I. Title.
  H97.L68 2008
  303.3—dc22

                                                                    2008015135

Printed and bound in the United States of America on acid-free paper that meets the standards of the American National Standard for Permanence of Paper for Printed Library Materials.

Designed and typeset in Minion by Straight Creek Bookmakers

12 11 10 09 08   1 2 3 4 5

Contents

≈⊛≈

The Biography of Arenas of Power

Pluralism at Yale and in New Haven

For a political scientist, Yale was the place to be in the 1950s. Although the Department of Political Science didn't know it at the time, it was present at the creation of a political theory that could be appropriate for the New Deal era.

There was competition for bragging rights at Columbia University, in the single, imaginative mind of David Truman, which he had labeled "group theory." Truman had unearthed in the late 1940s the virtually forgotten masterpiece of Arthur F. Bentley, *The Process of Government.* As Truman put it in the preface of his book, "My plans for [*The Governmental Process*] grew out of my experience in teaching from Bentley's work." But "group theory" was more method than theory. In Truman's words, "As the title of the present volume suggests, Bentley's 'attempt to fashion a tool' has been the principal benchmark for my thinking." As a consequence, *The Governmental Process* was devoted primarily to empirical validation of the group as the proper unit for a science of politics. Intimations of theory were present, as indicated by his one substantive reference to pluralism in the entire book: "The so-called pluralist school of political philosophers ... in the first quarter of the century were so bent upon discrediting prevailing conceptions of the state, that they frequently overlooked the central significance of their own point of view" (pp. 46–47).

In the early 1950s, there was no consensus at Yale, and Truman's 1951 book hadn't reached New Haven. Robert A. Dahl and Charles E. Lindblom's highly innovative book, *Politics, Economics, and Welfare,* published two years after Truman's, identified four "central sociopolitical processes," of which polyarchy is one, along with price system, hierarchy, and bargaining. Dahl and Lindblom's book was the single thing that drew me away from law into academia. I was fascinated by the rendering of state and government into "techniques of control," a formulation that has never left my mind and has rarely deserted me when in need of characterization of policies in order to determine "what this case is a case of." My choice of Yale was determined not only by reading Dahl and Lindblom but by two great mentors at Michigan State, Joseph

LaPalombara and Glendon Schubert, junior professors who had enough vision in 1952 to 1954 to see Yale as the place to be. And I owe my Yale Falk Fellowship, as well as my career choice, to their support. But pluralism was not yet a part of their vocabulary, or mine, or Yale's. It was hardly referred to in Dahl and Lindblom. Polyarchy was the key to their political process, and only a small portion of their treatment of polyarchy touches on pluralism; they referred to it as "social pluralism," with their proposition that "some degree of social pluralism is a necessary condition for polyarchy" (p. 303). That was hardly a treatment to light a fire under my thinking or, for that matter, anyone else's. (The only other references to the same phenomenon will be found toward the end of the book, pp. 498, 507–508.)

In fact, Dahl's first self-conscious effort as a political theorist did not come forward until 1956, with publication of *A Preface to Democratic Theory*. Late in 1956, while waiting for a table at a New Haven restaurant, I overheard a prominent competitor of Dahl, Willmoore Kendall, say to his companion, "This book makes Dahl the foremost theorist of our day." But it was definitely not a theory of pluralism or of pluralistic democracy. The closest he came to a pluralist theory as such was in his first chapter, "Madisonian Democracy." But pluralism in name or concept does not appear anywhere. He offers Madisonian democracy simply as the first of three democratic models, with the second being "populist" democracy, and the third "polyarchal" democracy. And he refers to the Madisonian model in the first chapter as the "American hybrid," and not pluralism or pluralist democracy.

Dahl's three models were tried out on the students (including me) in the first semester of his 1954–1955 seminar on "politics and policy making," which turned out to be a trial run for his Chicago Walgreen Lectures as well as his book. My best introduction to Madison, which served me well in my teaching and scholarship for years to come, came from Dahl's rendition of how "social pluralism" was a necessary check against tyranny. But it didn't make a pluralist out of Dahl or of me, at least not at that point. The second semester of that formative 1954–1955 seminar was dedicated (by unanimous vote of the members of the seminar) to a community study of the nearby town of Guilford. It had intrigued Dahl and us that the Guilford town meeting had rejected education bond issues in previous years and suddenly reversed itself. Questions of power, and the "scope of power," in Guilford were to become a trial run for his New Haven study and his highly influential *Who Governs?*

Pluralism at Yale did not become the focal point of empirical research and self-conscious theory until Yale in particular and pluralism in general found themselves under siege by a swarm of sociologists, packing weapons of social structure, elitism, and oligarchy, with implications not only for American communities but for the prospects of democracy itself. It started modestly as a purely academic project by sociologists truly interested in "community studies," of which there was a series of careful empirical reports on research carried out all during the postwar period. Nelson Polsby, the most intensive and thorough student of this sociological threat, referred to their point of view as "a 'stratification theory' of community power, since it suggests that the pattern of social stratification in a community is the principal, if not the only, determinant of the pattern of power" (p. 8). Polsby cites several dozen of these studies in Chapter 1 of what was to become his book, concluding with an appeal, prior to his intensive book-length criticism of their conclusions, that "it would be a great pity if disciplinary lines were to harden around the alternative political theories generated by stratification and pluralist presumptions" (p. 12). But that is exactly what happened, and Polsby was a major contributor to that polarization. If Dahl was the Marx of pluralism, Polsby was surely the Lenin, in *Community Power and Political Theory,* his doctoral dissertation, revised for Yale Press in 1963. The pantheon of the Yale pluralist vanguard has been thoroughly inventoried and evaluated in Richard Merelman's *Pluralism at Yale.*[1] By the end of my course work in 1956, I had become a pluralist political scientist. And I took my pluralism with me to New York and Columbia University, as a research associate for my Yale mentor, Herbert Kaufman, and his senior colleague, Wallace Sayre, on what was to become their masterpiece, *Governing New York City.*[2] My hope and their expectation was that I would also get a dissertation out of some of my research for them.

Work for Sayre and Kaufman completed my graduate education and made New York the opportunity of a lifetime. First, it provided an escape from New Haven without having to leave the Yale Ph.D. program. Second and more to the point, New York was an intellectual experience different in the extreme from that of New Haven and most other middle-size U.S. cities where community studies were staged. The difference between New Haven and New York was the difference between a city of the late nineteenth to the middle twentieth century versus a city of the late twentieth and the early twenty-first century. Those of my graduate cohort who remained in New Haven became pluralists and remained pluralists. I virtually commuted between New York and New Haven during the ensuing two years, but the study of New York was changing me in ways that I was yet to recognize.

Book I of Dahl's *Who Governs?* devotes seven short chapters to the history of New Haven, which he characterizes as "From Oligarchy to Pluralism." New Haven was portrayed as a city-state that had not expelled a social elite regime but had adulterated it with party leaders, new bourgeoisie, and "ex-plebes"—into a regime whose leaders drew power *from* politics through the local parties and interest groups involved in one or more policy issues. The political system of New Haven represented all of the social forces, the "sociopolitical processes," the "techniques of allocation," and the "techniques of control" that Dahl and Lindblom had cataloged so thoroughly in *Politics, Economics and Welfare.* New Haven was a pure case of the polyarchy described in their 1953 book as well as the pluralism portrayed in the ensuing chapters of *Who Governs?*

Polsby turned the New Haven case study into a more explicit pluralist theory, and he, accompanied by devastating articles by Raymond Wolfinger, directed the New Haven results against the "stratification theorists"—bold strokes for two young political scientists: The following are examples of some of the older, quite distinguished sociologists, drawn from a Polsby footnote: Floyd Hunter (the principal target), Robert Lynd, W. Lloyd Warner, E. Digby Balzell, Milton Gordon, and C. Wright Mills, whose "community power structure" studies "claim to have found this pattern."[3] The Polsby and Wolfinger critiques of these sociologists are severe and substantively correct but often dip into derision and ridicule. In brief, to the pluralists, the most galling part of "social stratification theory" is, as Polsby put it, that "power is a subsidiary aspect of the community's social structure" (p. 7). On this point I could not agree more—now as well as then—but that point is precisely what threw me out of pluralism altogether, because pluralists share the same fatal flaw: *the assumption that government (the state) is an epiphenomenon of social forces.* The pluralists located those formative social forces in what they call "the political process," to be distinguished from "the social structure."

In contrast, New York was to me more like a modern nation-state. Even in 1957, what struck me were not such pluralist characterizations as the prominence of "the political process" or the "participants who go about getting what the system offers."[4] Quite apart from the multitude of organized participants and the bargaining that produce equilibrium, there is a "power structure" composed of the gigantic, autonomous government itself—a product of history, with a highly differentiated, professionalized, bureaucratized apparatus, around which parties, interest groups, and other participants in the contest—the "sociopolitical process"—circulated and took its shape. New York City was of course very plural, indeed pluralistic, with multiple centers of power. But as a process, this multiplicity was flowing around established agencies, whose permanence very substantially *shaped the process,* rather than the other way around.

By comparison to New Haven, New York, even in the late 1950s, was truly a Hobbesian Leviathan. I quickly incorporated what I had learned from Lasswell with what I had learned from Dahl and Lindblom, especially to appreciate the truth of Mosca's brutally simple dichotomy of state development, from the feudal to the bureaucratic, as picked up by Carl Friedrich with "bureaucracy: the core of modern government." Feudal government—virtually an oxymoron—was one in which law and order were products of wealth and social status, with government the epiphenomenon of that preexisting social structure. The elitist theorists, mainly sociologists with a Marxist theoretical slant, saw "community power structure" precisely as a modern offshoot of feudalism. Their pluralist adversaries, mainly political scientists with an Adam Smith slant, *also* saw government or "the state" as a derivative; but for them it was a "power structure" produced by the repetitions of a more heterogeneous "political process" incorporating all sorts of social pluralism. These two schools of power turned out to be a "unity of opposites," a unity that can be subsumed in three simple, interlocking propositions: (1) process causes policy; (2) the distribution of the stakes, as a percentage of successes and defeats in the process, is a measure of community power; and (3) the scale and pattern of successes give the regime its name: elitist, pluralist, polyarchal, corporatist, or what have you. In all, politics causes policies.

New York, for me, turned their debate on its head—or back on its feet: I found that, in New York, the converse comes closer to the truth: *policy causes politics.* Through the study of New York I had become a statist—unaware, step by step, I was "bringing the state back in." Thirty years later, I thought back on this with greater clarity when I was preparing what was to become my APSA presidential address. Its title conveys accurately the principal argument of the address: "How We Become What We Study." I can now apply that thesis to myself: The 1950s through to 1970 (according to Merelman's account) seems in retrospect to have been an interlude— or a passage, or better yet, a desperate throwback—to democracy in which government *is* politics. We were entering a new republic. In 1979, for the second edition of *The End of Liberalism,* I gave it an appropriate subtitle, *The Second Republic of the United States.* This "new American state," to take a phrase from Stephen Skowronek (Cornell's contribution to Yale's political science department), happened in stages, and political science was adapting accordingly, with appropriate reactions against its advancement.

Still, with at least one foot in New Haven, I knew that I would try to contribute to the "community power" literature. But the dissertation could not, for practical reasons of scale, be a standard community study. My choice was shaped mainly by Lasswell, not from his 1955–1956 seminar but from his pilot study for a series sponsored by the Hoover Institute, *The Comparative Study of Elites*, in 1951. His introductory rationale gave me my own:

> The "leadership" of a society is a criterion of the values by which the society lives. The manner in which the "leadership" is chosen; the breadth of the social base from which it is recruited; the way in which it exercises the decision-making power.... By learning the nature of the elite, we learn much about the nature of the society.[5]

The choice of a recruitment study of the top political patronage in New York was doubly attractive because I could address many of the questions posed by the community studies but could go beyond them by placing their cross-sectional analyses in the historical context of U.S. political development.

I was ready for all of that, and my mentors were all on board. So were my Yale graduate student colleagues, who were familiar with my plan and endorsed its compatibility with Dahl's emerging New Haven study. I had been commuting between New York and New Haven for over a year to attend an informal seminar of dissertation-level graduate students that we had formed to present our prospectuses to each other. But I was not prepared for the surprise that was to come about a year into the writing. I learned later that my surprise is called serendipity, which I picked up from my third (or fourth) reading of Robert Merton's *Social Theory and Social Structure*: "the discovery through chance by a theoretically prepared mind of valid findings which were not sought for ... [and] which becomes the occasion for developing a new theory or for extending an existing theory."[6]

Pluralism at City Hall and in New York

The title of the dissertation and the book, *At the Pleasure of the Mayor,* was inspired by a clause found in many city charters, granting the mayor full discretion over appointments and removals. The population of political elites was the "cabinet level" officials, appointed as commissioners to head the departments stipulated in the city charter. There was no provision for an official mayoral cabinet, but this level remained stable for the sixty years covered by the study. The project had a very simple design. I began in 1898, with the first administration under the charter of the Greater City of New York, which was created by the state-imposed merger of Manhattan (New York County) with Brooklyn (Kings County), the Bronx, Queens, and Staten Island (Richmond County). The coverage ended with the end of the first term of Mayor Robert Wagner in 1958. In all, there were 1,200 appointees (some were of course reappointments) made by twelve mayors. The key personal attributes of each appointee were punched into IBM cards, for manipulation on the now extinct IBM countersorter device.[7] These appointees were indeed a significant part of the New York City political elite, and they would meet the criterion set by Lasswell in his elite recruitment series. Their selections for office were genuine policy decisions because of the attributes they brought with them. Those attributes were thus "exercises [in] decision-making power," and the distribution of politically relevant attributes represents the distribution of community power at large.

The obvious first step, which I took with passionate anticipation, was to run time series on the distribution of those attributes of each appointee that would tell us something about the mayor and the relation of each mayor to his successor. (No female mayors.) And, predictably, the very first attribute I traced out on the countersorter device was "party recruitment"; that is, the proportion of mayoral appointees who had held important party positions prior to appointment. Examples would include assembly district leaders, county committee members, elected representatives and candidates for elective office, legal counsel, major contributors, and prominent advisers.

Figure I.1 gives the history of party recruitment. The actual trend line is more saw-toothed, reflecting the two Republican-Fusion mayors John Purroy Mitchel (1913–1917) and Fiorello LaGuardia (1933–1945), but their reform efforts only slightly accelerated the secular pattern, which dropped from 92 percent[8] of all commissioners recruited from the party down to 45 percent at the end of Wagner's first term. This secular decline confirmed my expectation, based in part on general reading of New York political history plus interviews of old but still-living New York political hands. But I also expected such a pattern because I was still a pluralist, and I got a great deal of mileage out of its confirmation. If I had stopped simply with this, my book could well have been titled "From Oligarchy to Pluralism," a successful case study of Book I of Dahl's *Who Governs?* In plain and simple language, during the latter half of the nineteenth century into the first decade of the twentieth century, the party system—in particular, the majority party, the "machine"—held a "monopoly of access to government and to policy." But the decline "toward oligarchy" was easy to see by the onset of World War I

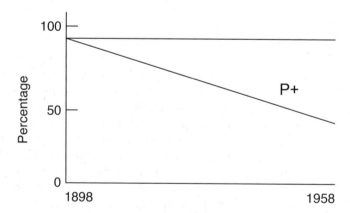

Figure I.1 Party Recruitment of the Top Patronage in New York City, 1898–1958 (percentage of party-recruited [P+] commissioners of the total at the cabinet level)

and had dropped undeniably toward pluralistic competition by the 1950s, with literally the end of the traditional machine by 1958.[9]

Party remained an important factor, but it was no longer *the* factor through which the social elites and the burgeoning economic elites had to work for access to city government. Albeit the most important party was by the 1950s one of the many "contestants for the stakes." And that showed up spectacularly well in my recruitment data: increasing numbers of appointees drawn from prominence in economic groups, professional groups, civic groups, religious and ethnic organizations, and from the city bureaucracies themselves, that is, top career civil servants. These appointees were indeed a representation of "multiple centers of power."

If I had stopped there, I would still have had a dissertation worth publishing. Moreover, I would have established a place for myself in *Pluralism at Yale* rather than ending up as an outsider, or, as the historian of pluralism at Yale defined me, a "resistor."[10]

I did stay with pluralism long enough to explore its causes in my dissertation, drawing from a rich literature. Parties declined as immigrant groups became integrated, moved up the social scale, and were no longer captured constituents. Another explanation was the merger of the Greater City itself, increasing difficulties with Albany and the significantly increased relevance of Washington. Another factor was the growth of corporations that were less and less needful of city government access. But it was inevitable that I would ask one more question that would put me beyond pluralism, beyond the role of "Yale Resistor," and into another orbit altogether.

From Pluralism to the Plural Forms of Pluralism

My minor subject in graduate school was public administration and public law, to which I had been drawn as an undergraduate by Glendon Schubert. I pursued this at Yale through Herbert Kaufman and James Fesler, and I had the good fortune of access to Wallace Sayre, David Truman, and Richard Neustadt at Columbia, who were so cordial despite my interloper status there. I was intensely aware that I was not only dealing with New York City as a political system but was dealing with the public administration dimension, because the appointees I studied were commissioners heading administrative departments and agencies, and each was accountable at the summit of rather large hierarchies, each as a single head or as a member of a multimember commission. My questions followed: What if I controlled for agency? With just a simple sort of the IBM cards, how different would the pattern on Figure I.1 be if I introduced the possibility of variation according to something about the world of public administration? That is, could some substantive jurisdictional or policy factor make any difference in the distribution of recruitment characteristics, or was I to remain in the realm of "multiple power centers" or "the interplay of group forces ending in equilibrium"?[11]

The step I took was "through the looking glass," into the world of agencies. And the language of that world required distinctions between and among agencies, beginning with a simple distinction between line agencies and staff agencies. I drew on terms from military usage, where line agencies deal with the enemy, while staff (overhead) agencies serve the line agencies. In like fashion, civilian line agencies deal with the public, and overhead agencies (such as budget, personnel, purchasing, planning) serve the line agencies. Public administration would also prefer to distinguish within line agencies according to a conventional distinction between service and welfare agencies versus regulatory (which I called regulation and property protection) agencies. A fourth category I called "input" agencies, which incorporate property taxing and assessment agencies. These four categories, being quite conventional, were safe and were endorsed readily by my faculty consultants.[12]

Figure I.2 provides only two trend lines because three of the four categories—the two line agencies and the overhead categories—produced almost identical profiles. Thus, for simplicity, I squashed them into one trend line, with the input category alone in the second trend line. The result was, then and since then, the most remarkably clean and clear pattern that I have ever encountered in the empirical experience of social science. No need for "tests of significance." Reflection on the quantitative consistency of the difference between the two trend lines over the entire sixty-year period was akin to Keats "on first looking into Chapman's Homer." The best case in point is LaGuardia, the crusading reform mayor who served longer than any other mayor in New York history. As a matter of principle, his appointments were made strictly on a nonparty basis; very often LaGuardia would disqualify a party leader even if he possessed the appropriate technical qualifications to a very high degree.[13] Yet, in the input agencies, LaGuardia made straight, Republican Party–recruited appointments. Thus, while the parties were losing their grip dramatically on most governmental agencies, they were holding fast to party monopoly in this one category of agencies.

Dramatic findings such as these require elaborate explanation, and the explanation has to be in terms of the classification scheme. That is to say, since the appointees were sorted according to the function of their agency, the explanation should be in the same terms: public administration and the public policy giving each agency its mission. This was the beginning of a forty-five-year stretch of political analysis and political theory grounded in policy and policy categorization.

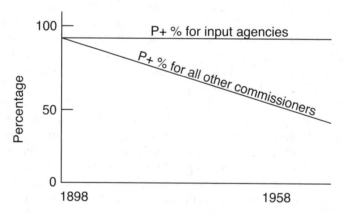

Figure I.2 **Party Recruitment of the Top Patronage in New York City, 1898–1958 (percentage of party-recruited [P+] commissioners, comparing heads of input agencies with heads of all other agencies)**

My approach was reinforced by the distribution of many of the other appointee characteristics. For example, the percentage of those with some training for office (which I defined as "job-oriented skills") increased throughout each administration. But the appointees with job-oriented skills in regulatory departments tended to be from the professions, as indicated by prominence in professional groups, while equally qualified appointees to posts in welfare and service departments tended significantly to come from movement upward within the bureaucracy of the department over which the appointee was appointed commissioner. Another interesting example is length of service (survival) in the job. Taking just the line agencies, tenure was about the same in regulatory and in welfare/service departments; but *re*appointment by a succeeding mayor was significantly higher for the latter than the former. This strongly supports the argument that it is immensely more difficult for regulatory commissioners to establish supportive relations with their clientele, while welfare and service commissioners, if they survive at all, tend to be kept on in a nonpartisan or nonfactional manner by the next mayor.

Over and over again, the distribution of important attributes varied according to the type of department. And at this point I began to find increasingly useful another of Lasswell's formulations: "arenas of power." *Arena* is for politics as *market* is for economics. In the real world there is no "pure market" just as there is no "pure power arena." Each concept is a mind game (like a pure vacuum in physics) in which *homo economicus* is treated as committed to the maximization of wealth over all of the values; so is *homo politicus* seeking political power over all other values.[14] However, my formulation is not for the entire field of politics. There is not one single "arena of power"; *there is a different arena, field of play, process, and power structure in each of the departmental categories.* I found myself having to reject the practice of political scientists to speak of "*the* political process" and "*the* power structure," as though there were only one of each for a whole political system. I also rejected the tendency of political scientists to choose a particular explanatory argument (or theory) for each and every kind of political phenomenon. Such an ad hoc explanation for each phenomenon or discovery may look very strong and may be very suggestive, but when causal factors are cumulated, on the assumption they belong to the same level of analysis, they can take on 300 percent, 400 percent, or more, of explanatory power. For example, congressional voting explained by psychological or rational choice factors, Appropriations Committee decisions by sociological factors, or Education Committee behavior by ideological factors may meet a "goodness of fit" standard, but these explanations cannot travel very far. Some attention has to be given to maintenance of a single level of analysis.

Consequently, my work led me to seek closure around a single level of analysis that was at or near the very core of politics. Although my own limited experience may have led me to the policy dimension and to variables constructed accordingly, I have stuck with this principle for forty-five years. As this idea matured, and as my confidence strengthened, I moved from policy in general to an insistence that *if policy determines the mission of each working unit of the state, the mission would be the key determinant of most of the relationships in politics.* Somewhere along the way, it came down to the single proposition, "policy causes politics." This is not a reduction down to a single causal explanation. But it is a reduction down to a four-causal explanation—one for each arena. It is a single level of analysis (policy or mission) in which there would have to be not one but four separate and distinct, logically related political arenas and four separate and distinguishable, logically related political processes. Indeed, four separate states-within-the-state.

Leaving Community Power and New York City

As I began to incorporate these ideas into my urban politics course at Cornell, I began to wonder whether my formulation would hold up outside the city. Despite my lowly status, I managed to get Social Science Research Council (SSRC) financing to take the project to Washington. JFK, the revival of positive government, and "the joy of politics" had drawn almost all of my Yale cohort from urban to national politics, institutions, and policies. Capitol Hill and Brookings were infested with political scientists. But I had my own personal reasons as well.

My four public administration categories were too narrowly empirical. "Regulatory" was a conventional designation whose boundaries and referents were well established and fully explored, especially by the public law and "business and government" specialists. "Welfare and services" was also well enough understood among New York City watchers to provide consensus on what departments should be included in such a category. But Sayre gave me a more connotative rationale: The welfare and service departments were responsible for programs that pitted "the money providers" against the "service demanders," which turned out to be a genteel way of saying "redistributive policies" and "class politics."

All of this meant that to move up from local to national would require moving upward toward a higher level of abstraction. And that required incorporation of another discipline altogether, *jurisprudence.* Each law (or policy) has a descriptive, empirical reality that must come from a plain, straightforward reading of the statute.[15] But this would have to be translated into a language of intent and a language of coercion. This is where the Dahl and Lindblom of 1953 became so valuable, by giving me the idea of "techniques of control." Every law (policy from here on)[16] seeks to shape some aspect of the future; it must identify the category of persons and conduct to be included (jurisdiction), and it must provide some method or procedure for implementation. Any policy that is weak in either of these standards is lacking in legal integrity and creates a problem of interpretation for citizens and for analysts like me.

This was probably my biggest and irreversible step away from pluralism at Yale. One of the many valuable insights from Dahl was his warning in studying power to ask the very simple question, "power for what?" Another formulation was Lasswell's "scope of power." As early as our 1955 Guilford study, Dahl's advice was to take into account the "issue area" that was the focus of our Guilford case study. But something was missing. "Issue area" was just too empirical, and it provided no closure. Any good definition of a concept must supply what the concept *is* and what the concept *is not.* Consequently, "issue area" gives no clue to *what the case is a case of.* In fact, if researchers and theorists stuck to "issues" as the unit of observation and analysis, they would create a *hyper*pluralistic tsunami from which we would never escape.

I took my project to Washington, but not to replicate my New York recruitment study or to interview key political players for their knowledge of who holds power on what issues. I hardly needed to be in Washington at all, because I spent most of my days in the Brookings library reading statutes. I did learn a lot about Congress and policymaking from my numerous colleagues who had also been drawn from a local to a national venue. Many were on the Hill, and I was ensconced at Brookings, a safe distance away. Most prominent in my memory were Nelson Polsby, Aaron Wildavsky, Raymond Wolfinger, George LaNoue (still finishing his dissertation at Yale), Randall Ripley and Kent Jennings (Brookings staffers), Hugh Douglas Price, and a host of other researchers who were not living in Washington but were passing through with additional information. Most memorable of these were Ralph Huitt and Warren Miller. Some combination of these worthy souls would meet occasionally for lunch in one of the Capitol dining rooms, and in two hours I would pick up virtually all the anecdotes and impressions they had garnered during their days and weeks of interviews between our meals. They were in effect my team of researchers. Meanwhile, I was plodding along in the U.S. Code, mainly reading organic statutes (as amended) that created a particular department or agency and gave it its mission, its powers, its jurisdiction. And I concentrated heavily on agriculture—not because it was first in the alphabet but because there had been so many excellent books and articles on "the politics of agriculture."

While I was suffering through the legal language, I encountered a book whose weaknesses and strengths would bring Arenas of Power truly into focus: Bauer, Pool, and Dexter's *American Business and Public Policy*. It was brought to my attention by Polsby; his enthusiastic recommendation of this book made it essential reading, because Polsby rarely praised a book he didn't write. It was a case study of international trade policy between 1953 and 1962. But it was the most thorough case study of public policymaking in the literature, coupling intense on-site coverage of decisionmakers in Congress with the workings of interest groups (the "old lobby") and mass campaigning (the "new lobby"). What was especially attractive to me was that the authors, by their own account, started out as pluralists (without using the term), expecting a rich context of well-organized interest groups competing for influence on this particular "issue area" in Congress. But they ended up as significant and compelling dissenters or resistors. They were struck by how much time group leaders actually spent just to develop and articulate a single voice for their group. As one admiring reviewer put it, "After a rather intensive study of the politics of U.S. trade policy [Bauer, Pool, and Dexter] concluded that interest groups were remarkable only in their ineffectiveness." Yet, the author continued, "Theodore Lowi argues that the intensive case study developed by [Bauer, Pool, and Dexter] could only be understood in a theoretical framework which they don't provide. Lowi does." Bauer, Pool, and Dexter tried to explain their surprising results with an argument that a "complex psychological mechanism" is at work, a concept related to "cue-taking."[17]

My critique was published in a lengthy book review essay, in which I laid out my first general design and an initial theory of Arenas of Power. First I embraced the findings that so surprised Bauer, Pool, and Dexter; but I then tried to demonstrate that a psychological theory is a departure from politics—an entirely unconnected, huge jump into another level of analysis altogether. Second, I tried to demonstrate that if they had fully examined the substance of the policies in traditional tariff legislation and then compared that to the substance of the policy in the 1959 legislation, they might have found as I did that the unexpected political process could be readily explained by the fundamental difference in the substance of the policies. Traditional trade policy was "distributive policy" as I called it then, which I later renamed "patronage policy" as a synonym but more self-explanatory. The later policy was moving toward regulatory policy, to replace policymaking as a residuum of bargaining among individual elites with legislative rules to control and stabilize trade at the sector level. I was becoming more clear and confident with my perverse, axiomatic argument that "policy causes politics."[18]

Having moved my policy categories to a slightly higher level of abstraction, with regulatory policy and distributive (patronage) policy, a jurisprudential logic between them enabled me to develop some kind of policy scheme with a third type, redistributive policy. This was attractive to me because of the point I had learned from Sayre, that these policies pit "service demanders" against "money providers." But these policies are not called redistributive because they actually redistribute wealth. My policy categories had to be a priori, not dependent upon reasoning backward from impacts that a policy may or may not have on the environment. "Redistributive" is not the perfect concept here because it sets off an immediate response as to the character of impact. It is redistributive for me because the "technique of control" in such legislation works through "the system" by broadly manipulating categories of people, through marginal changes in the value of money, the level of tax liability, and so on. A more accurate title for the third category would probably be "categoric" policy or "meta"-policy or "system manipulation" policy because redistributive policy seeks to influence conduct not one individual at a time but by altering the environment of conduct.[19]

My review of the international trade case gave me the bridge to the national level that I needed, while confirming my confidence that political analysis must begin with jurisprudence. And agriculture proved fortuitous for several reasons. First, I discovered policies should be read and analyzed comparatively, through clusters of statutes. (Students of politics using a case study method usually focus with very close attention on the policy at issue but do not read multiples of policies along with it to get a comparative view.) Out of this came another great moment of serendipity: There is no such thing as "agriculture policy." There is a subject matter called agriculture policies, and there are, by name, agriculture policies by the dozens, distinguishable by the kind of crop, the kind of market, and the culture of the average participant. But, other than subject matter, "agriculture policy" is heterogeneous, very plural. Some agriculture policies are regulatory. One of the largest and most expensive regulatory policies in our history is agricultural land-use regulation, to determine ceilings on how many acres of farmland can be used for wheat or corn or some other "surplus commodity," in order to stabilize prices at a level deemed beneficial to the farmers. Other agriculture policies are distributive (patronage), providing direct grants, goods, education, and other services to all farmers who can make the appropriate claim. And there are agriculture policies that are redistributive policies, those designating a category of farm and farmer poverty that, as a category, is given a favorable tilt (a form of affirmative action) with loans and other special privileges to those who fall into a category of serious need. It was with this simple inventory and classification that I could easily explain why the two leading works in "the politics of agriculture" were so at odds with each other.[20]

The *World Politics* piece put me in the middle, perhaps the forefront, of a new embrace of public policy—not only as "the policy-making process" or policy advocacy, but for its own sake, to be evaluated normatively for its meaning, as an opening to the evaluation of democratic government and the prospect of equity. Surely the move was brought on by the explosive growth of national public initiatives in the Kennedy and Johnson administrations. All of their policies or "programs" (clusters of policies) were a long-delayed completion of the "Roosevelt Revolution." And, given my own ideological leanings, I embraced the Democratic 1960s, approving the goals of virtually every Kennedy-Johnson initiative. But something else happened to me on the way, just from reading the statutes, which by then had extended beyond agriculture. Or, as an outsider, maybe I just couldn't be part of any movement, whether it was pluralism, or the Democratic party bandwagon, or liberalism itself. While reading statutes, I became slowly aware of two things beyond my search for types of policy.

First, I noted that most of the pluralism in the so-called politics of agriculture was a product of the policies, not the other way around. For example, the largest regulatory program in U.S. history still bearing the title of Agricultural Adjustment Act not only regulated how many acres of land each farmer could put into cultivation of certain "surplus products," but also provided *by law* a decentralized procedure of decisionmaking in which farmers and their associated agriculture interest groups were invited (quite explicitly) "to participate in the decisionmaking process." Then another large set of distributive policies, such as the 4-H programs or soil conservation, provided *by law* that private groups would be invited to participate in policymaking, and many of those very groups had been sponsored and fostered by the U.S. government. The most illustrious example is the Farm Bureau Federation, which was conceived at Cornell University and chartered in the very halls of the Department of Agriculture in Washington. Pluralism itself was a matter of policy, not a natural, spontaneous "group politics." That was not the pluralism at Yale or New Haven. It was more like the corporatism of prewar Italy.

Second, another feature that cut through all categories of policy in agriculture was the poor quality of statutory drafting. Each provision was open-ended, imposing few if any standards or guidelines on the agency responsible for implementation, thus leaving to the agency the ultimate policy decision. The apologists for these programs called this delegation of legislative power "filling up the details." I called these statutes "policy without law." Later I called the practice *legiscide,* and my concern for the rule of law and for liberalism itself took me on the highly normative detour away from the more empirical Arenas of Power. I was certain that these two paths would end up in parallel directions; nevertheless it was a major detour. Even as I was pursuing Arenas of Power with the joy of discovery, I was writing critiques of pluralism that had become (or always had been) too much like European corporatism—a state-sponsored version of pluralism. Even while writing the 1964 *World Politics* piece, I published one in a general periodical, "How Farmers Get What They Want."[21] These empirical thoughts about corporatism led me to think more broadly about liberalism itself, my own homegrown belief system that had been activated and sharpened by the shame of segregation in my hometown, which I fictionalized in my writing as Iron City.[22]

The detour was longer than expected. Jim Rosenau, who had read my *World Politics* piece, challenged me in 1966 to expand on it for a conference he was organizing on "the domestic sources of foreign policy." Arenas of Power was present in the argument, but actually subordinated to my concern for liberalism, as indicated by the summation of my argument, "making democracy safe for the world," an appeal that came back to haunt me not only for its applicability to Vietnam but also Iraq. This too became a chapter in *The End of Liberalism.*

By this time, I had begun to realize that I was committing political theory—in the spirit of "if Dahl can do it, so can I." For a while, I was tabbed as a political theorist, which is not necessarily a title of honor. But it was an exciting ride because the attack on pluralism had become a major movement within the student Left, whose leaders inducted me as a charter member of the Caucus for a New Political Science. The article that had put me squarely in that realm was "The Public Philosophy: Interest-Group Liberalism," which got still more mileage by its publication in the *American Political Science Review (APSR).* "Interest-group liberalism" quickly became a household word in the political science vocabulary, and from then on it was my fate to be reviewed by card-carrying political theorists—mainly from the Right. In any event, the *APSR* article was intended to be the end of my normative trek.

Evidence of my intent to get off the normative theory detour can be located in several citations of Arenas of Power as "forthcoming." This is why Arenas of Power earned the reputation as "the best known unpublished book in political science." The clinching evidence of my commitment came in 1966, in my prospectus for the application for a Guggenheim Fellowship. It was strictly and explicitly devoted to Arenas of Power. I went to Paris for the year, following the famous writers who wrote their great novel there. But in the end, Arenas of Power became *The End of Liberalism.*[23]

Realizing Arenas

Another challenging invitation came from Walter Dean Burnham in 1965, which produced a paper of great importance to me but also turned an acquaintance with Dean Burnham into a long and productive friendship. His invitation was wide open: to contribute something on the development of the party system, what came to be called American Political Development (APD). I chose to look in particular at the "golden age" of U.S. democracy, the Jacksonian period during which parties were accepted and recognized as essential to U.S. democracy and, in retrospect, when parties, through the overthrow of King Caucus, gave the president, through the invention of nominating conventions, a political base outside of and independent of Congress.

Given my growing commitment to a policy orientation (and my reading of Merton), I found myself asking about the function or functions parties performed in our system. What was original and for me most exciting was my answer, that the principal function of party was "constituent." It is a word I learned from France and their use of a "constituent assembly" to provide themselves with a new constitution. Constituent and constitution are virtually synonymous, both capable of being defined as referring to the makeup or composition of a thing. And this resolved for me the problem of how to distinguish U.S. political parties from the Westminster and European models of political parties. The old world parties are "responsible parties," programmatic parties, parties that are elected on policy or ideological agendas and proceed to discipline their members in order to adopt their "programme." U.S. parties are notoriously *non*-programmatic, irresponsible parties; but what is a positive, substantive rendering of that? Our parties "agree on what to disagree about." They command the "rules of the game." They control the procedures. They set the agenda. They make the legislature work. They organize and administer the transfer of power. They are policy brokers, not policymakers. "Constituent" was perfect for all this: Constituent was to me a second-order function much like the "overhead" agency functions I'd experienced in New York City. Constituent functions include distributions and restraints of power, rather than the substantive use of power. This argument for the constituent function was embraced by the conference participants, and became one of the chapters in a book that gave all of us a tremendous boost in our visibility; and the book has stayed in print for decades. Looking back on it, I see this book as one of the leading moments in the rise and success of APD.[24]

However, because of my fixation on the nonrelation or second-order relation of party to public policy, I failed to perceive the *policy* significance of "the constituent function," despite the fact that it was such a small step to *constituent policy*. There is no *tion* word for it, as there were for the other three categories—regulation, distribution, redistribution—indicating process, or state of becoming. I could have remained consistent with "constitution policy," but that had too many other connotations in the United States. Procedural rules in Congress, changes in the jurisdiction of the court, electoral and redistricting laws, establishing and expanding or attracting overhead functions, granting line-item veto to the president: all of these are constituent policies, concerning the makeup, the appropriation, and the division of powers. Parties are prominent in these matters, and decisions of this sort are policy decisions, including the overhead functions.

I did not come onto this until four years later, and it hit me like a ton of bricks. First, it was a new appreciation of the function of party and it enabled me to bring party into the discourse of policy. But of far greater importance, a fourth category of policy *closed the logic of my scheme*, giving me a system of public policy and a method of characterizing and reasoning in comparisons of policies *within a logical structure*. And, at last, the four categories taken together met the two requirements of logical classification: (1) *the categories must be mutually exclusive*; and (2) *together they must exhaust the possibilities*.

To initiate the logic, there had to be an element of circularity, because I already had discovered empirically the four categories without need of a logic. In other words, it was necessary to *deduce* the results I already had. But as the analysis got under way, it worked both ways. Empirical experience required categorization in order to compare. But to provide a logic for it, I had to have something paradigmatic that gave reason to experience. Once I had four categories I could see how each helped define the others by enabling me to state what each category was and what each category was *not*.

This kind of comparison led me back to the one fundamental characteristic that all policies share. And it is the one characteristic we liberals fear above all and yet tend to neglect or denigrate in our policy analyses: coercion. That was the central paradigmatic concept.

Government in the Western state tradition—at least since Hobbes and Locke—has been defined in terms of coercion. The social contract was for them a transaction in which the state agrees to protect the property rights of individuals in return for their consent to be governed in all other respects. And most every social scientist is fixed on Max Weber's definition of the state as "a human community that (successfully) claims the *monopoly of the legitimate use of physical force* within a given territory" (emphasis in the original). But if we stopped at that, we'd have little mileage and a lot of libertarian ideology. All it took to escape the definitional trap was to ask "what kinds of coercion are there?" My four categories were an appropriate answer, but without rationale.

At this point, it was necessary to create my own jurisprudence. First, I was confident that the classic form of government coercion is to establish rules of conduct, to impose those rules as obligations on individuals, and to back those rules by sanctions designed to get maximum observance. Thus, as I put it, some government coercion "works through" constraints on individual conduct. Once I had that in mind, I looked for its opposite, which I found in the economists' dichotomy of *micro/macro*. The *macro* side of that dichotomy required that there be a form of coercion that works at the level of the collectivity, or, as I put it, policies that "work through" the *environment of conduct* by manipulating some aspect of it. Occasionally I use "system" as a synonym, but that is more a matter of poetic license.

That dichotomy is a reasonable slice into reality, and it enlightens any argument about the use of government coercion. But dichotomies have minimal value on their own, because they do not encapsulate enough experience or logic. They aid in comparison, but only along one dimension, as in designation or description. But a dichotomy begins to take on great intellectual power when it is joined as an axis in combination of another axis in the delineation of a bounded space. My second dichotomy, concerned with some other aspect of coercion, gives logic, depth, and closure to the concept of government coercion. My second dichotomy was a common sense choice, the "likelihood of coercion" by government—high versus low probability. This is of course a most relevant dimension of coercion, and it enabled me to provide my first logical, paradigmatic method of categorizing and charactering all public policies. Taking these two dimensions as axes and "cross-tabulating" them creates four *property spaces*. And, within the logic of classification, these four categories produced by the cross-tabulation satisfy the requirements of classification, that the categories are (1) mutually exclusive, and (2) exhaustive.[25] However, there was all along a problem with "likelihood of coercion" because it is post hoc, requiring judgment based on knowledge of actual experience and impact. I held to it through a few lectures and publications but with growing awareness that it lacked jurisprudential value and encouraged circular reasoning. At this point, my scheme and I were saved by H.L.A. Hart.

Hart had upset the legal world by his objection to John Austin's classical definition of law as "the key to the science of jurisprudence." For Austin, said Hart, law is "criminal in form," setting a rule that imposes an obligation, and backing that rule by a sanction, usually some kind of punishment.[26] But Hart goes on against Austin to insist that Austin's law, criminal in form, "is not the only law, in spite of appearances to the contrary" (p. 24). Let me cut through Hart's many complexities to say that he opposed Austin's simple construct with a second category of law:

> But there are important classes of law where [application of the criminal form] altogether fails, since they perform a quite different social function. Legal rules defining the ways in which valid contracts or wills or marriages are made do not require persons to act in certain ways whether they wish to or not. Such laws do not impose duties or obligations. Instead, they provide individuals with *facilities* for realizing their wishes. (p. 27)

Thus, Hart insists, it would be "grotesque" to "reduce [law] to a single form" (p. 40), and he provides rules of two types. They are a simple dichotomy: *Primary* rules "impose duties"; *secondary* rules "confer powers, public or private" (p. 79). Note well that Hart's dichotomy is a priori; that is, we can know and classify a law or rule on the face of its provisions, not having to wait for the life of a policy to classify it.

Realization of a genuine logical scheme of policies was an enormous personal landmark in my life. Nearly fifteen years had passed since my work in New York City and the dissertation; and *The End of Liberalism* had overshadowed my life's true work, *Arenas*, because arenas had become my thoughtway, a mind game that drove not only my policy inquiries but virtually every other aspect of political institutions and processes that I confronted far beyond *Arenas*, in my teaching and in my tremendous involvement in textbook writing. A better balance with undergraduate teaching along with graduate teaching and scholarship was a factor in my return to Cornell from Chicago.

However, advancement of scholarly life outside the university also continued to beckon, and with the advancement of professional visibility came invitations, challenges, and dares to "apply the scheme." Several of my responses to those challenges will be found in ensuing chapters. I will hold myself to one example here, with apologies for some repetition in the later chapters. I selected it here as a case in point precisely because it is an application in a real life situation that was actually not a direct response to a challenge but was one from within myself, for use as a way of making federalism more dynamic in my classes, my texts on American government, and in my writing for lectures abroad and papers on globalization, eurofederalism, and corporatism, mainly under the auspices of the International Political Science Association.

The case in point is U.S. federalism, when I came to look at it afresh, with functional eyes. After some considerable surveying of the annual session laws of the U.S. Congress from the early and late decades of the nineteenth century, I found, without any fudging, an almost perfect map of the Arenas of Power scheme within the federalist framework. Table I.1 portrays the principal policy outputs of each level of government in the U.S. federal system. The list of policy items in Column 1 is much shorter than that of Column 2, which is a reflection of the virtually unanimous attitude of the framers that most of the governing should be done by the states. Although the national government appears smaller as a consequence, it is more important to recognize that national government was functionally specialized. Except for a few constituent policies (treaties with France and England, creating the courts, setting up departments), every legislative output at the federal level was distributive (patronage) policy. And that remained true for well over a century. Even the four-year Civil War, with its moratorium on the Constitution

Table I.1 The Traditional Federal System: Specialization of Functions Among the Three Levels of Government, c. 1800–1933

National Government Policies (Domestic)	State Government Policies	Local Government Policies
Internal improvements	Property laws (including slavery)	Adaptation of state laws to local conditions (variances)
Postal services subsidies (mainly to shipping)	Estate and inheritance laws	Public works
Tariffs	Commerce laws (ownership and exchange)	Contracts for public works
Public lands disposal	Banking and credit laws	Licensing of public accommodations
Patents	Labor and union laws	Assessable improvements
Currency	Insurance laws	Basic public services
	Family laws	
	Morals laws	
	Public health and quarantine laws	
	Education laws	
	General penal laws	
	Public works laws (including eminent domain)	
	Construction codes	
	Land-use laws	
	Water and mineral resources laws	
	Judiciary and criminal procedure laws	
	Electoral laws (including political parties)	
	Local government laws	
	Civil service laws	
	Occupations and professions laws	

Note: This table will be referred to throughout the book.

and its strong central government, did not alter the specialization of function. In sum, the national government is a major exception to the development orientation of APD. In other words, the national government of the United States did not change in any appreciable way between roughly 1800 and 1933. The exceptions that any good constitutional historian can bring up are so few that they confirm the rule. Equally clear is the distinctiveness of the state government level. The single trait common to all of the items in Column 2 is regulation; in other words, our states were specialized as "regulatory states." Column 2 also demonstrates that Americans were quite heavily regulated, and were accustomed to being regulated by government, long before the national government took on major numbers of regulatory policies after 1933. It was only then that the institutions and practices of the national government changed in any appreciable way from what it had been up until 1933. This is all very neat, but it is also quite realistic: *U.S. constitutional, governmental, and political history was formed by its pattern of policy outputs: distributive, regulatory, redistributive, and constituent.* And my career has been shaped accordingly.

—*Theodore J. Lowi*
2008

Part I

Arenas of Power

The Model

The development of Theodore Lowi's core conceptual framework, "Arenas of Power," has stretched from his early work on the politics of New York City in the late 1950s to the present. It has been used to explain historical changes in U.S. politics from the eighteenth to the twenty-first century and provides important insights into the process of political and institutional change. It has been applied to a broad spectrum of issue areas, including population policy, agriculture, tariffs, and the social movements of the latter half of the twentieth century. As such it provides a way to analyze political behavior and political structure independently from the vagaries of the issues of the day. The framework has brought together diverse scholarship on the politics of public administration, Congress, interest groups, federalism, political parties, and mass movements—tracing the impact of policy choices across these various institutional settings and demonstrating consistent consequences of policy choices.

Lowi's approach starts with two simple observations about public policymaking that focus on decisions about how public power is applied. Lowi's first conceptual contribution is that the analysis of public policy should focus on the choices about how to apply the power of the state and not primarily on what substantive goals the state should pursue. Building consensus in support of a public goal is, of course, an important part of the political process; but it remains rhetorical until a coalition is formed supporting a specific policy that directs the application of state power toward that goal. A description of a public problem, combined with an expression of concern and an appropriation of funds, does not constitute policy, Lowi argues. Legitimate coercion is the defining characteristic of the state, and public policy is made when some public authority indicates its intent to influence conduct by the use of positive or negative sanctions. It is the choice of sanctions and the choice of institutional mechanisms for applying them, combined with the specified intent, that constitute policymaking. As Lowi tells us, *a policy is a rule formulated by some governmental authority expressing an intention to influence the behavior of citizens, individually or collectively, by use of positive and negative sanctions.*

Policy analysis, then, is not about issues but about the ways in which the power of the state is made manifest. In early versions of his approach, Lowi argues that issues, the customary focus of policy analysis, are ephemeral and have no systematic or predictable impact on the political process. Issues must be categorized: What is each issue a case of? The substance of issue politics, he asserts, is data rich but theory poor and offers no theoretical insights for policy analysis, however important their goals, incentives, political mobilization capacity, and social-economic impact might be. In contrast, the application of public power through public agencies promises to reveal systematic variations in recruitment, political process, power structure, and even corruption across issue areas. Thus, a predictive political science might be built from a model rooted in the application of state power.

A second conceptual contribution of Lowi's work is bound up in the contention that policies create politics. Policy proposals about how to use public power in pursuit of public goals will, Lowi argues, largely determine in which arena the political battle will be engaged. The arena will, in turn, determine the institutional rules of combat and the access of various interests to the policy process. Ultimately, policy choices about the use of public power will determine the relationship of the citizen to the state, elite recruitment, and the structure of the state bureaucracy. *Policy choices are an independent variable in the political process.*

There is a strong assumption of rationality in this model. As such, readers may find many interesting links to the institutional economics literature. Political interests, like economic utility schedules, are driven by social and economic circumstances, values, and perceived opportunities. But political behavior is driven or structured by the institutional requirements of using different types of state power. Those who wish to wield state power will learn, over time, to adapt behavior to the institutional requirements. Political actors will attempt, when possible, to choose policies that optimize the use of their political assets, reduce their transaction costs, and effect desired changes in citizen behavior efficiently. The four types of policy identified—regulatory, distributive, redistributive, and constituent—represent the most basic choices for using the power of the state. (Lowi used different versions of the terms in different articles, so both "constituent" and "constitutive" are referred to in the following chapters.) This assumption of rationality, as in economics, greatly simplifies the analysis by eliminating the need to address individual motivation, values, and perception. This simplification is justified to the extent that the four policy types do, in fact, constrain behavior in the same way that the market constrains economic choices.

If the choice of policy drives both political process and institutional structure, it is analytically necessary to establish the policy type before examining either the process of making the policy choice or the mechanisms for executing the policy. This led Lowi to focus on the enabling (organic) legislation as the policy choice. There are two dimensions of choice, and when dichotomized and cross-tabulated, they produce four logically related property spaces. The categorization is based on simple principles of jurisprudence. If government is defined as legal coercion, the next question is: What kinds of coercion are there?

For the first dimension, Lowi made a conventional choice, one that most political scientists would appreciate: *the likelihood of coercion*—immediate or remote (see Table

2.1). This was dropped after trying the scheme in classes and the publication of a couple of articles, because the distinction between immediate and remote, thought intuitively satisfying, was too likely to depend upon post hoc considerations. The categorization had to be a priori and therefore had to reside in jurisprudence. Lowi chose H.L.A. Hart's emphasis on the nature of rules, in particular the necessary distinction between "primary" rules and "secondary" rules. In Hart's *The Concept of Law,* the classic understanding in law is a rule that imposes obligations backed by sanctions. But there is a second type of rule, he argues, one that confers powers or facilities.

The second dimension was inspired by the distinction in economics between the *micro* and the *macro* level. Jurisprudentially, the "level" has a quite different function, dichotomizing the universe of rules into rules that work on or through *individual* conduct (*micro*) and rules that work on or through the *environment* of conduct (*macro*).

From this cross-tabulation, the four types of policy are derived, and the resultant categories are deemed to be mutually exclusive and exhaustive: distributive, regulatory, redistributive, and constituent. Beyond that, each of these is a separate "arena of power," containing quite different patterns of politics and "power structure." The dynamic is less strictly causal, tending toward the Darwinian: each arena is an environment that is hospitable to some characteristics of politics and inhospitable to others.

The four-cell table that became the flagship of the enterprise was slower to come, as Lowi reports in his Introduction, and will be referred to in the sequence of chapters. In the New York study there were four categories, but they were not logically formulated; they were simply four conventional, empirical categories that were ubiquitous in mainstream public administration. And the first piece on national policy (Chapter 1) employed only three categories, because they were sufficient for the critique of "power structure" through use of the available case studies of policymaking. The possibility (and need) for a closed logical approach to all policies and power structures was not yet in the cards or in his head. Empiricism without a logical scheme was enough.

It seems remarkable that by 1961, Lowi's model was enjoying such visibility with so little of it published. His dissertation, based on recruitment for the top management positions in New York City, won the American Political Science Association's prize for the best dissertation in the field of state and local government, but when it was published in 1964 as *At the Pleasure of the Mayor,* its attraction seemed to have been his effort to tie the distribution of political characteristics to "the functions of the state" (whether local, state, or national government). The door from policy to politics was opened by his explanation of the decline of the party monopoly of access to government by the rise and specialization of governmental functions rather than by sociological factors (such as "the coming of age" of immigrants) or political factors (such as interest groups, progressivism, etc.). The "type of policy" seemed to account for most if not all the differences in the distribution of political characteristics.

Lowi's autobiographical introduction here, "The Biography of Arenas of Power," incorporates a lecture given at the University of Illinois in 1970, and published in 1971 in Oliver Walter's collection, *Political Scientists at Work.* However, almost forty years had rendered his first account somewhat passé; thus he has updated it for this book.

Chapter 1 in this volume is titled, "American Business, Public Policy, Case Studies, and Political Theory." This chapter was the beginning of the succession of efforts to establish Arenas of Power. It firmly established the Lowi model within the debates over political theory in the 1950s and 1960s. Also, it introduces the reader of this volume to the methodological issues associated with policy analysis—in this instance, the use of case studies. Finally, it firmly establishes the model as a tool for illuminating a particular policy area—tariff policy—in comparison and potential comparison with case studies of other types of policy.

Chapter 2, "Four Systems of Policy, Politics, and Choice," was the first formal introduction of Arenas of Power, as it would remain, despite numerous amendments, for the ensuing years. As reported above, the vertical axis on Table 2.1 (likelihood of coercion) was replaced with Hart's jurisprudential dichotomy (primary/secondary rule), but that enriched the scheme without altering the logic. Most importantly, the model becomes fully a priori in regard to the matters inside the box. The items at the margins outside the box were meant to suggest the political tendencies most likely to prevail. Lowi was simply following the lead of the Lasswellian "hypothesis-schema": "not formulation of established laws,... they are intended to serve the function of directing the search,... a 'speculative model,' which is useful in calling attention to deviations" (pp. xxii–xxiii).

The Lowi model does much to establish the boundaries of elite theory and pluralist theory and in the process strengthens both by establishing the limits of their applicability. Beyond that, the four arenas of power define the functions of the state and, through that, the parameters of political activity.

His theoretical contribution lies in the insights his model provides into the predictable institutional consequences of the policy choices made to move the pursuit of public goods into one or another of the four arenas. In all arenas of conventional politics—legislative, administrative, judicial, and civil society—the choice of policy mechanisms imposes predictable constraints on the outcome of public action and is not simply derivative from either the electoral process or the configuration of interest groups.

—*Norman K. Nicholson*

Suggested Reading

H.L.A. Hart, *The Concept of Law* (New York: Oxford, 1961), esp. Chapters 3 and 4.

Robert Spitzer, *The Presidency and Public Policy: The Four Arenas of Presidential Power* (Tuscaloosa: University of Alabama Press, 1983), Chapter 2.

Samuel Beer, "Modernization of American Federalism," *Publius*, Fall 1973.

Robert A. Dahl and Charles E. Lindblom, *Politics, Economics and Welfare* (New York: Harper and Brothers, 1953), esp. Chapter 4.

H. H. Gerth and C. Wright Mills, *From Max Weber: Essays in Sociology* (New York: Oxford University Press, 1946), Chapter 8.

Oliver Walter, ed., *Political Scientists at Work* (Belmont, CA: Duxbury Press, 1971).

Harold Lasswell and Abraham Kaplan, *Power and Society: A Framework for Political Inquiry* (New Haven: Yale University Press, 1950).

CHAPTER 1

꧁꧂

American Business, Public Policy,
Case Studies, and Political Theory

Case studies of the policy-making process constitute one of the more important methods of political science analysis. Beginning with Schattschneider, Herring, and others in the 1930s, case studies have been conducted on a great variety of decisions. They have varied in subject matter and format, in scope and rigor, but they form a distinguishable body of literature which continues to grow year by year. The most recent addition, a book-length study by Raymond Bauer and his associates, stands with Robert A. Dahl's prize-winning *Who Governs?* (New Haven, 1961) as the best yet to appear. With its publication a new level of sophistication has been reached. The standards of research its authors have set will indeed be difficult to uphold in the future. *American Business and Public Policy* is an analysis of political relationships within the context of a single, well-defined issue—foreign trade. It is an analysis of business attitudes, strategies, communications, and, through these, business relationships in politics. The analysis makes use of the best behavioral research techniques without losing sight of the rich context of policies, traditions, and institutions. Thus, it does not, in Dahl's words, exchange relevance for rigor; rather it is standing proof that the two—relevance and rigor—are not mutually exclusive goals.

But what do all the case studies, including *American Business and Public Policy*, add up to? As a result of these case materials, how much farther along the road of political theory are we? What questions have the authors of these studies raised, and what nonobvious hypotheses and generalizations about "who rules and why" would we have lacked without them?[1] Because of what it does, what it implies and what it does not do, *American Business and Public Policy* provides a proper occasion for asking these questions and for attempting once again to formulate theories that will convert the discrete facts of the case studies into elements that can be assessed, weighed, and cumulated. But, first, what theories have we now, and how does this significant new study relate to them?

Existing Notions: The Nontheories of Power in America

It was inevitable that some general notions about power and public policy would develop out of the case study literature. Together, these notions form what is variously called the group theory, the pressure group, or the pluralist model of the democratic political system (a model recently also applied to nondemocratic systems). No theory or approach has ever come closer to defining and unifying the field of political science than pluralism, perhaps because it fitted so nicely both the outlook of revered *Federalist Paper 10* and the observables of the New Deal. Group theory provided a rationale for the weakness of parties and the electoral process. It provided an appropriate defense for the particular programs pursued by the New Deal and successive administrations. And, more importantly, it seemed to provide an instant explanation, in more or less generalizable terms, of the politics of each decision. Analysis requires simply an inventory of the group participants and their strategies, usually in chronological form—for, after all, politics is a process. Each group participant is a datum, and power is attributed in terms of inferred patterns of advantage and indulgence in the final decision. The extremists have treated government ("formal institutions") as a tabula rasa, with policy as the residue of the "interplay of forces" measurable as a "parallelogram." More sophisticated analysts avoided the government-as-blank-key approach by treating officials as simply other units in the group process, where congressman and bureaucrat were brokers but with their own interests and resources. In group theory, all resources are treated as equivalent and interchangeable. And all the varieties of interaction among groups and between groups and officials are also treated as equivalent, to such an extent that only one term is employed for all forms of political interaction: the coalition. Coalitions, so the argument goes, form around "shared attitudes" and are extended by expansion of the stakes of the controversy. Two types of strategies comprise the dynamics of the process: internal and external. The first refers to the problem of cohesion in the midst of overlapping memberships; cohesion is a determinant of full use of group resources. The second refers to expansion of the coalition and the strategy of its use. Large coalitions beat small coalitions.

System equilibrium (of unquestionably high-priority value to pluralists) is maintained by the requirement of majority-size coalitions, which are extremely difficult to create but which must be created virtually from scratch for each issue. Thus, power is highly decentralized, fluid, and situational. There is no single elite, but a "multicentered" system in which the centers exist in a conflict-and-bargaining relation to each other.

As an argument that the group must be the major unit of analysis, pluralism excites little controversy. But controversy is unavoidable insofar as the pluralist model implies a theory of power or power distribution. Most importantly, the pluralist model has, until recently, failed to take into account the general economic *and* political structure within which the group process takes place.[2] On this basis, the leading type of critique of the pluralist model is a set of explicit propositions about power structure and elites. The typical answer to pluralism is a straightforward Marxian assumption that there is a one-for-one relation between socioeconomic status and power over public decisions. Perhaps the more sophisticated version is a combination Marx-Weber approach which specifies the particular status bases most closely related to power—i.e., the major "orders" of society (*ständen*) in our day are the military, the industrial, and the political hierarchies.

This is no place to enter into an elaborate critique of either of these approaches or of the pluralist approach itself. Suffice it to say that while the pluralist model has failed to take the abiding, institutional factors sufficiently into account, the "social stratification" and "power elite" schools wrongly assume a simple relation between status and power. Both of these latter schools mistake the resources of power for power itself, and escape analytic and empirical problems by the route of definition.[3] There is no denying, however, that the social stratification or power elite approaches can explain certain important outcomes in a more intuitively satisfactory manner than the pluralist model precisely because each emphasizes that, while coalition-forming may be universal, not all coalitions are equivalent. For certain types of issues (without accepting Mills's argument that these are all the "key" issues), it seems clear that decisions are made by high public and private "officials" in virtually a public opinion and interest group opinion vacuum. One does not have to go all the way with Mills and insist that behind all apparent conflict there is an elite whose members all agree on specific major policy goals as well as long-range aims. But the pluralist is equally unwise who refuses to recognize that "command post" positions in all orders of society are highly legitimate, and that the recruitment and grooming of these institutional leaders make possible a reduction in the number of basic conflicts among them, and equally possible (1) many stable and abiding agreements on policy; (2) accommodation to conflict by more formal, hierarchical means ("through channels") than coalition politics; and (3) settlement of conflict by more informal means (i.e., among gentlemen, without debates and votes) that maintain the leaders' legitimacy and stability.

There is still a third approach to power and policy-making, no less important than the others, which has not been self-consciously employed since its creation in 1935 because it was mistakenly taken as a case of pluralism. I refer to E. E. Schattschneider's conclusions in *Politics, Pressures and the Tariff* (New York 1935). Schattschneider observed a multiplicity of groups in a decentralized and bargaining arena, but the nature of relations among participants was not in the strictest sense pluralistic. The pluralist model stresses conflict and conflict resolution through bargaining among groups and coalitions organized around shared interests. The elitists stress conflict *reduction* among formal officeholders in a much more restricted, centralized, and stable arena. What Schattschneider saw was neither, but contained elements of both. His political arena was decentralized and multicentered, but relationships among participants were based upon "mutual noninterference" among uncommon interests. The "power structure" was stabilized toward the "command posts" (in this case, the House Ways and Means Committee), not because the officials were above pressure groups, but because the pattern of access led to supportive relations between pressure groups and officials. What may appear to one observer as evidence of a power elite appears to another as decentralized pluralism (to such an extent, indeed, that Schattschneider is often credited with an important share in the founding of pluralist political analysis). Schattschneider's masterful case study actually reveals neither. At one point he concludes: "A policy that is so hospitable and catholic as the protective tariff disorganizes the opposition."[4] In many important cases completely unrelated to the tariff and much more recent than 1930, we can find plenty of evidence to support this third or fourth[5] approach to a "theory" of power and policy-making. But as a general theory Schattschneider's conclusions would be no more satisfactory than any one approach identified earlier.

The main trouble with all these approaches is that they do not generate related propositions that can be tested by research and experience. Moreover, the findings of studies based upon any one of them are not cumulative. Finally, in the absence of logical relations between the "theory" and the propositions, the "theory" becomes self-directing and self-supportive. This is why I have employed the term "theory" only with grave reservations and quotation marks.

The pluralist approach has generated case study after case study that "proves" the model with findings directed by the approach itself. Issues are chosen for research because conflict made them public; group influence is found because in public conflict groups participate whether they are influential or not. Group influence can be attributed because groups so often share in the *definition* of the issue and have taken positions that are more or less directly congruent with the outcomes. An indulged group was influential, and a deprived group was uninfluential; but that leaves no room for group *irrelevancy*.

The elitist approach is no less without a means of self-assessment. If power distributions are defined as "inherently hierarchical,"[6] then a case of coalition politics either represents nonexhaustive research or concerns an issue that is not fundamental and so only involves the "middle levels of power."[7] One need not look for theoretical weaknesses in Schattschneider's approach because his interpretation was mistakenly thrown in with the pluralists. This is most unfortunate, because if the differences between Schattschneider's discoveries (especially his insights into a different *type* of coalition) and those of later case writers had been recognized, a more sophisticated kind of ordered pluralism might have resulted. This is coming close to the approach I will presently propose.

The controversies among the approaches to policy analysis, as well as the logical and empirical weaknesses I have identified, have engendered some of the best empirical work to be found in the literature. But since most of this work is based on the local community, only a collateral attack can be mounted from these findings against assumptions and propositions concerning national power. Only similarly careful and systematic studies of national political processes will lead to a balanced and well-founded attack and to a more productive approach to theory. The first step is certainly *American Business and Public Policy*. While the authors do not offer an adequate theoretical alternative to established approaches, their findings, either explicitly or by implication, are worthy of review in any effort to build such a theory.

American Business and Public Policy starts out as a study of "the flow of communications to and within groups involved in the foreign policy decision-making process" (p. 5). But while this is carried through for every type of participant and phase in the process, the authors are in a position to deal as well with the substance of the communications, perceptions of them by the recipients, and, therefore, with some of the vital aspects of influence. They have looked into the little black box of political relationships among all the influence-seekers which the pluralists say contains the reality of influence and the elitists say doesn't really exist anyhow. What they have found severely tests the assumptions of both schools of thought. Without significant adjustments, the pluralist framework (called by the authors the "pressure group model") will be able to encompass a great many of their propositions and findings only with extreme difficulty. For example:

(1) There is no one-for-one nexus between the policies at stake and interest group activation (chap. 9). Protectionists were more highly activated than antiprotectionists.

(2) The two "sides" of the controversy never met in a face-to-face conflict with a settlement by compromise. In large part, the basis of the protectionist coalition was a series of interests in individual tariff items, in a relation of "uncommon interest" rather than of "tangential interest." The basis of the antiprotectionist position was *general* opposition in line "with the ideology of the times" (pp. 15ff. and 209). The outcome depended not upon compromise between the two sides in Congress but upon whose *definition of the situation* prevailed.

If tariff is an instrument of foreign policy and general regulation for international purposes, the antiprotectionists win; if the traditional definition of tariff as an aid to 100,000 individual firms prevails, then the protectionists win.[8]

(3) Cohesion was found to be *directly* (not inversely) related to overlapping membership (pp. 333 and 338). Most of the well-organized "associations" were so heterogeneous on the tariff question that they took no stand at all (pp. 334–38). Those groups that were at all cohesive maintained their cohesion "by use of multiple group memberships for purposes which might produce conflict within a single given group" (p. 332).[9]

(4) Despite the strong saliency of the trade issues to many groups, little in the way of direct attempts to influence policy-makers could be found. Most group activity "involved interaction with people on the same side." "Scholars have assumed that interest groups had clear interests, of which they were aware. A number of the campaigns we have described show clearly that a pressure group's function is frequently to define the interest of its partisans" (p. 398).[10]

(5) Massive activity, expenditure, and influence by monolithic interest groups appeared to constitute an image that opposing groups create of each other rather than the reality of pressure practices (Part IV, esp. chap. 28).

(6) Most congressmen were found to have their own independent ideologies and interests and tended to read constituency support into their mail rather than to reflect the messages from the outside. Messages from constituents and groups are so numerous and conflicting that congressmen have a maximum-choice situation. And, groups were found to hold fairly strictly to the rule of contacting only those congressmen already known to agree with the group's aims. The predominant group role was found by the authors to be as "service bureaus."[11]

(7) Congress displayed no capacity for, nor did congressmen display any desire for, retaining the power of tariff and trade decision-making (esp. pp. 35, 37–38, 197, and 455–456).

But for every single problem that the tariff decisions of a decade pose for the pluralist model, they pose several for the elitist or the stratification approaches:

(1) There was never, throughout the entire modern history of tariff and foreign trade, any evidence that the top military played a role of any sort. This is true despite the fact that the effectiveness of military aid and military installations abroad was deeply influenced by the economic health of the recipient countries. The Millsian complex of military-industrial intimacy would make military participation in foreign trade decisions all the more probable.

(2) Only a minority of businessmen large and small ever felt themselves aligned with either side of the issue (p. 125). (This finding hangs heavy upon the elitists who argue that the top business leaders care and control, and upon the pluralists who assume that most business leaders are interested and compete.)

(3) Of 128 classifiable responses by big business leaders in their sample, the authors report that 56 per cent favored freer trade, 3 per cent favored raising tariffs, and the remainder favored leaving tariffs "as is." A more conservative estimate of the distribution of attitudes was a 3-to-1 preference for freer trade (chap. 8). Yet the protectionists won year after year following World War II.

(4) Many of the leaders of the largest firms refused to generalize at all and remained actively inactive throughout the decade because their firms were too diversified to have a clear interest. General Electric and DuPont were identified as "typical of large firms" who left their individual division managers to lobby or not as they saw fit (p. 125).

(5) Most other industrialists in the top "command posts" probably favored freer trade. The leading liberal trade group, the Committee for a National Trade Policy, was composed of many of the leading lights of the "establishment": Harry Bullis of General Mills, Joseph Spang of Gillette, John McCloy of Chase National, John Coleman of Burroughs, and Charles Taft and George Ball for themselves and many others. Their leading opposition, the Nationwide Committee of Agriculture, Industry and Labor on Export-Import Policy, was composed of such "middle levels of power" interest group leaders as representatives of the UMW, National Coal Association, Manufacturing Chemists' Association, and the Window Glass Cutters' League of America (chap. 3). The CNTP and its official parent, the Randall Commission (Inland Steel, etc.), had gone out of existence well before the 1962 Trade Act successes.

(6) The final outcome in the Trade Act of 1962 was the direct result of classic President-Congress interplay, involving many of the kinds of compromises that the most vulgar pluralist view of American politics would lead one to expect. Congressmen appeared to be more independent of constituents and groups than the pressure group model would allow. But, on the other hand, the degree to which the Executive would be able to use trade as an instrument of international politics was determined in Congress; and it seemed that such a relationship would continue (pp. 73–79).

Elitists might accommodate to the extraordinarily careful analysis and unimpeachable findings of *American Business and Public Policy* by treating the trade issues of the whole postwar period as "middle-level." But this avoids all the interesting questions and begs a few as well. It was the large industrialists and the high members of the political directorate themselves who defined the issue as fundamental, particularly in the late 1950s after the Common Market was seen to be an immediate rather than a future reality. These were the men who kept trade on the agenda for over ten years. Yet there is nothing in the politics of trade decisions to support the notion that power follows directly from selected, established institutional positions in industry or military and public administration.

Bauer, Pool, and Dexter discovered that the pluralist model was of little use to them. It seems equally clear that the elitist model would have been of even less assistance. But this is because neither approach is a model. Each is, if anything, a self-validating standpoint; the pluralist approach suggests what to look for and the elitist model suggests perhaps what not to look for. Since neither is a theory, neither has much bearing on specific cases. At the end of an empirical study, neither approach affords a means for cumulating the data and findings in coherent and logical abstractions with other findings; they merely provide the basis for repeating the assumptions of the beginning. The following example is drawn from one of the very best case studies:

> The realization of national policy in the United States depends upon the formation and maintenance of coalitions (often of a temporary nature) overcoming the separation of powers, overcoming the fragmentation of power within the legislative and executive branches of government, overcoming weak cohesion by joining elements of both parties and many interests, to accomplish a desired objective. There is no small group of men who, if they agree among themselves, can assure favorable decisions on all or most of the important national policies. Power in Congress is fragmented and dispersed. Bits and pieces of influence are scattered (unequally to be sure) among committee chairmen, party leaders, and many others.... National policy is approved or rejected by building a coalition majority through bargaining and the proposal of objectives appealing to a wide variety of interests.[12]

The comment "This is where we came in" would be appropriate not only for these general remarks in Wildavsky's study, but also for virtually all case studies and their generalizations since Bentley. In many respects, one can say of both pluralists and elitists what was said of Debussy, but say it here more meaningfully: They opened up a couple of new streets that have turned out to be blind alleys.

Arenas of Power: An Interpretative Scheme for Cases

American Business and Public Policy, despite its richness as a case study in the politics of foreign trade, suffers the one debilitating handicap of all case studies, the problem of uniqueness. The case casts serious doubts on the perspectives employed in most case studies because of the rare comprehensiveness and exhaustiveness of its analysis, which goes far beyond the storybook and paste-pot relations among participants usually contained in case studies. But still, how are we to know the extent to which the patterns the authors discover apply to all cases? How are we to know at least toward what class of cases we can generalize? The authors have too little to say about this. The subtitle of the book, "The Politics of Foreign Trade," implies that everything they say applies strictly to this class of cases. However, at one point in the book they argue that the case belongs to a much larger class, a class which probably includes all domestic decisions except "some really new and unexpected issue" (p. 461): "So, on the whole, our case seems to us typical of any issue having economic implications for a number of industries and where, through a historical process, institutional alignments and expectations have been established" (pp. 460–461). On the other hand, one cannot be entirely sure how inclusive a category the authors had in mind, for at another point they say: "the more an organization represents the business community as a whole, the more unlikely it is to become committed on such an issue as foreign trade policy" (p. 339). The qualification ("on such an issue as") would hardly be necessary if they took foreign trade policy as typical of all ongoing policy processes.

Thus, the authors are unusually clear about their research aim, and self-conscious and skillful as to appropriate techniques of research and data manipulation; but they are far less than clear or self-conscious and skillful about defining their case in terms of some general scheme of classification. If their findings are to be judged for their applicability to all of national domestic policy-making, then we are about where we were before the book was published, except for some healthy negative insights as to prevailing "theories." If foreign trade is part of a smaller category of cases, then we would have to know what the class is, how it is distinguished from others, and what attributes are special to that class and what are general to all classes. Rather than dealing with these problems, the authors came out in favor of cashiering the present approaches altogether and of adopting a communications or "transactional" approach.[13] So, despite the fact that Bauer, Pool, and Dexter have managed an outstanding empirical study, the job of "making something of" the findings still remains, as it has remained for some time.

It seems to me that the reason for lack of interesting and nonobvious generalization from cases and other specific empirical studies is clearly that the broad-gauged theories of politics are not related, perhaps are not relatable, to observable cases. In general, American political science seems to be subject to a continuing fission of theory and research, in which the empiricist is not sufficiently mindful of his role as system-builder and the system-builder is not sufficiently mindful (if at all) of the role that theory is supposed to play. What is needed is a basis for cumulating, comparing, and contrasting diverse findings. Such a framework or interpretative scheme would bring the diverse cases and findings into a more consistent relation to each other and would begin to suggest generalizations sufficiently close to the data to be relevant and sufficiently abstract to be subject to more broadly theoretical treatment.

An attempt at such a framework follows. For over two years prior to the publication of *American Business and Public Policy* I had been working on a general interpretative scheme.[14] The hypotheses drawn from the scheme have so far anticipated most of the patterns described in existing case literature, and few of those patterns not anticipated have been found to be inconsistent with a logical extension of the scheme. A review article as the first published use of the scheme for national politics seemed appropriate because Bauer, Pool, and Dexter's case study is the most elaborate case yet published, and it appeared long after most of my hypotheses had been developed.[15]

The scheme is based upon the following argument: (1) The types of relationships to be found among people are determined by their expectations—by what they hope to achieve or get from relating to others. (2) In politics, expectations are determined by governmental outputs or policies. (3) Therefore, a political relationship is determined by the type of policy at stake, so that for every type of policy there is likely to be a distinctive type of political relationship. If power is defined as a share in the making of policy, or authoritative allocations, then the political relationship in question is a power relationship or, over time, a power structure. As Dahl would say, one must ask, "Power for what?" One must control for the scope of power and look for elites, power structures, and the like within each of the predefined scopes or "issue areas."[16] My analysis moves in this direction, but farther. Issues as such are too ephemeral; it is on the basis of established expectations and a history of earlier government decisions of the same type that single issues are fought out. The study of single issues provides a good test of hypotheses about structure, but the hypotheses must be arrived at in some other, independent way.

Obviously, the major analytic problem is that of identifying types of outputs or policies. The approach I have taken is to define policies in terms of their impact or expected impact on the society. When policies are defined this way, there are only a limited number of types; when all is said and done, there are only a limited number of functions that governments can perform. This approach cashiers the "politics of agriculture" and the "politics of education" or, even more narrowly but typically, "the politics of the ARA bill" or "the politics of the 1956 Aid to Education bill," in which the composition and strategy of the participants are fairly well known before the study is begun. But it maintains the pluralist's resistance to the assumption that there is only one power structure for every political system. My approach replaces the descriptive, subject matter categories of the pluralists with functional categories. There is no need to argue that the classification scheme exhausts all the possibilities even among domestic policies; it is sufficient if most policies and the agencies that implement them can be categorized with little, if any, damage to the nuances.

There are three major categories of public policies in the scheme: distribution, regulation, and redistribution. These types are historically as well as functionally distinct, distribution being almost the exclusive type of national domestic policy from 1789 until virtually 1890. Agitation for regulatory and redistributive policies began at about the same time, but regulation had become an established fact before any headway at all was made in redistribution.[17]

These categories are not mere contrivances for purposes of simplification. They are meant to correspond to real phenomena—so much so that the major hypotheses of the scheme follow directly from the categories and their definitions. Thus, *these areas of policy or government activity constitute real arenas of power.* Each arena tends to develop its own characteristic political structure, political process, elites, and group relations. What remains is to identify these arenas, to formulate hypotheses about the attributes of each, and to test the scheme by how many empirical relationships it can anticipate and explain.

Areas of Policy Defined

(1) In the long run, all governmental policies may be considered redistributive, because in the long run some people pay in taxes more than they receive in services. Or, all may be thought regulatory because, in the long run, a governmental decision on the use of resources can only displace a private decision about the same resource or at least reduce private alternatives about the resource. But politics works in the short run, and in the short run certain kinds of government decisions can be made without regard to limited resources. Policies of this kind are called "distributive," a term first coined for 19th century land policies, but easily extended to include most contemporary public land and resource policies; rivers and harbors ("pork barrel") programs; defense procurement and R & D; labor, business, and agricultural "clientele" services; and the traditional tariff. Distributive policies are characterized by the ease with which they can be disaggregated

and dispensed unit by small unit, each unit more or less in isolation from other units and from any general rule. "Patronage" in the fullest meaning of the word can be taken as a synonym for "distributive." These are policies that are virtually not policies at all but are highly individualized decisions that only by accumulation can be called a policy. They are policies in which the indulged and the deprived, the loser and the recipient, need never come into direct confrontation. Indeed, in many instances of distributive policy, the deprived cannot as a class be identified, because the most influential among them can be accommodated by further disaggregation of the stakes.

(2) Regulatory policies are also specific and individual in their impact, but they are not capable of the almost infinite amount of disaggregation typical of distributive policies. Although the laws are stated in general terms ("Arrange the transportation system artistically." "Thou shalt not show favoritism in pricing."), the impact of regulatory decisions is clearly one of directly raising costs and/or reducing or expanding the alternatives of private individuals ("Get off the grass!" "Produce kosher if you advertise kosher!"). Regulatory policies are distinguishable from distributive in that in the short run the regulatory decision involves a direct choice as to who will be indulged and who deprived. Not all applicants for a single television channel or an overseas air route can be propitiated. Enforcement of an unfair labor practice on the part of management weakens management in its dealings with labor. So, while implementation is firm by firm and case by case, policies cannot be disaggregated to the level of the individual or the single firm (as in distribution), because individual decisions must be made by application of a general rule and therefore become interrelated within the broader standards of law. Decisions cumulate among all individuals affected by the law in roughly the same way. Since the most stable lines of perceived common impact are the basic sectors of the economy, regulatory decisions are cumulative largely along sectoral lines; regulatory policies are usually disaggregable only down to the sector level.[18]

(3) Redistributive policies are like regulatory policies in the sense that relations among broad categories of private individuals are involved and, hence, individual decisions must be interrelated. But on all other counts there are great differences in the nature of impact. The categories of impact are much broader, approaching social classes. They are, crudely speaking, haves and have-nots, bigness and smallness, bourgeoisie and proletariat. The aim involved is not use of property but property itself, not equal treatment but equal possession, not behavior but being. The fact that our income tax is in reality only mildly redistributive does not alter the fact of the aims and the stakes involved in income tax policies. The same goes for our various "welfare state" programs, which are redistributive only for those who entered retirement or unemployment rolls without having contributed at all. The nature of a redistributive issue is not determined by the outcome of a battle over how redistributive a policy is going to be. Expectations about what it can be, what it threatens to be, are determinative.

Arenas of Power

Once one posits the general tendency of these areas of policy or governmental activity to develop characteristic political structures, a number of hypotheses become compelling.

And when the various hypotheses are accumulated, the general contours of each of the three arenas begin quickly to resemble, respectively, the three "general" theories of political process identified earlier. The arena that develops around distributive policies is best characterized in the terms of Schattschneider's findings. The regulatory arena corresponds to the pluralist school, and the school's general notions are found to be limited pretty much to this one arena. The redistributive arena most closely approximates, with some adaptation, an elitist view of the political process.

(1) The distributive arena can be identified in considerable detail from Schattschneider's case study alone. What he and his pluralist successors did not see was that the traditional structure of tariff politics is also in largest part the structure of politics of all those diverse policies identified earlier as distributive. The arena is "pluralistic" only in the sense that a large number of small, intensely organized interests are operating. In fact, there is even greater multiplicity of participants here than the pressure group model can account for, because essentially it is a politics of every man for himself. The single person and the single firm are the major activists. Bauer, Pool, and Dexter, for instance, are led to question seriously the "pressure group model" because of the ineffectiveness of virtually all the groups that should have been most active and effective.

Although a generation removed, Schattschneider's conclusions about the politics of the Smoot-Hawley Tariff are almost one-for-one applicable to rivers and harbors and land development policies, tax exemptions, defense procurement, area redevelopment, and government "services." Since there is no real basis for discriminating between those who should and those who should not be protected [indulged], says Schattschneider, Congress seeks political support by "giving a limited protection [indulgence] to all interests strong enough to furnish formidable resistance." Decision-makers become "responsive to considerations of equality, consistency, impartiality, uniformity, precedent, and moderation, however formal and insubstantial these may be."[19] Furthermore, a "policy that is so hospitable and catholic ... disorganizes the opposition."[20]

When a billion-dollar issue can be disaggregated into many millions of nickel-dime items and each item can be dealt with independently, multiplication of interests and of access is inevitable, and so is reduction of conflict. All of this has the greatest of bearing on the relations among participants and, therefore, the "power structure." Indeed, coalitions must be built to pass legislation and "make policy," but what of the nature and basis of the coalitions? In the distributive arena, political relationships approximate what Schattschneider called "mutual noninterference"—"a mutuality under which it is proper for each to seek duties [indulgences] for himself but improper and unfair to oppose duties [indulgences] sought by others."[21] In the area of rivers and harbors, references are made to "pork barrel" and "logrolling," but these colloquialisms have not been taken sufficiently seriously. A logrolling coalition is not one forged of conflict, compromise, and tangential interest but, on the contrary, one composed of members who have absolutely nothing in common; and this is possible because the "pork barrel" is a container for unrelated items. This is the typical form of relationship in the distributive arena.

The structure of these logrolling relationships leads typically, though not always, to Congress; and the structure is relatively stable because all who have access of any sort usually support whoever are the leaders. And there tend to be "elites" of a peculiar sort in the Congressional committees whose jurisdictions include the subject matter in question. Until recently, for instance, on tariff matters the House Ways and Means Committee was virtually the government. Much the same can be said for Public Works on rivers and harbors.[22] It is a broker leadership, but "policy" is best understood as cooptation rather than conflict and compromise.

Bauer, Pool, and Dexter are astonished to discover trade associations and other groups suffering from lack of funds and support. They see as paradoxical the fact that "protectionism" as a policy could win out time after time even when a majority of businessmen and Congressmen seemed on principle to favor freer trade. (There are instances of this running clear back to the 1890s.) They see as purposive Congress's "giving up" tariff-making because the "power to dole out favors is not worth the price of having to beat off and placate the insistent pleas of petitioners" (p. 37). Astonishment and the detection of paradox and a "Congressional group mind" are evidences of an insufficiently broad point of view. There are good and theoretically interesting reasons for each of these phenomena. Distributive issues individualize conflict and provide the basis for highly stable coalitions that are virtually irrelevant to the larger policy outcomes; thousands of obscure decisions are merely accumulated into a "policy" of protection or of natural resources development or of defense subcontracting. And Congress did not "give up" the tariff; as the tariff became a matter of regulation (see below), committee elites lost their power to contain the participants because obscure decisions became interrelated, therefore less obscure, and more controversy became built in and unavoidable.[23]

(2) The regulatory arena could hardly be better identified than in the thousands of pages written for the whole polity by the pluralists. But, unfortunately, some translation is necessary to accommodate pluralism to its more limited universe. The regulatory arena appears to be composed of a multiplicity of groups organized around tangential relations or David Truman's "shared attitudes." Within this narrower context of regulatory decisions, one can even go so far as to accept the most extreme pluralist statement that policy tends to be a residue of the interplay of group conflict. This statement can be severely criticized only by use of examples drawn from nonregulatory decisions.

As I argued before, there is no way for regulatory policies to be disaggregated into very large numbers of unrelated items. Because individual regulatory decisions involve direct confrontations of indulged and deprived, the typical political coalition is born of conflict and compromise among tangential interests that usually involve a total sector of the economy. Thus, while the typical basis for coalition in distributive politics is uncommon interests (logrolling), an entirely different basis is typical in regulatory politics. The pluralist went wrong only in assuming the regulatory type of coalition is the coalition.[24]

One of the most significant differences between the pluralists and Bauer, Pool, and Dexter—the treatment of the phenomenon and effects of overlapping membership—becomes consistent and supportive within this scheme. In fact, it helps to clarify the distinctions I am trying to draw here. Truman, for instance, stresses overlapping membership as a source of conflict, the function of overlapping membership as the reduction of cohesion in any given group. In contrast, Bauer, Pool, and Dexter found that in tariff politics this very overlapping of membership was a condition for cohesion: "unanimity (or cohesion) is maintained by the use of multiple group memberships for purposes that might produce conflict within a single given group" (p. 332n). They observed that overlapping is a form of specialization allowing individual firms, or special constituent groups within larger associations, the freedom to pursue outside the association the goals that are contrary to other associated groups. Meanwhile the cohesion of the larger group is preserved for the goals that all the constituent groups share. The fact appears to be that both positions are correct. Owing to the unrelatedness of issues in distributive politics, the activities of single participants need not be related but rather can be specialized as the situation warrants it. But the relatedness of regulatory issues, at least up to the sector level of the trade association, leads to the containment of all these within the association and, therefore, to the dynamic situation ascribed erroneously by Truman to all intergroup relations in all issues. When all the stakes are contained in one organization, constituents have no alternative but to fight against each other to shape the policies of that organization or actually to abandon it.

What this suggests is that the typical power structure in regulatory politics is far less stable than that in the distributive arena. Since coalitions form around shared interests, the coalitions will shift as the interests change or as conflicts of interest emerge. With such group-based and shifting patterns of conflict built into every regulatory issue, it is in most cases impossible for a Congressional committee, an administrative agency, a peak association governing board, or a social elite to contain all the participants long enough to establish a stable power elite. Policy outcomes seem inevitably to be the residue remaining after all the reductions of demands by all participants have been made in order to extend support to majority size. But a majority-sized coalition of shared interests on one issue could not possibly be entirely appropriate for some other issue. In regulatory decision-making, relationships among group leadership elements and between them on any one or more points of governmental access are too unstable to form a single policy-making elite. As a consequence, decision-making tends to pass from administrative agencies and Congressional committees to Congress, the place where uncertainties in the policy process have always been settled. Congress as an institution is the last resort for breakdowns in bargaining over policy, just as in the case of parties the primary is a last resort for breakdowns in bargaining over nominations. No one leadership group can contain the conflict by an almost infinite subdivision and distribution of the stakes. In the regulatory political process, Congress and the "balance of power" seem to play the classic role attributed to them by the pluralists, attacked as a theory by C. Wright Mills, and at least seriously questioned by Bauer, Pool, and Dexter.

The most interesting thing about the work of Bauer, Pool, and Dexter, from the standpoint of my scheme, is that they studied a policy that was undergoing a transition from distribution to regulation. It is, I feel, for this reason that they find some support for the pressure group model but not enough to convince them of its utility. But it is this very transition that makes their case study so interesting. Beginning with reciprocity in the 1930s, the tariff began to lose its capacity for infinite disaggregation because it slowly underwent redefinition, moving away from its purely domestic significance towards that of an instrument of international politics. In brief, the tariff, especially following World War II and our assumption of peacetime international leadership, became a means of regulating the domestic economy for international purposes. The significant feature here is not the international but the regulatory part of the redefinition. As the process of redefinition took place, a number of significant shifts in power relations took place as well, because it was no longer possible to deal with each dutiable item in isolation. Everything in Bauer, Pool, and Dexter points toward the expansion of relationships to the level of the sector. The political problem of the South was the concentration of textile industry there. Coal, oil, and rails came closer and closer to coalition. The final shift came with the 1962 Trade Expansion Act, which enabled the President for the first time to deal with broad categories (to the sector) rather than individual commodities.

Certain elements of distributive politics remain, for two obvious reasons. First, there are always efforts on the part of political leaders to disaggregate policies because this is the best way to spread the patronage and to avoid conflict. (Political actors, like economic actors, probably view open competition as a necessary evil or a last resort to be avoided at almost any cost.) Second, until 1962, the basic tariff law and schedules were still contained in the Smoot-Hawley Act. This act was amended by Reciprocal Trade but only to the extent of allowing negotiated reductions rather than reductions based on comparative costs. Until 1962, tariff politics continued to be based on commodity-by-commodity transactions, and thus until then tariff coalitions could be based upon individual firms (or even branches of large and diversified firms) and logrolling, unrelated interests. The escape clause and peril point were maintained in the 1950s so that transactions could be made on individual items even within reciprocity. And the coalitions of strange bedfellows continued: "Offered the proper coalition, they both [New England textiles and Eastern railroads] might well have been persuaded that their interest was in the opposite direction" (p. 398).

But despite the persistence of certain distributive features, the true nature of tariff in the 1960s emerges as regulatory policy with a developing regulatory arena. Already we can see some changes in Congress even more clearly than the few already observed in the group structure. Out of a committee (House Ways and Means) elite, we can see the emergence of Congress in a pluralist setting. Even as early as 1954–1955, the compromises eventually ratified by Congress were worked out, not in committee through direct cooptation of interests, but in the Randall Commission, a collection of the major interests in conflict (p. 47). Those issues that could not be thrashed out through the "group process" also could not be thrashed out in committee but had to pass on to Congress and the floor. After 1954 the battle centered on major categories of goods (even to the extent of a textile management–union entente) and the battle took place more or less openly on the floor (e.g., pp. 60, 62, and 67). The weakening of the Ways and Means Committee as the tariff elite is seen in the fact that in 1955 Chairman Cooper was unable to push a closed rule through. The Rules Committee, "in line with tradition," granted a closed rule but the House voted it down 207–178 (p. 63).[25] Bauer, Pool, and Dexter saw this as a victory for protectionism, but it is also evidence of the emerging regulatory arena—arising from the difficulty of containing conflict and policy within the governing committee. The last effort to keep the tariff as a traditional instrument of distributive politics—a motion by Reed to recommit, with instructions to write in a provision that Tariff Commission rulings under the escape clause be final except where the President finds the national security to be involved—was voted down 206–199 (pp.

64–65). After that, right up to 1962, it was clear that tariff decisions would not be made piecemeal. Tariff became a regulatory policy in 1962; all that remains of distributive politics now are quotas and subsidies for producers of specific commodities injured by general tariff reductions.

(3) If Bauer, Pool, and Dexter had chosen a line of cases from the redistributive arena for their intensive analysis, most assuredly they would have found themselves in an altogether different universe, proposing different generalizations, expressing different doubts. The same would have been true of Schattschneider and of the pluralist students of regulatory cases. Compared particularly with the regulatory arena, very few case studies of redistributive decisions have ever been published. This in itself is a significant datum—which Mills attributes to the middle-level character of the issues that have gotten attention. But, whatever the reasons, it reduces the opportunities for elaborating upon and testing the scheme. Most of the propositions to follow are illustrated by a single case, the "welfare state" battle of the 1930s. But this case is a complex of many decisions that became one of the most important acts of policy ever achieved in the United States. A brief review of the facts of the case will be helpful.[26] Other cases will be referred to in less detail from time to time.

As the 1934 midterm elections approached, pressures for a federal social security system began to mount. The Townsend Plan and the Lundeen Bill had become nationally prominent and were gathering widespread support. Both schemes were severely redistributive, giving all citizens access to government-based insurance as a matter of right. In response, the President created in June of 1934 a Committee on Economic Security (CES) composed of top cabinet members with Secretary of Labor Perkins as chairman. In turn, they set up an Advisory Council and a Technical Board, which held hearings, conducted massive studies, and emerged on January 17, 1935, with a bill. The insiders around the CES were representatives of large industries, business associations, unions, and the most interested government bureaucracies. And the detailed legislative histories reveal that virtually all of the debate was contained within the CES and its committees until a mature bill emerged. Since not all of the major issues had been settled in the CES's bill, its members turned to Congress with far from a common front. But the role of Congress was still not what would have been expected. Except for a short fight over committee jurisdiction (won by the more conservative Finance and Ways and Means committees) the legislative process was extraordinarily quiet, despite the import of the issues. Hearings in both Houses brought forth very few witnesses, and these were primarily CES members supporting the bill, and Treasury Department officials, led by Morgenthau, opposing it with "constructive criticism."

The Congressional battle was quiet because the real struggle was taking place elsewhere, essentially between the Hopkins-Perkins bureaucracies and the Treasury. The changes made in the CES bill had all been proposed by Morgenthau (the most important one being the principle of contribution, which took away the redistributive sting). And the final victory for Treasury and mild redistribution came with the removal of administrative responsibility from both Labor and Hopkins's FERA [Federal Emergency Assistance Administration]. Throughout all of this some public expressions of opinion were to be heard from the peak associations, but their efforts were mainly expended in the quieter proceedings in the bureaucracies. The Congress's role seems largely to have been one of ratifying agreements that arose out of the bureaucracies and the class agents represented there. Revisions attributable to Congress concerned such matters as exceptions in coverage, which are part of the distributive game that Congress plays at every opportunity. The principle of the Act was set in an interplay involving (quietly) top executives and business and labor leaders.

With only slight changes in the left-right positions of the participants, the same pattern has been observed in income tax decisions.[27] Professor Surrey notes: "The question, 'Who speaks for tax equity and tax fairness?' is answered today largely in terms of only the Treasury Department" (p. 1164). "Thus, in tax bouts ... it is the Treasury versus percentage legislation, the Treasury versus capital gains, the Treasury versus this constituent, the Treasury versus that private group.... As a consequence, the congressman ... [sees] a dispute ... only as a contest between a private group and a government department" (pp. 1165–1166). Congress, says Surrey, "occupies the role of mediator between the tax views of the executive and the demands of the pressure groups" (p. 1154). And when the tax issues "are at a major political level, as are tax rates or personal exemptions, then pressure groups, labor organizations, the Chamber of Commerce, the National Association of Manufacturers, and the others, become concerned" (p. 1166). The "average congressman does not basically believe in the present income tax in the upper brackets" (p. 1150), but rather than touch the principle he deals in "special hardship" and "penalizing" and waits for decisions on principle to come from abroad. Amidst the 1954–1955 tax controversies, for example, Ways and Means members decided to allow each member one bill to be favorably reported if the bill met with unanimous agreement (p. 1157).

Issues that involve[28] redistribution cut closer than any others along class lines and activate interests in what are roughly class terms. If there is ever any cohesion within the peak associations, it occurs on redistributive issues, and their rhetoric suggests that they occupy themselves most of the time with these.[29] In a ten-year period just before and after, but not including, the war years, the Manufacturers' Association of Connecticut, for example, expressed itself overwhelmingly more often on redistributive than on any other types of issues.[30] Table 1.1 summarizes the pattern, showing that expressions on generalized issues involving basic relations between bourgeoisie and proletariat outnumbered expressions on regulation of business practices by 870 to 418, despite the larger number of issues in the latter category.[31] This pattern goes contrary to the one observed by Bauer, Pool, and Dexter in tariff politics, where they discovered, much to their surprise, that self-interest did not activate both "sides" equally. Rather, they found, the concreteness and specificity of protectionist interests activated them much more often and intensely than did the general, ideological position of the liberal traders (pp. 192–93). This was true in tariff, as they say, because there the "structure of the communications system favored the propagation of particular demands" (p. 191). But there is also a structure of communications favoring generalized and ideological demands; this structure consists of the peak associations (which were seen as ineffective in tariffs—pp. 334, 335–36, 337–38, and 340); and it is highly effective when the issues are generalizable. This is the case consistently for redistributive issues, almost never for distributive issues, and only seldom for regulatory issues.

As the pluralists would argue, there will be a vast array of organized interests for any item on the policy agenda. But the relations among the interests and between them

Table 1.1 Published Expressions of Manufacturers' Association of Connecticut on Selected Issues

	Number of References in Ten-Year Period (1934–1940, 1946–1948)	Percentage of Favorable References
1. Unspecified regulation	378	7.7
2. Labor relations, general	297	0.0
3. Wages and hours	195	0.5
Total expressions, redistribution	870	
4. Trade practices	119	13.8
5. Robinson-Patman	103	18.4
6. Antitrust	72	26.4
7. Basing points	55	20.0
8. Fair trade (Miller-Tydings)	69	45.5
Total expressions, regulation	418	

Source: Lane, *Regulation of Businessmen,* 38ff. The figures are Lane's; their arrangement is Lowi's.

Note: This table will also be referred to later in the book.

and government vary, and the nature of and conditions for this variation are what our political analyses should be concerned with. Let us say, in brief, that on Monday night the big associations meet in agreement and considerable cohesion on "the problem of government," the income tax, the Welfare State. On Tuesday, facing regulatory issues, the big associations break up into their constituent trade and other specialized groups, each prepared to deal with special problems in their own special ways, usually along subject matter lines. On Wednesday night still another fission takes place as the pork barrel and the other forms of subsidy and policy patronage come under consideration. The parent groups and "catalytic groups" still exist, but by Wednesday night they have little identity. As Bauer, Pool, and Dexter would say, they have preserved their unanimity through overlapping memberships. They gain identity to the extent that they can define the issues in redistributive terms. And when interests in issues are more salient in sectoral or geographic or individual terms, the common or generalized factor will be lost in abstractness and diffuseness. This is what happened to the liberal trade groups in the tariff battles of the 1950s, when "the protectionist position was more firmly grounded in direct business considerations and ... the liberal trade position fitted better with the ideology of the times" (p. 150).

Where the peak associations, led by elements of Mills's power elite, have reality, their resources and access are bound to affect power relations. Owing to their stability and the impasse (or equilibrium) in relations among broad classes of the entire society, the political structure of the redistributive arena seems to be highly stabilized, virtually institutionalized. Its stability, unlike that of the distributive arena, derives from shared interests. But in contrast to the regulatory arena, these shared interests are sufficiently stable and clear and consistent to provide the foundation for ideologies. Table 1.2 summarizes the hypothesized differences in political relationships drawn above.

Or, take the Wagner Act, well after the opening blast of the New Deal. It was of congressional origin and was dominated by congressional forces. President Roosevelt held out for a few changes in particularly objectionable parts, but he was dragged along more as an unhappy supplicant than as a leader of nation, government, and party.[14]

But Roosevelt does not constitute a sufficient case. The real question here is whether this differentiated pattern, set during the 1930s, became institutionalized into separate and predictable systems of policy and politics. Rather than concentrate only on the 1930s, it would be better to span the entire period since those formative days. Strong *and* weak Presidents have been in the office since then, and the test will be whether, regardless of that, they face the same kinds of politics when the policy conditions are the same. If this is true, it would mean that strong Presidents may increase the amount of political action or the level of intensity, but they are less likely to alter the pattern of politics except insofar as they pursue one type of policy overwhelmingly more than the three others.

The Record Since Roosevelt: Stabilized Variation

The "Summary of Case Studies" (Table 2.2) presents a pattern of stabilized variation. Once we began regularly to get a goodly number of policies of all four types, we also began to witness four quite different types of politics. Were it not for the possibility of overstating the argument, one could say that each is a distinct subsystem.

The summary is comprised of 17 published case studies. [Sources for these cases appear at the end of the chapter.] Many are book-length, all are very detailed, and each was written by a reputable scholar. Our task was essentially to "interview" each author by addressing certain questions to his case study. The questions are presented in shorthand across the top of the summary. For example, it was important to learn what each author had to say about the typical participant in his story (column 1)—if indeed the author was struck by anything worth reporting on that subject. As is clear, almost all authors did stress some characteristic of the participants that could be coded, as indicated by the adjectives running down column (1). To take one case, Bailey and Samuel were impressed by the quality of "every man for himself," in the formulation of the Rivers and Harbors Act of 1950.[15] For another that has been covered in enormous detail, the politics of the traditional tariff has by all observers been considered highly individualized.[16]

Each author, through his case, was also asked if he had anything special to report on how the actors seemed to relate to each other (column 2). Did they mainly engage in mutual back scratching? Or, does the author report that he found careful strategy over long periods along broad, ideological lines? Or was there careful plotting and coalition building but along sector or other more special lines of cleavage? Ideological ties and long and stable lines of cleavage were reported by McConnell in his accounts of Farm Security and Farmers Home Administrations, as did Munger and Fenno in the fight over aid to education. In contrast, all of the authors of the middle six grouping of cases reported unstable cleavages (coalitions) based on sector and trade lines. It was this type of case, of which there were so many in the 1940s and '50s, that provided the empirical basis for the formalizing of the pluralist interpretation of American politics.[17]

The President is most likely to perceive for himself the patterns reported on columns (5) through (8) of the summary. Here the authors were asked what they had to report about the relative importance of lobbying, congressional committees, the floor, and the White House, respectively, to the final outcome of the program. No author undertakes to write a policy-making case study unless he intends to have something significant to say about the relative importance of these "loci of power."

The first thing one is struck by in the returns from these 17 cases is their sheer variation. Yet, if we could really generalize about national politics, would there not be a great deal of similarity in these adjectives?

The second thing one is struck by is the pattern of variation. Other readers might use different adjectives, but that is not likely to change the pattern much, since the adjectives used here were either used in the original or were careful translations of longer accounts. Even if something is lost by converting a paragraph or section into a single, summary word, the repetition and regular variation of these words across 17 important cases cannot be taken lightly.[18]

What the Roosevelt watchers report as exceptions to the general rule of Roosevelt mastery, therefore, turn out on closer examination to be not exceptions at all, but the rule under certain conditions that can be known in advance and understood in theoretically and jurisprudentially interesting terms. In all four of the distributive cases—the top group on the summary—the authors report that the President was either out of the picture altogether or was in it as a very weak and striving supplicant. Often the only way the President has been able to get into this act has been to try to convert the legislation into something else besides pork barrel—as Roosevelt succeeded in doing once and no more on TVA, and as Kennedy succeeded once in doing with his emergency public works proposal, which he tied to fiscal planning and general redistribution. But usually the committees succeed in severing these redistributive features from distributive bills.

A variety of words describe Presidents in the six cases of regulatory legislation, but one thing runs dramatically through all of them: Whether the President is strongly involved (as in AAA legislation on parity), or is stalemated due to squabbles within his own branch and party (as was true in the case of Taft-Hartley), Congress dominates the regulatory process. And this is the parliamentary Congress—the floor, not the committees. Sometimes the President has presented full-blown draft legislation, and sometimes the relevant committee will draft the original version. But in either event, according to the authors of the six regulatory cases, there is likely to be a lot of rewriting on the floor, through the amending process, and through conference.

Table 2.3 is a statistical confirmation of the results in the summary. It is a count of the actual amending actions involved in the 13 post-1948 bills on the summary, plus all bills in the 87th Congress, First Session, that received roll call votes in both houses. We used eight types of amending activity, and we ranked them according to degree of difficulty: (1) number of amendments offered; (2) per cent passed; (3) number of important amendments offered; (4) per cent of those that passed, (5) number of amendments offered over objections of the sponsor; (6) per cent of those that passed; (7) number of important amendments offered over objections of sponsor; (8) percent of those that passed. The average amending activity, using each of the eight types, was tallied, and the results of three of these are presented in the table. We then attached weights from

Table 2.2 Variations in the Policy Process—Summary of Case Studies I: Actors and Their Roles

Case	Attribute			
	(1) *Primary* *Units*	*(2)* *Relationships* *Among*	*(3)* *Stability* *Among*	*(4)* *Insider* *Bureaucrats* *& Outsider* *Specialists* *Factor*
Distributive				
Rivers-Harbors 1950	Single	Logrolling	Highest	Some
Airports Aid 1958–1959	Single	Logrolling	Very high	Low
ARA	Single	Logrolling	Highest	Low
Tariff, 1950s	Single	Logrolling	Highest	Low
Regulative				
FDA, 1938	Tr. Assn.	Bargaining	High	High
Rent Control 1950	Tr. Assn.	Bargaining	Low	Low
Robinson-Patman	Tr. Assn.	Bargaining	Low	Low
AAA 1938	Tr. Assn.	Bargaining	Low	Low
Taft-Hartley	Tr. Assn.	Bargaining	Moderate[a]	Low
Landrum-Griffin	Tr. Assn.	Bargaining	Low	Low
Redistributive				
Farm Security Admin.	(Bu. only)	Ideology	High	Highest
Farmers Home Admin.	(Bu. only)	Ideology	Very high	Highest
Social Security 1935	Peaks	Ideology	Very high	Highest
Federal Aid to Education	Peaks	Ideology	Very high	High[b]
Employment Act 1946	Peaks	Ideology	Very high	High[b]
Excess Profits	[c]	Ideology	Very high	High[b]
Internal Revenue 1954 (exemption and rates)	Peaks	Ideology	High	Highest

Notes:

Sources have been moved to the end of Chapter 2.

Lobby role: *Very high* if prominent and creative in legislature, executive, and grass roots; *high* if prominent and creative at any point; *moderate* if only prominent; and *low* if no evidence of anything.

Committee role: *conduit, lobbyist, creative, determinative,* in that rough order of importance.

Floor role: *consensual, contentious* (if a lot of debate but little alteration of the bill), *creative* (if evidence of alteration).

Executive role: *passive, coordinative, supplicative, legislative* in that order.

a. Pros high, antis low. Votes for (mainly Republican) Taft-Hartley very stable; votes against (mainly Democratic) not stable, with conservative Democrats providing the two-thirds vote to override President Truman's veto.

b. Professionalism very high; agency personnel involvement as lobbyists or draftsmen not high.

c. No mention is made of any groups or associations. The "business community" is termed "unanimous" and "concerted" but not managed.

**Table 2.2 Variations in the Policy Process—Summary of Case Studies I:
Actors and Their Roles (continued)**

	Attribute			
Case	(5) Lobby Role	(6) Committee Role	(7) Floor Role	(8) Executive Role
Distributive				
Rivers-Harbors 1950	Very high	Determinative	Consensual	Supplicative
Airports Aid 1958–1959	High	Determinative	Consensual	Supplicative
ARA	High	Creative	Consensual	Supplicative
Tariff, 1950s	Low	Creative	Contentious	Supplicative
Regulative				
FDA, 1938	Low	Creative	Very creative	Supplicative
Rent Control 1950	Low	Creative	Creative	Supplicative
Robinson-Patman	Very high	Creative	Creative	Passive
AAA 1938	Very high	Creative	Not ascertained	Coordinative
Taft-Hartley	Very high	Creative	Creative	Passive (stalemated)
Landrum-Griffin	High	Conduit	Very creative	Coordinative & supplicative
Redistributive				
Farm Security Admin.	Very high	None	None	Legislative
Farmers Home Admin.	High	Lobbyist	Not ascertained	Legislative
Social Security 1935	Moderate	Conduit	Consensual	Legislative
Federal Aid to Education	High	Lobbyist	Contentious	Inactive[d]
Employment Act 1946	Moderate	Very low	Very creative	Legislative
Excess Profits	Moderate	Lobbyist	Contentious	Supplicative
Internal Revenue 1954 (exemption and rates)	Moderate	Low-creative[e]	Contentious	Legislative

Notes:

d. Failed passage. As a general rule, if executive activity is low on a redistributive activity, the bill is probably doomed. This is not true of the other two types.

e. Joint Committee on Internal Revenue Taxation very creative—especially its staff; but it is not a legislative committee. The Ways and Means Committee and Finance Committee were much less creative, much more ratifiers of accords reached between JCIRT and Treasury lawyers.

1 to 8 to these categories to reflect roughly the degree of difficulty a member would have in getting each type of amendment adopted, and the "weighted mean" for each chamber is presented in the last column.

First, we can see that floor activity jumps up dramatically from distributive to redistributive bills. Since other evidence (see the summary) indicates presidential dominance over redistributive legislation, this finding suggests that on redistributive bills we get something like an acting out of the intent of the framers: direct communication between Executive and Legislative Branches. But the evidence in Table 2.3 is really classic for regulative bills. The goose egg for significant creativity in distributive legislation tends to dramatize the fact that on 67 per cent of all regulative bills at least two significant amendments were added during floor debate in the House despite the objections of the sponsor, who is usually the committee chairman. Indeed, that is a lot of rewriting, a lot of creativity, especially in the era of the "rise of the presidency" when Congress's reputation for creativity has declined.

The "weighted mean" adds considerable confirmation.[19] Obviously the overall level of floor action was much higher in the Senate, where smaller size and permissive rules prevail. But within the Senate the amounts of floor action, i.e., the evidence of floor creativity, varied from policy type to policy type, in a predictable way.

In House and Senate the dramatic jump upward was from distributive to regulative. This is much more significant in the House because of the many rules that discourage access to the floor under any circumstances. But even in the Senate, the reputation for floor creativity would hardly exist if we went back to the period when federal legislation was all distributive.

Finally, in the Senate, as in the House, there is a significant jump from distributive to redistributive, in evidence of floor creativity. This finding will bear further examination. Since history and the cases have revealed the special role of the Executive on redistributive matters, and since we now see also the considerable creativity of Congress as well, we might be led to reformulate our notions of policy and institutions, and how they relate to each other. It is quite conceivable that political scientists can develop criteria for policy choice in terms of predicted and desired impacts on the political system, just as economists, biologists, and the like attempt to predict and guide policies according to their societal impacts.

Implications for Prediction and Choice

Neither these data nor data of any other sort would support a drastically diminished interpretation of presidential power. His freedom to commit us to war, his command of secret information and diplomacy, his power to use executive agreements are all too impressive. But these impressive powers have overshadowed real variations even in that area defined, quite erroneously, as "foreign policy."[20] One need only note the amount of revision of factual and normative interpretation about presidential power since the Vietnam failures to realize the variability that was probably masked in the political science of national power during the 1950s and 60s. All of this is to say that presidential power, and all other political phenomena, must be put in proportion and perspective. Whether we are concerned about

Table 2.3 Evidence of Floor Creativity: Straight Amendment Counts

	(1) Average Number of Amendments Offered per Bill	(2) Percentage of These Passed	(3) Percentage of Significant Amendments Passed Over	Weighted Means, a Summary of All 8 Levels of Amending Action	
				House	Senate
Distributive Bills (N = 22)	5.8	41.8	0	.05	.16
Redistributive Bills (N = 25)	9.1	62.4	24	.15	.45
Regulative Bills (N = 15)	12.8	48.9	67	.46	.50

the issue of presidential power or the issue of adopting a regulatory approach to a social problem, and whether we are concerned with the objective business of prediction or the normative business of choosing a particular outcome, perspective must reside in at least two considerations: (1) prediction or choice must begin by recognizing the possibility of more than one pattern, and by pattern we must mean whole models rather than incremental differences in specific behavior patterns; and (2) if predictions can be made at this massive, institutional level, then they can, and inevitably will, become a major criterion for policy choice—i.e., really good theory is unavoidably normative.

(1) If this chapter has shown anything, it is that almost any generalization about national politics is inapplicable to as many as two-thirds of the cases of policy formulation. If we reverse the generalization by adding a "not," the new generalization would also tend to be inapplicable to about two-thirds of the known cases. This analysis was of course completed before the fourth arena—constituent policy—was put in place. The policy framework provides a basis for stating the conditions under which a given proposition is applicable, rather than merely helping improve the batting average from .333 to .335, or something of the sort. The policy framework locates the smaller universe where the batting average might be .677 or higher, and additionally it puts each of the generalizations into a theoretically orderly relation to all others. In turn, this produces new insights but, more important, it builds the propositions toward whole models rather than merely stringing out specific x-y statements.

One example alluded to earlier, where whole models of government and politics are seen to be involved, has to do with the conventional wisdom that American politics is all subsumed under a "presidential system," with exceptions. The cases and statistics here suggest first that several models have been masked over by the notion of a single system with multiple centers of power. One of the worst consequences of this assumption is its central construct, the "rise of presidential power, the decline of legislative power." *Sub rosa* it is then recognized that presidential power is not unilateral, nor is it even remotely equivalent to executive power; but those ambiguities are left theoretically unsettled. When one allows for multiple models rather than multiple power centers in a single model, many tendencies that must be left as ambiguities or anomalies can be brought explicitly to the center and handled rather easily. At least two such models involve a very strong Congress, and in one or perhaps both of these, presidential and congressional power are consonant, not zero-sum.

This bears further pursuit. Evidence of floor creativity is stronger for strong Presidents, such as Kennedy and Johnson, than for weak Presidents, such as Eisenhower, or Truman during his first three years in office. And floor creativity, as Table 2.2 shows, is high for redistributive bills, when the presidential role is most pronounced, for strong as well as for weak Presidents. What this really means is that the levels of political responsibility in the two branches tend to be consonant, and that they exist together in counterpoise to the administrative or bureaucratic levels of both branches. When the President is weak it is his bureaucracies and the congressional committees—the levels of low political responsibility—that tend to dominate the process; when the President is strong it is because he controls the bureaucratic levels.

(2) If the policy scheme developed in this chapter, or some superior one to come along, can predict when a President will be strong and weak, as well as when other

gross institutional patterns will prevail, then it is no step at all to a policy science for political scientists. This kind of wisdom provides criteria for choosing among policies, criteria that do not require the imposition of private goals upon legislators or the people. To illustrate, if two policies have about an equal chance of failure or success in the achievement of some social purpose the legislature has agreed upon, then that one should be preferred that has the most desirable impact on the political system. It should be the expertise of the political scientist to specify these kinds of consequences, and a policy framework would be necessary to do this. This is science, yet it reaches to the very foundations of democratic politics and the public interest. Let us pursue both, the second first.[21]

For a public interest to be involved at all, at least one of two properties must be present: The policy should be large enough in scope to affect a large number of people in a consistent way. This could be true of constituent policies, where a basic structural change in the system tends to create a class even where it does not directly define one, as for example in electoral reforms.

Or, the policy must, regardless of its scope, express a clear rule of law. A rule of law identifies the citizen in each person, the public part of each of us. The making of a real law (as contrasted with a policy without law) is an act of setting a public morality upon some action or status hitherto considered private.[22]

Distributive policy, in this context, clearly comes closest to being a complete privatization of the public. Much of it is intended to be *sub rosa*, and usually succeeds, given the capacity of these policies for continual fission according to the number of individuals making claims. To take but one contrasting example, regulatory politics that embody even vague rules of law cannot be fully privatized. The directly coercive element introduces public concerns of increasingly general applicability.[23] The overriding point is that these policy considerations, within the arena's framework, provide a systematic and plausible basis for defining good and bad legislation—without holding one moral code absolutely above another.

We can also judge public policy as good or bad in still another sense, a sense that leads toward fundamental questions about the relationship between public policy and democracy. If we want an open and public politics, we are limited to certain kinds of policies—regardless of whether the manifest goals of these policies are fulfilled. Again we would try to avoid distributive policies, because nothing open and democratic can come of them. But more nuance can be added. There can be moments in history, or changes of fashion, where the presidency is thought to be too powerful—perhaps we live in such a period today. In such a situation, Keynesian fiscal policies should be resisted, and regulatory policies should be preferred, for the latter tend to bring things to Congress and tend to invigorate interest group action. If anxiety about unlimited presidential power in international affairs continues to grow, regulatory provisions could even be tied to treaties or executive agreements. To trace this out is to illustrate rather dramatically the possibilities of looking at politics through policies: The best way, in other words, to open up the presidency and to expose the relations he is developing with another country is to put into policy terms some reciprocal commitments that require internal controls in both countries. For example, a provision requiring exchange of stock between two or more corporations, or their countries, in order to deal with air or water pollution would destabilize the politics of both countries, at least enough to gain entree into what is going on. Requirements for inspection of financial institutions dealing in our foreign aid would do about the same thing. Finally, if we wished to introduce strong national parties into our system, we might try to pursue more goals through constituent policies—like effective public propaganda in the birth control field, or dealing with monopolies by changing the rules protecting their limited liability rather than by adding regulations affecting their conduct.

The point is that if we can discover empirically the policy conditions underlying our political patterns, we have a basis for better public policies as well as better political science. Should we regulate? If there is the slightest contribution to political theory or policy science in this chapter, it would be in having established a basis for actually answering that question.

Sources for Table 2.2

Sources of the summary of cases cited in Table 2.2:

Rivers and Harbors Act of 1950. Stephen K. Bailey and Howard Samuel, *Congress at Work* (New York: Holt, 1952).

Airports Aid, 1958–59. Randall P. Ripley, "Congress Champions Aid to Airports," in F. N. Cleaveland, *Congress and Urban Problems* (Washington, D.C.: Brookings Institution, 1968).

Area Redevelopment Act. John Bibby and Roger Davidson, *On Capitol Hill* (New York: Holt, Rinehart and Winston, 1967).

Tariff. Raymond Bauer et al., *American Business and Public Policy* (New York: Atherton, 1963).

Food, Drug, and Cosmetic Act. David Cavers, "The Food, Drug and Cosmetic Act of 1938: Its Legislative History and Its Substantive Provisions," *Law and Contemporary Problems* (Winter 1939).

Rent Control, 1950. Bailey and Samuel, op. cit.

Robinson-Patman. Joseph C. Palamountain, *The Politics of Distribution* (Cambridge: Harvard University Press, 1955).

Agricultural Adjustment Act. Charles Hardin, *The Politics of Agriculture* (New York: Free Press, 1952); and Gilbert Fite, *George Peek and the Fight for Farm Parity* (Norman: University of Oklahoma Press, 1954).

Taft-Hartley. Bailey and Samuel, op. cit.

Landrum-Griffin. Alan McAdams, *Power Politics in Labor Legislation* (New York: Columbia University Press, 1964).

Farm Security and Farmers Home Administrations. Grant McConnell, *The Decline of Agrarian Democracy* (Berkeley: University of California Press, 1953).

Social Security. Paul H. Douglas, *Social Security in the U.S.* (New York: Whittlesey House, 1936); and Edwin E. Witte, *The Development of the Social Security Act* (Madison: University of Wisconsin Press, 1962).

Aid to Education. Frank Munger and Richard Fenno, *National Politics in Federal Aid to Education* (Syracuse: Syracuse University Press, 1962).

Employment Act of 1946. Stephen K. Bailey, *Congress Makes a Law* (New York: Columbia University Press, 1950).

Excess Profits. Bailey and Samuel, op. cit.

Internal Revenue. Stanley S. Surrey, "The Congress and the Tax Lobbyist: How Special Tax Provisions Get Enacted," *Harvard Law Review* (1957), pp. 1145ff.

Part II

✦✦✦

Public Policy, History, and a Theory of Political Development

P art II focuses on Lowi's application of his Arenas of Power model to political
development in the United States. He suggests that there has been a linear pro-
gression since the establishment of the U.S. Constitution in the predominance of
the four policy types in U.S. politics. Not surprisingly, constitutive (constituent) policies
predominate in the first few years as the basic structure of government is established.
Starting with Jefferson, however, and extending well into the early part of the twentieth
century, distributive policies provided the bedrock of U.S. politics at both the national
and local levels and greatly influenced the evolution of U.S. political institutions. In
the 1880s, regulatory policies began to increase at both the state and national level,
reaching unprecedented levels during the New Deal era and the 1960s. The New Deal
also constitutes a watershed in U.S. politics with an explosion of redistributive policies
at the national level. This story is well documented in the four chapters in this part
and suggests that the sequence is not, indeed, an accident of American history. Making
explicit the logic of the sequence is central to determining the broader applicability of
the Arenas of Power model and whether it can inform a theory of political change.

Clearly the four types of policies can coexist, albeit in different combinations, in different eras. It is also clear that the policy mix can vary vertically from national to state to
local levels of authority. For example, the national government may employ distributive
subsidies and extension services, regulatory acreage allotments and price controls, and
redistributive tax breaks as part of a strategy to address agricultural problems. It is also
the case that both citizens and political leaders can, within limits, choose to address
demands for public action selectively in one or another arena. Lowi reports that farmer
demands to address threats to rural livelihoods in the late nineteenth century through
redistributive policies were met with distributive policies that included support services
and publicly subsidized rural infrastructure. In short, policy choices are, or should be,
part of a conscious political strategy about the use of state power. This being the case,
the story is more complex than a simple unilinear evolutionary sequence.

How then does one explain the set of choices that produced systematic shifts in
policy choices from distributive to regulatory policies in the late nineteenth century

or the massive expansion of redistributive choices starting in the 1930s? Lowi does not proffer a specific theory of political change, but the chapters in this part do illuminate some of the factors.

First, growth and social-economic integration are explicitly powerful forces in these chapters. With constitutional arrangements that focused national responsibility on interstate commerce, trade, and defense, combined with a whole continent to master, it made sense to facilitate the expansion of the national economy. Lowi reports that Hamilton's call for "internal improvements" became national doctrine by 1814. Land grants and economic infrastructure became the currency of national policy in the nineteenth century—distributive policies. However, not a few national governments, from ancient history to the present, have used labor gangs and forced resettlement to accomplish the same result. The policy *need* did not determine the policy *choice*. By the late nineteenth century the policy objectives had been largely met. The continent was settled, interstate commerce had grown apace, but state-by-state regulation of product and labor standards, licensing issues, and the conditions of doing business were increasingly a problem for a national economy. National interest groups began seeking national regulatory solutions. The demand for policy and institutional change was outpacing the supply, a problem widely recognized throughout the developing world today. It is also not an uncommon situation where new problems and issues confront any regime.

Second, taken together, the four chapters in this part make a good argument for viewing the federal government as a case of arrested development, a political equivalent of a low-level productivity trap. Lowi identifies distributive, or patronage, politics as practiced in nineteenth-century America as political underdevelopment. This is not because there is not a legitimate place for distributive policies in any polity, but because a system dominated by distributive politics limits the aggregation of problems into demands, and demands into issues. A distributive system, as Lowi suggests, dissipates problems and thereby reduces political transaction costs, economizes on political resources, and although it may well increase conflict, it is contained at the local level. But in theory, and in practice, the institutional arrangements for distributive policies can be either salutary or perverse. The free distribution of scarce irrigation water in poor countries can evince all the perverse characteristics that Lowi would anticipate. Scarce, but free, water is wasted (with serious environmental consequences in hot climates); consequently, monitoring of use and system maintenance is shoddy, and most water goes to the powerful. Conflict ensues but is localized. In contrast, an investment in local, participatory irrigation associations can reduce the transaction costs, manage the resource efficiently and equitably, and mitigate conflict. Both are distributive policies, but institutional arrangements make the difference. Clearly not all social and economic problems benefit from disaggregation and decentralization. So it is still important to ask why it took a century and a half for the United States to develop a national administrative capacity and a policy framework for national regulatory and redistributive policies. However, in the last chapter in the part, "The Europeanization of America?" Lowi raises questions about the efficacy of pursuing the "European" model headlong into national redistributive policies and Europe-wide regulatory policies. Perhaps, as with distributive policies, the answer lies in the choice of institutional arrangements associated with the policy choice.

Third, the four chapters in this part invite an explicit exploration of the interaction of supply and demand for policy and institutional change. Efforts at both regulatory and redistributional policy changes at the state level in the period between the Civil War and the Depression provide considerable insight. Constituent policies were attempted at the state level to reduce the transaction costs of recurrent legislative battles in state after state. Urban home rule and municipal reforms predated national and even state reform efforts. But as the chapters recount, farmers, labor, even industrialists eventually found that the costs of distributive solutions exceeded the benefits. There were, indeed, political and economic returns to scale in switching from distributive to regulatory policy alternatives as problems grew beyond local boundaries. The problem, it would appear, lay with the policy *supply.* Not the party system, not Congress, and not the president had the capacity to respond. Further, Washington had neither a national bureaucracy in place nor an institutional alternative to such a bureaucracy. In contrast, even a "developing" country such as India at independence had a national revenue and police administration in every district in British India that became the initial, if minimal, foundation of its development efforts.

Finally, these chapters offer rich evidence about how institutions relate within policy arenas. The executive branch, legislatures, political parties, and interest groups interact within the "rules" of regulatory, distributive, or redistributive policies in ways that influence both the choice of arenas and the efficacy of the policy outcomes. But at any point in time these key political institutions may be part of the problem or part of the solution. If Lowi's argument is correct, political parties, as distinct from political partisanship, have failed to contribute to policy solutions for a century or more. The capacity for change of both state and national executives seems much higher than that of the legislatures. The transformation capacity of interest groups seems the most flexible. As we shall see in Part V, mass movements have the capacity to mobilize and focus demand, inducing changes in the supply of policy and institutional change.

"Parallels of Policy and Politics" (Chapter 3) systematically interprets the policies, institutional structures, and political process of historical eras of U.S. history within the Arenas of Power framework—focusing on the impact on the national government. It contains probably the single best treatment of constituent policies, especially from the immediate postrevolutionary era when the fundamental constitutional arrangements were made and key national institutions were established. The chapter documents the slow expansion of national regulatory policy, largely derivative from the responsibility granted to the national government in the Constitution for interstate commerce. In the post–World War I era, this trend was continued, Lowi suggests, by the spread of national interest groups. Although Lowi does not make the point, one is inclined to speculate that the nineteenth-century practice of protecting interstate commerce interests at the state level through constitutional amendment was simply overcome by economic growth and national economic integration. However, the revolution in the U.S. government occurred in the 1930s with the massive expansion of national redistributive policies and the institutional and political changes associated with it.

"American Federalism: A Demonstration of the Categoric Character of Policy and Politics" (Chapter 4) begins with a discussion of the unique character of the U.S. Constitution and the institutional and political context that evolved from it. Power and policy were concentrated at the state and local levels, with the national government limited to foreign policy, defense, interstate commerce, and the institutional arrangements necessary to support commerce—such as currency and physical infrastructure. To the states were reserved public health, labor and immigration rules, economic institutions of property of all kinds, codes and standards, police power, regulation of financial and commodity markets, and family law. Lowi argues that this functional division of labor moved both regulatory and redistributive policies to the state level. Constituent policy was undoubtedly more active at the state level in the nineteenth century than at the national level. Distributive policies and associated patronage politics dominated national policymaking and, of course, were endemic at the local level. This arrangement, post–Civil War, contained social and economic conflict at the state level. This clash, in turn, determined the evolution of the U.S. political party system and interest group politics, and it delayed the appearance of national bureaucracy, national political organization, and national interests for a century or more.

"A New American State, and Four Different Roosevelts" (Chapter 5) was a contribution to a collection of essays on Mario Einaudi's book *The Roosevelt Revolution,* and provides interesting commentary on Roosevelt's role in American political history. However, the chapter is included here for the insight it provides into Lowi's concept of political change. The predominant policy accomplishments and budget priorities of the New Deal, Lowi argues, were traditional distributive politics and were in no way revolutionary. The revolution was engendered by regulatory and redistributive policy innovations at the national level. The creation of the National Labor Relations Board, followed by the Employment Act of 1946 and the establishment of the Council of Economic Advisors, combined to destroy economic federalism, Lowi argues. Alongside this constitutional revolution, the federal bureaucracy expanded, policy initiative shifted to the national executive branch from Congress, and interest groups replaced parties as the core of national politics. In short, the Roosevelt revolution laid the foundations and established the policy patterns for a modern American state.

What makes these changes more than an American political accident? First, the Roosevelt revolution was composed of a complex set of changes—constitutional, institutional, shifts in policy types, and changes in power structures at the national level. Thus, it was not merely that the national government grew, but its character also dramatically changed. The word that Lowi chooses to describe this change is "differentiation," and he attributes the concept to both Samuel Huntington and Gaetano Mosca. One might easily also have pointed to Talcott Parsons in sociology or most of the field of development economics, which equated modernization with growing complexity and scale manifested in structural differentiation, division of labor, and specialization. What Lowi adds to this line of analysis is the suggestion that both political structure and policy types also evolve to keep pace with structural changes in society and the economy. But although social and economic change, differentiation, can create a *demand* for political and governmental change, the *supply* is determined by both leadership (it was a Roosevelt revolution) and policy choices. The lesson to be drawn from this chapter is that to understand the process of political change, one needs a framework and vocabulary for understanding changing policy choices—changes in the way the power of the state is employed to effect the relationship of the citizen to the state.

"The Europeanization of America?" (Chapter 6) completes the story begun in the previous two chapters by bringing the evolution of the modern nation-state in America into the 1970s. Lowi suggests that the United States lagged well behind most of Europe in adopting the centralized, bureaucratic state with the concomitant expansion of national power in the lives of citizens and communities. He further suggests that once the change in political culture and governing institutions appeared in the 1960s, both political parties embraced the power of the modern nation-state with a massive explosion of federal regulatory and redistributive policies.

The chapters in this part contain an implicit theory of political change. The driving force in the evolution of the U.S. political system, stated loosely, is globalization: the increasing economic scale of the United States, first nationally and then globally. This creates a "demand" for institutional and policy change that induces a "supply" from political actors—globalization is not the demand, it induces the demand. The factors that drive demand are largely exogenous to the polity and historically linear: a growing population, an expanding market economy that included all the factors of production, and rapid technological change. However, Lowi's theory of change is never made explicit. This omission is certainly not a fatal flaw. Grand theories of political and economic change are not currently in vogue, and we are awash in heated debates about why much of the world's population has not followed the transatlantic path to prosperity and democracy, a condition that clear theory would presumably resolve. What is clear, however, is that much of the world's population has failed to make choices in response to both the opportunities and shocks of globalization. Lowi's work offers the reader a major contribution to a theory of political choice—how societies respond to the "demands" for change, however induced. The reader is invited to explore links to the voluminous literature on development (or poverty) and, in particular, to some important contributions to the theory of political and economic change.

Suggested Reading

Douglass C. North. *Structure and Change in Economic History.* New York: W. W. Norton, 1981.
   The concept of "demand" for institutional and policy change is nowhere better stated than in Douglass C. North's seminal work and is articulated in shifting factor prices (land, labor, and capital)—with or without a market economy.

Hans P. Binswanger and Vernon W. Ruttan. *Induced Innovation: Technology, Institutions, and Development.* Baltimore: Johns Hopkins University Press, 1978.
   Citing earlier work by North and others, Binswanger and Ruttan apply their model of economic change directly to the institutional, policy, and technical changes embedded in the Green Revolution in Asia.

David Feeney. "The Demand for and Supply of Institutional Arrangements." In Vincent Ostrom, David Feeney, and Hartmut Picht, eds. *Rethinking Institutional Analysis and Development: Issues, Alternatives, and Choices,* ch. 6. San Francisco: International Center for Economic Growth, 1988.
   Neither North's *Structure and Change in Economic History* nor the Binswanger and Ruttan volume, however, addresses how "demand" might be articulated through nonmarket

mechanisms. In addition, both books treat the "supply" of change (institutions, policies, and technologies) as a black box. It is precisely these supply side, black box issues that Lowi's careful historical attention to the process of policy choice illuminates. David Feeney brings demand and supply together in this important article.

E. L. Jones. *Growth Recurring: Economic Change in World History*. Ann Arbor: University of Michigan Press, 1988.

Jones reminds us that there are numerous examples of dramatic "extensive" economic growth (i.e., total production), but that "intensive" growth (i.e., growth in productivity) has been less common and historically proved unsustainable. The European experience with the Industrial Revolution, and by implication the recent experience with globalization, reflect a somewhat unique set of policy choices that seem to have, with blips, sustained intensive growth for an exceptionally long time. Thus, the economic, demographic, and geographic variables common to change models may well explain the demand for change, but do not yield a theory that explains either the supply of sustainable improvement in the human condition or the structure of such an efficacious response.

The East Asian Miracle: Economic Growth and Public Policy. New York: World Bank/Oxford University Press, 1993.

A quite different set of policy and institutional choices than those in Europe and America produced the Asian Miracle, as documented in this important World Bank study.

Thomas Friedman. *The World Is Flat*. New York: Farrar, Straus, and Giroux, 2005.

This bestseller articulates a strong case for the uniformity of the globalization process of the twenty-first century, a perspective widely shared. We are tempted to conclude that, thanks to globalization, we now have the convergence of conditions that makes a theory of change possible, and in consequence, the European and American experience seminal.

Nancy Birdsall. *The World Is Not Flat: Inequality and Injustice in Our Global Economy*. WIDER Annual Lecture 9. Helsinki: UNU, 2005.

Nancy Birdsall quickly challenges Friedman in this major address. The emphasis on inequality within a global economy is simply another way of saying that the globalization process is not uniform, does not yield uniform institutional and structural choices, and does not guarantee uniform benefits. Perhaps the world is not "flat" after all.

Alan Winters and Shahid Yusuf. *Dancing with Giants: China, India, and the Global Economy*. Washington, DC: World Bank, 2007.

The recent experience of two of the world's fastest-growing economies does not appear to reflect a "flat" world if that implies uniform responses to uniform conditions. These authors offer two new potential "success stories" with yet two different sequences and choices of both policy and institutional arrangements.

As emerging economies join the global economy, applying the Arenas of Power framework to policy watersheds continues to be a productive enterprise. It helps us understand the choices that affect the supply of change and shows us how different conditions induce different institutional and policy mixes.

CHAPTER 3

❦

Parallels of Policy and Politics

The Political Theory in American History

Origins do not reveal truths. The past does not speak for itself. History is rewritten in each generation because each generation imposes on the past a different language and a different need. One persistent need, however, is to use the past as a testing ground for the present. For the proper study of mankind, history is a tool made necessary by the absence of controlled laboratory conditions. To use history as a surrogate laboratory, the student must go to it with an established idea about society, or seek through history to develop an idea about society—or both. My intention is to establish reciprocity with history. The "Arenas of Power" idea, though only rudimentary in its development at this point, will be tested with the data drawn from the history of public policy and politics; therefore as an hypothesis it will guide in the choice and treatment of data. At the same time, the testing will be used to sharpen the scheme, to bring it to further maturity, so that it will be a better instrument for dealing with the present.

For the past, as for the present, the central perspective is the same—that the state, or system of government, produces a politics consonant with itself. If this does not happen naturally, it will happen unnaturally. Consequently, developments of policy and politics ought to be parallel, to such an extent that a single line of explanation ought to suffice for both. The method is a simple one. It consists of going through the public policy enacted by the U.S. Congress and trying to find dominant patterns of policy output from one era to another. Are there distinguishable eras, and do the policies within each era have something significant in common? The next step is to describe independently the prevailing political patterns, if any, for each of the eras. This phase of the effort is based largely on secondary materials, not merely because of the wealth of political histories but also because these independent treatments will necessarily be innocent of the uses to which they will be put here. A third step will call for the imposition of the "Arenas of Power" model upon the parallel developments in order to see first how much of those developments the scheme can rationalize, and, second, in order to bring the past in an appropriate form through a full-scale reinterpretation of the present.

The Constituent Period

When the Federalists took office in 1789 they were explicitly committed to four cardinal goals. These were the encouragement of manufactures, establishment of the public credit, extension of and protection of the frontiers, and staying out of foreign wars.[1] The first two of these being the domestic portions of their program, they commissioned the young Secretary of the Treasury, Alexander Hamilton, to write reports for their guidance. The results were two of the most important State documents ever composed: the *Report on Manufactures* and the *Report on Public Credit*. However, the force of events in the new nation pushed Congress away from the first, "the development of the national estate," toward the other three goals, including public credit. Consequently, Hamilton's report on credit was presented to Congress in January of 1790 and his report laying out a program of encouraging industries did not even reach the Congress until 1792.

The most immediate pressure was simply one of fleshing out a new government, including establishment of actual executive departments and the judicial branch. This being done to a large extent in the First Congress, First Session, the Second Session (1790–91) concerned itself primarily with the debt built up during the war. This included legislation providing for the repayment of debts owed to foreign governments—the least controversial part of the problem. It also included legislation providing for repayment of debts owing individuals and States geared to commitments made by the provisional government during the war. A great part of this was owed to soldiers and officers themselves; another portion was owed to farmers and merchants as a result of purchase for otherwise worthless paper by troops in the field; another portion took the form of bonds actually purchased by wealthier patriots. There seems to be little question that legislation would provide for full repayment, despite the fact that many domestic and foreign speculators had been trading in this paper at the expense of the original patriots. Legislation was eventually enacted to cover the most controversial dimensions of the debt, that which was owed by the States. The question was whether the Federal government would "assume" those debts. On this point debate lasted in Congress for at least six months. It polarized the members of Congress, leading, as we shall see, to party organization in Congress; and the ultimate compromise affected a whole variety of things, including a deal whereby Virginia would be given the site for the national capital on the banks of the Potomac, after a ten-year period in Philadelphia. Although the amount of State debt to be assumed was estimated at $21.5 million as compared to the more than $40 million owed directly by the national government, and $10 million owed to foreign governments, the assumption issue was the most divisive.[2]

Succeeding sessions of Congress passed the first Militia Act, created the Bank of the United States, created additional departments of government, and ratified the important Jay Treaty, which established regular commercial and diplomatic relationships with Great Britain. This polarized the Senate still further, along the lines already forged by the assumption issue; the treaty was ratified in 1795 only by virtue of Federalist solidarity in support of Washington's position. Congress also concerned itself during those years with the creation of a national monetary system and the establishment of the national government's authority to lay and collect taxes, especially to collect taxes.

The Bank of 1791 was followed in 1792 by Congress's decision to designate the dollar as the money unit, with a decimal basis and with an assigned value stated in precious metals. "Congress underlined the definition of the dollar as an act of sovereignty by making its own choice of a metal content for this unit different from that of the Spanish coin then most familiar among foreign pieces circulating in the country."[3] The most important purpose of this monetary legislation was to standardize the forms of money rather than to affect its substance or distribution.[4] As for taxation, the key throughout this period was the issue of establishing the power to impose tariff on imported goods and to both impose and collect excise taxes upon selected domestic commodities, particularly whiskey. The whiskey tax was literally chosen as a test of the power of the federal government to exercise any kind of coercive control over States or individuals, in contrast to the absence of such ability under the Articles of Confederation. Although Congress did reduce the size of the whiskey tax in response to organized farmer opposition to it, the tax was maintained and Congress went so far as to authorize the President to call out the militia to enforce its order to all insurgents to submit to federal authority. Washington called out over 13,000 militiamen from Pennsylvania and nearby States, and the Whiskey Rebellion quickly disintegrated. Several were tried for treason; two were convicted but were ultimately pardoned by the President. Once the Federal government had demonstrated its intentions and its powers, the President was able to express the generosity of the sovereign.[5]

The Policies: A Characterization

If there is a common thread running through these various Acts of Congress during the first decade, it is "state building." Each piece of legislation appears to have been part of an effort to erect a national structure within which private action could take place. These were legislative efforts in large part to implement one of the most basic intentions of the Constitution, to overcome the weaknesses of the Articles by lowering if not eliminating the barriers erected by each of the States to the flow of commerce within the continent. Only one of the basic pieces of legislation, listed on Table 3.1, involved the federal government in a direct exercise of governmental coercion over citizens. This was the Whiskey Excise Tax, and even here it is the consensus of scholars that the underlying problem was one of establishing once and for all the right and power of the federal government to impose such an excise. This is emphasized by the fact that sufficient revenues could have been raised by tariffs alone.[6] Virtually all of the other important legislative efforts were aimed one way or another at creating a capacity or a structure within which the later governmental actions might effectively follow. This was as true of the international actions, such as the Jay Treaty, as it was of internal domestic actions, such as providing the criteria for calling up the state militia or creating the administrative structure within which customs could be collected, federal revenues could be deposited, or the miniscule departments could be administered.

Some of the early legislation had a more complex character. For example, the manner of dealing with the war debts would inevitably and unavoidably have a definite and immediate impact on the distribution of wealth in the country. Nevertheless, this

Table 3.1　Actual Policies Adopted by Congress: The Founding Period, 1789–1803

State-Building Policies	"Foreign" Policies	"Fiscal" Policies
Bill of Rights	Jay Treaty	Tariffs
Incorporation of U.S. Bank	Pinckney Treaty	Excises
Provide Common Currency	Louisiana Purchase	Assumption of Debts
Establish Postal Service		Colonial
Admit New States		State
Create Cabinet Departments		
Create Federal Judiciary		

was incidental to the primary and literal purpose of funding and assumption of debts, which was to establish in the first instance a national and uniform monetary system and at the same time to gain legitimacy through the standardization of the monetary units and through the cooptation of the support of the more influential persons who were or might eventually become creditors.

Constituent policy is a term to be preferred over state-building because the characteristic or the function in question does not disappear once the state is built. Constituent is not intended to imply only voters, their representatives, and the district wherein they reside, although legislation defining such constituencies are examples in point. The term constituent is used in its European sense, having to do with the makeup of a thing, as in the case of constituent assemblies brought together to draft a new constitution and to create a new government. After all, the term constitution itself has to do with the makeup or construction, as well as the desired construction, of a thing. Constituent policies are policies formally and explicitly concerned with the establishment of government structure, with the establishment of rules for the conduct of government, of rules that distribute or divide powers and jurisdictions within which present and future government policies might be made.

Laws dealing with debt and currency, similar to or identical with laws passed during the 1790s, will ultimately be treated in a separate category—redistributive policy—because they deal directly with citizens, their wealth, or their ability to produce and dispose of wealth. However, two considerations have influenced the decision to emphasize the constituent character of public policies during the entire period of the 1790s, even to the extent of including debt and monetary policies in the constituent category. First, they were so few, and purely constituent policies were so many, that the entire context of government was set by constituent policy. Second, and of greater importance to a logic of the analysis, in the 1790s, these debt and monetary policies were unprecedented organic laws concerned primarily with the establishment of the structures themselves. Though nothing in government is ever neutral, such structures as the First Bank, the Mint, the new U.S. bonds, the Treasury Department, and the collection agents were necessary for their own sake if a government of commerce as well as justice were to be founded at all. For one example, the Constitution had given Congress unambiguous power to coin money and to "regulate the value thereof"; yet, all Congress attempted to accomplish in its original monetary policy was simply the standardization of units and practices. Thus, by creating the Mint in 1792, Congress sought to standardize units of money not by imposing a single coin of the realm but by making coinage a service, with no fees attached. Later, compulsion was exercised by federal law to impose acceptance of paper money as well as to force the elimination of privately minted coins. But this emphasizes further the constituent character of the original monetary policies.[7] This is a good opportunity to emphasize once again that the definition or categorization of policies in this analysis is based as much as possible upon only the formal provisions and not upon any consideration at all of the direct impact the policy may have had upon the society or individuals in it.

The Politics of the Constituent Era

James Madison in *Federalist 10* warned against political parties. Washington in his Farewell Address warned against parties. Hamilton sincerely condemned the idea of party and at no time saw himself as a man building a party. There did not even exist a model of party to go by. Yet, these original leaders produced a party and a party system no less directly and surely than if they had intended to do so. Every student of the period has come away impressed with the extent to which the politics of the 1790s was a politics of party and party formation. By the end of the decade, over 90 percent of the members of Congress were clearly affiliated Federalists or Republicans.[8] So well mobilized were the parties that they completely dominated the 1800 presidential election; party regularity was so great that a tie between Jefferson and Burr in the Electoral College produced a political crisis that called forth the Twelfth Amendment of the Constitution and changed forever the meaning of the Electoral College itself.

It was also a period of classic competition between the Executive Branch and Congress; the Founders must have been delighted to see the Separation of Powers working so soon and so well. The first Standing Committee of the Congress, the Ways and Means Committee, was established in order to contend on a more or less equal basis with the Secretary of the Treasury, Alexander Hamilton. President Washington was rebuffed in his effort to use the Senate as a truly advisory body in the negotiation of treaties. (Washington and his Secretary of War during the very first session went to the Senators with important papers concerning negotiation as well as approval of the treaties. This was the first and last time such a collaborative effort was attempted.) A strong minority in Congress attempted strenuously to limit the powers of the President to remove heads of Executive Departments. And most of the proposals for legislation listed in Table 3.1 received extensive and emotional debate on the floor of one or both chambers. In fact, it was these debates, their intensity and their character, that virtually produced the abiding political coalitions around which the parties formed. As we shall see time and time again in association with constituent policy issues and not with, say, distributive policy issues, political differences during those early years were expressed in broad ideological terms, and the divisions of legislators tended to be consistent from one issue to the next. The issues were explicitly defined in the larger terms, of executive versus legislative, of Federalist versus Anti-Federalist or Republican, of aristocracy versus democracy. White reports that even before any departments had been established or any Secretaries appointed, one member of Congress had already raised the banner of congressional independence: "Are we, then, to have all the officers the mere creatures of the President? This thirst of power will introduce a treasury branch into the House, and we shall have ministers obtrude upon us to govern and direct the measures of the Legislature and support the influence of their master."[9]

Cleavages among members of the legislature were not only consistent but seemed to be cumulative; some expressed them in terms of abstract theories of republicanism, some identified the issue in terms of executive versus legislature, or Washington versus Jefferson, or Hamiltonianism versus Jeffersonianism. In whatever form, there was enough stability of political division to provide a basis for party organization, and it was party based upon broad principles rather than party based upon coalitions of interest and convenience as it became in the Second Era. Some students of the period report that there was a measurable amount of class or class-based political mobilization during that first decade or so of the history of the Republic. However, this mobilization was nevertheless largely in party terms. Farmers, and debtor groups in general, moved with increasing frequency toward Jefferson, while creditors and the mercantile class in general tended to hold closely to the Federalist line. Although the separations were always blurred by sectionalism, strong social class tendencies were present. But during this period they tended to express themselves through party interests and party structures. The close parallelism between class and party at that time can be seen in the awareness of the leaders themselves that important differences along class lines were involved and that the newly established parties were serving important class interests.[10] Class politics in America became much stronger a century later, as policies of redistribution increased in number and importance. Yet, when class politics did emerge at the later time, it was expressed outside and independent of political parties. This is one of the fundamental differences between the politics of constituent policy and the politics of redistributive policy. The joining of class and party in the 1790s was not merely a coincidence of thoughtful statesmen coping with a young republic. What gave their political relationships their special flavor—especially considering that these very statesmen sincerely opposed the formation of political parties—was the particular kinds of issues they had to deal with. With some important exceptions, the main issues, and the main terms of cleavage, were constituent policies.

The peculiar distinctiveness of these political characteristics—emergence and persistence of two-party conflict, the subsuming of philosophic and class dimensions within the party system, and the formal competition between the two main Branches—and the intimate relationships between these political characteristics and the prevailing policies of the national government at the same time, can be appreciated only through their contrasts with later periods of policy and politics.

The Second Era: Distributive Policies, Logrolling Politics

The end of the Federalist Era came dramatically, in a momentary realization of the worst fears of the Founders: The dominant party, indeed a party, had attempted by law to suppress the party of the opposition. In June and July of 1798, the Federalists enacted the infamous and patently unconstitutional Alien and Sedition Acts. These were four measures adopted ostensibly to deal with the French Revolution, and in fact only the fourth of four measures dealt directly with domestic sedition. After rejecting a provision declaring every Frenchman an enemy of the United States—making treasonable any extension of aid to such a person—Congress provided for severe punishment against any attempt to interfere with the enforcement of the laws, to make scandalous and malicious statements against the government, to try to stir up hatred among the people, or to publish anything unfriendly to the government.

Jefferson was probably the most appropriate third president conceivable. He was the father of Republicanism, he was orthodox in his Republican principles, and yet he proved not only flexible in practice but also compatible to a surprising degree with the Federalist program. As the vice president he not only denounced the Alien and Sedition Acts as deeply unconstitutional and repugnant, he collaborated secretly with Madison, John Taylor, and others in the drafting of a formal attack upon those Acts and on the very power of national government to pass such legislation. These sentiments were expressed eventually in the Virginia and Kentucky Resolutions, which embodied virtually a preconstitutional theory that "each State acceded a State" and that "the government created by this compact was not made the exclusive or final judge of the extent of the power delegated to itself"; consequently, each State "has an equal right to judge for itself, as well of infractions as of the mode and measure of redress." The Kentucky Resolution went so far as to declare the right of a State to nullify unacceptable actions taken under color of the Constitution. Yet Jefferson who collaborated in those Resolutions was nevertheless, as President, a person capable of living comfortably within the Federalist mold. Many of his earlier policies were constituent policies, taken on as an effort to maintain our neutrality with the British and the French. A number of other fundamentally important constituent policies came, however, more from conviction than from the dictates of the European war, such as for example the encouragement of the admission of new States and the organization of new Territories. There were several distinctively Republican efforts, of course. For example, all domestic excise taxes were repealed. And although the provisions for dealing with the national debt were not repealed, the Administration made every effort to accelerate liquidation of the debt, to satisfy Republican antagonisms toward it.[11] However, at the same time, Jefferson was beginning to commit himself and his Administration to "internal improvements" despite Republican theory that such activities were unconstitutional for the Federal government to engage in. Purchase of the Louisiana Territory was an especially extraordinary thing for Republicans to do. But this gigantic single act overshadows many other essentially distributive policies that, in theory, were also too much for the national government to take on itself. These included provisions for the Cumberland Road, for other military and post roads, for development of ports, for delivery of mail. They also included the first efforts to provide tariffs to protect specific "infant industries." Also included were provisions to give land not only as claims for services rendered to government but also to encourage local school programs.

During Jefferson's own eight years, these distributive policies were modest and were taken on with certain misgivings. But as time passed and the European war, including our own small share in it during the War of 1812, fizzled out, the Republican misgivings about the desirability and constitutionality of internal improvements fizzled out also. Hamilton's master plan for a national role in the economic development of the country, which had been postponed due to the force of circumstance in the 1790s, was going to be dusted off and applied vigorously after 1814. Many "strict constructionists" remained within the leadership of Republicans in Congress. But they became known as the "Old Republicans," and after the War of 1812 the dominant group was distinguished as the "New Republicans."[12] For them the future lay in a much more positive and vigorous national government, and the result was a regular and significant increase in the number of policies enacted by the U.S. Congress providing for a variety of internal improvements, for subsidies to shipping, for land grants to encourage various kinds of venture, and for many of the other purposes laid out so well and in such detail by Hamilton in his *Report on Manufacturers* written and circulated during the height of Federalist power. The culmination of Republican commitment to domestic policies of this nature probably came in 1828 when a Republican Secretary of the Treasury, Richard Rush, invoked Hamilton himself to emphasize the desirability of positive public policies for the Federal government: "[Hamilton's] comprehensive genius, looking into futurity, and embracing in its survey all the interests that go to make up the full strength and riches of a great empire, saw the truth, now in course of corroboration by our own experience, that the protection and increase of manufacturing labor, far from stopping the springs of our commercial power, would but multiply and diffuse them."[13]

In 1819–20, well before the end of the first decade of peace under the Republicans, the entire complexion of Federal government activity had changed. This can be seen dramatically by little more than a quick scan of the Public Acts of Congress enacted by the Sixteenth Congress of the United States (1819–21). As in previous years, there remains a very large proportion of constituent policies, providing for Courts, providing for the organization of new States and Territories, apportioning representatives following a new Census, acts establishing or reorganizing major Cabinet departments, acts providing for the printing and circulation of the laws of the United States. But we now also see as many as one-half of the total output of the Sixteenth Congress to be comprised of such enactments as provisions for trading houses with Indian tribes, provisions for the sale of public lands, provisions for additional land offices for purposes of selling such public lands in one State or Territory after another, laws providing for the relief of specific settlers in specified Territories or Districts, acts authorizing new post roads and the alteration of others, an act providing for a coastal survey, and various acts providing for the relief of settlers, either through land or cash payments. Similar measures were passed in each succeeding year, including a few important innovations such as direct subsidies to railroads, the coastal trade, and ocean-going mail carriers. By 1850 over 2,500,000 acres were granted alone through the State of Illinois for the construction of the Illinois Central Railroad; over 1,100,000 acres went to the Mobile and Ohio line in Mississippi and Alabama for the extension of its railroad. In 1856 and 1857 equivalent grants were made to as many as 45 different railroad companies, directly or through the States, to help finance construction of rail lines.

This is not to say that the Federal government had become a major force in American social and economic life. As we shall see in the next chapter, State government was truly the linchpin of government in the American system. The point here is that the Federal government, whatever its importance may have been relative to the States, had taken on a new function after 1800 or perhaps 1815. When the Republicans had established themselves as the single governing party, they began to share views expressed by such people as President Madison in 1815 when he held forth on the "great importance of establishing throughout our country the roads and canals which can best be executed under the national authority.... [No] ... objects within the circle of political economy so richly repay the expense bestowed upon them."[14] The pattern was accentuated by Adams and also by Jackson, who even chose to fight national banking largely by judicious political distribution of federal deposits in varieties of State banks.[15] The pattern was accentuated still further by particular use of the tariff; for, once the power to enact tariffs had been fully established, it became strictly a matter of using the tariff power on an item-by-item basis in response to demands made from individual manufacturers.[16]

What may be even more remarkable is that during more than two decades following the Civil War, there was very little change in the composition or relative importance of the Federal government. Congress continued to respond to the needs and demands of the country by either constituent policies dealing with the structure of the government itself or by distributive policies as these were described and illustrated throughout this chapter. And it is of equal significance to report that Congress persisted in its avoidance of regulatory and redistributive policies. Occasionally one encounters an act of Congress providing for public health around ports and waterfronts or for the liability of captains of seagoing vessels. But these were very infrequent until well beyond the end of the Second Era.

The Peculiar Character of Distributive Policies

These policies that comprised the Hamilton program have a number of very significant characteristics in common. Perhaps the most striking is the concern of each policy for the expansion of alternatives. Generally these policies are benign. They are concerned with the husbanding of resources, the spreading of benefits toward universality. It is for this reason that the category was labeled distributive. An appropriate synonym would be subsidy policy; another appropriate synonym would be patronage policy, if by patronage we comprehend the general notion of to patronize.

A second fundamental characteristic of these policies is that they embody no rule of law that requires a discrimination or an invidious distinction between or among statuses, attributes, or behaviors. The rule simply provides for a facility or for a privilege, or for explicit grants of money or land, which combine aspects of facility and privilege. A third fundamental characteristic of all distributive policies is that each one can be broken up into a larger and larger number of smaller and smaller units for purposes of distribution. This capacity for disaggregation into smaller and smaller units for distribution derives directly from the absence of a rule of discrimination. But whatever the source, the fact remains that disaggregation gives a distributive policy a capacity to spread itself toward universality. No principles of exclusion are involved, and if the governmental resource at stake is a facility or a privilege or a fund of land or money, disaggregation is likely to take place as long as there are vigorous individual or organized claims for inclusion.

Disposal of public lands is probably the best illustrative case; moreover, it was the case around which the term distribution was coined for the entire category of policy. According to Gates, original land policy was designed to produce revenue for the Federal government. Consequently, prices began high, there was competitive bidding, and tracts were relatively large. However, very early in the Republican Era, the Administration redefined the purpose of land distribution to include encouragement of western settlement as well as revenue. Thus, the facility, or resource, was simply made available to virtually all of those who wished to avail themselves of it by going to where the public lands were available. From that time onward, the price per acre began a downward trend that did not end until the Civil War and the Homestead Act—at which point most public lands were being distributed without any charge whatsoever. The same process of disaggregation affected size of tract as well as price of acreage. At first, the minimum tract was 40 acres. By 1840, the law had switched from minimum size to maximum size, which was put at 160 acres. Thus, the floor under size of unit had been eliminated altogether. By that time, moreover, settlers were allowed to improve their land even before they had earned title to it. Thus, by 1850, the size and the price of a unit of land had dropped so far that public lands had become almost universally available. This is clearly a pure case of disaggregation.[17]

The same pattern may be clearer still in the history of the tariff. Once the Federal government established fully its authority to use the tariff as a policy of protection as well as revenue, the tariff became an elemental distributive policy. With but one exceptional period (1842–56), there was for 100 years after 1833 a steady and dramatic increase in the number of items to which tariffs were attached. Tariff rates increased and decreased according to the party in power, but tariff policy itself was well accommodated to the partisan struggle. Between 1832 and 1932, the number of pages in the tariff schedule of the U.S. Congress increased from below 10 to nearly 200. The number of items in those tariff schedules increased from a few categories of goods to over 150,000 separate dutiable items.[18]

The land distribution policies and the tariff policies of the Federal government in the 19th century had a significant impact on our society. The one encouraged and shaped western expansion; the other encouraged and shaped American industry and at the same time freed the American citizens from some of the more burdensome taxes that could have undermined the foundations of the new country. Nevertheless, there was never a land policy or a tariff policy enacted by Congress explicitly to produce the results attributed to land distribution and tariff. "Land policy" was never more than an accumulation of such land policies as "An act making further provision for the sale of public lands" (1820); or "An act granting the right-of-way, and making a grant of land, to the States of Illinois, Mississippi, and Alabama, in aid of the construction of a railroad from Chicago to Mobile" (1850); or, "An act in relation to donations of land to certain persons in the State of Arkansas" (1850). Western development was virtually incidental. Western expansion, although very much in the rhetoric, was not in a single, discriminating policy providing for development of the West as a fundamental social choice. Western development was an outcome of piecemeal distribution of land—land distributed mainly for revenue, to pay off war debts, or to respond to the clamor for land. And the greater that demand, the smaller were the subdivisions of the units of land to be distributed. That is distributive policy, and land distribution was the source of the label for this category of public policy.

Politics in the Distributive Era

The original Arenas of Power formulation, which applied the logic of the scheme to contemporary cases, hypothesized the politics of distributive policy as one of logrolling and "pork barrel." It was hypothesized as a politics without cumulative issues, without ideology, without program. It was hypothesized as a politics in which political parties are prominent, but political parties of a particular sort. These were parties based upon nonideological forces; in effect, they were parties that were little more than institutionalized pork barrel coalitions, where the members had almost nothing in common beyond their agreement that hanging together was better than hanging separately. Before testing out those hypotheses with additional contemporary cases and data, it will be useful to test them with facts about the politics of the 19th century in light of what would be predicted from the premise that distributive policies were overwhelmingly the most important policy outputs of the federal government during an era extending from around 1815 through the end of the 19th century. Political facts about that era will be drawn from the assessments of important political historians. Their assessments are quite consistent with each other, are completely independent of the Arenas of Power hypotheses, and were also totally innocent of the uses to which that would be put in this analysis.

Leonard White reported that the change in the politics of the national government began very soon after 1814. Despite their common political views, Republicans began to fall into "chaotic factionalism" which "drove difference of principle off the stage of public affairs."[19] Party politics remained important; in fact, it was during this period that the Republican Party collapsed into two separate parts, Whigs and Democrats. But the basis of party and party differentiation was entirely different from that of the "first party system." Richard McCormick characterized this second party system as "artificial" because the cleavage between the two national parties "bore no direct relationship to the reality of sectional antagonism."[20]

Both parties attempted to be national in scope, and both parties had powerful Northern and Southern wings, so that "intraparty tensions were greater than the tensions between the two parties." They lived together as parties by avoiding the divisive issues.[21]

Herbert Agar's entire book on that period is literally based upon an appreciation of the same phenomenon. For Agar, these nonideological parties, governing the nation, were "the price of union."[22] His observations were both confirmed and explained by more recent research of Samuel Beer, who characterized the entire period between 1828 and 1860 as the period of "pork barrel coalitions." Members of these pork barrel coalitions had no common interests, or only vague interests, reports Beer. It was unnecessary to agree on common goals, and the effort to find common goals could be divisive.[23] However, these logrolling, pork barrel coalitions and the two political parties based upon them had to have some institutionalized location in the national government. During the Constituent Era, this locus shifted back and forth between President and Congress in a classic expression of the separation of powers. But toward the end of the Constituent Era Congress became the overwhelmingly dominant institution. Given the existence of a single political party and its domination of the presidency as well as of Congress, the United States might well have developed its own version of a Cabinet or parliamentary system of government if the new two-party system and the presidential nominating conventions had not emerged. During the era of distributive policy, Congress remained the more powerful institution, but on a changed basis. The new locus of power was the Congressional committee system, in part but not entirely as we know it today. Distributive politics is so individualized and localized that representation of interests before the full House or Senate became an impossibility. At the same time, members of Congress had a very large stake in participating in the actual implementation of the arrangements that had been legalized in each of the public laws providing for a distributive policy. The committee structure turned out to be an ideal means by which local and district interests could be efficiently considered before passage of distributive legislation and could then also be effectively supervised during the course of implementation by administrative agencies.

Congress got along with almost no standing legislative committees for the first 25 years of its existence under the Constitution. The House got along with three during the first decade—Ways and Means, Agriculture, and Commerce were all established as standing committees in 1795. Another committee was added in 1805 and two more in 1808. Then four were added in the House between 1813 and 1816. Before 1816, the Senate had created no standing committees whatsoever; and then in that year alone eleven standing committees were created. From that time on, however, an average of five or six standing committees were added each decade in each Chamber, until by the end of the century there were over sixty standing committees in the House and seventy in the Senate. One other fact should be added here. Virtually each and every one of these standing committees was designed to parallel the jurisdiction of a major department or agency in the Executive Branch. This proved to be the preferred method of dealing with the separation of powers: No longer would the attempt be made to compete as an institution with the presidency; standing committees would enable Congress to make policies and then supervise their implementation in each of the departments, regardless of presidential efforts. No wonder by 1895 Woodrow Wilson, as a professor of political science, could conclude that "Congressional government is committee government."[24]

It was not until the 20th century that committee government in Congress undermined party government. During this Second Era the two reinforced each other, and their relationship comprises a very important dimension of the politics of the Distributive Era. The presidency, and national programmatic parties, were submerged in the morass of millions of individual dispensations provided for in distributive statutes. The parties, as institutionalized logrolling coalitions, remained the fundamental force in Congress. In fact, party discipline, as measured by a consistency of roll-call voting, reached a level of effectiveness in the peacetime decades between 1850 and 1900 that we have never experienced since that time.[25] The parties were a congeries of individual interests, but they were able to hold themselves together when questions of the distribution of public domain were concerned, and they worked most comfortably off the floor and inside the committee structure. At the same time, since majority votes were needed to pass legislation, the role of the Speaker and the other elected parliamentary party leaders was also of considerable importance. In this sense, the dominant power of national government was the logrolling party system, which controlled policy-making through the Speaker and tight discipline on roll-call votes, controlled policy formulation and the representation of interests through dominance of the committee system, and held just short of the lion's share of control over administration through that same Congressional committee system. It is no mystery that "strong presidents" were the rule until Jefferson and were the very rare exception thereafter. And it is no paradox that national politics could remain extremely stable throughout that century in spite of the most dynamic economy in the history of the world and in the face of almost catastrophic changes in the society.[26] Part of the explanation for this paradox will have to await the next chapter, because it has so much to do with the delegation of fundamental social choices to the State governments. But part of the explanation also lies here: The domestic functions that were left to the Federal government were—until there had been a fundamental reinterpretation of the Constitution—essentially distributive functions; and, except where the whole system falls apart in civil war, distributive policies will tend to produce a highly stable politics. To refer back to New York City, the political machine is, after all, an example of extremely stable politics. And machines were based upon the kind of patronage that makes up the essence of distributive policy.

The U.S. Congress did not concern itself exclusively with distributive policies. Nearly half of its output during the Distributive Era was, in fact, constituent policy. However, two points can be made in response that can also facilitate linkage to the contemporary analysis of later chapters. First, constituent policies did in fact develop their own separate political subsystem during this era, and it is quite distinctively different from the political subsystem of distributive policy. It was simply not the prevailing one during the era in which distributive policy was overwhelmingly the prevailing function of government. Second, during this entire era, as observed earlier, almost no regulatory or redistributive policies were enacted by Congress at all. This meant that the United States had not yet become a modern nation-state and was not exercising to the fullest all of the powers and functions inherent in modern nation-states. When, in the 20th century, the United States began to exercise all of the (four) types of governmental functions, the politics of the national government began to differentiate into four separate political subsystems; but this can only be confronted after the survey of its historical development is completed.

Regulation: A Third Era of Policy, a Third Layer of Politics

National regulatory policy suffered a series of abortive beginnings and remained a dwarf creature until the New Deal. Until the late 19th century there was little demand for national intervention through regulatory policy. The Supreme Court was against it, the prevailing theory of federalism was against it, and the orientation of most social movements was still turned away from it, toward the States. Consequently, until the end of the 19th century and the first 100 years of our Republic, federal regulation "had been confined to foreign commerce or water-borne domestic commerce, and had for the most part been concerned with mere detail."[27]

There was no absence of demand for governmental intervention. The period following the Civil War was peppered up and down the country by intense social movements, responding primarily to industrialization. The agrarian reaction to commercialization was probably the most important and widespread response, but various labor movements added important class as well as regional influences to the last decades of the 19th century.

Yet it would be impossible to gain any awareness or understanding at all of these social movements by studying the laws of the national government. The public policy of the national government continued to be distributive, as though virtually unresponsive to highly assertive interests. But two interrelated developments were ultimately going to put an end to the almost exclusive tradition of conducting national politics over the pork barrel. The first of these was the nationalization of the economy to such an extent that the States became practically and constitutionally incompetent to respond to the demands of social movements. The second of these was the spread of certain of the social movements beyond their State borders in response to national or interstate commerce. All of this came to a head in 1886 with *Wabash Railway v. Illinois* in which the Supreme Court held that States could not lawfully regulate interstate commerce, even that portion taking place within its own borders.[28] This created a virtual no man's land, where States could not and Federal government, as yet, would not.

There had, of course, been a few Congressional efforts to regulate commerce. A tax had been passed immediately after the Civil War to eliminate State bank notes from the economy. In 1875 Congress enacted the Civil Rights Act which made it a misdemeanor for any individual to discriminate on the basis of race against the enjoyment of a variety of public accommodations. The Supreme Court's decision to declare this Act unconstitutional helped produce the regulatory no man's land, because it was in this opinion that the Court made unmistakably clear that the Fourteenth Amendment was a prohibition only upon the States and did not give the Federal government the right to regulate the behavior of individuals or enterprises even where a clear deprivation of civil rights could be shown.[29] Congress had passed a law regulating the importation of tea in 1883 and within two years had enacted the first of its regulations against colored margarine and adulterated butter. In 1890 and 1891, Congress passed its first laws attempting to regulate the slaughtering and curing of animals for sale. But the primary sanction in these laws was inspection; nearly twenty years would pass before more detailed regulations in the food and drug industries were to be enacted. Something as dramatic as the *Wabash* case was necessary before Congress was to make any serious effort to provide specific regulations for specific business behaviors. For, almost immediately following *Wabash*, in 1887, Congress enacted the historic Interstate Commerce Act, which turned the corner in the history of federal regulation. This was followed three years later by the Sherman Antitrust Act. Almost every year thereafter, some movement or interest group culminated its effort in a series of national legislative proposals. In the 1880s and 1890s, at least 190 bills were introduced in Congress concerned with food alone.[30] The first important and lasting food and drug regulations were enacted in 1906, but other efforts to draw the federal government into the economy were succeeding before and after that time in other areas. The Elkins Act of 1903 stiffened federal regulation of Interstate Commerce, as did the 1906 Hepburn Act and especially the Mann-Elkins Act of 1910, which attempted to restore some of the power of the ICC over long- and short-haul pricing that had been undermined by an earlier Supreme Court decision. These efforts were extended and essentially codified by the important Clayton Act and the Federal Trade Commission Act of 1914.[31]

The Character of Regulatory Policy

Two characteristics distinguish regulatory policies from virtually all the policies that had been traditional for Congress to enact. Regulatory policy brings government into (1) directly coercive relationships (2) with individual citizens. (The second characteristic becomes important as a distinction between regulation and redistribution.) Regulatory policy involves a classic use of the "police power" on the basis of which a sovereign has the right to protect the health, safety, and morals of the community. In all of the instances identified even in this earliest period of federal regulation, each policy is a matter of placing a moral definition upon conduct and then backing that definition with sanctions. Although each policy is stated in very general terms, each works upon individual conduct and must await individual conduct before being applied. The original Civil Rights Acts made it a misdemeanor for an individual to interfere against any other individual, on the basis of race, in their enjoyment of public facilities and accommodations. It was precisely because of the element of federal coercion against an individual that the Supreme Court came down against the Civil Rights Acts. The Court at the that time was still holding to the view that such coercive policies against individuals were strictly within the province of the States except under the very limited conditions that the behavior to be affected was in interstate commerce or that the individual to be regulated was a State official operating as an official. This is why so much early federal regulation concerned transportation as such or goods destined for export-import markets and therefore unmistakably in interstate commerce. By this definition, federal subsidies to farmers would also be unconstitutional, because farmers are no more in interstate commerce than are workers in factories. Yet, the constitutionality of federal subsidies was not questioned while virtually all federal efforts to regulate factory conditions were invalidated virtually until after the Depression of 1929. Apparently the Supreme Court recognized the very same distinction we are making here, between federal policies that are directly coercive and those federal policies which are in the short run only facilitative. Except for the original disposal of public lands—which were of course coercive only as regards the natives from whom they were conquered—even distributive policies are coercive in the sense that the goods distributed are drawn from a taxation system and the privileges distributed are drawn from earlier restrictive legislation that created the privileges. But this is an indirect form of coercion as compared to regulation. In the short run, and in terms of the plain meaning of the statutes themselves, the coercive element is indirect for distributive policies but quite direct for regulatory policies. Policies can be vague or specific, they can create new and effective administrative instruments, or they may be more active or passive in their approach. But one thing all regulatory efforts have in common is that they declare certain actions good or bad, they impose certain duties in regard to public programs, and they anticipate the application of some kind of sanction. There is a principle of exclusion involved here, even though it is often vague. There is a morality involved, and there is a sense that some things are in the public domain and some things are not. This was clearly true of the antitrust legislation, of the food and drug legislation, and of the child labor legislation (declared unconstitutional). It was because of this element of public morality placed upon certain actions that the question of constitutional power emerged at all. But the issue is raised here only to underscore the great difference between the three kinds of government action so far identified— those that grant powers, those that provide facilities or other resources, and those that impose duties or moralities upon individual conduct.

The Impact of Regulatory Policies on Government and Politics

Things were changing even as they appeared to remain the same. The "Republican Era," labeled by Leonard White and identified as having extended from 1869 to 1901, may differ in a number of respects from the pre–Civil War period, but to a very large extent it is a culmination of a 19th century pattern of party and congressional dominance, of government subordinated to politics, and of a presidency dominated by the other Branches. Toward the end of the Republican Era, however, the 19th century political pattern was beginning to show signs of breaking loose. Grover Cleveland, for example, began to display signs of a strong President, although his strength most frequently took the form of vetoes against congressional enactments.[32] According to presidential historian Wilfred Binkley, even President Harrison showed some signs of presidential dynamism. And more to the point, though weaker than Cleveland's, Harrison's presidency is associated with a period when "the House of Representatives began to take on some semblance of a deliberative body."[33]

Although neither Harrison nor Cleveland sought any changes, and in fact believed that the President should be guided by Congress and by his party in Congress, fundamental changes did begin to take place in the late 1880s and 1890s. These changes were enhanced and accelerated, if not demanded, by the more assertive presidencies, increasingly assertive presidencies, of Harrison, Cleveland, and McKinley—despite the fact that all three of them are known as members of the conservative wings of their parties.

Since a number of scholars will go so far as to locate the beginning of the "modern Congress" with the late 19th century, the coincidence with the advent of regulatory policy is too strong to resist. The Speaker, though always important in the House of Representatives, was joined in the 1880s by a Minority Leader. Although a party office, its purpose was more effective use of Congressional parties and would almost guarantee an increase in the importance of the parliamentary level rather than the committee level of Congress. Of more fundamental importance, but fully parallel with the resort to a Minority Leader, was the effort by both parties and their leaderships to bring some orderliness to floor proceedings. As H. Douglas Price describes the 19th century House, "Members often used bitter and outrageous language ... Outbreaks of physical violence were not infrequent, and guns and knives were on occasion carried into the Chamber."[34] The attempt to gain decorum in floor behavior turned mainly to reform of the rules by which the two chambers conducted their business. And, except for important reforms during the Reconstruction, the basic reforms in the Congress's rules were attempted and instituted during the era of regulatory policy, from the mid-1880s until 1911. Those rules changes involved such fundamental features of Congress as the power of recognition and of appointments to committees in the Speaker, such as strengthening of the Rules Committee over the conduct and allocation of time for debate, the outlawing of dilatory motions and of filibustering in the House, clarification of the jurisdiction of the Standing Committees, rules governing placement and withdrawal of bills from a calendar. All are examples of the efforts being made within Congress during that period to make itself more suitable for the conduct of business at that time. And virtually all of these rules reforms led toward one very fundamental goal: restoration of the integrity of the floor, that is, of the parliamentary level of Congress, and of the ability of Congress to cope as an institution with the new responsibilities of making fundamental social choices for the society rather than leaving those with the States.[35]

Another development specifically of that period, related to rules reforms and also to the particular problems of dealing with regulatory policy, is the beginning of an unbroken secular decline in the strength of political parties. This is a definitive turning of a corner away from the golden age of party government in the 19th century. The most obvious evidence of this change can be found in the second wave of reforms in Congress itself, beginning in 1903 and ending in 1911. This was the period during which the Speaker—a party leader, unlike the House of Commons—had his wings clipped. A revolt in the House against Speaker Joseph Cannon took away some of the important powers of the Speaker by establishing a Consent Calendar and a rule providing for committee access to the floor under some conditions without approval of the Speaker (Calendar Wednesday). The revolt also produced a rule removing the Speaker from the all-important Rules Committee, whose rules governed the amount and character of debate on each bill. This became primarily an elective rather than an appointive committee. Additional rules provided for election by the full House of the members and chairmen of standing committees, an attempt to remove from the Speaker virtual autocratic power over the all-important committee memberships.

No rules changes of comparable significance were made in the Senate during that period. However, a number of other fundamental changes in the power of political parties, inside and outside Congress, affected the Senate as well as the House. For example, the weakening of the Speaker is directly associated with the efforts in both chambers to strengthen the committee system at the expense of parties—therefore, to sever the intimate relationship between parties and committees that had prevailed all during the 19th century. In brief, this is the period in which committee seniority became virtually the sole criterion for committee power. Polsby's figures show that in the pre-1880s period, it was typical for over 90 percent of the committee chairmanships to be filled without regard to seniority. After 1887–88, departures from seniority dropped toward

at the same time in a manner that would attract attention in Washington, and so did a number of important unions. Many such groups, such as Boards of Trade, farm commodity organizations, and craft unions, predate the era of national regulatory policy, but their presence in Washington is not remarked upon until virtually the 1890s. By 1912 there was a regional and national association for most industries and sectors, for many of the important trades representing labor, and for most of the commercial farm commodities. By the end of World War I, there were at least a thousand trade associations alone, organized on a nationwide basis, representing some important trade, industry, or industrial sector.[40] In agriculture the same pattern is observable in the rise of organized commodity associations. From the 1890s onward professional observers note a major increase in the number of such organizations on a state and regional level who then began to emerge as claimants for national policies before, during, and after World War I. For example, organized interests representing corn, dairy products, cooperatives, dairy product producers (creameries), grain elevator operators, wheat, etc., became so active on the national scene that, in 1925, at least 20 of them met and formed the Grain Belt Federation of Farm Organizations (better known as the Corn Belt Committee) to fight first for tariff legislation that would favor farmers and eventually for the principle of "parity" that ultimately became the core of the New Deal policy to help the farmers by regulating farm prices.[41]

A trade association, a union, or an organized farm commodity association serves its members in a number of ways, only a proportion of which are political. A profoundly important function of business trade associations is to exchange information to help members better control their market. Provision of cheaper insurance has always been an important service of unions and farm organizations, and each such association usually publishes one or more journals or newsletters to keep each individual member alert to opportunities and rights.[42] However, when these narrowly organized trade associations and their cousins among workers and farmers turn to politics, it is extremely likely to be for the purpose of advancing a regulatory policy against a competitor, or defending itself and its members against regulatory policies that were imposed upon them by other groups. These narrowly organized trade associations, farm commodity associations, and specific trade unions are to be distinguished from the broad "peak associations" such as the Chamber of Commerce, AFL-CIO, and the American Farm Bureau Federation, which are "groups of groups." As we shall see time and again, regulatory policies tend to discourage activities by these peak associations, because regulatory policies tend to cut across and differentiate among members, corporate and individual, of the peak associations. In contrast, a narrowly defined trade association tends to be homogeneous with regard to specific regulatory policies and proposals and is unusually cohesive with respect to these. Thus, it is no coincidence, according to the Arenas of Power model, that such trade associations and sister organizations emerged in such number to deal in Washington after the 1880s; and this relationship between regulatory policy and interests organized at the trade association level will be confirmed in case study after case study of contemporary politics. It is possible to go farther and say that the rise of such groups to prominence in Washington politics helps explain the decline of power of political parties. Groups cut across geographical constituencies, and the clamor and continuity of groups in the policy-making process reduce the ability of political parties to use the committee system for logrolling. The interests of trade associations are too broad and too principled for log-rolling and tend, therefore, to spill over onto the floor and into public view. Just as in the case of New York where the machine lost its grip on regulatory and service agencies while maintaining it over the highly specific assessment agencies, this tends to be confirmed, at least at this gross survey level, with regard to regulatory policies at the national level. More specific and more quantitative data will be needed to put this association to the test, but this will be offered in due course. For the moment this issue can be left with the proposition that the change of the national government with the adoption of a number of important regulatory policies is associated with changes in the politics of the national system indicated best by the intrusion of large numbers of highly organized special inter-ests, the reform of Congress to meet these special interests, and the weakening of party to accommodate the participation of these interests in the policy-making process.

None of this is supposed to mean that as soon as regulatory policies reached the federal agenda the entire political system was transformed. What seems to be happening is that with the increase in the frequency of national regulatory proposals, the system of distributive politics moved over and was joined by still another system of politics, the two now coexisting with each other. Given the overwhelmingly larger number of distributive bills passed by Congress after the 1890s as well as before, the politics of the national level continued to be primarily one associated with distributive policies. But a small increase in the number and regularity of important regulatory policies passed by the Federal government had a very large effect on that government, and it is one that can be observed more and more easily as the national government expanded with additional important regulatory policies after 1933. The important point to emphasize here is that as the Federal government adjusted to these new functions it did not neces-sarily amalgamate the new politics into a single political system. The entire thrust of this book is the contrary, that the adjustment took the form of the establishment and maintenance of independent subsystems of politics. Each area of government policy, therefore, would tend to develop its own separate subsystem or "arena" of power. The purpose of this history of policy and politics is to show how these areas and arenas could develop naturally out of the history of the national government. Social scientists are quick to observe and accept the differentiation of functions and institutions as a distinguishing mark of modern societies. There is no reason at all to expect that the political system in a modern society will not differentiate itself proportionately to all the other institutions and processes. In fact, it would be quite remarkable if the political system resisted such differentiation.

Redistribution: Macropolicies and Macropolitics

Although the Fourth Era had its origins alongside the Third, these origins are mere traces. The relative prices of gold and silver—a version of hard and soft money policy—were a national issue going back at least to the Coinage Act of 1792. And there were times when debate over a national bank gave the appearance of hard (national) versus soft (state) monetary policy. There were, of course, serious and sustained fiscal and monetary policies during the Civil War, and there were sustained national government actions dealing with the war debt afterwards. But an organized confrontation of inflationists favoring national fiscal and monetary policy can be said to have begun in earnest after the Civil War, with real evidence of results in national statute law coming still later.[43]

Concerted efforts by Congress to affect the economy appeared in 1878 with the Bland-Allison Silver Purchase Act. This Act authorized the U.S. Treasury to buy silver and to restore and maintain both the price of silver and its status as part of the monetary system (bimetalism). This presumed success for debtors, especially farmers holding mortgages, was only a compromise, falling far short of unlimited free coinage of silver; but it met such demands for vigorous federal involvement in management of the economy. The Sherman Silver Act of 1890 was still another such venture—pro-silver and pro-inflation, but still short of soft money policy sought by those favoring free coinage of silver. A conservative turn in 1893 repealed the Sherman Silver Purchase Act and intensified farmer-debtor agitation, leading towards a brief Bryan–Free Silver epoch in the Democratic Party. During this period, Congress even attempted to enact in 1894 the first peacetime income tax, which the Supreme Court in 1895 promptly declared unconstitutional on two grounds: first, that it was a direct tax and must therefore be levied among the states according to population; and second, that since it put an ungraduated 2 percent levy on all incomes above $4,000, it violated the constitutional requirement that all taxes must be uniform.[44]

Except for the Gold Standard Act of 1900, which sealed up the coffin on the Bryan silver movement, more than a decade was to pass before there would be further and serious Congressional action in the area of redistributive policy. Fiscal policy during this period was mainly a question of how to deal with the surplus produced by tariffs. But national policy-makers became aware of the need to modernize fiscal and monetary affairs after the crisis of 1907. The Sixteenth Amendment, proposed by a Republican-dominated Congress during 1909, was adopted by the necessary 36 States just as the Democrats were returning to office in 1913; and efforts to modernize the national banking situation, which had begun soon after the 1907 panic, were coming into maturity that same year. Thus, two of the most important redistributive policies ever adopted by the Federal government, and certainly the first important ones since the 1790s, were developed and adopted by Congress in almost record time. These were the Federal Reserve Act and the graduated Federal Income Tax. The income tax was adopted so promptly that the Federal government was able to tax incomes for 10 of the 12 months of 1913. However, except for important wartime policies, such as increased income taxation and borrowing under the War Finance Corporation, there were to be no more important redistributive policies until the New Deal.[45]

The Redistributive Era had arrived irreversibly by the end of the first 100 days of the Roosevelt Administration and took its place as an equal category of public policy well before the end of Roosevelt's first full Administration. Some of the most important redistributive measures of that period were: suspension of the convertibility of dollars into gold; suspension of gold export; the Emergency Banking Act of 1933, loosening accessibility of Federal Reserve loans to member banks; dollar authority to issue unsecured greenbacks up to $3 billion under the Thomas Amendment to the AAA; temporary deposit insurance (subsequently made permanent); presidential authority to purchase up to $2 billion of gold, foreign exchange, or government securities as part of an easing of money supply. This was far from the end of New Deal fiscal and monetary efforts but only illustrates a very large and significant beginning.[46]

Of many additional New Deal redistributive policies, the highlights would include: the Social Security Act, plus the revision of the Internal Revenue Code, the various work programs for those already on relief, the Farm Security Administration (later Farmers Home Administration) with its provisions for loans to needy farmers at rates of interest well below the market, the entire Farm Credit System, and original provisions for home mortgage guarantees in the Federal Housing Administration (FHA) which were to be expanded so greatly in various areas of investment guarantees in the 1960s and 1970s.[47]

Redistributive Policies: A Characterization

Despite the apparent heterogeneity of these examples, they clearly belong to the same species, and this species is distinctively different from the three others identified before. Each of these policies works through some fundamental discrimination among attributes in the society, or it so creates or manipulates some structural feature of the economy that large aggregates of the economy or society are divided by it. Redistributive policies involve "primary rules" just as do regulatory policies, but with the enormous difference that the primary rules of redistributive policy do not depend upon or wait for the behavior of individuals before being applied. Redistributive policies therefore involve involuntary groupings of people and automatic or self-executing groupings of people. This happens in at least two ways: Individuals cannot escape the application of a rule defining a negative category, such as the income brackets of the Internal Revenue Code; and, second, individuals cannot by their own choice get themselves included into a positive category established by a redistributive rule, as in the case of welfare programs. Federal Reserve manipulation of the interest rates will affect the housing mortgage market regardless of the particular behaviors of individuals inside or outside that market. Limiting public works jobs to those already on relief, or limiting indemnities to those who have passed the age of 65 and have quit work, or moving tax rates up with each income bracket are all examples of redistributive policies, of a positive or a negative type of categorization, because they deal in attributes of citizens and structures of citizens without regard to individual performance.

No judgment is involved here on whether these policies actually do redistribute values. A very sophisticated analysis covering many, many years would be required to assess the actual impact of any policy on the society or economy. Policies included within this type are redistributive only on the basis of the formal provisions of the laws. "Redistribution" probably is not a good name for this category because of its connotation. "System manipulation" might be a better term. "Macropolicy" might also be a better term; in fact, "environment of conduct," which is used to help define redistributive policy, is almost synonymous with the notion of "macro." Welfare is macro because it works through attributes without having to wait for individual actions, etc. I will hold to the term redistribution because I have already used it in certain publications and because I have found no altogether better alternative. However, the notion of macropolicy ought to be kept in mind.

Redistributive Politics

From the very beginning redistributive policies have been associated with social classes and social movements. Reference was made earlier to intimations of class politics during the 1790s in association with some important redistributive policies, despite the fact that that era was dominated by constituent policies. Since that time, agriculture is the most interesting case in point, first because agriculture interests were the first to make important redistributive demands on the government in the late 19th century, and second, because there is such a neat fit between changes in the demands of agriculture and changes in the structure of agriculture politics. When an all-agriculture movement first formed after the Civil War in the United States, it was quite clearly in reaction to the commercialization of agriculture, and it took the form of demands for inflation as a matter of national policy. The price of silver and the coinage of silver, and the easy money policy in general, were the policy demand, and around these demands agriculture built such a broad, class solidarity that they made a tremendous amount of political history during the late 19th century. For a while they were in fact a national political party with a presidential candidate, and after that, again for a short while, their interests dominated the Democratic Party. This is the beginning of a new phase of "movement politics" in the United States, and it was soon to be joined by a national labor movement, whose early demands were also of a redistributive nature. But note immediately for agriculture that as the national government responded with subsidy and educational programs rather than redistributive policies, the agriculture movement became decentralized back toward its many state organizations and commodity groups. National government actions culminated in a sense with the Extension Service in 1914. The politics around the Extension Service was primarily the local "farm bureaus," which were organized to make the Extension Service programs work in each county, and five years after the foundation of the Extension Service in 1914, the Farm Bureau Federation (FBF) was formed, and the FBF immediately became the dominant political force around agricultural services. Yet the FBF is not like the earlier agriculture movement at all; rather, it is a logrolling coalition of state farm bureaus, composed mainly of rather prosperous farmers and farm service organizations. A third form of agriculture politics, the tightly organized farm commodity organizations, came eventually to dominate the regulation of agriculture standards and the regulation of land uses in the "parity" programs of the 1930s. Both of these are regulatory programs.

Even business politics took on a class or social movement form around these early redistributive policies. In the battle to repeal silver purchase policies and to reestablish the Gold Standard, the Boards of Trade in 17 cities west of Ohio and north of Missouri called a conference for January of 1897, at which 26 of the 45 states in the United States at that time were represented by 500 delegates. A commission was formed and some serious studies by economists were commissioned in order to produce draft legislation for reform proposals. This went to the newly elected President McKinley, who put the prestige of his office back of the proposals, leading to enactment of the Gold Standard Act of 1900.[48]

The passage of the Gold Standard Act indicates another important aspect of redistributive politics that could already be seen early in the era of redistributive policy but can be seen increasingly clearly in our own day. This is that redistributive politics is highly executive-centered. Even weak presidents found themselves the center of attention when issues of this sort arose. At a time when there were no strong presidents, President Cleveland, who had virtually abdicated leadership to Congress, found himself taking the lead on two important issues during his Administration: the repeal of the Silver Purchase Act and the issue of interest charges on U.S. bonds. On these two issues, Binckley reports that Cleveland was inextricably the political center, to such an extent that he had to compromise with "his theory of separated powers," according to which he tried to leave all policy-making to Congress. According to Woodrow Wilson, a contemporaneous observer, Cleveland "thought it not part of his proper function to press his preference in any other way [than by recommendation in a message] upon the acceptance of Congress," yet, we see him taking a lead in two important redistributive demands.[49] At another time, in 1895, when gold was being exported at too fast a pace, President Cleveland "took matters into his own hands" and arranged with a consortium of New York bankers, headed by J. P. Morgan, for a sale of $65 million, to be paid in gold imported from Europe.[50] As the frequency of redistributive proposals and policies increased, so did the definition of the presidency and of President-Congress relationships. Theodore Roosevelt defined the presidency in terms of a "stewardship" in which a President ought to be able to do anything that is not expressly forbidden. Woodrow Wilson's concept of the presidency was one of a strong British-type prime minister who would have a program, attempt to get it through Congress, and would "go to the country" if Congress failed to do his bidding. Similarly, Roosevelt referred to the presidency as a "bully pulpit"; and Roosevelt was already using the notion of an "administration bill," which became a regular description during the Wilson administration. An administration bill was given privileged status in the House and Senate, and there were leading members of Congress who were known as administration representatives and were expected to carry the administration program through.[51] Although by no means all of Wilson's legislative proposals were redistributive, many of them, especially the important early ones, were in fact redistributive.

The behavior of agriculture and labor groups around redistributive policies suggests still another important characteristic of redistributive politics, which is that it is far more ideological than any other kind of politics. The "Cross of Gold" rhetoric may have been personal to William Jennings Bryan, but that level of appeal was actually typical, and remains typical, of redistributive politics. The agriculture movement was filled with rhetoric about fairness and justice and equality. The "decline of agrarian democracy" so eloquently chronicled by Grant McConell can be seen as the decline of egalitarian ideology. The high level rhetoric became less and less appropriate as the national government responded less with redistributive policies and more with such distributive policies as agricultural extension. And without the intense egalitarian ideology, the agriculture movement itself cooled into a problem of organization and was transformed into a congeries of agriculture-based groups with concrete interests too narrow to be called ideological.[52]

The same was true of the labor movement after the Civil War. It was led by highly militant and ideological leadership until it was transformed in structure and in demand by Samuel Gompers and his literally antimovement notion of "business unionism." As a consequence, labor became a movement in name only, eventually resembling the cold remains of the agriculture movement—a congeries of individual craft and, eventually, industrial unions. Later it will be shown in more detail how these specialized unions are compatible with distributive and regulatory policies, coming back together in a solidarity House of Labor mainly on welfare and general unemployment (redistributive) policy demands.

Business, although cooler in style, has not been immune to ideological appeals and ideological points of view, literally in the form of a movement politics. The National Association of Manufacturers (NAM) itself was an industry-wide general anti-union organization. And, in its retreat from power during the New Deal, business made appeals that can only be counted as heavily ideological, in their attempt to unify all of the various and otherwise competing business interests. Robert Lane shows in his intensive study of the reactions of big business to the New Deal that it started out in the 1930s as highly ideological but within a few years became much more concretely interest-oriented and instrumental. As will be shown, this phenomenon observed by Lane is not merely a matter of the passage of time but is closely related to the issues themselves, such that some ideological appeals remain against the most redistributive aspects of the New Deal and the Fair Deal while the rhetoric of business was a good deal more cool and instrumental in response to regulatory policies.[53]

Other aspects of politics changed also to make a place for redistributive policies, but because these were joining a government already modernizing by significant growth plus the accretion of the almost entirely new function of regulation, the precise changes attributable to redistribution cannot be singled out as a separate era. Congress, as reported, was already responding to these governmental changes. Accretion of redistributive functions brought on still more changes, though these will eventually be appreciated as quite distinctive. For example, redistributive policies had a special impact upon Congress precisely because these policies are so much more compatible with the White House and with professionals and bureaucrats inside the government and in the corporations and universities. For example, the 1890s fight over silver not only gave us a temporarily assertive presidency but was accompanied also by a dramatic though temporary shift in Congressional behavior—not toward submission to the President but simply away from committees and parties toward the floor and toward broader, nonparty confrontations. According to Myers, "the cleavage in both Houses was along sectional lines rather than party lines, and both parties were badly split."[54] And "sectional lines" especially at that time were strongly associated with basic differences in relationships to capitalism and agriculture. Moreover, although the conservative Gold Standard Act of 1900 was a presidential proposal, drafted by professional university economists, Congress nevertheless took the draft and changed it in significant ways before adoption.[55] Hurst, looking at the same Act, was struck by the fact that while most policies of that period were "opportunistic bargains" rather than integrated policy, Congress "asserted its right to control the money supply." And the examples Hurst gave of Congressional assertion were precisely the several redistributive efforts made by the national government extending back to 1875 and culminating with the Gold Standard Act of 1900.[56]

CHAPTER 4

᚛᚛

American Federalism

A Demonstration of the Categoric
Character of Policy and Politics

A national government without regulatory and redistributive policies may have been unique in the development of all modern states. The national government of the nineteenth century United States was just such a government; and the political consequences of such a government, as well as the consequences of modernizing that government, have now been reviewed. What remains is the question of where the other primary functions of government were being performed and whether predictable and explicable patterns of politics developed there.

The Constitution, the Federal Structure, and the Division of Functions

If there was a single, unquestioned principle at the 1787 Constitutional Convention, it was that the states would be the foundation of the Republic. The position of the states under the Articles of Confederation had been even stronger; indeed, one of the purposes of the new Constitution was to get the states to relinquish some of their powers to the national government. Nevertheless, none of the states were prepared to relinquish very much, and consequently there was little conflict among the delegates over the final resolution of the federal structure of the Constitution, that there were to be two sovereigns in the American system. The national government was, of course, to possess the foreign affairs power, small for a country bent upon avoiding international involvements, yet expandable. Beyond that it was to be a government of delegated and expressed powers, as outlined in Article I, Part 8. These were not inconsiderable powers, and successive generations of national leaders discovered the elasticity of the expressed powers that had been granted. However, most of the early generations of leaders interpreted these grants of national power relatively narrowly. The intention of strict construction of national powers was underlined by the Tenth Amendment of the Bill of Rights (ratified December 15, 1791): "The powers not delegated to the United

States by the Constitution, nor prohibited by it to the States, are reserved to the States respectively, or to the people."

The Constitution produced two sovereigns in theory but also in fact. Since the states already existed, this was something of a recognition of realities. Nevertheless, the Constitution placed an entirely new reenforcement upon state government even as it was creating a far stronger central government than many had thought they had fought for in the Revolution. The Republic under the Constitution began with and continues to have, or to tolerate, two separate layers of government: two separate sources of law; two separate sources of legitimate control; two almost completely separate sets of restraints upon and protections of human beings, their rights, their obligations, and their security. The states were of course not made completely autonomous from each other or from the national government. The Supreme Court is the supreme court of the United States and not merely of the national government. Conflicts between citizens of two or more states are beyond the power of any one state. Conflicts between a state law and a federal law immediately become the province of the federal judiciary. States are beholden to the treaties made by the national government, and states are severely limited in their power to entice or control business enterprise. There turned out to be ample means for making a national economy and for keeping the many, and growing number of, states tied to the nation as the first among equal sovereigns. Where federalism expresses itself most clearly as a separation between two sovereigns or two layers of government is in the ultimate division of functions as these can be seen concretely in the very different types of public policies produced by the states and by the national government. And the results flowing from this division could hardly be more fundamental in the shaping of the American political system.

Table I.1 is a straightforward inventory of the division of functions between the states and the national government during all of the nineteenth century and most of the twentieth. And, although national government has, as we have seen, taken on significant regulatory and redistributive functions in the twentieth century, Table I.1 continues to be a fair, even if declining, representation of the division of functions in our own times. Column 1, a summary of nineteenth-century national government policies, needs no further treatment here. Columns 2 and 3 are the significant additions and will be the focus of this inquiry.

States and Cities: The Real Division of Powers

The key to federalism is not to be found in the special layering—the states—between the national and local levels. That is merely a restatement of federalism. The key lies with what it was the states were empowered to do and with what the states ended up doing in fact. One of the most interesting features of modern American government and politics is that so much of it operates precisely as the Founders had intended.

The states were expected to retain most of the so-called police power in our system—that is, the power to make policies concerning the health, safety, and morals of the community, and that meant to exert control over persons and property. This is precisely what the states have been doing for 200 years, and that will be the key to the states as well as to the cities. The merest glance back at column 2 of Table I.1 will give an adequate picture of the real division of powers between federal and state and between state and the city. It shows clearly that the states did almost all of the governing, and still do most of it. All of the property and commerce law has been in the laws of each state; the preponderance of property and commerce law is still in the state statutes. That is also true of the marketing laws, the credit laws, the insurance laws, and the land use laws. This means that the states created capitalism in the United States and that capitalism is inconceivable outside the cumulation of hundreds of laws concerning property and its exchange. That of course includes all the corporation laws, which have been and in largest part still are state laws. Take as a single case the activities of the State Assembly of New York in 1850. The Assembly passed 380 laws, of which 65 percent dealt with local governments and business corporations. Cities and counties in the state were recipients of 179 laws; and, although most of them dealt with relatively trivial matters in response to requests made by representatives of the local governments, many fundamental laws are included, as for example, the complete city charter for the City of Brooklyn and the fundamental public health laws of the City of New York, which was at that time only Manhattan. Business corporations were the subject of at least 70 laws, of which 17 dealt with the regulation of some aspect of railroads, and 13 laws provided for various regulations of the banking industry. One law was a general railroad corporation law; several of the laws had to do with improvements on the chartering of banks; several laws concerned the charters and permissible behaviors of mutual insurance companies in the state.

By 1850, states like New York already had effective public health laws on their books, and that is interesting considering that this is before there were any accepted theories of epidemiology. States also developed construction codes, standards for street openings in cities and in towns, regulations concerning public conveyances within cities, and the all-important regulations affecting families, estates, marriages, disposition of children, and so on. The regulation of the electoral process was still another area in which states were virtually the exclusive government.

The states, therefore, have made the fundamental social choices for the society. The states have provided most of the framework within which modern life is taking place, life as economics, life as family, life as community social order. The importance of the states can be further emphasized by including the fact that there is no national common law in the United States. Each state's judicial system has dealt with all matters not covered strictly by legislation, and has also been the interpreter of last resort of state statutory law. The state assemblies have in turn codified the many decisions of the state courts into later legislation. This has been an expanding and self-reinforcing system of making, interpreting, and extending the fundamental social choices in our country. And into this system the Supreme Court and the U.S. Congress enter only occasionally and sporadically. Some state laws have conflicted with national laws or with the U.S. Constitution. Citizens of two states may in a suit in the federal courts implicate still other state laws. But these moments of intervention by the federal courts are tiny in comparison to the total flow of fundamental social choices being made by state legislatures, enforced by state courts, and later codified by state legislators as state statutes. This has been the law of capitalism as it was the law of slavery. This has been the law of property and virtually all of the other arrangements held dear enough by the American public to lead them to support severe, authoritative, and clear commitments by the government through law. This is how the division of powers between national and state government became a division of function. Sovereignty was lodged at the national level, but for every type of public policy other than foreign policy, the action of the national government was contingent upon a domestic consensus that rarely existed—as anticipated and desired by Madison in *Federalist 10*. As we have already seen, consensus at the national level for domestic policy was usually a logrolling consensus based upon uncommon rather than common interests. In contrast, all the remaining domestic policies were left to the states, where fundamental social choices had to be made whether there was consensus or not. The states were left to deal with matters that Justice Cardozo once described as closest to "the concept of ordered liberty." This is a police power. This is the power and the obligation to regulate individuals for the sake of creating and maintaining public order.

Where does this leave the local government? It is well known that all local units, from villages to counties to the largest cities, are mere creatures of the state government. Over 40 percent of all of the legislative action in New York in 1850 concerned itself with the structure or functions of local government, and neither New York nor 1850 was unique in this type of activity. Nevertheless, cities and counties have always been important units of government. The special role of the state government simply put local governments in an unusual situation. Since we were a federal system, cities were freed from many of the types of controls that central governments exercise over cities in Europe. There was no large administrative presence representing a national government, no Ministry of the Interior, no national police force. On the other side, while cities and other local governments were subject to state laws, local governments were not treated only as administrative units of the state government. Local governments have operated under narrowly delegated authority, within which they were left to apply state laws to their own local conditions. The principle of municipal law that once guided virtually every state court was the so-called Dillon Rule, which held that "Any fair, reasonable, substantial doubt concerning the existence of power is resolved by the courts against [city government], and the power is denied."[1] But this still gave cities sufficient leeway to develop their own peculiar and distinctive type of government. That is to say, the cities were given a special, though small, sphere of freedom, and this shaped their governmental development profoundly. The states, in effect, had given the city the power to grant privileges. Fundamental social choices in each area were made by the states, and therefore the city was saved from the most agonizing feature of governing.

Therefore the city, especially the large city, could concern itself entirely with the distributive side of social choices. State government delegated to cities certain powers to apply the state laws and to make allowances in terms of local needs. Those applications and allowances became privileges that the city governments could hand out on an individual basis as a reward for services, as a reward for political support, as a benefit to members of one's own family, and so on. That is to say, the major role of local government has been to take that which has been declared illegal by the states and to grant it to individuals, item by item, as a privilege.

This has been the essential character of local government until recent decades. The fundamental social choice as to what shall be declared illegal was made in the State Assembly; the city government could then dispense with the allowances, the variances, and the permissions on an individual basis. In the broadest sense, this is licensing, and that was the basis of city government as well as the basis for most of the valuable patronage for which city governments and city political elites have been famous. A license—or a permit or franchise—is a permission to do something that is otherwise illegal. This licensing power is an essential aspect of the police power and was, in the name of public order and justice, applied to the use of lands, the construction of buildings on those lands, the operation of inns and public conveyances, and to a wide variety of businesses and occupations. There is nothing intrinsically or inherently outside the reach of state power to declare an activity illegal and then to grant permission to individuals to engage in that restricted activity. There is, therefore, almost no limit as to patronage as a policy. This power to declare things illegal and then to grant them as privilege is the power of kings, the power of sovereigns. There is probably no other instance in history where this power of kings has been given up to such an extent to lower units of government. State governments and the national government can of course exercise the licensing power, and do; but it is extraordinary that so much of this power has been delegated to the local governments, and it is all the more significant because it comprised so large a proportion of the city government activities during the first 150 years or more of American history as a national republic. And this licensing power, or the power to grant exceptions and variances to general prohibitions, is an especially significant basis for city government because it is almost infinitely expansible and renewable. At any point when available patronage resources are shrinking, cities need only go to the State Assembly and get another one or more enterprises or occupations declared illegal. This immediately renews the patronage resource.

City government, therefore, has a deeply distributive basis. As with distributive policies described for the federal government, local government policies can be disaggregated into hundreds and thousands of individual units, each of which can be dispensed within virtual isolation from the other units. This is true whether we are talking about licenses granted to restaurants, variances granted to enterprises seeking to build a certain type of building in a particular area where it is otherwise forbidden, permits granted to individual cab drivers, or franchises granted to large corporations to operate exclusive railroad or other public conveyance services in all or part of the city. And it may be important to repeat here that these governmental policies require almost no confrontation with fundamental social choice. The fundamental choices were made by the state legislature at the time when it was decided to declare the practice of law or medicine illegal, or the sale of taxi rides illegal, or the provision of water illegal, and so on.

An inevitable conclusion from all this is that the power to provide variances and exceptions to state law was almost miraculously well suited for the type of politics that came to be associated with cities and counties. But the truth is almost precisely the other way around: The power to create and grant privileges antedates the local political patterns we are aware of today; in fact, here is another instance where the prevailing pattern of public policy caused the observed political patterns. Many of the important distinctive features of American cities can be shown to be directly attributable to the setting up of local governments as patronage dispensers. And when city governments began to take on important regulatory and redistributive policies, as part of their advancement toward "home rule," they lost some of their distinctive nineteenth century features and took on some brand new twentieth century features. In each instance the changes in policy and eventually in politics will confirm the theoretical structure of this volume.

The Specialization of Politics Within a Federal System of Divided Functions

The number of state and local units in the United States would appear to defy generalization. Nevertheless, there are a few consistent patterns of association between the dominant policy pattern for each level and the prevailing political patterns. Some of these, although by no means all, will be consistent with the Arenas of Power scheme and could have been predicted by an extension of the logic of that scheme. Despite many exceptions and anomalies which may or may not be accounted for, there is one overriding fact, and this is that state politics is different from local politics, and states have more in common with each other than any one state or regional designation of states may have with its own and neighboring cities. The policy scheme will be confirmed to the extent that this proposition is confirmed, because most states are most like each other, and are most different from cities, in terms of the policies they are making within the federal system; and they are most unlike each other, and should most resemble their own and neighboring cities, in terms of the cultural and historical characteristics of their geographical location.

Politics in the States

The origins of most of the characteristics of modern politics can be traced back to the period of the Founding, the spread of suffrage, the spread of the industrialization of work, and the commercialization of agriculture. But what is most striking about the politics, considering the immensity of the social forces out of which the politics generated, is the differential impact of those social forces upon each of the levels of government. The contrast between national politics and state politics will be found to be extensive and fundamental, as will be the differences between state politics and local politics. The best way to capture the differences throughout the nineteenth century is by contrasting the state with the pattern of national politics as captured so well by Samuel Huntington: "The institutional framework established in 1787 has ... changed remarkably little.... [T]he American political system of the twentieth century still bears closer approximation to the Tudor polity of the 16th century than does the British political system of the twentieth century."[2] As we have already seen, it was the national political structure that did not change appreciably during the entire nineteenth century and part of the twentieth century. These patterns seemed even to survive the Civil War. And they gave the national government a stability that is quite astonishing when put in context of the violent and disruptive social changes going on during the same period.

It would of course be quite mistaken to conclude that politics was somehow insulated from this social dynamism. The fact of the matter was that America had not insulated itself from social dynamism but had managed to focus that dynamism away from Washington and upon the state governments and state political systems, where, in largest part, it was successfully absorbed. America was not nonviolent in its politics. America did not enjoy a happy and peaceful Lockean consensus. America enjoyed a Madisonian consensus, which meant the pushing of fundamental issues and fundamental political confrontation away from the center, either to keep them from being settled at all, or to be sure that a majority solution in one area of the country could not become, except with great difficulty, a national majority settlement. The buck stopped with the states, at the state level, because that was where a solution could, in fact, be written into law. This was almost certain to produce a distinctive set of institutions and political practices. This distinctiveness can be located along at least four different dimensions. Even though the manifestations of each will vary from state to state and region to region, there will be ample documentation of one kind or another in virtually all the states. And, although each of these dimensions or factors is intimately related to each of the others, they can with little damage be separated out for purposes of analysis. The four dimensions will be taken up in the following order: party and partisanship, groups and corporations, constitution versus legislature, violence.

The Role of Party and Partisanship

Party organizations have been almost nonexistent at the state level in the United States. The states tended to develop strong partisanship, not strong party organizations or institutions. Here we immediately see the situation that is almost the reverse of the national and the local levels in the United States. As the suffrage spread and as party organizations formed, they formed around districts where elections were to take place. In a well organized party situation in the United States, there is some kind of party committee for every district in which an election is to be held. A formal picture of party organization in the United States is a very complex affair. The informal, or real, party organization is a simpler version of exactly the same thing; that is to say, there is a high correspondence between formal and informal party structure in the United States, in which one or more of the levels of formal party organization become the key and central unit. Ordinarily this is the ward or assembly district, at the lowest level, and the county at the intermediate level. For most states, that has been pretty much the story in a nutshell. Each of these wards and counties would gain some kind of representation at a state convention for the purpose of nominating candidates for governorship and other statewide elective offices. But it would be very difficult to find a state party apparatus or any regular, vertical, or hierarchical articulation between the lower levels and the "state central committee." Some state central committees have enjoyed power, and on rare occasions a state political leader may have been called a state boss. That was usually a misnomer. Party organization in the United States is almost entirely and exclusively a local phenomenon.

Now, to this extent, the state and the national political systems tend to resemble each other, in that both are highly derivative, and the effectiveness of continuity of each depends upon the occasional consensus that a central or national committee leader might enjoy among the local party organization leaders. But here resemblance ends, because state politics is, and has been, heavily and consistently partisan despite the absence of statewide party organizations.

Distinctions between the two national parties in the nineteenth century were also consistent, and were strong enough to influence the presidency, Congress, and national administrative organizations. But the division between the parties, as already shown, was mostly a matter of convenience, dominated by logrolling, comfortable within the context of distributive policies of the day. Partisan politics in the typical American state was far more intense and cumulative across a variety of issues. At every turn it is impossible to miss this intensity. State politics has been an all-stakes game, a politics of exclusion, a politics frequently peppered with violence, a politics not far removed from conquest. Partisanship has been polarized even though not organized. At the risk of doing grave injustice to a few important exceptions, this polarized partisanship has displayed itself in at least three forms—one early in the nineteenth century for all the states at that time, and two for the late nineteenth and into the twentieth century—one for the South and one for the remaining states. But despite these different forms, it will be quite possible to use the same vocabulary, because so much about the politics in each of these states has been the same. As Richard McCormick puts it, "Between 1836 and 1852, as in no other period in our history, each of the parties was truly national in its extent."[3] Prior to 1836, according to McCormick, organized partisanship had put the Federalist party in the overwhelmingly dominant position in the New England states, while the Republicans possessed an almost equal supremacy among southern states. Thus the two decades after 1836 were almost an interlude, although a very significant one indeed. During that time, the two major parties were represented in virtually every county and principality in the country. In only two of the then twenty-five states—New Hampshire and Maine—did the dominant party carry more than 90 percent of all the counties in the election of 1836. In twenty-two of the states the second party carried at least 20 percent of all the counties. Party polarization was, therefore, organized and in virtually all of the localities of the United States of that time.

Following the Civil War some of that same partisanship was to return to many of the states, but it was declining toward a different kind of polarized partisanship altogether. The first of these forms was, of course, a return to the system of one-party states of the pre-1836 period. By the end of the nineteenth century, there were many states in which the second party was almost nonexistent. New England and some of the Middle Atlantic States were entirely and consistently Republican, and the states of the confederacy were by that time so Democratic that Republicans hardly bothered to offer candidates at all. In the South, the minority party was forced out because of the tremendous urge of white people of all social classes and regions to maintain consensus against blacks. Other divisive issues were handled by the device of the white primary, and this further obviated the functions of a second party. This device was sufficient to deal with important economic and social differences among whites, and it was resilient enough to handle the near-violent forms in which southern politics often emerged because of racial fears and the reactions to the coming of modern capitalism.[4]

Factors leading to the suppression of the Democratic party in New England and other parts of the North were only a little less violent than those of the South. Part of it was the memory of the Civil War and the issues that gave rise to it. And part of it was the much more contemporaneous but equally serious business of rural-urban cleavage. As long as rural interests continued to be dominant, the Republican party was likely to be dominant in these states. As Samuel Hays put it, "Rural-urban conflicts were as strong, if not stronger, than the hostility toward corporate wealth."[5] This was going to keep the farmers and workers at each other's throats and was at the same time going to contribute to the suppression of one party or another wherever rural interests continued to dominate.[6] The point here is that the stakes were so high in state politics that for a long period of time, organized and routine party politics was done away with almost altogether, in favor of different forms of very intense, high-stakes, near-violence partisanships. Elites might be urban or rural, corporate or individualist, reactionary or progressive. But for many states during many decades, politics was literally too intense for the cool workings of electoral organizations and skillful party professionals.

Even during the very period of "sectionalism," where many states were under the exclusive control of a single party, there were some states which gave at least the appearance of maintaining the two-party competition the entire country had experienced for a short while in the early nineteenth century, and were again to experience after 1932. But for most of these states, the appearances are deceiving. The actual form of partisanship in these states was closer to the one-party states than to the actual two-party competitive states. What was actually happening here was a kind of intrastate sectionalism, where one section of the state was almost completely dominated by one party and another section of the state was almost completely dominated by a different party. For statewide offices, especially governor, this gave the state politics an appearance of organized, two-party competition, when, in fact, the opposite was almost certainly the case. Sometimes this was the result of a deep and abiding rural-urban split. At other times it was the result of differences in patterns of original settlement, with part of the state drawing its original population from New England and another part drawing its population from the deep South. But whatever might explain it in particular states, the fact of the matter was that a significant number of states were one-party Republican in one part, and one-party Democratic in another, with the minority party in each half virtually suppressed. For example, the State of New York is well known for its close two-party competitiveness for gubernatorial and senatorial elections. Yet, this is clearly the result of an urban-Democratic New York City and Buffalo, where Republicans rarely got more than crumbs, and an "upstate" where Democrats were a hopeless case. That is a clear case of rural-urban cleavage that virtually eliminated direct two-party confrontation, but left organized partisanship extremely strong. Or take Oklahoma, in which for most of its history as a state the Republicans dominated all the counties in the northern half and the Democrats dominated the counties in the southern half of the state. This was the result of differential migration reinforced by different types of agriculture in the two halves of the state.[7] Illinois was a variant of both the Oklahoma and the New York cases, since it combined a north-south split based upon sources of migration with a rural-urban split between Chicago and "out-of-state." Thus, the Democrats have been overwhelmingly dominant in Chicago and in the southern counties, whereas the middle, most rural, and agricultural counties have been overwhelmingly dominated by the Republicans. That there have been many such states can be indicated by the fact that so many states have lived under systems where the governorship is consistently held by one party and the two legislative houses were under control of the opposite party. For example, this was the case between 1931 and 1952 for at least 12 important states. In 3 such states (Massachusetts, Nevada, and Connecticut) there was such a split in 14 of the 20 years. In 4 states (Rhode Island, Wyoming, Indiana, and New York) there was such a split for 12 of the 20 years. And in 5 states (Colorado, Delaware, Montana, Washington, Missouri) 10 of those 20 years were lived under such conditions.[8] A great part of this pattern is attributable to intrastate sectionalism. Other factors also contributed to it, such as direct suppression of the minority party, collusive relationships between a dominant party and a minority party in order to sweeten the rewards of defeat, and, of course, systematic gerrymandering. But all the factors add up to a single proposition, "Most American states have developed a wondrous damper on party government."[9]

Intense partisanship based upon sectionalism, urban-rural cleavages, racial cleavages, intra-agriculture and infra-industrial cleavages, reinforced by Civil War memories, were most often too hot for party. And if this were to the extent observed here true in the developed East, it was all the more true in the new states of the West, where the large corporations and industrialization preceded people as well as parties. California, which has been famous for "nonpartisanship" because of the ultrafragmentation of political parties, has actually been a case of partisanship in the extreme. The so-called nonpartisanship has really been a mask for intense but nonparty partisanship. While older states may have suppressed their second party, there was at least one party and a memory trace of a party system. In California, party was not allowed to develop at all. From an organizational standpoint, California is more comparable to many Third World developing countries than to the other American states. A few major corporations, such as Southern Pacific, were the only organized force in a new state that was large, rich, growing, and politically amorphous. Movements, vigilantism, sporadic party organizations, and direct political violence provided an ostinato accompaniment to regular domination in Sacramento by a few corporate barons. As California developed away from that primitive stage, it still did not develop parties, but did develop partisanship—in fact, a rather stable four-way partisanship of infrastate sectionalism reinforced by economic cleavages. One student of California politics divides the state into four major geopolitical areas: (1) the Bay Area Complex, plus coastal regions up to Oregon and down to the Tehachapis (25 percent of the population); (2) the Southern California Sun Belt, including Orange County, San Diego, and the six other Southern California counties, but excluding Los Angeles (about 45 percent of the population); (3) the City of Los Angeles and immediate environs (about 15 percent of the population); and (4) the Interior Agricultural Plateau (about 15 percent of the population).[10] Successful state politicians in California—from Hiram Johnson and Earl Warren through Richard Nixon, Ronald Reagan, and Jerry Brown—have been intensely partisan; nonpartisanship has been a misnomer for nonparty. They played the partisanship game or they perished. And they used the same intensely partisan but nonparty tactics used in other one-party or nonparty states, especially of the South—strong rhetoric, personal followings, mass appeals, class and racial and regional fears, etc., because these grew upon California's long memory of railroad and other corporate domination, the importation of cheap labor, the surge and then abandonment of labor supplies, and, in general, poverty amid prosperity. It is a myth that party and stable electoral processes prosper in this kind of environment. To repeat, the politics of the states in the United States was consonant with the kind of job the state governments had to do.

The Role and Place of Groups

Since this is almost the correlative of the party, or nonparty, situation, little detail is necessary. Whether one is observing the Southern Pacific, the oil corporations, or the mining companies of the West, or whether one is observing the trusts, the utilities, or the trade associations in the East, an ever-present reality of state politics is corporate pluralism. During long stretches of the political histories of most of the states, the political machines around the state legislatures were corporate rather than party, and were based upon wealth and organization and access rather than voters and electoral districts. The "Big Four" of California politics for over a generation following the prosperous 1880s were corporate giants whose basis of power was the railroads. In 1908, for example, a San Francisco newspaper referred to "the railroad company machine," with "an expert political manager" in every California county, as still the dominant force in California politics. But at the very same time, even in the advanced industrial economy of New York State, there was broad consensus that the State Assembly was dominated by the equivalent corporations, there simply being more of them in an advanced economy. A famous cartoon by Keppler depicts the State Senate in Albany as a motley collection of meek little fellows at their desks under the shadow of several enormous, bloated, top-hatted creatures around the rear of the chamber with the following labels prominently written across their distended bellies: Steel Beam Trust, Copper Trust, Standard Oil Trust, Iron Trust, Sugar Trust, etc.

Corporate pluralism is far more compatible with partisanship than with party. Organized groups either represent or can maneuver in order to appear to represent existing interests that underlie partisanship. Consider, for example, the many workers who preferred the iron trust in the East or the railroad bosses in the West over the dirt farmers in their own neighborhoods despite the similarity of their experience with class exploitation. Moreover, partisanship as well as corporate groupings are both more appropriate than parties or the politics of state police power as this is expressed in regulatory policies. At the state level, groups and partisanship took their shape around the fact that the Assembly could exclude an entire race of Chinese (immigration was almost entirely under state law until the twentieth century), the state could grant a monopoly, could authorize a private army, could allow or disallow strikes, could constrict or expand corporate freedom. In the Midwest and South there may have been less obvious control by corporations acting as plural machines, but there was still more organized pluralism than organized state parties in both regions. The Grange, for example, was a state-by-state movement, well organized along fraternal lines. It appeared to be a national or large regional movement; but that was a superficial interpretation of regional influences that moved from state to state, within each state, from Minnesota to Mississippi. Even where the Grange was present the South was less pluralistic than the other regions of the country, and most everyone will agree that this is attributable to the suppression of many natural differences in order to maintain state control of race relations. In an important sense this is a further confirmation of the rule that policies shape politics, inasmuch as the problems for a long period of time in most southern states had to do with the suppression of one race by another—an ugly but true type of class-oriented, redistributive, or reredistributive policy.

The Role of Violence

H. Rap Brown, an early leader of the Student Non-Violent Coordinating Committee (SNCC), turned out to have been one of the better historians when he observed during the turbulent 1960s that "violence is as American as cherry pie." Despite our image of ourselves as a consensus society, as a melting pot society, political violence has been a regular feature of American history and has been responsible for some of the most important and lasting changes in American history. One does not have to rely only on the Civil War for examples. The long history of labor in the United States more than confirms the notion. It has been called "the bloodiest and most violent ... of any industrial nation in the world."[11]

Violence, is, of course, inherently local. But it can be more or less relevant to governments at different levels. The patterns suggest that it has most frequently and intensely been relevant to state governments and their agencies, next after that relevant to large cities, and only relatively, mildly, and remotely to the federal government and its agencies except insofar as the federal government steps in to back state action after it seems to have failed.

Except for the Whiskey Rebellion in Pennsylvania early in the establishment of the Constitution, the frequent outbreaks of agrarian violence and near-violence have most often been aimed at the state government or agencies of the state government. Agrarian movements spearheaded the attack against monopolies and were responsible for some of the most important regulatory legislation ever attempted against industrialization and corporate enterprise.

Organized violence in the South was almost always motivated by the desire of whites to suppress Blacks, and this often meant literally illegal supplement to local government action. Nevertheless, the most concerted and lasting results of the Ku Klux Klan and other southern efforts to organize for violence and rebellion were the so-called Jim Crow laws—state laws attempting to establish and to enforce the separation of the races. One example that highlights the special place that state governments held is the case of Alabama, where, as far back as anyone can remember, and as far forward as the present, members of the southern aristocracy and upper bourgeoisie were traditionally elected through calmly conducted campaigns to the United States Senate and the House of Representatives, whereas candidates speaking for the lower white classes ran for and were elected to state office on the basis of highly agitated, racist, semiviolent campaigns.

A not unrelated pattern can be observed throughout the West, including California—vigilantism. As with the Ku Klux Klan, the immediate perceptions of vigilante committees and vigilante movements were local disorders and the need to use violence to pacify lawless communities. A lynching or a tar and feathering might, through fear, provide some respect for order. Nevertheless, as with the Ku Klux Klan, the main focus for lasting influence of vigilante movements was the provision of laws to produce a more dependable stability. In stable communities, the vigilante movements attempted to influence state laws. In less organized communities, vigilante committees actually provided miner's codes and criminal codes in the absence of any property law or criminal law. Once the territorial or state governments established appropriate codes and extended them to the localities, the extralegal or illegal informal governments tended to disappear.[12]

Among all the examples of political violence in American history, the most significant will be found in the labor movement. Before there was a concerted effort to organize workers in corporate trade unions, there had been many worker-based movements, and the probabilities may have been equal as to whether such a spontaneous and sporadic uprising would focus upon city hall or upon state agencies. More than enough examples of both can be found in the literature.[13] Most such efforts were for the immediate relief of grinding poverty and starvation, and as often as not the violence was initiated by the local police and militia rather than by the poor people themselves as they took to the streets to manifest their discomforts.[14] However, the issue became entirely different once there were small initial successes in organizing workers into unions in order to control the market for labor and the price for labor, as well as the conditions of the workplace. From this time forward, it became a matter of "the state" against the unions, and most of the time this meant the actual states of the United States as well as the abstraction, "the state." Labor unions were capable of using violence as a technique of advancing their interests; and whether or not they were using violence at a particular moment, agencies of the state government were also perfectly capable of using violence as an instrument of their own, either directly through their own police forces and militia or indirectly through the toleration of private police forces, such as the Pinkertons. It is especially significant that the various labor movements did not become regularly relevant to the national government until long after they had become an established fact in the states. Until the mid-nineteenth century, unions were treated as criminal conspiracies; but even when this posture crumbled, unionism was subjected to heavy state control through the injunctive process. While organizing and striking were no longer criminal per se, a state could, at the request of the employer, issue an injunction to cease and desist the questioned activity. If the injunction was not observed, the offenders were subject to summary punishment for contempt of court, and this was an invitation to intervention by private (company) policemen as well as local police, state militia, sheriffs, and others, who could continue to attack with impunity until order in the community was restored. Until the very end of the nineteenth century, violent action was handled primarily by the state governments and their agents; regular use of federal troops is a very recent phenomenon. National Guard armories, those huge edifices that stand out so prominently in the center of many American cities, were not even constructed until the end of the nineteenth century, following a number of very violent and very deadly mob scenes.[15]

Collective protests and disobedience by workers, the unemployed, and the poverty-stricken are local and will always be dealt with locally in the first instance, even where the

state and federal authorities eventually intervene. Although it has already been stressed
- as significant that even when local, the authority has been from the state government
and the responsibility has also been fairly quickly focused upon state governments,
there is another aspect of this which will tend to confirm still further the distinction
between the politics of the state governments and the politics of local governments. As
the employed and unemployed workers began to organize into trade unions or worker-
type political parties, they were very often integrated into the regular, local political
system even as they were being attacked and severely regulated under state law. New
York City has a long and distinguished history of absorbing workingmen's groups and
parties into established political organizations. It is significant that the term "boss"
arose first out of workingmen's groups. Some claim that its first explicit use was for
"Boss Laborer" Hughey McLaughlin in the Brooklyn Navy Yards during the middle
nineteenth century. McLaughlin went on to become leader of the Brooklyn Democratic
Organization. Or, across the East River, Tammany Hall emerged as the major political
organization in old New York City precisely because of its willingness to recognize and
induct neighborhood worker organizations. The same is observed of Philadelphia and
Boston; this is all part of the melting pot image, and there was a certain amount of
truth to it where worker organizations were concerned.

The tendency to induct worker organizations into normal, local politics can be found
in the unorganized West as well as in the highly organized eastern cities. For example,
the Workingmen's Party under the leadership of Denis Kearney became a major force in
San Francisco politics in the late 1870s. It declined during the prosperous 1880s, and its
adherents as well as its leaders were mainly absorbed by the local Democratic party, such
as it was. But within a decade, a labor party began to emerge once again, and by 1901 the
newly formed Union Labor party elected itself a mayor, Eugene Schmitz. The dominant
figure was Abe Ruef, and for a time Ruef operated as the boss of San Francisco. But he
was not a classic eastern boss because his Union Labor party was not much of a party,
and was certainly not a political machine, the way in which that term is understood
east of the Mississippi. As Shefter puts it, Ruef's power did not rest upon his command
of the disciplined party organization but derived from his position as a broker between
businessmen and the local governments.[16] The only thing close to a machine in California has been the railroad corporations,[17] and it is interesting how their relationships to
a leader like Ruef varied as between San Francisco and Sacramento. Ruef, and Kearney
before him, had managed to make their peace with the railroads as well as other local
businesses in San Francisco itself, despite the reigning importance of San Francisco as
the central city of the developing state of California. At the very same time, these local
leaders were extremely anti-railroad in Sacramento. They drummed up massive demonstrations against the railroads for importing oriental workers—the "Yellow Peril"—and
they sought with every legal means at their command to eliminate railroad influence
altogether from state politics. They spearheaded the movement for the direct primary;
the direct election of U.S. senators; the establishment of initiative, referendum, and
recall; the cross-filing system; the revitalization and extension of the powers of the State
Railroad Commission; and the institution of prohibition on child labor and in favor of
workman's compensation laws. The contrast between labor politics at the local level and
labor politics at the state level could hardly have been more clear.[18]

The Role of Constitutions and Legislatures

One of the most striking and widespread manifestations of state politics for keeps has been the involvement of state constitutions in efforts to displace the state legislatures. It was neither natural nor coincidental that state constitutions have always had a tendency to grow long, detailed, and large; nor that there continued to be frequent public as well as legislative initiatives to amend the constitution for a particular legislative purpose. When the political game is being played for keeps, group and party leaders seek safer refuge for their interests, and that safety is often sought in the extraordinary processes of constitution making and amending. This safety has been sought by any and every type of interest, but especially by those once-in-a-decade social movements, such as the farmer and labor movements of the nineteenth century, fearing, as they did, that entrenched interests may already own the legislature. The purpose of so many of these constitutional amendments was legislative; the intensity of state politics so often escalated the legislative activity toward the level of constitutional amendment.

Everywhere the politics of the states seemed to be too big for legislatures and therefore sought legislation through the extraordinary processes of the Constitution. This was not a pattern limited to the East or any other region. Lawrence Friedman put it extremely well:

> There was great diversity in state constitution-making. Region differed from region, state from state; but some clear patterns emerged.... Most of the states had come to feel that public order demanded more of a constitution than a bare frame of government; and particularly that a legislature could not be trusted to make proper laws. This trend had appeared before 1850; it now grew stronger. The constitution would control the problem of bad laws through its own, overriding superlaws ... hence, the constant inflation of constitutions continued. Indeed, it was almost out of hand.[19]

Friedman goes on to review in rich and useful detail many of the instances of constitutional inflation, and most of the instances confirmed the extraordinary and intense character of state politics. Louisiana, for example, had gone through eight constitutions before 1900, six between 1852 and 1900. Since 1879, constitutions ran to 326 articles, many of which were clearly substantive legislation.[20] Some parts of each state constitution were indigenous, while other parts were copied from other states. Some of the most popular items of legislation that were elevated to constitutional amendments included restrictions on long-term agricultural leases, railroad rate regulation, banking regulation, eminent domain, water rights, taxation of mines, divorces, and, among southern states, race. It was also popular to attempt to curb the power of the state legislature by setting tax limitations, debt limitations, and so on. Whatever the source of these provisions, each one was probably put into the constitution, despite the fact that it was mere legislation, because it was thought to be too important to be left to the whims of a legislature. In California, in the late nineteenth century, the key issues were the interlocked ones of railroad power and Chinese immigration; in other western states the issues were the railroads, the mines, watered stock, and rights of access to real water. In the Grange states of the Midwest, the issues of prevailing importance were railroads, grain elevators, and other commercial services to agriculture. In each of the states, as the issue became important, the urge was to raise the level of politics away from the legislature toward the constitution.[21]

Politics in the Cities: A Separate Stairway, the Tradition

Although cities are constitutionally creatures of the state, they have enjoyed more political autonomy than their counterparts in Europe. No Prefects or Subprefects have had them under control. No Interior Ministry has had them under regular surveillance. No national police force has operated independently of City Hall. And cities were free of the burdens of making fundamental social choices for their own residents. Cities were therefore relatively free to develop their own political system on the basis of the exceptions and variances they could make within the fundamental social choices made by the state governments.

One indication of the political autonomy of cities is Sayre's Law of the Mayoralty: Mayors come from nowhere and go nowhere. Formulated by Wallace Sayre to fit the New York City experience, Sayre's Law turns out to apply with almost equal force to the entire population of cities in the United States. Since the beginning of modern New York City in 1898, no New York mayor has ever escaped the city's constituency—and many of the 15 mayors have tried. Mayor Robert Wagner's 1956 nomination for the Senate was the only nomination for higher elective office ever received by a New York mayor, and this fractured the Democratic party at its very foundation.[22] In the 80 years between 1870 and 1950, 995 persons were elected governor in the United States. Among these, only 118 had had any local government experience whatsoever, and only 74 had gone directly from a local office to a governorship—and at least a proportion of these were not mayors at all but were commissioners, or city council presidents, or county commissioners.[23] In fact, there were more governors who came directly to the office without any governing experience at all than who came directly from the mayoralty.

This suggests that cities are indeed a separate stairway and that even cities which have a preponderance of a state's population do not have a constituency to build upon. There have been many political heavyweights among mayors, of New York and elsewhere. But in recent years, the only significant exceptions to Sayre's Law would be Hubert Humphrey (mayor of Minneapolis, then senator and vice president), Joseph Clark (mayor of Philadelphia, then senator), and David Lawrence (mayor of Pittsburgh and eventually governor of Pennsylvania). And it is with extra special significance that all three of these exceptions had been leaders of major, statewide political organizations or independently formed movements well before election as mayor. That is to say, the mayoralty did not provide them with a base, but their broader base gave them the mayoralty. Nevertheless, they are exceptions, but their rarity tends to prove the rule.

Though no specific demonstration can prove it definitively, this separation of constituencies between cities and the states is indicative of two very different, inconsistent, perhaps antagonistic ways of going politics. This in turn is related to two very different traditions of public policy; and this, we argue, is where the discontinuity rests. The states have been making the fundamental policy choices and have, therefore, been involved in the enunciation of rules that are broader than specific decisions. The cities were saved much of that obligation, and therefore their institutions and their politics could thrive in a highly particularistic environment, each decision being made in isolation from other decisions, each agency operating pretty much in isolation from other agencies, and each locality operating as its own end. Only in cases of severe financial or social crisis has the discontinuity between states and cities been broken. This autonomy, coupled with the highly particularistic policy environment, provided a favorable climate for machines and other stable political arrangements, whether these were parties or whether they were corporate management. In the East, where populations preceded large corporations, particularistic politics played its way out as machines and other stable electoral organizations. In the West, especially where large business corporations actually brought the populations to the territory, political machines did not develop, and the tradition of political parties has always been weak. However, other kinds of highly particularistic politics did develop, and the points of political stability or political power were corporate, not organized parties but corporations and trade associations operating in a political way: the railroad corporations in California; rail, mining, and other corporations in many areas of the Southwest; and perhaps smaller corporate enterprises elsewhere. Local politics, precisely because of its particularistic functions, could accommodate to whatever institutional arrangements existed. Violence has, of course, always been a regular urban phenomenon; however, when it has lasted beyond a momentary outburst, and especially when it has been converted into a political manifestation, it has quickly escalated from local to state politics, with a state focus, a state responsibility, and a process that ends in state policy decisions.

Modern Cities: Changing Policies, Changing Politics

Early in the twentieth century, and increasingly with each decade, local governments began to acquire new functions—at least new for local governments. This acquisition had begun in association with the Progressive movement, which had a strong local reform orientation. Home Rule was among the best known of all of the reforms sought by the Progressive movement and was certainly the best known aspect of the demand for a change in the status of local governments. But it may be the least significant of the reforms. Home Rule did provide cities with something of a guarantee against the intervention by state legislatures into the affairs of local government with legislation applicable only to a particular city. Home Rule permitted cities, within strict limits, to choose their own governmental structures and to write their own charters. Since all of this relieved state legislators from many of their burdens, they were not altogether loath to cooperate in Home Rule reform. However, of far greater significance was the cooperation of state legislators in what might be called functional Home Rule, that is to say, the delegation of specific power to cities to make their own policies in a specified subject matter. One of the earliest examples was state legislation delegating power to local governments to abate nuisances—to pass local ordinances regulating certain minor offenses. Other delegations of state legislative power to local governments followed, especially to the larger cities. Yet there were few such delegations of power from state to cities by the beginning of the twentieth century, so few that eastern cities began lobbying for more such local authority, and western cities still occasionally had to turn to vigilantism to deal with local problems of police power. More delegations of power did follow. States began to delegate to cities the power to pass their own ordinances regulating slaughter houses, regulating and establishing public transportation facilities, providing for new street openings (early land use regulation), regulating local markets and trade centers, providing for fire prevention and building quality standards, and regulations of certain aspects of gambling and prostitution. States continued to set limits on the breadth of each delegation of power to cities, and so did the courts with their continued application of the Dillon Rule. But these limits were successively weakened at the same time that additional powers were being delegated: powers over local public education, powers over public health, broader powers over markets, broader powers of general land use regulation, and so on. Some cities were later than others to receive these powers—Chicago was far later than New York. Some cities got more from the state legislature than others: Los Angeles was early to enjoy delegated powers, but many of the powers were delegated directly to autonomous agencies in the city or county rather than to City Hall itself. And, within each city in the United States, there has been and continues to be a range of degree of delegation, from extremely broad and almost unlimited delegation to the almost complete retention of power at the state level: For example, public health and land use regulations are almost entirely in state hands, whereas police departments, operating under criminal codes, are held much more narrowly to state legislation. Public education holds a sort of middle ground, where each school district can enrich and experiment in a variety of ways according to its own choice, but minimum standards of education, teacher recruitment, and facilities are still outside local discretion and are held tightly by state legislators and state educational authorities.

Yet, with all of this variation, one common fact remains: All local governments, especially large cities, have been granted increasing numbers of opportunities to make fundamental social choices for their own people. This is precisely what is new about the modern city, and it will be found to be behind the transformation of city politics. But it is very recent, a product of the twentieth century, if the twentieth century can be said to have begun after 1912. There was a transformation of politics in the cities not because the federal government took over the distribution of spoils from city politicians, but because cities took on functions for which their governmental and political institutions had not been equipped to handle. Historically, Boards of Aldermen were notoriously unlegislative. Aldermen were generally composed of spoilsmen, or lackeys for spoilsmen. There were few administrative agencies; even police and fire departments were not professionalized among the older cities until well into the nineteenth century, and one of the most important keepers of local order, fire insurance, was altogether in the hands of private corporations, which also had the biggest stake in operating volunteer fire clubs and companies. Leonard White, one of America's most distinguished students of administrative history, once observed that as late as the beginning of the twentieth century, the most distinctive thing one could say about the mayor as chief executive is that he was chief of little and executive of nothing.[24] Quite suddenly, city legislators were being asked to legislate and mayors were being asked to participate in legislation and to preside over serious administration. The right to make fundamental social choices for the community was a burden which, once sought, could never be cast off; and the consequences for each city as a political system were incalculable. But they are patterned, and they are predictable.

City governments, in a fundamental way, have become modern governments—not merely because their administrative structures have been modernized, and not merely because the government and the rest of the city were technologically advanced. City governments became modern because they began to perform a large number of regulatory and redistributive functions. Prior to this time, cities had participated only as interest groups in making of state (or federal) policies. And, as cities modernized in this sense, they also tended to differentiate, along the lines already suggested. Many aspects of this differentiation were already identified. The point is this, that as regulatory and redistributive policies were added, new political characteristics followed.

In the larger cities particularly, the center of gravity moved away from electoral organizations toward professional bureaucracies. Politics moved away from party-centered, family-centered, and corporate-centered elites to bureaucratic-professional elites. As in New York, the older structures of political power did not necessarily disappear, but their domains were severely reduced to make room for new bases of power and new forms of politics. Some departments or areas of public policy, as we have seen, continued to be dominated by electoral organizations, often party machines. In some areas, classic corporate interest groups seemed to be the dominant force. In many, and growing numbers of areas, the bureaucracies themselves became the "new machine."[25]

Other observers have found counterparts and parallels in other cities. Harrigan, for example, draws on his own work and the work of others to document the differentiation of cities such as Cleveland, Oakland (California), Newark, St. Paul, Los Angeles, and Boston.[26] Marshall Langberg, in a replication of my New York City study, and an extension of it to Chicago and San Francisco, found 15 years after my original study a strongly similar and parallel set of patterns in those three cities. He reports that Chicago was not as far along this path as New York or San Francisco but that some differentiation was already appearing well before the end of the Daley era as traditional boss of the city. It should also be repeated that Chicago is much later than the other two cities to be granted by the state legislature a maximum amount of autonomy in the making and implementing of basic public policies. But even so, in spite of the mastery of the city by Richard Daley, Langberg was able to detect certain important areas where new forms of politics had already emerged. While Daley held tight to public works, he had pretty much given up on welfare. Blacks had been making considerable progress in housing policy, and the bureaucracies themselves had gained considerable autonomy in education and elsewhere.[27] It will be very interesting and significant to watch the development of Chicago now that the Daley era is over and now that the recently adopted Illinois Home Rule constitution has had a chance to take effect.

It is in this context that the national government began to heap upon cities, beginning in the late 1930s, the new resources and the new direct decision-making authority. It should be no mystery therefore why there has been since that time a "crisis of the cities." Functional Home Rule delegated to cities by state legislatures, coupled with new resources and some additional decision-making authority delegated to cities by Congress, contributed to the differentiation of city politics without any guarantee that local institutions could handle all this. That is to say, that politics responded by differentiation but the central decision-making institutions were not necessarily able to withstand the shock. The only mystery about all this is why there was any optimism about the capacity of cities to take these broadly delegated responsibilities for making social policies, why there was any optimism that cities could spend money in a more efficient, more responsible, and more equitable way than states or the national government could. Most of the changes in social relationships to be found in recent American cities were likely to have been forced upon cities by governments above and outside themselves. This was noticeably true among southern cities in the question of racial integration, but it is beginning to be increasingly true of northern cities in the area of racial integration and also in such areas as environmental protection, energy conservation, and so on.

Cities may ultimately develop the institutions of government appropriate to these new responsibilities and to the unaccustomed forms of politics. But in the meantime, it is at least worth considering whether the country might not be better served by reverting to provision of these basic choices by state governments. Such fundamental choices may be too destabilizing for cities and may in fact work against the otherwise well known ability of American cities to develop and foster communal relationships. But these are questions of social policy and of normative analysis that should be deferred until a later point. What is important to stress at this point is the patterns of relationships themselves—between public policies and politics, between areas of governmental activity and arenas of power.

CHAPTER 5

~~~~~

A New American State, and Four
Different Roosevelts

Einaudi's *Roosevelt Revolution* bears the special mark of original intent: it was planned and executed as "a book aimed at those Europeans who think and worry about modern America and are confused about its meaning." His goal was a large and ambitious one: that "the Roosevelt Revolution should become more fully part of the remembered experience of the western world ... [and] that only a balanced and reasoned understanding of the respective grounds upon which they stand can provide [Europeans and Americans] an authentic basis for the solidarity so needed in their future relationships." Europeans, in Einaudi's view, have "often forgotten that if America is paying a price for its present way of life, this is because America has dared to identify and accept some of the unavoidable conditions for the survival of a democratic community in the 20th century." In effect, the New Deal saved capitalism, as most Europeans do appreciate. But the New Deal did something more, which most Europeans have not appreciated: it saved democracy. In Einaudi's book, *The Roosevelt Revolution* is seen, in the first place, as an effort to reestablish the sense of community in a free industrial society and to come to terms with its requirements, and, in the second place, as the most important attempt in the 20th century to affirm the validity and central role of the political instruments of democracy.... While democracy was being routed all over the world by the totalitarians and the technicians, it triumphed in the United States. Those who proclaim their attachment to democracy ought to consider how this was done.[1]

It is only the beginning of analysis, however, to say that capitalism and democracy were saved by the New Deal. One of the most remarkable things about Roosevelt scholarship is the disparity of assessments of the consequences of the New Deal and, especially, the character of the Roosevelt leadership and the Roosevelt legacy. Lincoln is one of the few American leaders who has been more researched than Roosevelt; but there is a good deal less disparity in the range of Lincoln assessments. The Roosevelt assessments are not so much in disagreement with one another as simply not focused on the same things; they are more disparate than they are contradictory. A review of these assessments will make a start toward a clearer sense of the nature of the real contribution that the New Deal made to the "new American state."

Who Was the Real Roosevelt?

A good place to begin is with Einaudi's disagreement with James MacGregor Burns's assessment of Roosevelt's overall leadership. To Burns, Roosevelt failed as a "creative leader." Roosevelt did no more than leaders have to do at a minimum to be leaders, which is to be a strategic role player or "role-taker": "While role-taking is traditionally viewed as a device to enable the leader to present different faces to different publics in the time-honored fashion of the politician, it is also testimony to the influence of environmental factors that compel the leader to recognize their demands and expectations. Roosevelt is an excellent case in point." "The creative leader" must transcend the role-taking requirement and the environmental forces that impose the role:

> A test of the more dominant or creative leader ... is the extent to which his role-taking is a means of implementing a central purpose independent of those roles.... Role-taking ... implies finally the absence of leadership.... [The role-taker] mirrors society rather than transforms it. The creative leader, on the other hand, stands somewhat apart from society and assumes roles ... as a tactical means of realizing his long-term strategic ends.[2]

It is in this sense that Roosevelt fell short.

Einaudi's response could hardly be more in opposition:

> To deny the central position of Roosevelt throughout the Roosevelt Revolution indicates a readiness to go all the way either with a wholly chance view of the nature of history ... or with a deterministic view ... or with an elite theory view. Leadership within this context cannot mean the lifting of the leader above and outside society. The democratic leader is the man who is able to express the urge of his society to achieve common and deeply felt needs.... In this sense, Roosevelt has been the supreme democratic leader of our time.[3]

Burns carries his assessment into the specifics of policy making, where he found that on the all-important issue of labor regulation Roosevelt was neither a lion nor a fox:

> Quite unwittingly [Roosevelt] acted as midwife in the rebirth of labor action. Neither he nor Miss Perkins had much to do with [Sec. 7A of the National Recovery Act (NRA)]. Framed mainly by congressmen and labor leaders, it was simply part of a bargain under which labor joined NRA's great "concert of interest." ... Roosevelt failed to see the potentialities of an enlarged labor movement.... [The Wagner Act of 1935] was the most radical legislation passed during the New Deal ... yet ... [Roosevelt] threw his weight behind the measure only at the last moment, when it was due to pass anyway.[4]

Historian William Leuchtenberg begins on a point of agreement with Burns and then takes a distinctly different tack: "The New Deal was a Broker State, [yet this] clashed with the fact that [Roosevelt] was agent, both willingly and unwillingly, of forces of reform that business found unacceptable."[5] In other words, Roosevelt was a broker among corporate interests and yet a social democrat and leader of a movement antagonistic to business as a class.

Political scientist Wilfred Binkley jumps in on Einaudi's side, stressing Roosevelt's unprecedented popular leadership, yet when facing a "crucial test" over the economy bill,

Binkley was so moved by Roosevelt's party leadership that he was led to stress this element as the aspect of leadership that made the difference: Roosevelt the party leader.[6]

To scholars such as Robert A. Brady, Roosevelt was a centrally placed leader but of a new corporate state of sponsored partnership between labor and capital at the expense of the public at large.[7] Einaudi takes profound exception to the corporatist designation—understandably, given his experience with the real thing in Fascist Italy—yet he agrees with everything else except the label: "The NRA was, on the other hand, an attempt to strike a bargain between government and business ... [showing] the extent to which the New Deal remained within the framework of what has been loosely called the capitalistic system ... provided it recognized its social responsibilities."[8]

Other analysts contribute to these disparate and conflicting interpretations of Roosevelt and the New Deal. Paul Douglas's autobiographical account of Social Security shows Roosevelt's power as based in the executive branch, fully in control of Congress, especially in the most creative aspects of policy making.[9] Richard Hofstadter projects a picture of Roosevelt operating at first with "practically dictatorial powers," and beyond that he was operating on the basis of a leadership of the most numerous classes of society against the upper classes, who themselves polarized the situation into class terms: "It has often been said that he betrayed his class; but if by class one means the whole policy-making, power-wielding stratum, it would be just as true to say that his class betrayed him."[10] In contrast, James Landis, in his autobiographical account of the Securities Acts and the Public Utility Holding Company Act, is so impressed with Congress's creativity that surely a reborn Woodrow Wilson would have been able to insist, on the basis of Landis's two case studies, that the New Deal was another era of "Congressional Government."[11]

All these characterizations of Roosevelt and the New Deal are accurate and true. But note that each observation tends to be offered in a tone that makes one expect to see the word *yet* following; sometimes, as with Leuchtenberg, it does so within the space of the same paragraph. Roosevelt *was* a mass leader, yet also a broker. He *was* an agent of reform, yet also innocent of the significance of the emerging reform movement. He *was* a social democrat, yet also a corporatist. He *was* a leader of a programmatic administration, yet also head of a completely nonprogrammatic political party. He *was* the supreme leader of an integrated administration, yet made a virtue of pluralistic administration of relatively independent agencies operating with conflicting jurisdictions constantly in need of reorganization. ("The president needs help.") Each characterization simply applies to a different New Deal. Roosevelt was neither lion nor fox. He was an elephant surrounded by blind analysts trying to generalize on the basis of one part of the corpus.

Antecedents: The Old American State

The best way to put Roosevelt back together is to allow him and the New Deal to emerge out of the state developments that preceded him. Aside from the obvious Great Depression, to what was the New Deal a response? And aside from the economy, which we know was not directly transformed by the New Deal, what was transformed by the New Deal? If it was the state, then from what to what was it transformed?

Table I.1 presents a quick overview of the old American state (see page 18, this volume). The very first impression is how small the U.S. domestic government was (column 1) compared to the state governments (column 2). Leave aside that this was as intended by the Founders. Beyond that, it is important to note two traits common to the policies in column 1: (1) their common purpose was to promote commerce (we were rightly referred to as a "commercial republic"); and (2) the common technique of government was patronage. This is to be understood in the medieval sense of patron and client, where patronage was a relationship between a superior who was in command of resources and a subordinate who sought to share in the allocation of those resources, where the patron could allocate them at his discretion on an individualized and personalized basis. The term was confined in normal American usage to the handing out of jobs to the party's faithful; but that is obviously one very small example of patronage when properly understood. There was discretion in the allocation of these resources as long as the national government stayed away from directly coercive relationships with citizens and with rules of law that bound the resources to a priori conditions of their allocation.

The narrowness of the specialization of policy and function of the national government can be most easily clarified by quick reference to the state government functions during this same period (column 2). These policies are a reflection of the constitutional provision that all powers not explicitly delegated to the national government were "reserved" to the states or to the people, who in their wisdom could vote to delegate any of those retained powers to the states. As a result, the states did most of the fundamental governing, and the states were in particular responsible for those aspects of government that require directly coercive techniques. In our modern parlance we would tend to call this "regulation."

This old American state as outlined in Table I.1 prevailed for nearly a century and a half. Anyone familiar with U.S. history will immediately interject such famous exceptions of domestic policy as the Fugitive Slave Laws, Reconstruction, the Interstate Commerce Act, and the Sherman Act. But those are so exceptional as to confirm the rule. The Fugitive Slave Laws were the first national intervention and accomplished nothing but the polarization of Congress and the inability of Congress to avoid war. Reconstruction was terminated by congressionally ordained demobilization, and with that, the return completely to the status quo ante bellum. Looking at congressional output in the 1880s, one would hardly be able to recognize that there had been a war at all. The Interstate Commerce and Sherman acts did persist, but were extremely narrowly defined. In fact, the shadow of constitutional doubt was spread so darkly across those acts and the regulatory legislation of the Woodrow Wilson period that all of these exceptions to Table I.1, column 1, were restricted to an extremely narrow conceptualization of the "interstate commerce clause." Consequently, it was not until the 1930s that Congress began to adopt domestic regulatory policies with such frequency and scope that they put traditional constitutional limits to the test at all.[12] Pre–New Deal exceptions are intimations of a new American state only if we impute to them our post–New Deal knowledge of what ultimately happened.

In sum, for the first 150 years, the national government stayed on the reservation to which it was relegated by the Constitution or by early interpretations thereof. Elsewhere I have covered the implications of this for president-Congress relations, for parties, and for pluralism and the group process.[13] At the level appropriate to Einaudi's own inquiry, the most important question is: To what extent did the New Deal produce a new American state?

Building the New American State[14]

The domestic New Deal was born in 1933 and was buried toward the end of 1939 with the onset of mobilization for war. During those six years, the federal service was expanded from 572,000 to 920,000 employees, a rate of increase of 58,000 employees per year. The budget grew from $4.6 billion in 1933 to $8.8 billion in 1939, a rate of increase of about $700 million per year. But where was the Roosevelt Revolution? In the four preceding years, the Hoover administration expanded the civil service from 540,000 to 572,000 employees, an increase of about 8,000 employees per year. And the Hoover budget expanded from $3.1 billion to $4.6 billion, a rate of increase about half that of the New Deal rate. And for that, Hoover had earned the denunciation of candidate Roosevelt as "the greatest spending Administration in peacetime in all our history."

Indeed, where was the revolution? Of the $6.7 billion in the first New Deal budget, $2 billion was allocated to the Works Progress Administration (WPA) and $1 billion to the Public Works Administration (PWA) with another half billion dollars budgeted for the Civil Works Administration (CWA). These three programs alone accounted for nearly 53 percent of the 1934 budget, 46 percent of the 1935 budget, and 41 percent of the 1936 budget. Although these programs were proposed as recovery and relief programs, and indeed did provide a lot of relief work, they were essentially expansions of the patronage state as shown in Table I.1, column 1.[15]

The Roosevelt administration might well have responded to the Depression by expanding only those types of functions to which the national government had been accustomed during its traditional century and a half. And it is conceivable that such an approach might have been just as effective as the approach Roosevelt ultimately adopted. After all, given the sorry condition of the country in 1939, Roosevelt might have done no worse if he had stuck with traditional means. If he had chosen that approach, however, and even if he had succeeded at it, he would have left no legacy at all and we would hardly concern ourselves with a Roosevelt Revolution.

Table 5.1 shows what the New Deal actually did. In section 1 are the policies adopted by the New Deal which can be considered direct extensions of the traditional system of the national government. These are all essentially patronage policies. Section 2 is made up of policies that definitely do not fit comfortably in the same category with those in section 1. They do resemble the occasional efforts at regulation tried by the national government between 1887 and 1932, but they more closely resemble the kinds of policy traditionally associated with the state governments, because the regulatory policies of the New Deal went well beyond the narrow interpretation of interstate commerce employed in the earlier national efforts and attempted to go directly to those local conditions that the Supreme Court, until 1937, had definitely put outside and beyond the limits of national government power. We call these regulatory policies because each of them seeks to impose obligations directly on citizens and back those obligations with sanctions. In other words, for the first time in any systematic way, the national government established a direct and coercive relationship between itself and individual citizens.

Section 3 includes New Deal policies that do not fit comfortably in the same category as those of sections 1 or 2. In the first place, these policies are patently different from traditional patronage policies in that they possess an element of direct coercion. Second, although the coercive factor makes them comparable to regulatory policies, they do not work on the conduct of individuals in the same way as regulation. They are called "redistributive" here in order to imply this difference. The best way to convey the difference explicitly is: while regulatory policies seek directly to influence individual conduct,

Table 5.1 The Political Economy of the New Deal

Program (Policy/Agency)	Acronym	Year
Traditional Policies		
Civil Works Administration	CWA	1933
Public Works Administration	PWA	1933
Civilian Conservation Corps	CCC	1933
Works Progress Administration	WPA	1933
Tennessee Valley Authority	TVA	1933
Rural Electrification Administration	REA	1933
Soil Conservation Service	SCS	1935
Regulatory Policies		
Agricultural Adjustment Administration	AAA	1933
National Recovery Administration	NRA	1933
Securities and Exchange Commission	SEC	1933
Public Utility Holding Company Act		1935
National Labor Relations Act and Board	NLRB	1935
Fair Labor Standards Act	FLSA	1938
Civil Aeronautics Act and Board	CAB	1938
Redistributive Policies		
Federal Deposit Insurance Corporation	FDIC	1933
Bank Holiday		1933
Home Owners Loan Corporation	HOLC	1933
Devaluation		1934
Federal Housing Administration	FHA	1934
Federal Reserve Reforms	FED	1935
Social Security Act	SSA	1935
Farm Security Administration	FSA	1935
Internal Revenue Tax Reforms	IRS	1935
Organizational (Constituent) Policies		
Judiciary Reform		1937
Executive Office of the President	EOP	1939
Budget Bureau	OMB	1939
White House Staff		1930s
Administrative Law		1930s
Federal Bureau of Investigation	FBI	1940s
Joint Chiefs of Staff	JCOS	1940

these so-called redistributive policies seek to influence individuals by manipulating the "environment of conduct" rather than "conduct itself." These policies seek to create new structures, to manipulate existing structures in order to change the value of property or money, or to categorize people according to some universalized attribute, such as level of income or age or status of occupation. Call these categoric policies.

Although the Income Tax and the Federal Reserve acts were adopted 20 years before the New Deal, they nevertheless confirmed the distinctiveness of the New Deal in other ways. First, the income tax did not confront the Constitution with any real test, because it was enacted by Congress following an entirely new constitutional amendment adopted precisely to confer on Congress the power to enact an income tax. The Federal Reserve also did not confront the Constitution, because it came clearly within the provisions of Article I, Section 8, conferring on the national government the power to coin money and regulate the value thereof. More to the point, both of these policies were given their real scope, scale, and administrative muscle during the New Deal. And by 1939 they were only two of many absolutely fundamental additions to the apparatus of the new national state (as shown in Table 5.1, section 3).

The novelty of the policies in sections 2 and 3 of Table 5.1 can be conveyed by the fact that both put the Constitution itself to the test and required a fundamental adjustment to the Constitution by Supreme Court decisions. The reality of the distinction between the policies in section 2 and those in section 3 can be confirmed by the fact that they required separate constitutional validation. Regulatory policies were validated in a line of cases beginning with *NLRB v. Jones and Laughlin Steel Corporation,* 301 US 1 (1937). The redistributive policies in section 3 required separate testing and validation, in *Helvering v. Davis,* 301 US 619 (1937) and *Steward Machine Co. v. Davis,* 301 US 548 (1937). When validating the regulatory power of Congress, the Supreme Court concentrated on the commerce clause of Article I, Section 8 and rejected as artificial the distinction between interstate and local, arguing as follows in the *NLRB* case: "When industries organize themselves on a national scale, making their relation to interstate commerce the dominant factor in their activities, how can it be maintained that their industrial relations constitute a forbidden field into which Congress may not enter when it is necessary to protect interstate commerce from the paralyzing consequences of industrial war?" For redistributive policies, the Supreme Court relied on an entirely different part of the Constitution; in fact, for the first time it recognized the "general welfare" clause of the Preamble and of Clause 1 of Article I, Section 8, of the Constitution. The Court also based its case on recognition that there is no limit to congressional spending power except Congress's own wisdom, but that was itself colored by the very recognition of the almost unlimited character of the two "general welfare" clauses.

The Roosevelt Revolution 1: Central Tendency

"Revolution" is a useful exaggeration. It puts the emphasis not merely on change but on discontinuous change, a break from the past. In this context, the Roosevelt Revolution can and should be broken down into four separate aspects, each with its own special relationship with the past: (1) the constitutional revolution, (2) the governmental revolution, (3) the institutional revolution, and (4) the political revolution. The first three concentrate on discontinuities at the broadest, most general level of political phenomena. Although the fourth shares some of that character, it has its own character and will be dealt with separately. In the words of the statistician, the first three changes focus on "central tendency." The fourth focuses primarily on "dispersion" or, more accurately, differentiation. Since the first three have been the focus of most attention, by others as well as myself, I deal with them briefly in this first section. More attention is reserved in the following section for the fourth change, because it has been least recognized.

The Constitutional Revolution

Some constitutional historians actually refer to 1937 as the onset of the First Constitutional Revolution. (The Second Constitutional Revolution usually refers to the period beginning at some point after the 1954 school segregation case.) Although the *NLRB* case (cited above) is the watershed decision, it was reconfirmed in other decisions where Congress reached even further down into local conditions and into situations involving individual farmers and not merely large, essentially interstate corporations.[16] If there was any doubt after the Filburn case that economic federalism was dead, it was dispelled in the cases validating the Civil Rights Act of 1964, in which the Court argued that Congress could reach a single restaurant in Birmingham for refusing to serve blacks even if it could prove that the restaurant did not serve interstate customers. The Court reasoned that Ollie's Barbecue could constitutionally be regulated because a substantial portion of the food served by the restaurant came from outside the state of Alabama.[17]

The Governmental Revolution

The governmental revolution can easily be defined as the addition of the new functions listed in Table 5.1 and by the addition of the directly coercive factor behind those new policies. This is precisely what was being validated in the constitutional revolution. But the discontinuity of government goes beyond even that. It includes the fact that all the hundreds of thousands of new civil servants were "covered in" and made permanently tenured employees of the national government. It would take a veritable counterrevolution to return to anywhere near the previous levels of federal employment.

Another aspect of the governmental revolution was the establishment of an elaborate apparatus of overhead agencies for management. A quick glance at section 4 of Table 5.1 will reveal a sense of determination to control all the agencies but, more important, to make them a rational force. In addition, the governmental revolution includes the virtual permanence of all the agencies and functions that had been established in the 1930s. It is extremely significant that not a single important government agency or program established during the 1930s was terminated after World War II, despite the death of Roosevelt, the succession of a very weak President Truman, and the election in 1946 of a very large Republican majority whose leaders were antagonistic to the New Deal.

Finally, the governmental revolution includes the commitment on the part of all the leadership, Republican as well as Democratic, to make the new apparatus a "positive state." With the adoption of the Employment Act of 1946 and its promise to make the national government responsible for getting a job for everyone who wants one, along with its establishment of the Council of Economic Advisors, the national government was determined not to be merely a reactive government but to take initiatives to head off economic disasters and personal injuries.

The Institutional Revolution

The institutional revolution is basically a revolution in the separation of powers. The most prominent institutional feature of the traditional system of national government was the centricity of Congress with its committees and parties. With a few exceptions during emergencies involving military actions, there was legislative supremacy, as intended by the Constitution. Stronger presidents vetoed a lot of legislation, but the source of the legislation, the creativity at the national level, was congressional. Nothing changed more completely or dramatically than this during the 1930s. In order to meet the demands of the Depression, Congress authorized the executive branch to undertake all the activities identified above, and it delegated those powers to the president with almost no guidelines on how those powers would be used. Technically, this practice is called the delegation of power. And at the beginning, members of Congress and prominent jurists attempted to rationalize the delegation of power by arguing, first, that the emergency required it and, second, that administrative agencies were staffed by experts who were merely "filling in the details" of programs that Congress had constitutionally legislated. But there came a point fairly soon when most people were willing to admit that these new agencies, especially the regulatory ones, were making coercive policy decisions about individuals which Congress itself ought to be making. In 1935 the Supreme Court ruled that such broad and unguided delegation of power was unconstitutional.[18] That constitutional rule has never been overturned explicitly by later Supreme Court decisions, but it has never been followed either.

Out of this revolution in institutional relationships the modern presidency emerged— or sprang.[19] Some would argue, following Arthur Schlesinger, that the modern presidency is based on the rise of the national security state and the discretion required to run it. Although it is impossible to disagree about the importance of that development, the truth is that the presidency in the new American state began in the 1930s on the *domestic* side, with the very large number of domestic policies predicated on broad and unguided delegations of power from Congress to the executive branch.

The Political Revolution

Part of the political revolution comes under the rubric of central tendency, so I discuss it briefly here before going on to differentiation. The most dramatic way to put this is the decline of the parties and the simultaneous rise of interest group politics and mass politics. There have always been interest groups in American politics. Madison referred to them as "factions" and treated them as a mischievous force requiring careful constitutional creativity. But interest groups have become a very special phenomenon in the 20th century for two reasons. First, with the decline of political parties, interest groups gained direct access to Congress and the executive branch. They are no longer mediated by parties; their demands no longer go through modification and compromise before being processed in congressional committees and executive agencies. Second, the status of interest groups has improved tremendously, from a mischievous force in Madisonian theory to a positive virtue in the liberal theory arising out of the 1930s. Thus, interest groups now not only enjoy access to government unmediated by parties but actually enjoy direct and official sponsorship by government agencies, often in the official statutory obligations of these agencies. Einaudi may be justified in his opposition to the use of the term "corporate" to describe these patterns. (Up to a point, I agree. This is why I coined the alternative concept, "interest-group liberalism.") The practice in the United States, however, at least approximates corporatism to the extent that the government encourages and often sponsors the involvement of organized interests in the policy-making process.

The second central tendency produced by the political revolution, the rise of mass politics, can best be seen in the politics of the presidency. With the decline of political parties and the building of the massive statutory base of presidential power, the presidency itself began in the 1930s to develop its own independent base of power directly among the masses of the American people. President Roosevelt tried to modernize the Democratic party by transforming it into a truly programmatic national party along European lines of programmatic concerns and membership discipline. But it was in this very effort that Roosevelt experienced his most stunning political defeat in 1938, when he tried to purge the disloyal members of his own party. Once he failed to accomplish that, Roosevelt to a large extent abandoned the Democratic party and instead went over the heads of the party and congressional leaders directly to the American people. This has now become a normal and accepted relationship, and it is reflected in the methods of nominating presidential candidates. But this is too obvious a point to belabor here. Let us turn instead to the dispersion or differentiation dimension of the political revolution.

The Roosevelt Revolution 2: Differentiation

Differentiation means simply "the unlikeness of parts." It has been taken by many as a fundamental aspect of modernization, because many of the observable forms of differentiation seem to reflect rational organization of society toward goal achievement. The first entire book of Adam Smith's *Wealth of Nations* is devoted to the division of labor, which for Smith is a manifestation of humankind's ability to use reason. Differentiation can be taken, first, as one of the central tendencies not only in the 20th century United States but everywhere that modernization has spread. For example, Samuel Huntington treats "differentiation of structures" as one of three fundamental patterns of modernization throughout the world, in particular in the West.[20]

But applying the general tendency to the specific context of the Roosevelt Revolution brings it down below the central tendency to actual and sustained differences in governmental functions and in political processes and structures. All these were introduced by the New Deal and not before. It is useful to review once again the patterns of policy in Table 5.1. Each of its four sections is a distinguishable category of public policy, and each represents—or one might say each is a measurement of—the differentiation of governmental functions. If differentiation is the mark of modernization, then clearly the New Deal in a scant few years modernized the governmental system of the United States. There were other elements of modernization, such as the reform of the civil service and the introduction of varieties of skills, training requirements, and modern management techniques. All of this could have happened in a government in which virtually all the policies were of the type listed in section 1, the patronage policies that were the tradition of national government. In that case, there would have been a great deal less modernization than in the actual case, which involved sections 2 and 3 as well as an expansion and enhancement of section 4.

This, however, remains modernization by definition only. It is necessary now to look at the cumulative results of this differentiation of functions. The general hypothesis is as follows: each basic function of government, once it is stabilized and repetitive in its policies, becomes a kind of regime and fits the general tendency of any regime, which is to *develop a politics consonant with itself.* Using the terms established here, we can reconstruct Roosevelt and put some order into the disparate assessments of his contribution.

First, take Roosevelt as party leader. This is very much the view of him as seen through the traditional cases of patronage policy. In my own work I generally call it the "patronage state" to dramatize the intimacy of the connection between the type of policy and the type of politics. The so-called Roosevelt coalition or New Deal coalition was indeed an electoral coalition built on logrolling among many different, often conflicting, constituencies and groups. In this matter, Roosevelt might well be understood as a lion, using to the best of his ability as a party leader the large and growing amount of patronage available in both established "internal improvements" policies and newly created ones. Logrolling is a political relationship in which the participants have absolutely nothing in common except their understanding that each will support the other without questioning too hard what the partner is seeking. This was the basis of the political parties and the party system of the 19th century. They were patronage parties thriving in a patronage state. Roosevelt inherited this system; he was socialized in it through his recruitment and grooming in the politics of New York State. He had long ago made his peace with the leaders and the politics of New York City, including the best and the worst of Tammany Hall.

This is the Roosevelt the Republicans most feared, because an effective use of all that patronage could possibly enable Roosevelt to create a national machine; after all, it was the same type of resource on which the urban machines were built. No wonder the Hatch Acts were passed in Congress amid expressions of denunciation of Jim Farley and the fear of a dictatorial president. But this national machine failed to happen— not because of the Hatch Acts or the opposition and fears of Republicans, but because Roosevelt became involved in other areas of policy in which a patronage party and a leadership based on it were not effective. As we shall see, when Roosevelt tried to mobilize a large working class or to capitalize on it for the purpose of Social Security and monetary reform (shouting about the "economic royalists" and the "malefactors of great wealth"), he risked losing his party leadership altogether. As pressures of mobilization were mounting, Senator Burton Wheeler (D, MT) confronted a White House aide: "Who does Roosevelt think he is? He used to be just one of the barons. I was baron of the Northwest. Huey Long was baron of the South. [Other leaders were also mentioned.] He is like a king trying to reduce the barons."[21]

Roosevelt the broker in a broker state is the definitive characterization of Roosevelt when dealing with group coalitions, and anyone looking at the regulatory category of policies would have seen this kind of leadership rather than party leadership. Perhaps this is Roosevelt the fox, but in any event, this is the view one would get if one limited one's observations to cases of regulatory policy. A good starting point is a review of Burns's interpretation of Roosevelt's role in the passage of the Wagner Act. The same can be said of Roosevelt's role in adoption of the National Industry Recovery Act. This was built on brokerage among trade associations and unions, giving them access to the new agency and the opportunity to write their own tickets—if only they could agree among themselves. Another instance is the adoption of the Agricultural Adjustment Act, giving commodity associations the power to write their own tickets—once again, if they could agree among themselves. Some have called this the pluralistic system and others have called it the corporatist system, but either way, the Roosevelt role is a distinctive one, dealing with organized elements of the capitalists, but never with capitalists as a class. And the public constituency for his operations here was not a general mass constituency at all but a limited, albeit highly intense, constituency of organized leaders, primarily capitalists, contending among themselves, trying desperately to maximize their influence by agreement among themselves, succeeding only a sector at a time.

The third Roosevelt was the anticapitalist Roosevelt, or the savior of capitalism—depending on one's values and point of view. Each view stresses a leadership role in the context of social movements, class politics, and "historic forces." Here we see Roosevelt the Social Democrat. Here we see Roosevelt seeking a constituency among the masses, not among groups or group leaders. Here we see Roosevelt as part of history—responding to it, being led by it, and in fact, at least to some, shaping it.

Those who have seen this Roosevelt have been looking through the spectacles of redistributive policies. This was the Roosevelt as seen by Paul Douglas, Edwin Witte, and Frances Perkins during their experiences with the mobilization of forces necessary to adopt the Social Security Act. It was in cases such as this and cases of monetary reform, devaluation, and agricultural resettlement that Roosevelt was prompted to denounce capitalism's "malefactors of great wealth."

Since the Tennessee Valley Authority (TVA) was one of the gold star cases of Roosevelt leadership in Einaudi's view, let us take it as a case study in the discontinuity across these differentiated domains of policy or function. Einaudi, more than any other Roosevelt scholar, was impressed by the TVA as a new instrument of government and as an indicator of Roosevelt's leadership. Roosevelt did indeed sincerely view the TVA as a social experiment, in which electric power was to be a "secondary consideration."[22] The true nature of the TVA as a *type of function*, however, won out over Roosevelt's public definition of it. The TVA was really nothing more than an ambitious version of traditional internal improvements policies, and it was aimed at the very core of the traditional constituency of the Democratic party: Tennessee, Alabama, and Georgia. After 1933, as more of the New Deal got into gear, the TVA became the only such regional development, and as a "social experiment" it abruptly ended in favor of local flood control, local electric power, and local land development—in a word, it ended in favor of local constituency interests.[23] This is typical of politics in the patronage state.

Assessment

Einaudi's assessment of the Roosevelt Revolution begins with the basic dilemma of democracy, as identified by Alexis de Tocqueville exactly 100 years before the Roosevelt Revolution got under way:

> Tocqueville had no illusions about the advance of the equalitarian movement, to him the essence of democracy. Equality of status was the basic fact of modern times everywhere in the Western world. Democracy, conceived as equality, was both inevitable and desirable in spite of the longings of Tocqueville for the aristocratic societies of the past. "The nations of our time cannot prevent the conditions of men from becoming equal, but it depends upon themselves whether the principle of equality is to lead them to servitude or freedom." ... This, then, was the problem to which Tocqueville addressed himself: "The problem of the survival of the individual, in a democratic society where essential doctrine was that of the rule of the majority ... which, no matter how formed and by what issues ... would strive to assert itself and to stamp out the minority."
> [Also developing] rapidly in a country in which democracy was flourishing was a new and harsh aristocracy, identified by Tocqueville as the aristocracy of industry. The danger was that the business class would first impoverish and debase the men working under it and then abandon them to the charity of the public.... Tocqueville remains one of the earliest critical commentators of our industrial age to have seen the problems of business controls over the community, and the dangers of the probable failure of the industrial classes to accept the responsibility that went with power and to which earlier aristocracies had submitted. [This] represents a remarkable feat of prophecy.[24]

Einaudi then repeats the theme with which he had opened his book, with a sense that the book had confirmed it:

> Most of the trends forecast by Tocqueville came true in the next century.... The vitality of American democracy which Tocqueville had felt joined hands with constitutionalism to subdue the industrial monster to the medium of constitutional principle ... may well be listed as one of the permanent accomplishments of the Roosevelt Revolution.... Democracy had indeed been successful, while at the same time freedom had been able to maintain itself.[25]

Not content with this happy verdict, Einaudi went the long step further with Tocqueville: "Once possessed of the answer, Tocqueville imagined himself ready to advise his countrymen and to help a democratic France and Europe to follow the path of freedom rather than that of despotism." Some sense of Einaudi's purpose can be drawn from the following brief passage:

American economic policy since 1933 ... [is a] demonstration of the irrelevance of the theories and practices of the Soviet revolution in the affairs of an industrial society.... There have been many and persistent voices in the West bent upon proving our indebtedness to Russia in so far as planning and state intervention were concerned. The belief that the Soviet pattern of action had to be applied in times of trouble was an ingrained one. It took John Maynard Keynes's eloquence and theoretical constructions and Franklin Delano Roosevelt's practical political manipulations to provide proof of the inapplicability of the Soviet experience to the West.[26]

This was a bold and important message for the 1950s. The Soviet model was popular on the Left. The Communist parties of France and Italy were the largest outside the USSR. A Socialist federation with the Communist party was still in the future of France, and Eurocommunism was still to have its brief day. The break between the Socialist and the Communist Left in France was not to come until the 1980s. Andrew Shonfield was writing with the 1950s freshly in mind when he observed that "the United States is indeed one of the few places left where 'capitalism' is generally thought to be an OKAY word."[27]

Thirty years after the publication of *The Roosevelt Revolution,* the European countries (and there is no need to limit this to the European countries) have moved, for them, significantly to the right, but toward Einaudi's precious liberalism rather than toward fascism, as Einaudi feared they might as they fell out of love with the Soviet model. Indeed, by U.S. standards, the move toward liberalism is in a rightward direction only because the European intellectual tradition takes the attitude toward capitalism as its litmus test of Left versus Right.[28] But that is an egregious oversimplification equivalent to the U.S. practice of taking one's attitude toward government as the litmus test to distinguish between conservative (Right) and liberal (Left). It would be more accurate simply to call the recent European embrace of capitalist methods Americanization. But it would be equally accurate to characterize the U.S. embrace of a Keynesian model as Europeanization. Europeanization refers to the building of a large governmental presence, but with a politics consonant with that. This is the new American state. It is a positive state, one that does not react to but rather attempts to initiate action in regard to social and economic problems. It is a state filled with the rhetoric and a great deal of the reality of mobilization toward social justice and equity. It is also a government whose politics tends toward polarization and mass mobilization.

The United States is far from Europeanized, especially given the long-term decline of organized political parties; but it has been on a Europeanizing course since the New Deal. The growth of the governmental sector and of the public bureaucracy could be seen almost immediately. The political implications were not seen for a while, some indeed not until the 1970s and 1980s, with the emergence of a genuine right wing at the national level. The 1980s has seen a polarization of Right and Left on a national scale in the United States which is certainly unique in this century.

This first aspect of Europeanization has been recognized by many political scientists, and one group has urged a "return to the state" as the proper way to study politics and government.[29] Up to a point this is a good development, but there is a tendency to reify "the state," to approach it as though the state were a particular quality that can be measured as to its strength, its autonomy, and so on. This is an unfortunate extreme.

The state, like power, is a term of art, directing the observer toward a certain level of discourse. Moreover, stress on the state as a characteristic more or less present tends to expose the second important dimension of Europeanization (or "state development") in this review of the Roosevelt Revolution. It is a good point on which to conclude.

Differentiation is what is really meant by modernization. Modernization is not to be understood merely in terms of advanced technology, the increased recruitment of skills, and the elaboration of management techniques. This aspect of modernization was developing before the Roosevelt administration and was not something to which the Roosevelt administration was strongly committed. As a matter of fact, most of the important technological advances made by the Roosevelt administration occurred during World War II, with the integration of science into policy and policy making. In any event, differentiation is the more important dimension of modernization. Thus, the Roosevelt Revolution opened up two new streets for Americans: the positive state and the modernized or differentiated state. And these should be the main thoroughfares of political science research for the rest of this century and beyond. But for both of these directions there should be a single concern, so well expressed by Einaudi toward the end of *The Roosevelt Revolution*:

> What we have seen in the United States has been the systematic and inventive search for solutions to the difficulties of industrial mass democracy, a search intended to realize the ideals of community without collectivism, the ideal of freedom without anarchy, the advantages of technology without the loss of humanism.... What the Roosevelt Revolution has done has been to keep the door open so as to permit to our generation a chance to decide in liberty what we must do.[30]

The research we do today must keep that door open.

CHAPTER 6

The Europeanization of America?

From United States to United State

Among the large nation-states of the 20th century, the United States is the oldest constitutional republic and has the youngest consolidated national government. The modern, positive national state in the United States is a product of the years since 1933. Our institutions of government are still adapting themselves to their new functions and new relationships. Even the vocabulary of analysis has been adjusting itself to the state and related concepts, which had once been rejected as too abstract, formalistic, legalistic, and European to have any precision or utility in the American context. Once we were unique as a large nation where government was almost a matter of politics. In the 1960s and 1970s, government became the central presence and politics a peripheral, occasionally significant, collection of activities oriented toward influencing the government—i.e., the apparatus of the state.

Between 1789 and the 1930s the national government was not such a significant force in the economic or social life of the citizens of the United States. The most important principle in the Constitution of 1787 was Federalism, and for well over a century, despite the Civil War and abolition, Federalism was one of the dominating realities. Given their intimate knowledge of European political theory and experience, the Founders certainly must have selected the *term* "state" as the name for our lower units of government in order to indicate where most sovereignty was expected to reside. Comparison of national and state legislative activities in any year after 1800 will show that the states did almost all the governing in the United States. The domestic policies of the federal government were almost entirely concerned with subsidies, bounties, and claims. Land grants were piled upon land sales at low prices, and these were piled upon still additional land grants until the frontier ran out. Subsidies in the form of money and privilege were granted to the coastal trade, the railroads, and other common carriers. Tariffs were handed out to virtually any manufacturer or producer who could gain effective representation in Congress. The federal government was spending about 99 percent of its domestic effort husbanding commerce. In the meantime, the states were held responsible for the entire use of the "police power," which referred to the authority and obligation of governments to provide for the health, safety, and morals of the community. Through the police power the state governments provided for all of the property laws, the estate and family laws, the commerce laws (including ownership and exchange), family laws (including morals), public health laws, occupation and professions laws, construction codes, water and mineral resources laws, electoral laws, banking and credit laws, insurance laws, most of the criminal laws—in sum, virtually all of the legal and governmental framework for civil society.

It is no paradox at all, as some would like us to believe, that the national political system of the United States was so stable despite the instability and dynamism of the society and the economy during all the formative years of the Republic. The fact of the matter is that all the fundamental social choices involving the coercive powers of government were being made at levels of government far below the national. The Constitution, quite deliberately, had delegated the fundamental social choices to the lower level and therefore had delegated or suppressed or diffused political conflict. We had not, for lack of a feudal system to overthrow, merely lucked up on political peace, class harmony, and intergroup consensus. We had really designed a means by which the opposites of peace, harmony, and consensus could be institutionally dispersed. *Federalist 10*, understood in the context of constitutional Federalism and the actual comparative functions of government, was the most successful planning document in the history of the world.

Liberal historians are nevertheless correct insisting that the United States was never free of government and that our economy was never for an instant laissez-faire. Our economy was free, but only within an elaborate and stable framework of government. Moreover, it was not merely a government-as-umpire, although the use of government positively to enforce contracts was absolutely essential. Government during the era of our liberal economy was far more positive than this, and any images to the contrary are pure mythology. However, it would be equally mythological to argue that the role of government today is the same as the role of government in the 19th century. In a very important sense the New Deal was a "Roosevelt Revolution," as Mario Einaudi put it in the title of a very important analysis from a European perspective of the 20th century American experience with government. And the New Deal is significant far beyond its contribution to the size and scale of the national government, measured in budgetary terms. Although it is true that federal domestic expenditures increased from 0.8 percent of GNP in 1929 to 4.9 percent in 1939, the factor of far greater significance is the change during the New Deal in the *functions* of the federal government. Subsidy policies continued to be enacted by Congress; in fact, growth in subsidy programs accounts for a large portion of the general budgetary growth. However, the federal government was adopting two new kinds of functions, new at least for the federal government. These two new functions are *regulation* and *redistribution*. With the adoption of a very large number of important regulatory policies the federal government discovered the "police power." The second function is usually recognized as fiscal and monetary policies, but these bland labels mask the true significance of the new redistributive function.

Regulatory and redistributive functions and their respective policies are different from each other in a number of important respects. However, they have one very important thing in common which distinguishes the two of them from almost everything the federal government was doing prior to the 1930s. *They require the direct and coercive use of power over citizens.* With the adoption of such policies on a large scale, it was no longer possible for the federal government or its professional observers to hide from themselves the fact that "policy" and "police" have common roots. This is what is fundamentally new in the new, positive national state. There are, of course, well known precedents for both of these new kinds of policy, but the New Deal is the transition into the new state because of a number of such policies adopted at that time and because of the establishment once and for all of the constitutional right of the federal government to take on these new functions.

The New Deal was at most a transition, however, because a very large proportion of the policies adopted at that time were justified by the emergency conditions and might well have been repealed or weakened after the emergency had passed. After all, probably a minority of 1930s Democrats were intensely positive toward all the new interventions. Signs of permanent acceptance of the entire apparatus were few in the postwar years. The Employment Act of 1946 is the most significant sign that attitudes toward large positive national government had changed, but these signs were balanced by many negative signs, such as the softening of the Wagner Act by Taft-Hartley, and the softening of public housing with the much more private-sector oriented urban redevelopment. Attacks on TVA, welfare, and the alphabetocracy of the regulatory commissions were common throughout the 1946–1960 era. One can say therefore, that the new national state was not forever ensconced until the 1960s.

The return of the Democrats in 1961 brought with it far more than a commitment to the completion of the unfinished New Deal and Fair Deal programs. Of far greater significance was the new attitude they brought with them. Whereas the rhetoric of the 1930s had conceded that the new interventions were departures from tradition, and whereas even the New Deal Democrats attempted to justify many new programs as necessary evils, the leadership of the New Frontier accepted the positive national state—and its programs—as a positive virtue, as something desirable for its own sake and patently necessary for the society. There was great optimism about the ability of the national government to set the world to rights. There was optimism that the interests of all groups and classes were basically in harmony and that conflicts among these interests were never so far apart that they could not be adjusted by systematic, noncoercive governmental interventions. There was optimism about the ability of professionals and technocrats to define society's basic problems and to identify or invent the mechanisms appropriate for their solution.

Out of these attitudes grew the extremely optimistic and positive role of the national government we now accept as a commonplace fact about the Kennedy and Johnson administrations. What is less well appreciated is the continuity between those administrations and the Nixon-Ford administrations. The accompanying tables are a good overview of the policies and problems dealt with in this volume. But they are significant beyond that because they indicate that the positive national state is no longer simply a Democratic program. The national state is no longer a partisan matter at all. Republicans represent a different set of interests; Republicans may be stingy where Democrats are generous; Republicans may favor one mechanism and Democrats another. But there is no longer any variation between the two parties in their willingness to turn to the positive state, to expand it, and to use it with vigor whenever society's problems seem pressing and whenever governmental inaction may jeopardize electoral opportunities.

Table 6.1 is a listing, not necessarily exhaustive, of the important federal regulatory laws enacted by Congress since 1970. This looks more like a binge than a Republican retrenchment. Granted, some of these were pushed upon a reluctant president by a Democratic Congress. On the other hand, these did not require passage over a presidential veto. Moreover, the most significant regulatory program of that decade, and one of the most significant in American history, was the Economic Stabilization Act of 1970, which, although passed over presidential objections and signed into law accompanied by expressions of presidential misgivings, was used elaborately and vigorously by President Nixon as soon as the rate of "stagflation" began to threaten the economy and the 1972 election.

Although people disagree intensely in their interpretations of the motives and significance of the Republican efforts in the field of redistribution, especially welfare policy, no one can deny the fact that Nixon was a very active president in the welfare area and that the net effect of his effort was a rather significant increase in the positive national state. One book-length account of Nixon's welfare policy activities opens with the following sentence: "Anyone who had predicted that Richard Nixon would be the first president to propose a guaranteed income for families coupled with wage supplements for poor fathers, would have been dismissed as mad."[1] Thus, although the increases shown on Table 6.2 were mainly mandated by commitments made prior to the 1970s—loosened eligibility rules, increased rates, inflation clauses, and so on—the Republicans were making their own contributions to further growth of welfare and would have expanded it even further, had the Democratic Congress been more cooperative.[2] Congress rejected Nixon's Family Assistance Plan by an unusual coalition of liberals, who, always suspicious of Nixon, felt the plan did not go far enough, and conservatives, who feared the plan would go far beyond the existing welfare structure, which was already far beyond the acceptable conservative limits. But Democrats and Republicans accepted the second most important Nixon proposal in the field of redistributive policy when they enacted General Revenue Sharing and then on top of that accepted several of Nixon's requests for "Special Revenue Sharing" to consolidate a large number of existing categoric grant-in-aid programs. From the fiscal standpoint, General Revenue Sharing is not all that significant. It committed the federal government to $30 billion over the first five years of operation and has never contributed more than 5 percent to the operating budgets of any local government. Special revenue-sharing proposals were not greeted with cheers by the Democratic majority in Congress, but eventually two of the seven requests were adopted. These were the Comprehensive Education and Manpower Act of 1973 and the Housing and Community Development Act of 1974. The first of these collapsed the existing 10,000 federal manpower contracts into 50 state and 350 large city "bloc grants." The second replaced seven major categoric grant programs with a single Community Development program grant.

A good argument can be made that the motivation back of this special revenue-sharing approach was not merely to consolidate the many categoric grant-in-aid programs, but also to mask a net reduction in the total federal support for local governments. Nevertheless, there is a profound continuity between Democrats and Republicans which

Table 6.1 Federal Regulatory Laws and Programs Enacted, 1970–1976

Year Enacted	Title of Statute
1969–1970	Child Protection and Toy Safety Act Clear Air Amendments Egg Products Inspection Act Economic Stabilization Act Fair Credit Reporting Act Occupational Safety and Health Act Poison Prevention Packaging Act Securities Investor Protection Act
1971	Economic Stabilization Act Amendments Federal Boat Safety Act Lead-Based Paint Elimination Act Wholesome Fish and Fisheries Act
1972	Consumer Product Safety Act Equal Employment Opportunity Act Federal Election Campaign Act Federal Environmental Pesticide Control Act Federal Water Pollution Control Act Amendments Motor Vehicle Information and Cost Savings Act Noise Control Act Ports and Waterways Safety Act
1973	Agriculture and Consumer Protection Act Economic Stabilization Act Amendment Emergency Petroleum Allocation Act Flood Disaster Protection Act
1974	Atomic Energy Act Commodity Futures Trading Commission Act Consumer Product Warranties— FTL Improvement Act Council on Wage and Price Stability Act Employee Retirement Income Security Act Federal Energy Administration Act Hazardous Materials Transportation Act Housing and Community Development Act Pension Reform Act Privacy Act Safe Drinking Water Act
1975	Energy Policy and Conservation Act Equal Credit Opportunity Act
1976	Consumer Leasing Act Medical Device Safety Act Toxic Substances Control Act

Table 6.2 Federal Social Welfare Expenditures (in millions)

	FY 1965	FY 1970	FY 1976
Social Insurance	21,806	42,245	120,809
Public Aid	3,593	9,648	33,244
Health and Medical Programs	2,780	4,775	9,353
Veteran's Programs	6,010	8,901	18,790
Education	2,469	5,875	9,168
Housing	238	581	2,427
Other Social Welfare (Vocational rehabilitation, child nutrition, OEO, and ACTION)	812	2,258	4,534
TOTAL	37,708	77,433	196,325

Source: Social Security Bulletin (Washington, DC: Government Printing Office, January, 1977), pp. 5–7. For a more discriminating statement of federal social welfare expenditures, see Lawrence A. Lynn, "A Decade of Policy Developments in the Income Maintenance System," in Robert Haveman, A Decade of Federal Anti-Poverty Programs (Madison: Institute for Research on Poverty, 1977).

outweighs the minor difference in degree of generosity. The fact is, the Republicans were not opposing positive national government at all; quite the contrary. *Despite any reductions in the total amount of money they were willing to make available, they were actually tying the local governments closer to the national government than they had ever been tied before.* How is this possible? They did it by making the federal government more discretionary than it had been before. Under traditional grant-in-aid programs, there is a moderate limitation to discretion inherent in the fact that each grant-in-aid program was tied to a particular subject matter category. This is why we came to call them "categoric aid" to distinguish them from general bloc grants. Under General and Special Revenue Sharing, the Republicans took what little discretion there was in the categories and eliminated that almost entirely. This means that each of the 39,000 communities eligible for revenue sharing can take whatever grants they get and decide for themselves whether the money should go to tax relief, to new public works, or to the purchase of General Sherman tanks. From the other side, this means that the federal government is all that much more able to use grant-in-aid appropriations on a patronage basis to buy the support of mayors, governors, and urban lobbies. In the very short run, this increased discretion, which increases the opportunities to use federal monies as patronage, will produce "clientele relationships" between the national center and the 39,000 local principalities. This changed or intensified relationship is far more important than marginal increases and decreases in the total amount of money available. In this sense, the national presence has been extended, and the direct national-local relationship has been cemented. Thereby our positive national state has been perpetuated in virtually the same manner as earlier national states cemented and eventually perpetuated the relationship between the central prince (*primes inter pares*) and all of the other feudal lords.

Although it would be impossible to overlook the growing power and presence of the national government through the conventional fiscal and monetary policies, one aspect of this has generally been overlooked: investment guarantees and insurance. The so-called Lockheed loan of 1975 is a good illustration of this kind of national power, precisely because it was not a loan but was widely understood to be a loan. Lockheed, on the brink of actual bankruptcy, was neither allowed to dissolve nor saved by a direct subsidy. The government took positive steps, but it spent no money, granted no loan, made no direct transfers at all. The government action was merely a signature by a representative of the Emergency Loan Guarantee Board on a document which stated that the federal government would guarantee up to $250 million that Lockheed could borrow from private sources. With that guarantee—and it was no more than a signature by a public official on a slip of paper—Lockheed could go to private banks and get money at relatively low interest rates or money that was not otherwise forthcoming at all. The authority of the Board, established by statute in 1970, was as follows: "The Board, on such terms and conditions as it deems appropriate, may guarantee, or make commitments to guarantee, lenders against loss of principal or interest on loans that meet the requirements of this Act." The so-called requirements in that passage were simply that the Board must find that in its opinion the economy would be seriously affected if the applicant was not able to continue operation.

Table 6.3 gives a quick sketch of the scale and variety of this particular policy activity in the 1970s. And stress should be put upon the fact that this is a listing only of the discretionary investment guarantee activities. The table does not include other programs of investment guarantees and insurance that are nondiscretionary.[3]

Table 6.3 shows a striking growth of the accumulated commitments of all the agencies. Note should be taken especially of the accelerated growth of this kind of national commitment since 1970. Obviously this is a technique of national government which the Republicans prefer, while the Democrats seem to prefer direct regulatory involvements or conventional fiscal and monetary policy. But for neither party is it any longer a question of *whether* the national government should maintain and expand its presence in the economy and the society. Both are regularly using government vigorously and positively, and both parties prefer a discretionary approach to these things, even in fiscal and monetary fields where we have had a great deal of experience and success in constructing clear and detailed nondiscretionary programs called "automatic stabilizers." Why this preference for discretion as well as scale and positiveness? One does not have to pierce the inner thought processes of elites to appreciate the advantages inherent in discretionary programs—to be crassly brief, how much more intimately this ties the prospective recipients to the dispensing government. The discretionary element of these investment guarantee programs, therefore, adds a particularly important element of leverage to the size of this sector as measured by the figures in Table 6.3. In the case of investment guarantees and insurance, the ties are to corporations and organizations in the private sector rather than to local governments. But here is another extremely important dimension of the national presence and how it is being established, perpetuated, and institutionalized.[4]

There is no room left for doubt that a large, positive, interventionist, national state is finally and forever the central feature of the American political system. It is also

Table 6.3 Discretionary Fiscal Policy: Federal Investment Guarantee Activity, 1976 (in millions)

Program	New Guarantees	Total Guarantees Outstanding
International	$ 1,412	$ 2,502
Farmers Home Administration	4,391	17,847
Rural Electrification Administration	860	1,114
Maritime Administration	1,169	3,431
Economic Development Assistance	1	160
Defense-Tanker charters	0	180
HEW		
Health	215	1,061
Education	1,397	6,849
HUD		
Low rent	7,660	13,607
FHA	8,316	88,988
Communities	210	2,799
GNMA	8,999	25,610
Other credit	0	549
Interior		
Indian Programs	29	29
Transportation		
Railroads	264	670
WMATA (DC Transit)	0	997
Aircraft	78	100
Treasury	1,260	0
General Services Administration	24	956
Veterans Administration—Housing	10,250	64,116
Emergency Loan Guarantee Board		
(Lockheed)	0	185
Export-Import Bank	5,147	5,273
FDIC	0	1,144
Small Business Administration	1,768	4,979
Other Agencies	13	68
TOTAL	53,463	243,213[a]

Source: Special Analyses, Budget of the U.S., FY1978, Sec. E.

Note: a. Several agencies, including the Government National Mortgage Association (GNMA), the Federal Financing Bank (FFB), and several federally sponsored private enterprises, including the Federal National Mortgage Association (FNMA), formerly a public agency, actually buy up many guaranteed loans from the banks, converting them essentially into direct government loans. In 1976, $25 billion, nearly half, of the loan guarantees were so converted; and enough conversions take place to reduce the accumulated figure from the $243.2 billion on the table to $169.8 billion. Budgetary policy at OMB prefers the lower figures, arguing that otherwise there is double counting. But I prefer the larger figure because (1) it indicates the scale of this activity and (2) because all of it, converted or not, is discretionary and "off-budget." These intermediary or secondary institutions are a form of "backdoor" credit.

times, if indeed there ever are normal times in the United States. And the point of more pressing importance is that during this period we had nationalized local disorders. The national presence had extended itself throughout the length, breadth, and depth of the land. How it will express itself will certainly depend upon whatever is special to each era. But there is no longer any doubt about the national presence and the fact that it will express itself.

Sayre's Law (after the late Wallace Sayre of Columbia University) holds that the gains of any change are immediate and the costs are cumulative. Review of the many programs in this volume suggests that it is high time we start evaluating long-run costs along with short-run benefits and cost. The long-run costs may be directly empirical in their nature, but they also may require certain philosophic posture. Nevertheless, we must somehow approach them, because the welfare of the entire society may be at stake. We have become Europeanized at least to the extent that the United States has become a united state, and we are going to have to prepare ourselves for the consequences. Louis Hartz was only half right in his famous thesis that the liberal tradition in America arose out of the good fortune of not having a feudal system to overthrow. The other half of that thesis is that we were also blessed with not having a large and positive state to defend the basic interests of the ancient regime.

Since we cannot reenact our history and give ourselves a feudal order to overthrow, we may be safe to that extent from the loss of our liberal tradition. But we can still lose that liberal tradition if the large and unified national state we have now created is allowed to fail either through falling too short of its promises or through allowing itself to be captured by any combination of elite and corporate interests. Such a state will so confirm the most antagonistic theories of the liberal society that it may produce not an antistate movement but an antiliberal revolutionary movement that will simply attempt to free the state from one set of interests and enslave the state with another set. We as citizens would then have exchanged one set of masters for another. In its most fundamental meaning the liberal tradition is worth defending. To what extent is it endangered by the very state that modern liberals have produced? Though we must approach this kind of issue philosophically, we cannot deal with it unless we have concrete empirical materials about the behavior of the modern state, the policies of the modern state, and their consequences. It is our expectation that this volume will contribute to such an analysis, and it is our hope that through such an analysis an appropriate and effective philosophical position will emerge.

Part III

※※◎◎◎※※

Bureaucracy and Arenas of Power

The basic thesis of this part is that the four types of policy arenas include not only a characteristic policymaking (input) component but also a characteristic policy implementation (output) component. This is, of course, implicit in Lowi's definition of policy, a definition that includes both the statement of a rule or intent and the specification of a mechanism for applying the power of the state. In the modern world, Lowi suggests, the implementing mechanism is the state bureaucracy. A key contribution of this analysis, however, suggests that not only is there not a single public administration system, but that there are indeed four types shaped by the four types of public policy they must implement.

Chapter 7 introduces the basic conceptual argument that is central to the Arenas of Power model. Policy results from the actions and interactions of political actors in pursuit of their interests, but although those actions tell us a great deal about issues and problems, the desired outcomes, and the demand for policy, they do not define policies. The definition of policy requires first that one examine the authorizing language—the delegation of authority to implementing agents. Second, the conditions must be established for the application of state power to influence citizen behavior, including the target behavior or population and the institutional arrangements for exercising power. The definition of policy employed here also makes it clear that policy is not defined by the actual outcomes achieved. The classification of policy is not changed by the probability of success of the policy in question. This is a critical point in Lowi's argument, because our understanding of the characteristic impact of policy types in different settings can help us make choices among policies and institutional arrangements. The outcomes of policy and their overall effect on the polity and on citizens are indeed part of our process of evaluating policy choices.

The next step in the argument is the assertion that government agencies are shaped by the type of policy they implement. This seems reasonable. Regulatory agencies must be able to find the behavior and people they need to regulate, apply rules to individual behavior, and directly apply sanctions (or rewards). Similar arguments can be made about distributive, redistributive, and constituent policies. Lowi strengthens his case considerably by demonstrating that in both France and the United States, regulatory agencies (and other types) share common characteristics of staffing, management systems, and structure that are dictated by the type of policy they implement. In fact, one can make reasonably predictive statements about the impact of distributive, regulatory, or redistributive agencies across a wide variety of political systems and, with adequate knowledge of the institutional arrangements and conditions, anticipate success, failure, forms of corruption, and the character of citizen participation.

Chapter 8, dealing with U.S. agriculture, makes it clear that a given organization may, indeed, encompass a variety of different policies that employ greatly different institutional mechanisms. One question that Lowi does not address is what the implications are of attempting to have single organizations implement different types of policies. Organizations that implement multiple policy types are not a null set. Experience in developing countries with integrated rural development programs, for example, is instructive. In response to extremely limited administrative capacity in rural areas and in the name of simplifying access and reducing transaction costs for farmers, rural administration often combined regulatory duties and extension services as an integral part of the operation of rural credit programs designed to support agricultural modernization. Typically either the distributive ethos overcame the regulatory one (regulators became trapped in factional politics) or, more often, the distributive policy was subsumed to the regulatory one (national cropping priorities captured distributive services to farmers).

The Arenas of Power model has enormous potential for comparative analysis. Part III, focusing as it does on state administration, provides the easiest jumping-off point for such an effort. Although one can see potential insights from comparative work on political change (Part II), sectoral analysis (Part IV), and mass movements that take politics outside the box (Part V), the analytical challenge seems considerably greater than in the case of comparative administration. There are two sets of variables that will impact any comparative analysis using the model. First, macroeconomic structure and policy do set conditions within which the other policies work. Lowi is correct that macroeconomic policies are a policy choice (for example, inflationary policies), but they also influence the broader interests and perceptions of citizens and the efficacy of regulatory and distributive policies. In other words, the arenas interact. Second, microeconomic policies and institutional choices directly affect transaction costs of any of the four policy choices. For a country without private property and land markets, land titling (even without land reform) is a dramatic constituent policy choice. But the institutional arrangements for establishing ownership, adjudicating disputes, and overseeing available land-use contracts impact enormously on the initial constituent policy choice. Again, the interaction of policy choices and the specific institutional choices made within each are a key to the empirical analysis.

"The State in Politics: The Relation Between Policy and Administration" (Chapter 7) is a key piece in the development of the Arenas of Power model. First, it is the most explicit application of the "primary rule" and "secondary rule" distinction in describing the application of state power in building Lowi's fourfold typology of policy types. Second, an explicit link is made in this chapter between policy types and the organization and functioning of the state bureaucracy. Third, it is the only comparative application of the model outside the United States. For all these reasons, it deserves special attention.

The chapter is very much in the tradition of Lowi's earlier work in New York City. It focuses on administrative agencies and builds on the methodology of the New York study. It begins with the development of a classification methodology for differentiating administrative agencies. The data for this classification are the enabling statutes. It should be noted that the classification is, therefore, based on intent and authority granted the agency, not on what it actually does. Thus, if the statute is vague and there is no remedy (e.g., committee reports), the case is rejected. Information is then collected from each of the classified agencies regarding recruitment patterns, career paths, management systems, and structure (e.g., centralized and decentralized). The strength of the study is the impressive similarity between France and the United States in virtually all of these characteristics within the agency types. The line of reasoning is then presented for each of the four types that the predominant policy type in the agency defines the task of the agency (intent) and also its structure and management system required to exercise distributive, regulatory, constituent, or redistributive activities (coercion).

"The Case of Agriculture: Four Kinds of Policy, Four Kinds of Politics" (Chapter 8) examines the complex activities of the U.S. Department of Agriculture through the lens of the Arenas of Power model. Large bureaucracies that impact both directly and indirectly on citizens are a defining characteristic of the modern state and the instrument through which policy choices are implemented. A federal agency such as USDA may execute programs directly through federal staff in the field, through the land grant colleges as in the case of the extension service, through the cooperative movement, or even through commodity and financial market operations. Thus, it manages a mix of distributive, regulatory, and redistributive policies, typically in discrete administrative units under control of the Secretary of Agriculture. Lowi notes here, as he does frequently elsewhere, the characteristic U.S. penchant for congressional delegation of authority to implement policies to administrative discretion. The legislative authority establishes the basic rules of the game by designating the policy choice—distributive, redistributive, or regulatory—and, therefore, the power relationship between the citizen and the state. But many of the institutional arrangements, technical programmatic details, are decided by the bureaucracy or fed into the policy decision by the bureaucracy.

The evolution of the mix of agricultural policies is also instructive. Farmer movements in the nineteenth century focused on a redistributive policy, inflationary macroeconomic policy, as we have seen in Chapter 4. What evolved, over time, was a mix of distributive services, regulatory activities that manipulated agricultural markets in the farmers' favor, and microeconomic manipulation of financial markets through subsidized, but targeted, loans for productive activities, investments, and rural infrastructure. In the context of Part II, what is striking here is the increased complexity and diversity of policy instruments combined with greater ability, in all types of policy arenas, to target populations, problems, and strategic economic activities or transactions. The USDA case also documents the ingenuity and growing diversity of institutional arrangements for effecting policy goals in all arenas.

Lowi's argument in this part, that policy choices among the four arenas of power fundamentally affect the institutional arrangements of the state employed to reach the public objectives, is important in understanding current debates on the role of governance in economic development and the consequence of the proliferation of fragile states within the international community. Since the 1990s, governance has replaced both capital accumulation and macroeconomic policy reform as the key to development and the answer to global poverty. The governance literature is clearly a growth industry and demonstrates varying degrees of empirical grounding and analytical sophistication, but we have never had a richer environment for testing Lowi's model in diverse environments. Further, it is evident that prescriptions for the improvement of governance that do not grasp the requirements for implementing the four policy types are likely to be disappointing.

—*Norman K. Nicholson*

Suggested Reading

Useful descriptions of the "governance" problem include:

Francis Fukuyama. *State-Building: Governance and the World Order in the 21st Century*. Ithaca: Cornell University Press, 2004.
> After two decades in which the development community focused on paring back the state and effecting a better balance between market and state institutions, Fukuyama makes a strong case that it is precisely the weakness of the state and the absence of key state function that restrain development and suggest that fragile states have become the central problem in international politics in the twenty-first century.

Hernando de Soto. *The Mystery of Capital: Why Capitalism Triumphs in the West and Fails Everywhere Else*. New York: Basic Books, 2000.
> De Soto emphasizes the failure of many states to keep up with the legal and institutional requisites of a modern, globalized, capitalist economy, with the result that extralegal arrangements fill the gap.

Building Institutions for Markets. World Development Report 2002. Washington, DC: World Bank, 2002.
> The 2002 World Development Report provides a comprehensive statement of the institutional requirements of the modern state in ensuring competitiveness in the modern global economy.

Pranab Bardhan. *The Role of Governance in Economic Development: A Political Economy Approach*. Paris: OECD Development Center, 1997.
> In this brief paper, Bardhan addresses how corruption, overcentralization of the state, and uncontrolled ethnic conflict can fall into a "failed" institutional "equilibrium" that prevents adaptation to a global economy.

Nicolas van de Walle. *Overcoming Stagnation in Aid-Dependent Countries*. Washington, DC: Center for Global Development, 2005.
> Van de Walle echoes Bardhan's arguments about institutional failure that produces corrupt leadership and inept states. He argues further that foreign aid (distributive policies of donors) fails to alter these conditions and may even make them worse.

Daniel Kaufmann and Aart Kraay. *Growth Without Governance*. Washington, DC: World Bank, 2002.

This empirical study has been seminal in establishing the parameters of a dialogue about the relationship between governance and growth. There is at present no dominant paradigm for the comparative analysis of governance. However, in the context of related work on institutional change, Lowi's Arenas of Power model greatly clarifies the importance of policy choice.

Vincent Ostrom and Elinor Ostrom. "Public Goods and Public Choices: The Emergence of Public Economies and Industry Structures." In Vincent Ostrom, *The Meaning of American Federalism: Constituting as Self-Governing Society,* ch. 7. San Francisco: Institute for Contemporary Studies, 1991.

Vincent Ostrom and Elinor Ostrom make an important contribution in that they focus, like Lowi, on the exercise of the power of the state, but take as a key dimension the nature of the goods and services (public, mixed, private) provided.

Oliver E. Williamson. *Markets and Hierarchies.* New York: Free Press, 1975.

Oliver Williamson, with many others in the institutional economics tradition, emphasizes transaction costs as a key determinant in the choice and evolution of institutional arrangements that embody the implementation of policy choices.

There is also a growing empirical literature on the interaction of policy and institutional choice, or governance, with diverse political and economic environment. These include:

Lee J. Alston, Thrainn Eggertsson, and Douglass C. North. *Empirical Studies in Institutional Change.* Cambridge: Cambridge University Press, 1996.

Elinor Ostrom. *Governing the Commons.* Cambridge: Cambridge University Press, 1990.

Hernando de Soto. *The Other Path: The Invisible Revolution in the Third World.* New York: Harper and Row, 1990.

Robert Bates. *Beyond the Miracle of the Market: The Political Economy of Agrarian Development in Kenya.* Cambridge: Cambridge University Press, 1989.

Robert Wade. *Governing the Market: Economic Theory and the Role of Government in East Asian Industrialization.* Princeton: Princeton University Press, 1990.

Mustapha K. Nabli and Jeffrey B. Nugent. *The New Institutional Economics and Development: Theory and Applications to Tunisia.* Amsterdam: North-Holland, 1989.

Norman K. Nicholson. "Analyzing Bureaucracy and Rural Development Policy Implementation: The Limits of Hierarchy." In Derick W. Brinkerhoff, ed., *Policy Studies and Developing Nations,* pp. 113–137. Greenwich: JAI Press, 1997.

Norman Uphoff, ed. *Puzzles of Productivity in Public Organizations.* San Francisco: ICS Press, 1994.

Empirical and conceptual work is informing international development practice. See, for example:

Making Services Work for the Poor. World Development Report 2005. Washington, DC: World Bank, 2004.

The conclusion emerging from this body of literature is that the polity is not simply an epiphenomenon driven by exogenous natural and economic forces, but rather that, by enabling collective choice, it shapes society's response to changing conditions. The proactive role of government now being presumably obvious, we need to begin to build a theory of governance that combines an understanding of policy, of institutional arrangements, and of the impact of governance on global forces. Two studies, in addition to the materials presented in this volume, appear particularly helpful:

Douglass C. North. *Institutions, Institutional Change, and Economic Performance.* Cambridge: Cambridge University Press, 1990.

This important contribution to the institutional economics literature by Nobel Laureate Douglass North provides considerable insight into institutional change and how institutions effect change, positive or negative.

James G. March and Johan P. Olson. *Rediscovering Institutions: The Organizational Basis of Politics.* New York: Free Press, 1989.

This work reestablishes the state as an independent actor in political change and serves to bring institutional analysis back into the study of the state.

CHAPTER 7

※⊛※

The State in Politics

The Relation Between Policy and Administration

Anyone who studies political systems today must be struck by the presence of the state in all avenues of life. Yet, American political science has not fully integrated this fact. Although political science is rich in theories that help give meaning to political experience, none of these has tried to construct a politics on the basis of the state and its functions.

A state-centered theory of politics is based on a simple assumption—that every type of state, or regime, creates a politics consonant with itself. But one can look in vain for the state. What one generally sees are rules—actual rules, or actions emanating from rules—rules that are highly formal and explicit or rules that are implicit in uniforms or other official paraphernalia. The most important and formal rules are called by many names, such as laws, statutes, decrees, regulations. Most recently, the general category is referred to as policies, or public policy.

To extend the line of reasoning, the state, although an abstraction, can be experienced through the policies pursued by institutions that possess political authority. And, if policies are the state in action, then, if properly classified, they are types of regimes, each of which is likely to develop its own system of politics. This line of reasoning involves a considerable shift in theoretical perspective, from the assumption that politics causes policy to the assumption that policy causes politics. In operational terms, the causal arrows run from a policy proposal to its formulation to its implementation, and back again through group reaction to policy and administrative adaptation. The policy becomes the boundary conditions within which political action takes place. In brief, the theory requires the following analytic procedure: first, to identify and categorize public policies in their most formalistic and legalistic terms—literally as types of state or regime; second, to attempt to understand, explain, and predict political patterns, with politics defined as everything in the political system *except* the formalistic, legalistic policies. That is, the independent variables are the policies, properly categorized; the dependent variables are all other phenomena thought of as politics (again assuming that they are properly defined).

The larger purpose of this effort is to develop a political science of policy analysis—a politics rather than an economics of public policy, indeed, a politics of economics rather than an economics of politics. Up to now, political science has had very limited success in the theoretical or practical side of policy analysis. Many political scientists have become important political advisers, but aside from their skill in polling and in aggregate electoral data analysis, their success has come from good personal instincts more than from direct application of knowledge and theory drawn from political science and applied to public policy. In the area of policy evaluation, political scientists have been limited to helping politicians get votes for the passage of a bill through Congress or have played second chair to biologists, engineers, geologists, economists, and many others in the evaluation of actual impact of policies on the society. Political science may best make its pro rata contribution to good government on the basis of its ability to help define what government is, for purposes of analysis, and to evaluate the significance and impact of each form of government action *on the political system itself*. The reasoning is as follows. It takes many years for a policy to have an effect on the society, and once enough time has elapsed to warrant an evaluation of this effect, it is extremely difficult for even the most skillful analyst to isolate the particular contribution of the policy from the many other factors that could explain the outcome. In the meantime, however, each policy choice will have an almost immediate effect on the political environment. This important area is one in which political scientists are presumed to have expertise. Thus, if there is more than one policy approach to a given problem, political scientists ought to be able to advise policymakers on which approach would have the most desirable or the least undesirable effect on political institutions.

State into Policies: The Problem and Purpose of Classification

Once policies are appreciated as outward manifestations of the state, they cannot be adequately defined by mere designation of the subject matter with which each policy deals. Such designations as agricultural policy, educational policy, or industrial policy are, at best, indications of the interests of citizens and groups seeking something from governments. A proper definition of policy must be built not in terms of the interests of citizens but in terms of the forms of state action and the formally expressed intentions of the state. In the long run, state actions and private interests cannot remain far apart. Most policies are responses to interests or to demands made on the basis of interests. But policies are not themselves mere interests; they are state interests. If individual perceptions, interests, and organizations are made part of the definition of policy, there would be no way to explore the relationships between the two. A definition of policies must therefore be divorced from all interests other than those of the state itself.

A divorce of policy from all other aspects of politics requires two elements: the language of law and the techniques of control. Since the highest and most lasting forms of state action are expressed in legal language, so too must the definition of policy be expressed in that language. This is not merely a matter of vocabulary. The content of policies is law or lawlike. Rulers—no matter what their number, the nature of their selection, or their methods of policymaking—must delegate much of their power to agents. If the agents are not to become the rulers themselves, the delegation of authority must be made in language clear enough so that the delegates follow the intentions of the rulers and not their own. Consequently, the essential problem of active rulership is how to use language to maintain some connection between the intent of the rulers and the actual implementation by agents. In an important sense, the language *is* the policy.

Thus, the policy must intend—and it must address—a future state of affairs for a class of cases or actions. But if it is a public policy, it will also contain a coercive element. Coercion, following Weber, is basic to all state action. Unlike private institutions, the institutions of the state are not merely actors in their environment. State institutions have the right and the obligation to improve the probability that the future will resemble the intent of the original policy. A great part of the ultimate success of a public policy may be attributable to the mere statement of the preferred future state of affairs. The purpose of good citizenship is to make public policies virtually self-executing. But most policies are accompanied by explicit means of imposing their intentions on their environments, and in all policies some techniques of control are implicit.

A policy, then, is a rule formulated by some governmental authority expressing an intention to influence the behavior of citizens, individually or collectively, by use of positive and negative sanctions. This definition closely resembles the accepted definition of *rule* in jurisprudence. According to Roscoe Pound, a rule is a "legal precept attaching a definite detailed legal consequence to a definite detailed statement of fact."[1] Friedman and Macaulay see this as breaking down into two parts: the statement of fact and the statement of consequences. A third part is implicit: Friedman adds, "within some normative order or system of governmental control."[2] In other words, the third part of the definition amounts to a provision for implementing the intention and imposing the consequences. Today, that usually means a government agency. It is this third part of the definition that so often creates problems, because rules must be formulated in such a way as to provide standards and guidelines for these agencies. In the modern age of large government, laws, or legal rules, rarely communicate directly to citizens but, rather, to administrators.

A policy defined as a legal rule with these characteristics is obviously different from a specific decision or order, which derives from a rule but is not the rule itself. It is also different from a sentiment, which may express a desired end but embodies no rule. The preambles to statutes, full of important rhetoric, are often mistaken for policies. Finally, policy defined this way is obviously not intended to include observed changes in actual citizen behavior (such as increased savings or reduced racial discrimination), which, though they may have been the intent of the policy, are not necessarily attributable to that policy.

As clear and simple as the definition is, it does not locate a single, homogeneous class of phenomena. There is more than one type of policy, because there is more than one way the state can express an intention and more than one way the state can use its coercive powers through administrative agencies.

An important case in point is regulation, or regulatory policy. In his constitutional law treatise, Tribe[3] tends to equate regulation with government control and state action. He leaves open the question of what follows regulation, or what regulation is not. Thurow is probably typical of economists in taking regulation as a concept that needs no definition and then dealing theoretically and empirically with the impact of regulation on society.[4] Regulatory policies raise the incomes of some people and lower the incomes of others. But there is no concern for forms of government action other than regulation and therefore no opportunity to clarify the concept for purposes of political theory.

Others, including some political scientists, make some worthwhile distinctions among types of regulatory policy but fail to define regulation itself. In an important article, Wilson indicates, without explicitly stating, that there is a threefold distinction among government policies—government regulation, government ownership, and deference to the private sphere.[5] He then presents a more systematic scheme that becomes the center of an important part of his book *Political Organizations*. This scheme is concerned with the variation in political patterns within the various types of regulatory agencies according to whether the policy concentrates or disperses costs and benefits. Although very interesting, this does not sharpen the distinction between regulation and other types of state action.

Roger Noll devoted an entire essay to the question of "What Is Regulation?" and was only able to come up with a clearer distinction between regulatory and nonregulatory public policies.[6] First, the regulatory authority is not a party to the transactions it regulates but is a referee of transactions between other parties. (By contrast, the cost-reimbursement formulas for Medicare or Medicaid are not regulatory, because they are written by the purchaser of the service.) Second, regulation operates by cases and procedural rules. There are some problems with the second characteristic, but this definition gets closer than any other to a formal definition of regulation that is clean and clear of the many political and social variables one might wish to study in relation to the policy.

Nonregulation, however, remains merely the residual category. This is an important substantive issue. If we are to study regulation in any sense other than the technical one of the cost-effectiveness of particular agencies, we must have clear categories of comparison.

Some legal theorists help pierce through the dense atmosphere (the nonregulation sphere) of public policy. The less they are directly concerned with regulation itself, the closer they seem to come to theoretically helpful formulations. Summers and Howard provide a fivefold categorization of the nature of law, which can be taken as virtually synonymous with state action: (1) law as grievance remedial instrument, (2) law as a penal instrument, (3) law as an administrative regulatory instrument, (4) law as an instrument for ordering governmental conferral of public benefits, and (5) law as an instrument for facilitating and effecting private arrangements.[7] The first three categories include parts of what others often consider regulation, the first being court-made law for tort action; the second mainly legislative laws for conduct deemed evil in itself; and the third mainly legislative-administrative law for conduct deemed evil only in its consequences. The fourth category is a mixture of subsidy and welfare benefits, and the fifth concerns laws that distribute powers between the public and the private sphere. Summers's categories are asymmetrical, and he does not provide a logic for the distinctions or for their significance. But his scheme is rich in distinctions, and is a step toward defining areas of state action that are nonregulatory.

The logic absent from Summers's categorization can be found in the work of legal theorist H.L.A. Hart.[8] Hart begins with a critique of the traditional Austinian definition of *law* as "a rule that imposes an obligation and then applies a sanction for noncompliance." It is "criminal in form." He criticizes traditional jurisprudence for adhering to such a one-dimensional definition and identifies a second basic type of rule whose distinction from the first will immediately appeal to anyone who has examined legislation. Hart refers to the first or classical definition as a Primary Rule and then distinguishes it from a Secondary Rule, which fulfills Roscoe Pound's definition of a legal rule yet imposes no duties directly upon citizens. Rather, it confers powers or facilities on them. As an example of Secondary Rules, Hart suggests laws on marriage. This is a particularly good example, because some laws on marriage are Secondary Rules and some are Primary Rules. Marriage laws that confer facilities and processes to make marriage, marriage contracts, and marriage records available are examples of Secondary Rules. Laws that oblige husband and wife to observe the provisions of the contract, such as to refrain from adultery or bigamy, are examples of Primary Rules. Here we can see clearly the distinction between two basic types of laws or policies and at the same time can see the weakness of trying to distinguish among policies according to subject matter. That is to say, "marriage policy" is not a meaningful category.

Yet, powerful though Hart's dichotomy is, it does not appear to exhaust all the possibilities, especially when considering legislation instead of the judge-made law with which students of jurisprudence tend most to concern themselves. For example, some policies may appear at first to fit the definition of the Primary Rule in that they are involuntary, but they fall outside the definition in that they do not attempt to impose obligations directly on individuals. That is to say, some patently coercive rules do not seem to work through individual conduct but instead seek to influence the individual by working through the environment of conduct. This distinction between individual conduct and the environment of conduct is more easily recognized in the study of legislation than in the study of judge-made law, because judge-made law tends to work through individuals in individual cases (except when appeals courts review legislation). For example, a change in tax law can influence individuals without any concern for specific individual conduct or even the identities of individuals. Indeed, some provisions of the tax law are pure Primary Rules (regulatory)—for example, the obligation to file a return. But some tax provisions are clearly *not* regulatory, in that they deal with some aspect of the environment of conduct—for example, the definition of taxable income, the rate structure itself, general categories of deductions, general categories of exemptions, general statuses such as marriage and dependence. (Tax law also contains examples of still other types of policy, but these categories have not yet been identified.)

The concept of environment of conduct is not simply a third category to go along with Primary and Secondary Rules. It introduces an entirely separate dimension. This obviously breaks Hart's dichotomy into a four-celled typology, as indicated in Table 7.1. Simply put, this gives us two kinds of Primary Rules and two kinds of Secondary Rules, summarized as follows.

Table 7.1 Categorization of Public Policies

Form of Expressed Intention	Form of Intended Impact	
	Works Through Individual Conduct	Works Through Environment of Conduct
Primary Rule (imposes obligations or positions)	*Regulatory policies:* Rules impose obligations; rules of individual conduct, criminal in form *Synonyms:* police power, government intervention *Examples*: public health laws, industrial safety, traffic laws, antitrust	*Redistributive policies:* Rules impose classification or status; rules categorizing activity *Synonyms:* fiscal and monetary policy, overall budget policies *Examples:* income tax, Federal Reserve discount rates, social security
Secondary Rule (confers powers or privileges)	*Distributive policies:* Rules confer facilities or privileges unconditionally *Synonyms:* patronage, subsidy, pork barrel *Examples:* public works, agricultural extension, land grants	*Constituent policies:* Rules confer powers; rules about rules and about authority *Synonyms:* overhead, auxiliary, government organization *Examples:* agencies for budgetary and personnel policy, laws establishing juridical jurisdiction

Regulatory Policy

Primary Rules are regulatory when they work directly through individual conduct, where identities and questions of compliance and noncompliance must be involved. Regulatory rules impose obligations and sanctions. They are criminal in form. If effectively implemented, they may create an environment of conduct conducive or nonconducive to compliance. That, however, is a behavioral hypothesis about the political or societal impact and has nothing to do with the definition of the legal rule itself.

Redistributive Policies

These are Primary Rules: they impose something on the private sphere but work through the environment of conduct rather than directly upon conduct itself. Rules impose classifications or statuses; individual membership in a classification is involuntary and by definition (i.e., categoric).

Distributive Policies

These are Secondary Rules: they work through individual conduct but do not impose obligations. Patronage and subsidies are Secondary Rules in that they confer privileges or facilities. They are a special type of Secondary Rule because they make privileges or facilities available on a personal, individualized basis. People approve or disapprove of such policies according to their judgment or hypotheses about the cumulative effect of these privileges. Such judgments and hypotheses are part of the politics or economics of policy analysis and should not be included in the definition itself.

Constituent Policies

These are Secondary Rules: they work through the environment, either by making services and facilities generally available or by conferring powers or jurisdictions. These are referred to as rules about powers or rules about rules.

An operational definition of each of the four categories of policy is developed in detail below, but one further point should be made here. Because this approach is based on a formal concept of the functions of the state, the classifications here deal only with the formal language of the statute (or other formal expression of policy). They are in no way concerned with the actual impacts of policies on the society, polity, or economy. If the classifications (which we are taking as the independent variables) were to include such elements, any theory developed from them would be circular. To avoid this, the definitions self-consciously avoid any elements of politics about which later hypotheses may be formed. Thus a statute can be classified, say, as redistributive even if after 20 years of operation no actual redistribution has taken place as a result of the statute. The labels adopted for each of the four categories may be unfortunate if they are taken to imply hypotheses about impact. The strong caveat here is that the reader avoid such interpretations: classification and the ensuing analysis require that the categories of public policy, that is, the independent variables, be understood as efforts to grasp the intentions of rulers as expressed in the established formal language of government.

Policy Classifications and Agency Missions

If the initial assumption—that each type of public policy, i.e., regime, tends to develop its own distinct political structure and process—is to govern the analysis, then it follows that four distinguishable types of policy ought to produce four distinguishable *arenas of power*, that is, four identifiable clusters of political characteristics. This is the route from classification to theory.

The U.S. Congress has been explored on the basis of this scheme, using two different kinds of data. First, a reanalysis of seventeen published case studies of the formulation of important legislation revealed dramatic differences in the way the legislative process operates, depending on whether the bill in question is regulatory, redistributive, distributive, or constituent.[9] For example, distributive (pork barrel) bills show Congress as an institution dominated by its committees, with the floor and the parliamentary dimension playing a very passive and uncreative role. The typical regulatory bill shows the committee system much less dominant and the floor far more active and creative. Second, by use of statistics developed from the frequency of floor amendments of committee bills, a quantitative study of committee floor relationships strongly confirmed the patterns of variation developed by reanalysis of the published case studies. These not only confirmed predicted variations in the internal workings of Congress but showed consistent patterns of relationships between Congress and the executive branch.[10]

Among all the opportunities available for empirical exploration of the relationship between the state and its political environment, the concern here is with administrative phenomena—how the data on administrative structure and process vary from one policy category to another. Administration, despite the fact that it is the core of modern government, is one of the least systematically researched areas in politics. A rich literature of description and case studies was developed between the 1930s and the 1950s. Political scientists studied agencies as units of action in their political environment. From there the jump to organization theory and decision-making was made without going through intermediate levels of empirical research. Nothing was done comparable to what Key and others did for the study of elections by use of aggregate data within geographical units. Most of the systematic comparative study of administrative structure has been done by sociologists from sociological perspectives. Little political content can be found there.

This is not meant as a criticism. It simply underscores the need for similar work in political science. Administration is not only politics in its most serious form, it is also the most quantifiable form. Administration has at times been defined as voluminous, routine business. No routines are more important than administrative routines. Administration not only lends itself to quantification, it provides better reality checks on itself because so much can be known about administrative agencies independent of survey data.

Thus the study of administration must be central to the study of the relation between the state and politics. Differences among bureaucracies are significant for organization theory and for political practice but are most important for political theory, because observed variations can and must be explained by reflection on the way states and regimes shape their environments.

Rationale for the Classification

The agencies chosen for analysis are located at the first operating level below the top of each department or ministry. In the United States this is called the bureau, the first level below the Secretary and a phalanx of deputy and assistant secretaries. Independent commissions are included. In France, the comparable level of agency unit is called the *direction*. Each such agency, or unit, with few exceptions, operates within a jurisdiction delegated to it by a higher authority. The form of that delegation is an organic statute or similar instrument. It is usually a single statute or decree that extends, with occasional amendments, throughout the life of the agency. Because the organic statute can be taken as the mission of the agency, each agency is automatically classified once its organic act is classified. Thus, an agency is classified as regulatory if and only if its governing statute has been so classified. All personnel in the agency (if they are in the sample) are grouped according to the agency's mission, regardless of their individual tasks. What proportion of an agency's personnel is actually performing tasks directly relevant to the mission (versus auxiliary, support, or management tasks) is an empirical question, and an interesting one.

The first step, then, is to conduct an exhaustive inventory of the basic policies in each country and to concentrate on those that give agencies their mission and jurisdiction. These are then classified according to guidelines and procedures laid out below.

Classification: A Problem of Content Analysis

It is impossible to operationalize the definition of each category of policy in such a way as to make the classification task automatic. However, it is possible to minimize the inconsistencies of classification. Policies do not present problems of content analysis different in principle from those encountered in attempts to classify materials drawn from interviews of individuals. We have followed the procedure of survey researchers in setting up panels of coders to read and cross-check each policy as it is classified. Experience so far with nearly two hundred agencies and their policies in the United States and in France has produced nearly 90 percent intrapanel agreement on policy classifications. The guideline questions for the panel are provided in Table 7.2. These were derived logically from Table 7.1 and were revised and sharpened in response to the experience with the legal language confronted in actual U.S. and French laws. Table 7.2 is essentially an interview schedule of policy materials.

Disagreement among two or more panel members has been dealt with according to the following procedures:

1. Some statutes are omnibus laws that combine two or more separate subjects or functions in the same official enactment. Because each subject or function is given a separate title or chapter, each such title or chapter can be classified separately. However, in a few instances separately classified policies are given over to a single agency, and in a few other instances more than one separate statute delegates an additional and separately classifiable function to an agency. These agencies are, for our purposes, multifunctional and therefore impossible to place exclusively in one of the four categories. Such an agency is dropped from the aggregate analysis and is dealt with as a single case study.

2. Some statutes are so vaguely written that very different intentions can be inferred from them, and panel disagreement is very high. Additional materials are then collected, including, where possible, the official legislative history. If panel disagreement persists, the agency is eliminated from the aggregate analysis and is examined intensively for effects on the agency of operating under such vague legislative language. Vagueness in legislation is a serious problem for modern government, and it points to one of the normative or applied aspects of this study: How widespread is the practice of writing

Table 7.2 Guidelines for Content Analysis of Statutes

Question	Responses, Comments
1. Does the rule of the statute (or decree) apply to persons or conducts in the private or in the public sphere?	If in the public sphere, the policy is almost certainly constituent. If private, it could be any of the other three types.
2. Does the rule set conditions or impose obligations and provide penalties for nonperformance?	If yes, the policy is regulatory. This applies even to public officials because in matters of crime and tort all persons are private citizens.
3. Does the rule set conditions without sanctions?	If yes, the policy could still be regulatory if there is an implicit sanction such as exposure or publicity. The policy could be distributive, if the policy sets a process in train or provides for a facility without setting any conditions of performance for participation.
4. Does the rule pertain to individuals and deal with them by name or provide specific facilities without providing general standards from which the privileges or facilities derive?	If yes, the policy is almost certainly distributive; a clear example is a "pork barrel" act authorizing projects by name.
5. Does the rule create an agency?	If yes, the policy is constituent.
6. Does the rule provide an agency with jurisdiction over other agencies?	If yes, the policy is constituent; a clear example is budget bureau.
7. Does there appear to be a rule without contemplation of action by public or private persons?	If the rule sets a public process in train or defines the jurisdiction of an agency, it is a constituent policy. If the rule provides for a process for all or a large, defined aggregate of persons, it is probably redistributive. (See also question 9.)
8. Does the rule ignore individual conduct and concentrate on characteristics or properties of individuals; i.e., does the rule attempt to discriminate among defined aggregates of persons without regard to their conduct?	If yes, as in identifying all persons below a certain income or age, and if the category is invidious and involuntary, the policy is almost certainly redistributive (e.g., tax categories, welfare classification).
9. Does the rule provide for or alter a process or structure that is economy-wide?	If yes, the policy is almost certainly redistributive (e.g., Federal Reserve system; low-interest loan programs). In such cases, the entire citizenry is the category defined in the rule.

statutes that cannot be understood? And how can the legal integrity of such statutes be improved? These questions are extensively examined in Lowi [*The End of Liberalism*].[11] ...

Initial Results

The governing empirical question follows simply and logically: Do important characteristics of agencies or their personnel distribute themselves significantly differently from one category of agencies to the next? To put the matter another way: When agencies are arranged according to this fourfold scheme, does the distribution of their characteristics present a clearer and theoretically more interesting pattern than groupings of agencies according to alternative classifications?

Selection of empirical materials was aided substantially by two major surveys of administrative personnel carried out independently in the United States[12] and France.[13] Reanalysis of their data produced findings that strongly confirm the scheme.

The system in France is older and more formal than in the United States. France has a highly unitary concept of civil service (*function publique*), applying many laws and regulations to all areas, even including professors in public universities. Specialization is provided for in a formal and orderly way through the *corps*, which tie schooling to job specialties, careers, and status. This gives French bureaucracy diversity as well as uniformity. The diversity may well outweigh the uniformity, despite efforts to the contrary.

Of the various corps, as grouped in Table 7.3, the most significant are the *grands corps*. In prestige, personnel of the grands corps may appear to be a senior civil service, but they are not truly so because they are not evenly distributed across the top of all agencies. Only 1 percent served in the top management of regulatory agencies, and an equally small proportion served in distributive agencies, leaving 98 percent in the top management of constituent and redistributive agencies. A very different pattern obtains for the other two prestigious corps, the *corps techniques* and the *corps des services extérieurs*—not opposite in either case, but asymmetrical and very different.

Table 7.3 French Corps Personnel, Distributed by Type of Mission of Their Agency

	Grand Corps (%)	Corps de Control Administrative (%)	Corps d'Administration Centrale (%)	Corps Techniques (%)	Corps des Services Extérieurs (%)
Constituent	53	43	47	40	75
Distributive	1	11	17	43	—
Regulatory	1	17	14	11	25
Redistributive	44	30	22	5	—

Note: Totals do not equal 100 due to rounding of percentages.

The grands corps can be defined as including the career personnel in the Conseil d'Etat, the Cour des Comptes, and the Inspection Générale des Finances.[14] These corps go back generations, emerging out of the ancient *fonctions régaliens*—the king's requirements for maintenance of the realm in its civil life (accounts, records, the court itself, etc.). In farthest contrast, the corps techniques arose out of essentially military functions. They are engineers and other technicians who are responsible for roads and other public works, the post office, the mines, and so on. The prestige of these personnel is as high as that of the personnel of the grands corps. Entrance to their schools, called the *grandes écoles,* is intensively sought after by students from all classes, but especially the upper middle class. Though it is reasonable for agencies to draw staff from the grandes écoles, those high-powered trades schools, it is not so clear why graduates from the grandes écoles hold the top managerial positions. The answer cannot be merely that the tasks of such agencies are technical. Building a road is no more technical than designing and managing social security (redistributive), yet few technical specialists reach high management there. The contrasting distribution of services extérieurs personnel is made more interesting by the inclusion in this category of the *corps préfectoral.* Regulatory and constituent agencies delegate more policy and rule-making responsibility to the field (extérieur)—more will be said of this later.

No comparable data exist on the United States, because there is no corps tradition. However, some roughly equivalent data will be found in the center column of Table 7.4. Although drawn from aggregate Civil Service Commission data and one step removed from individual personnel, these data are nevertheless strongly confirming. The only agencies where substantive specialists are at all prominent in top management are distributive agencies. Moreover, although 4 percent seems a minuscule cutoff point, these figures are roughly cumulative. That is to say, any agency with at least 4 percent of each of these specialties will show over 15 percent of the combined use of the specialties in their top positions.

This pattern is further confirmed by the center column of Table 7.4. Only among the respondents in distributive agencies was there a strong tendency to rate outside professional training as of high value in promotion to top management.

The French data are clearly consistent with those of the United States. First, reading from Table 7.3, 43 percent of all corps techniques personnel in top management were in distributive agencies. The same data in a cross-cutting direction reveal that of all personnel in the top management of distributive agencies, 54 percent were from the corps techniques (versus none for corps des services extérieurs).

Table 7.5 is the only view offered here of variations in tasks, but it is an extremely important dimension. The task in question is that of coordinating the work of others in the agency. Coordination is the key to agency conduct and efficiency. Without effective coordination almost none of the advantages of bureaucratization can be realized. Yet there are limited methods of coordination available to policymakers, and some methods may be mutually contradictory. Only a few types of methods can be imposed on a reanalysis of the American or French data but several others are conceivable and will be identified and investigated in future research. Meanwhile, the few in Table 7.5 are sufficient to make the point.

Table 7.4 Professionalism: Use and Value of Technologists in Top Management, United States and France

	United States					France
	Percentage of Agencies in Which at Least 4 Percent of Top Managers Are:				Average Rating Given to Value of Outside Professional Training (1 high, 6 low)	Percentage of Top Managers Recruited from Corps Techniques
	Biomedical Specialists	Engineers	Physical Scientists	Social Scientists		
Distributive	36	50	25	21	2	54
Regulatory	11	17	6	11	6	21
Redistributive	7	14	14	14	6	6
Constituent[a]	—	—	—	—	—	19

Source: John Corson and R.S. Paul, Men Near the Top (Baltimore: Johns Hopkins University Press, 1966), interview data.
Note: a. Analysis of U.S. categories was developed before "constituent" category was created.

Table 7.5 Mechanisms of Administrative Control: Agencies Rely on Different Means of Coordinating Agency Conduct

United States

	Distributive	Regulative	Redistributive
Overhead mechanisms Agencies in which over 10 percent of the top personnel are in budgeting and accounting	7%	17%	43%
Close supervision Executives rank supervision activities as important (1) to unimportant (6) in a typical week's work	6	5	2
Bureaucratism (1) Rank on bureaucratism scale (promotion within rank, etc.)	4th	2nd	1st
(2) Rank on procedure scale (typical week involved staffing, negotiating, or representing)	1st	1st	3rd
Hierarchy Agencies in which at least 15 percent of HQ personnel are G315 and above	32%	72%	50%
Agencies in which 40 percent of top personnel are in the field	11%	39%	21%

France

	Distributive	Regulative	Redistributive	Constituent
Top personnel drawn from the two major overhead corps	6%	13%	45%	24%
Top personnel required to report to three or more superiors	15%	24%	24%	19%
Top personnel drawn from corps de services extérieurs	0%	21%	0%	16%
Top personnel who spent no time in field (services extérieurs)	61%	58%	71%	63%
Numbers of separate units or divisions within each direction	1–9	10–21	21+	1–9
Personnel who have departed from precedent or introduced an innovation	55%	51%	44%	49%

Note first the prominence of overhead mechanisms in redistributive agencies in the United States and France. Close supervision is also prominent among redistributive agencies in both countries: U.S top personnel in redistributive agencies rate supervision activities second in importance; and in France the respondents in redistributive agencies reported the narrowest span of control, an almost certain indication of relatively close supervision. Redistributive agencies also rate high on coordination through what (for lack of a better term) we have called *bureaucratism,* i.e., building careers strictly within the agency, with entry at the bottom, promotion through the ranks, and the internalization of norms and policy preference. Although no directly comparable data were available for the French, the French did demonstrate a consistent tendency to recruit top management in redistributive agencies fairly strictly from headquarters careers. This would tend to give the managers common values and also push them to rely still more heavily on overhead and direct supervisory methods (and precedent— note percentages for field control).

Some contrasts with coordination patterns in other agencies are visible. Regulatory agencies rely far more heavily on procedural and authority mechanisms. Not only do regulatory agencies rely heavily on proper procedure for coordination, they also structure these agencies so that there are both relatively high proportions of rank at headquarters and high proportions of rank in the field, serving presumably as policy-makers and as direct supervisors.

Syntheses and Hypotheses

On the basis of these and a few other data, rough models of administrative structure can be constructed. The task is akin to primitive archeology, where whole creatures were reconstructed from a few bone fragments and fossils. Though later refinements of theory and measurement exposed a great range of error in the original reconstructions, those first guesses provided the rationale for the hypotheses and the guidelines used to eliminate the errors.

The Regulatory Agency Model

Regulatory agencies are responsible for implementing the classic control policies of government, formulating or implementing rules imposing obligations on individuals, and providing punishment for nonconformance. This requires at a minimum that administrators know the main rules and share interpretations about how and when to impose them. Others, including courts, may be ultimately responsible for applying the sanctions, but only after the administrators have set the process in train by finding the individual, deciding that the conduct is contrary to the rule, and bringing that individual, by arrest or exposure, to the attention of the sanctioning authority. Interpretations of rules of conduct are passed along as operating rules of the agency officials, incorporating their reading of the statute with their understanding of legislative intent, court rulings, or executive orders. Other operating rules come from previous cases. Use of precedents produces a kind of common law in regulatory agencies. The fact that direct controls and punishments of individuals are involved creates an environment in which citizens will compare agency decisions for consistency and fairness. This leads to stress on rights, formal procedures, and a standardized relationship with higher authorities through rules and additional formal procedures. Although each regulatory decision is an individual case, the cases are tied by reference to one or more rules or precedents. Thus, although regulatory policies work through individual conduct (see Table 7.1), they cannot be disaggregated to the level of single individuals, each taken as a separate unit. That is a feature of distributive, not regulatory, policies.

Regulatory agencies will, then, show distinctive organizational features, some of which can be found through examination of the special distributions of personnel data. Regulatory agencies should be the most rule-bound (rather than tradition-bound, authority-bound, status-bound, or hierarchy-bound). Thus, for example, only 1 percent of all the top management in regulatory agencies in the French data were drawn from the grands corps, while 46 percent were drawn from the middle-status corps d'administration centrale and 21 percent each from the corps techniques and the corps des services extérieurs. The latter means primarily the prefectoral corps, whose members are more likely to be experts on process and procedure than on substance. Add to that the earlier data showing the heavy emphasis in regulatory agencies on coordination by procedure. Add also the practice of placing top managerial personnel directly in the field. Surely this is an expression of the need to maintain a balance between two conflicting requirements: to give ample discretion to workers on the line to decide which individuals are not conforming, and to maintain some appearance of consistency with rules and precedents. Sometimes high-ranking field officers are there to supervise the discretion of lower-ranking officials—for example, captains of police over patrolmen. At other times high-ranking officials are put in the field to make the decisions themselves, as in the United States is the case for hearing examiners, who in recent years have had their status upgraded (or finally recognized) with the new designation *administrative law judge*.

Table 7.6 suggests a few other hypotheses logically derived from this line of thought in dimensions of agency life for which data at present do not exist but could fairly easily be collected. For example, because citizen conduct is being controlled and sanctioned by rules, regulatory agencies should tend to be more specialized by units than by individual job specialties.[15] One case in point: a separate unit might be highly specialized, working only on rate charges or toxic substances while within each unit all employees may be doing the same kind of work. By the same logic, control-oriented, rule-laden regulatory agencies are likely to have the most intense and unstable relationships with their larger political environment (see Table 7.6). Intense involvement with organized interest groups should produce enhanced efforts at mutual cooptation and exploitation which should take the form of lateral entry, i.e., a tendency to recruit personnel from the outside directly into upper-middle and upper ranks. Lateral entry should tend to be practiced in distributive agencies also; however, these lateral entrants would be subject specialists (engineers), whereas in regulatory agencies they would tend to be process and procedure specialists (lawyers). To summarize, regulatory agencies are hierarchical but the hierarchy is flatter and more truncated than in Weber's model. They have large proportions of high ranking managers, many of whom are in the field carrying policy

Table 7.6 Guidelines for Hypotheses

Organizational Characteristic or Concept	Definitions, Indexes, and Comments	Hypotheses: Examples and Comments
A. Formal Structure		
Specialization (of labor): Unit differentiation	Controlling for size of agency, how many distinguishable work units are there, and in how many distinguishable layers? Are units divided by jurisdiction, or process or area? Some measures of "shape" are being considered.	Logic and experience suggest that regulatory agencies will rate highest on measures of unit specialization, with constituent agencies also high.
Specialization: Task specialization, division of labor	How many formally identified tasks are there? (See definition of occupational families—aggregate data.) How much pre-training and how much certification are required? How many different tasks (and what kinds) do senior administrators perform in a typical week?	Distributive and redistributive agencies will be highest in measures of task specialization, but since this is true for different reasons, more specific hypotheses will be framed to capture the different measures of specialization.
Organizational dispersion	What proportion of the agency's personnel are in field rather than HQ units? What percentage of top management have had field experience prior to HQ? What percentage of senior managers are serving in field units? What is the normal chain of command between field and HQ—e.g., between functional specialists, or strictly from unit chief to agency chief?	Distributive and regulatory agencies ought to show highest, and constituent agencies lowest (with concentration at HQ). But regulatory agencies should also show highest in average civil service ratings serving in the field.
Chain of command (operational centralization and decentralization)	What kinds of rules are there, and how strictly observed are they, pertaining to communications between layers and units, superiors and subordinates? Are horizontal linkages discouraged in favor of vertical linkages? How formalized and specific are requirements to notify and to record communications (e.g., to initial, to send carbons, etc.)?	Redistributive agencies ought to show highest policy decentralization on any measure of chain of command. Most extreme general policy decentralization should be found among distributive agencies, least among redistributive agencies. But different types of delegation must be allowed for—e.g., there is broad delegation
Delegation of authority (policy centralization and decentralization)	How much responsibility is delegated to field units? How carefully and explicitly do agency rules circumscribe discretion? How much freedom of action do personnel at different levels feel they have? How closely tied are these rules to the statute (and legislative intent)? How closely tied are procedures to decisions?	in regulatory agencies, but it tends to be accompanied by general guidelines and more procedural limits. Constituent agencies are also broad.

(continues)

Table 7.6 continued

Organizational Characteristic or Concept	Definitions, Indexes, and Comments	Hypotheses: Examples and Comments
B. Distribution of Responsibilities		
Coordination (types of centralization and decentralization)	What methods and devices does the agency rely upon most heavily to coordinate work? Overhead controls? Direct supervision? Formal clearance? Committees? Professional norms and common schooling? Explicit rules ascribing work, status, interdependence, etc.? How narrow or broad is the span of control (as measured by superior-subordinate ratios)?	One of the most important findings of the pilot study is that these various coordinating devices are inconsistent and often inversely related. Hypotheses concern not whether but which devices are used, and in what combinations. The findings tend to produce different types as well as degrees of centralization for each category of agency.
Internal accountability	How does the agency review responsibility for decisions and their outcomes? Are rewards and punishments meted out explicitly for performance? To what extent do personnel feel that promotion is tied to good decisions or good performance? Are there routines for monitoring individual performance?	Central substantive review would most likely be found among regulatory agencies. Performance and expenditure review more likely among redistributive agencies. Least surveillance among distributive agencies.
External accountability (formal)	How much departmental oversight is there? To what extent through agency chief or functional specialists? How much and what kind of congressional oversight is there? Is it budgetary or substantive? What level or status is permitted to deal directly with the department? With Congress and committees? With the public? How litigious is the agency? What kind of judicial review does it get, and how frequently? How strict and extensive are procedural rules? Do they apply only to individual cases? To public participation in policymaking? How hard or easy is it to get information from the agency? How often are Freedom of Information Act requests dealt with, and to what result?	Here again the type of external relationship is as important as the degree. Constituent agencies are likely to rate highest on formal relations with virtually all governmental agencies, but regulatory agencies tend to rate highest on requirements to relate to nongovernmental groups and to congressional committees. Lowest on formal (but high on informal) should be distributive agencies. Lowest on formal relations should be redistributive agencies.

(continues)

Table 7.6 continued

Organizational Characteristic or Concept	Definitions, Indexes, and Comments	Hypotheses: Examples and Comments
B. Distribution of Responsibilities continued		
Environmental relationships (informal)	Without regard to agency rules, what percentage of each level of agency reports direct contacts with the department? With congressional committees? Individual members of Congress? Interest group representatives, etc.? What percentage of top personnel entered laterally? Vertically through the agency? If laterally, from what source (e.g., other federal agencies, private sector, state government)? How active are top personnel in their professional association? In political parties or interest groups or major clientele firms or groups (present or former)?	Constituent agencies expected high here, too, for governmental units, but tend to be low on lateral entry. Regulatory agencies higher in lateral entry and in various other informal relations, especially the practice of lower administrators having direct relations with outside. (Distributive agencies rate high here too.)
Management style	What percentage of the managers are from subject specializations? What percentage from more general administrative occupations and careers? What percentage had direct field experience? How important is specific management training? Do agency heads tend to be agency careerists or lateral entrants? How public has the career of the head or top echelon been—e.g., in newspapers, *Who's Who?*	Distributive agency personnel tend to rate highest in preference for subject specialists in top management, regulatory lowest. Constituent agency personnel tend to come from higher social statuses and from more general career categories. Lateral entrants in top management least likely among redistributive agencies.

responsibilities, and many horizontal linkages among lower units as well as vertical linkage to headquarters and the courts.

The Distributive Agency Model

In mission, distributive agencies are almost the opposite of regulatory agencies. Although like regulatory agencies in being responsible for policies that work directly on or through individuals, the relationship is one of patron and client rather than controller and controlled. Consequently, distributive agencies can operate in their political environment almost as though they had unlimited resources. There are no integrative rules of conduct, only rules designating facilities, which do not require elaboration of intermediate rules or standards for agency decisions. Consequently, these agencies can respond to political conflicts by disaggregation. That is to say they can take each decision or facility, each unit of output, and treat it as separate and distinct from all others. Few criteria or precedents tie decisions together or provide a direct basis of comparison, especially across regions of the country. For example, the typical public works (pork barrel) statute is composed of dozens of individual authorizations to build, design, or inquire into proposals for specific, named projects. The only connection among the projects and proposals is the agency authorized to take the actions. These agencies can make peace with their constituencies because agency constituencies correspond to congressional constituencies, which can be placated by adding authorizations for further projects. Even when expansion is not possible, conflict can be bought off by subdividing existing units, particularly of commitments to run studies and cost-benefit analyses on proposals that could later become authorizations. In contrast, losers and winners are closer together in the regulatory agency environment, and rules or standards of conduct provide a basis for comparing agency decisions, thereby inhibiting the agency from disaggregating decisions into separate units.

Once again, organizational consequences ought to flow from the peculiarities of mission. Distributive agencies, while not the precise opposites of regulatory agencies, are likely to be far apart on a number of important characteristics. Organizations are too complex to be put on a single continuum, but it is possible to say at least that the absence of responsibility for imposing authoritative rules affects distributive agencies. The absence of rules is compensated for in large part by professionalism. Most hypotheses about these agencies will revolve around these and related characteristics.

We have already noted the heavy use of corps techniques personnel in the top management of French distributive agencies. Similar data were found in U.S. agencies, and further confirmation is expected in future studies. Professionalism is partly a solution to the problem of consistency without rules and partly a solution to the problem of coordination. Common schooling, common texts, common "cookbook" formulas, equations, techniques, and computer programs help give these personnel the same premises, so that when confronted with the same problem they are likely to make the same decision despite the absence of policy guidelines. Even though professionals may enter top management laterally, they presumably can fall right into step.

Like regulatory agencies, distributive agencies delegate a great many responsibilities to the field, but along functional rather than management (generalist) lines. To deal with this functional decentralization, more specialists are likely to be elevated to top management positions (see Table 7.6). Procedure is also likely to be as heavily stressed as in regulatory agencies—but, again, it is of a far different kind. Here are to be found fewer formal legal procedures and less due process, but a far greater number and variety of decision rules such as letting decisions rest on cost-benefit ratios, outcomes of environmental impact statements, or citizen participation.

A visualization of the hierarchy of typical distributive agencies would show them relatively flat, like regulatory agencies. But there the resemblance would end. The hierarchy is not truncated but integrated along functional lines. Professional discretion is permitted in the field, but horizontal linkages among field units are expected to be minimized while vertical linkages are maximized. The vertical linkages here are quite distinctive, passing through professional norms on the one hand and congressional committee oversight on the other. In contrast, vertical linkages in redistributive agencies are more likely to be internal and hierarchical (see Table 7.6). The relatively flat hierarchy has a double apex corresponding to the dual administration of functional and managerial authority.

The Redistributive Agency Model

Redistributive agencies maintain and manipulate categories of human beings. Their rules or the rules for which they are responsible affect society on a larger scale than any others. And although it is true that all rules discriminate, rules of redistributive agencies discriminate along broad class lines. As a matter of formal policy as well as informal politics, redistributive rules discriminate between the money providers and the service demanders, e.g., rich versus poor, young and employed versus old and unemployed, savers versus consumers.

This responsibility for making or maintaining rules that cut broadly along class lines ought to be a determining factor in the organizational structure of redistributive agencies. The general political environment of these agencies is likely to be stable, but for reasons far different from those stabilizing distributive agencies. Redistributive agencies have the stability of careful balance of organized conflict among major class interests, where small changes at the margins threaten large shifts of advantage in the economy (e.g., a fraction of a percent in the discount rate; the change of a word in the definition of eligibility; a change of one item in the composition of the CPI). These factors contribute to a declassing of the agencies. Great stress is placed on having the best management at the top, including people and professions of high social status (e.g., high proportions of grands corps in French agencies), coupled with tight control on entry and conduct throughout the agency. These agencies are, relatively speaking, severed from society by heavy stress on recruitment at the bottom, low lateral entry, and internal, bureaucratic careers. Internal career life is emphasized even more by the practice of promoting to top management people who have had experience only at headquarters. Virtually every type of coordination will be utilized to keep the field units working consistently with central policies: these agencies are expected to be as rule-bound as regulatory agencies and as professionalized as distributive agencies, but as a result of internal careers, not common schooling. In addition, very narrow spans of control will be maintained: many units within divisions and bureaus, close supervision, few subordinates per superior, stress on recordkeeping and clearance, and so on (see Table 7.6). In addition, there will tend to be heaviest stress on overhead methods, including preaudit, postaudit, performance, and efficiency reports.

A picture of redistributive agencies would come closest to the classic, narrow, high-peaked pyramid. The sharpness comes from narrow spans of control, where one superior has a minimum number of subordinates. Rules keep discretion to a minimum, and the concern for consistency with the rules produces strong vertical linkages plus efforts to discourage horizontal linkages. The American pattern will have to be adjusted for the federalistic structure of its welfare programs, where state agencies may be operating as local units. In these agencies, even more stress is put on overhead controls. And, although they fail in real-world situations, top management in Washington is likely to produce a lot of evidence of effort to maintain vertical linkages and to discourage horizontal ones.

The Constituent Agency Model

Although least has been done empirically on constituent agencies, some patterns can be drawn from the logic of the scheme, from contrasts with the three other types, and from case studies in the published literature. The missions of these agencies come closest to maintenance of sovereignty, what the French call *agences régaliens*. There is minimal responsibility for making or implementing rules that pertain directly to citizen conduct or status. Rules of these agencies apply to other government agencies, whether these are rules of jurisdiction or operating rules about budgeting, purchasing, recruiting and promoting personnel, or writing contracts or conditions for payment and nonpayment of contracts.

For reasons of both function and tradition, agencies with constituent missions are most likely to live by the older ideal of the good administrator as a person of good breeding, good general education, and the ability to make decisions. Almost everything happens at headquarters, and there is not likely to be much hierarchy, although these agencies support hierarchy in all other agencies (see Table 7.6). And although managers in these agencies are given a great deal of discretion, there are strong vertical linkages. The difference is that these are less likely to be superior-subordinate linkages than ones of collegiality and trust extending beyond the agency chiefs to cabinet and chief executive. A pictorial rendering yields no pyramid: there are too many generals and too few privates. An approximation would be a diamond shape with lines of authority and communication indicating a network rather than a hierarchy. The network includes linkages to the other three types of agencies, over which constituent agencies hold their special type of authority either directly through their ability to withhold resources or indirectly through their special access to the chief executive and others at the highest political levels.

Conclusion: Comparative Studies of Policy and Administration

Let it be said forthrightly that these findings and hypotheses, being based on reanalysis of data produced from old and independent studies, are intended to serve only as the groundwork for a large new comparative study. These fragments of bone and fossil were sufficient as long as they permitted extension of the original argument that regimes through their established policies make their own politics. But extension to other phenomena as well as further confirmation of patterns already observed is essential if progress is to be made along theoretical, empirical, or practical lines.

As many as half the questions in the Darbel-Schnapper and Corson-Paul studies can be replicated. This means that the original surveys can be used as a pretest as well as a basis for longitudinal analysis covering nearly 20 years. (The original interview schedules for both studies are available from the authors.)

It should be clear from earlier data and from the survey questions that the variables and methods to be utilized in such a study are simple and direct. Because the conventions of systematic empirical analysis of bureaucracy are not well established and the impressionistic work is very rich, it is essential that the variables stick close to sensory experience. For the same reason, the methods ought to be simple. And what makes simplicity possible is the presence of a theory. The most dynamic and relevant aspects of the analysis are inherent in the policy categorizations themselves. The Arenas of Power scheme has been widely utilized in the political science literature, and at the same time it has been criticized even by some of its users as being too difficult empirically. Much progress has in recent years been made on the definitional aspects of the theory, which should make it more useful empirically. No theory in political science has ever received more thorough published discussion and testing than this one prior to its application to systematic research. The time is ripe for application. Moreover, though the theory itself is closed as to its categories and the general nature of the hypotheses, the research project is quite open to other approaches. The data drawn from the country surveys will be useful to political sociologists who are interested in mobility and the social backgrounds of modern functionaries. The data will be valuable to students of organization who approach them without an explicit theory. The data will be even more valuable to those who approach public agencies with a different policy theory or different sets of policy categories. One obvious comparison to make is between regulatory agencies and all others, ignoring any systematic distinction between the two. Another might be a comparison of characteristics as they are distributed between agencies that deal only in domestic policy and those that deal in foreign policy or foreign and defense policy. Within the broad area of regulatory policy, another set of comparisons can be made between departmental and independent regulatory agencies. The analytic possibilities, though not infinite, are certainly numerous enough to satisfy a wide variety of interests and, we hope, are valuable enough to justify foundation support in the United States and abroad.

CHAPTER 8

✦✦✦✦

The Case of Agriculture

Four Kinds of Policy, Four Kinds of Politics

Analysis of informal behavior patterns in politics cannot proceed without first understanding the formal-legal context within which the patterns are formed. This is particularly true in political behavior, because the formalities also comprise most of the stakes or the incentives of behavior. And in a modern political system, most of the stakes are governmental in the strictest sense of the word. We have seen this to be true time after time in case studies focused upon one or another subject matter, although the principle itself is seldom made explicit. Case studies are usually staged around a particular policy decision, so that the political battle can be characterized as the "politics of education" or the "politics of agriculture," and the authors usually go to some lengths to describe the economics, technology, and other formal intricacies of the issue. Beginning with Schattschneider and Herring in the 1930s, the proper form for the political case study required a rather elaborate description of the "setting" of the case, including the substance of the issue. But then, the conclusions and generalizations were made for all of politics. Awareness that the conflict that comprised the story was limited to one issue did not lead to limitations on the applicability of the conclusions. In this sense, the formal policies or issues did not play a role in analysis; they were merely part of the description itself.

Obviously, staging analyses within the confines of a single issue, if generalization is intended, does not allow for the possibility that the issue may be the determinative factor in the ensuing informal process. If one assumes this as a possibility, then several issues must be taken on separately but simultaneously. But in order to do this, problems of definition immediately arise. There has to be some *a priori* characterization of the nature of the issues, the particular stakes involved in each, or else there will be no basis for later assessment and comparison of the outcomes in political behavior and relationships among actors.

One way to define issues is, conventionally, in terms of the subject matter of which it is supposed to be a part. Issues and agencies involving soil conservation become "the politics of agriculture";[1] and most certainly, the Department of Agriculture and representatives of agricultural interests are the central actors. A decision (or non-decision) on federal aid to schools is "the politics of education" and on highways "the politics of transportation." What troubles me about this method of definition is that things appear so different if "the politics of agriculture" is looked at through price supports or farm credit rather than soil conservation, or if "the politics of transportation" is approached through rate regulation or certification rather than grants-in-aid. The conventional subject matter as an approach to definition cannot be totally abandoned, since it immediately tells us the substantive interest of the participants and the segments of society most likely to be represented. But to it must be added some additional distinguishing characteristic. The characteristic to be added here is *the impact or intended effect of the policy in question on the society.* Each of the established domestic departments plus a few independent agencies must be taken as the subject matter categories. The bundle of policies and programs within the jurisdiction of each department must then be taken apart, each major policy or program then being assessed in terms of its impact, real or intended, and then each must be properly categorized.

Agriculture as a Case Study

The Department of Agriculture has always been known as a "holding company" agency containing a congeries of relatively autonomous, often unrelated, activities. Each bureau or service within the department is known to have developed a constituency peculiar to itself. It would hardly be surprising, then, to find that the "politics of" any one of these bureaus or any issue involving it is not the "politics of agriculture" but a "politics of" something else. But first it is necessary to see how these agencies and their programs differ substantively.

Regulation

1. The most important agriculture program since the 1930s has given the impression that "government-and-agriculture" implies regulation through acreage, formulas, loans, and price supports through the Agricultural Stabilization and Conservation Service (ASCS, a lineal descendant of Triple-A), the Production and Marketing Administration, and the Commodity Stabilization Service.

The principal ASCS activities are (1) price support, which is carried out through commodity loans to farmers or through direct purchases of agricultural commodities from farmers and processors on the basis of the "parity" formula; (2) production adjustment, which is carried out through marketing quotas, acreage allotments, and/or stabilization payments for surplus commodities (cotton, tobacco, rice, peanuts, wheat, corn, and other feed grains), and through incentive payments for two commodities for which there is a national deficiency (sugar and wool); (3) conservation assistance, carried out through sharing the cost of certain conservation practices with individual farmers, and through the Soil Bank; (4) management of the inventories of the Commodity Credit Corporation; and (5) emergency disaster relief. Except for (5), activities listed above and lesser ones not listed are all subordinated to and put to the service of (1), the stabilization of farm prices and maintenance of these prices at a level which achieves a farm purchasing power close to that of other groups in the society. If necessary, this price will be set above market price, so that various means must be employed to push market price up toward parity price. Otherwise, the Commodity Credit Corporation, at even greater expense to the Treasury than has been the case, would own and sell virtually all the crops covered by the legislation. Real prices are kept up toward parity prices largely through manipulation of supply, which is effected in largest part by control of the amount of cultivated land.

Price support operations involve several levels of decision and enforcement. Beginning with the Agricultural Adjustment Act of 1938, with significant amendments since then, Congress set forth the basic principle and formula of parity. It starts with an "adjusted base price," which is a ratio of the 10-year average price received by a given commodity to an index of general farm prices in a given year compared with the same in the period 1910–14. This is multiplied by a "parity index," which is a ratio of the farmer's "cost of living" in a given period to the same in 1910–14 (1301 U.S.C., Title 7). Congress also set down a schedule of minimum and maximum price support, ranging from 75 percent to 90 percent of parity depending for most covered commodities upon "supply percentages," or the relation that normal supply bears to the estimated total supply of a commodity for the coming year. A large carry-over of CCC stocks or an expected bumper-crop year pushes parity down from 90 percent (1428–41 U.S.C., Title 7).

In carrying out the purposes of the legislation, the Secretary of Agriculture is left with vast areas of discretion. It is he who determines the specific items that comprise the parity indices. It is he who determines the estimates for "supply percentages" and the level of price support in advance of planting. (His "forward prices" can be raised later in the season, but they cannot be reduced. 1426 U.S.C., Title 7.) The Secretary also is left to decide when the acreage allotments, the setting of which allows broad discretion as well, are to be converted into marketing quotas for purposes of a referendum concerning whether crop restrictions are to be mandatory. (See, for example, 1344 U.S.C., Title 7, on corn.)

But the essence of the program emerges in its administration and the means available for supporting prices at the levels stated in legislation and by the Secretary, for these are not and were not intended to be self-executing goals. In general, the process begins with a proclamation by the Secretary of a national marketing quota for a given commodity, the amount needed to balance supply with demand. The national quota is converted into acreage allotments which are divided according to past yields among the states. State allotments are subdivided among farms on the same basis. Direct dealings with farmers are a responsibility of state and county Agricultural Stabilization and Conservation Committees. State committees consist of three to five members appointed by the Secretary of Agriculture, plus the State Director of the Agricultural Extension Service. County committeemen are elected annually by farmers from among their company, and are supervised by the state committee. All serve on a per diem basis. The county committee checks the eligibility of farmers for price support, makes adjustments and reviews complaints on acreage allotments, determines whether there has been compliance with allotments and quotas, and supervises records keeping, storage facilities, and the like of individual farmers. Committees are also responsible for informing farmers of upcoming referenda and usually campaign on behalf of the department for acceptance of mandatory quotas (requiring two-thirds vote). Complaints are reviewed by *ad hoc* local committees of farmers (but not those on the original committee), the state committee, and the Secretary. Upon exhaustion, appeal may go to the U.S. District Court or to any state court of general jurisdiction (1364–65 U.S.C., Title 7). When price support and acreage restriction are not mandatory (having been rejected by referendum, or when applied to such "permissive-support" commodities as cottonseed, flaxseed, soybeans, etc.), price support falls automatically to 50 percent and then only to those who voluntarily restrict cultivation to their allotment. The county committee is empowered to verify compliance again. When support is mandatory, non-compliance involves cash penalties of up to so much per unit of excess. When support is permissive at 50 percent of parity, non-compliance means only loss of title to CCC loans and purchase agreements.

With all its peculiarities in comparison to other regulatory programs, price support is in essence regulatory. It is an effort to manipulate individual output in order to manipulate the market. In its direct purpose it, therefore, differs from such regulation as securities and trade, where specific practices and their encouragement or prevention are ends in themselves. Price support is more like fair trade or Robinson-Patman policies where the purpose involves the whole market rather than the specific regulated practices themselves. Peculiar enough in purpose, price support is probably unique in the pattern of techniques made available to ASCS: (1) Regulation is self-imposed and periodic. Mandatory quotas require enactment by referendum, and such restrictions once accepted are effective from one to three years. (2) Regulation is not only self-imposed but directly purchased by the offer of higher parity with mandatory restrictions or by at least some support when restrictions are voluntary. (3) The program is largely self-administered through the network of state and local farmer-committees. (4) Finally, not only does it work more by incentives than by sanctions, these incentives are individualized through the provision of conservation payments, the Soil Bank, and so on.

But price support is regulatory despite its focus on the total market and despite the addition of carrot to stick. The impact of price support is directly upon the alternatives of farmers in the use of their lands. In full operation the program is clearly regulatory. In partial operation the impact is the same but the techniques change more toward incentive over sanction. Essentially, the program is an attempt to create among farmers the capacity to control their market that businessmen have without the loan of sovereignty. Farmers at first tried to solve their problems by seeking and getting government regulation of those who they felt were the cause of their problems—railroads, other monopolies, and banks. They also sought redistribution through cheap money, a boon to all debtors. These failing, they sought the route of distributive politics by trying to "make the tariff work for agriculture" through McNary-Haugenism. This failing, they sought to regulate themselves.[2] ASCS is also responsible for a proportion of the conservation program, including the Soil Bank, export subsidization, and disaster relief (all distributive), but the character of the agency and its work is set by its regulatory functions.

2. Programs administered by the Agricultural Marketing Service are also essentially regulatory. In fact, they are closely geared to the needs of the price support program. The

original Agricultural Adjustment Act of 1933 created three basic elements, "production adjustment," "income adjustment," and marketing controls. The former two are responsibilities of ASCS. Part of the latter one is also in ASCS, but largely it is under AMS and it comprises the most important part of the work of AMS. AMS has some regulatory power over all commodity areas. Under the Grain Standards Act of 1916, the Packers and Stockyards Act of 1921, the Cotton Standards Act of 1923, and others of later vintage, AMS is empowered to establish standards of quality and classification by quality and condition of a variety of products. In the past AMS has regularly raised standards of quality, especially in plentiful years, to help reduce surpluses. ("Surplus" does not include inferior goods.) Its regulatory power is further extended by the Warehouse Act of 1916 and others, which allow for inspection and licensing of all handlers and processors and for the licensing of samplers and classifiers of products. AMS may revoke licenses and administer other penalties for discriminatory pricing, fraudulent advertising, or other deceptive or harmful marketing practices.

AMS has additional power over certain commodities, particularly of a perishable type which cannot be included under acreage allotments, through use of marketing agreements and orders. On approval of two-thirds of the producers of a crop (usually in a local area) or by the producers of two-thirds of the crop, the Secretary may sign market agreements with handlers to limit the total quantity marketed, to allocate quotas among handlers, to dispose of surpluses and equalize the burden among producers and handlers, to declare "shipping holidays" during glut periods, to control "unfair practices," and to employ other such means of regulating the market through the middlemen. For milk, there is also an elaborate price-fixing scheme. Agreements when signed are binding. And all agreements are extended only to specific commodities and to areas of limited size.

Here clearly is a regulatory agency. Its marketing research services and grant programs are minor compared to the scope and impact of the regulatory ones. Again, the essential element is direct control over the alternatives and practices of private individuals.

3. Another clear case of agriculture regulation is the Commodity Exchange Authority under the Commodity Exchange Act of 1922. Its jurisdiction extends to the trading in futures of some 17 agricultural commodities and to the persons and institutions dealing in such trade (6 U.S.C., Title 7). The Authority designates what are to be lawful "contract markets," controls excessive speculation, fixes limits commodity by commodity on the amount of trading in futures there will be, and controls fraud and misrepresentation. The Authority registers commission merchants and floor brokers and can suspend trading up to 10 days to hold hearings or enforce its orders.

4. Most bureaus, services, or equivalent agencies, the highest operational levels below the Secretary, are unifunctional. They are usually created by and operate within a single or a few related statutes with amendments and can, like the three agencies above, be rather easily classified as distributive, regulative, or redistributive. The Agricultural Research Service is one of several exceptions. It combines, close to half-and-half, services of a distributive nature and regulation. It was established in 1953 as an effort to consolidate most of the physical, biological, chemical, and engineering research in the department regardless of whether the research involved plant, dairy, or animal products. But it took

over most of the federal regulation of these products as well, and only a small part of the Service's research is devoted to the problems of regulation. Meat inspection and grading, eradication and control of animal and plant diseases in interstate commerce and importation, and inspection and quarantine for such purposes are all carried on directly by the Service in cooperation with state regulatory programs.

But as a result of these two separate functions, the Service has become divided organizationally. There is a Deputy Administrator in charge of regulatory programs, and there are four Deputy Administrators in charge of the various divisions of research. Within the Service, the distinction between its regulatory and research activities is clearly understood. One Deputy Administrator described the Service as being comprised of "two categories." Analytically these two categories will be kept separate.

The above agencies and programs exhaust the important regulatory aspects of the Department. They are all "agriculture," but in many significant ways their impact on agriculture or the society at large cannot be assumed to be the same as the other programs that follow.

Distribution

5. The Federal Extension Service is responsible for the diffusion of useful information on farming and home economics, particularly to farmers without benefit of higher education. It is cooperative in the sense that the Service only shares the expenses of extension work with the states, the land-grant colleges, the county governments, and the local agricultural associations (in the beginning typically called "farm bureaus"). Its county agents serve the farmers; its home demonstration personnel serve farm women; its 4-H and other programs serve farm youth.[3]

The Extension Service was an extension and expansion of the Morrill Acts for land grants and aid to agricultural education. Until the New Deal, extension was a primary activity of the USDA and the primary channel through which all governmental activities reached the farmer. Unlike the programs listed above, Extension services were always freely available without regulatory strings attached. As evaluated by a 1940 Brookings study, "A large farmer actively in touch with government agricultural services might receive gratis during a year some hundreds of dollars' worth of laboratory or consultative service ... whereas other farmers might continue to follow as primitive or slovenly methods as they chose except as the harmful results of such practices might call for the imposition of certain regulatory measures."[4] In addition to the capacity of a program of the Extension type to roll with the punches of individual farmer demands, it can be extremely flexible among groupings of farmers at local, county, state, and regional levels. Extension services have simply been made available to the degree provided by Congress; the actual pattern of services has always been determined by the degree of interest and organization in each geographic area. The Extension Service from the beginning encouraged the creation of local farmer associations by requiring that localities with the aid of the states provide part of the expense if they were to employ a county agent. Thus, individual farmers on their own account and farming areas, by hiring a county agent, could receive services "on demand." The entire establishment was set up to work that way and almost exclusively that way. As it came out of the pre–New Deal constitutional period, Extension works on a grant-in-aid basis under conditions of greater decentralization than, for example, the comparable Soil Conservation Service (SCS). Decentralization is further strengthened by the extremely strong supportive relationships among federal Extension officers, the land-grant colleges, and the state and local farm bureaus. This easily extends into the agriculture committees and appropriations subcommittees by the fact that so many Congressmen in farm areas have used the local Extension system as a prime constituency base.

6. The Soil Conservation Service, in formal contrast to the Extension Service, is a "direct line" agency. It plans and executes its programs directly through its own rather large technical staff and soil management administrators. The organic act empowers the SCS (1) to conduct surveys, etc., to disseminate the results and to carry on demonstrations; (2) to carry out erosion prevention measures and to cooperate with any agency or person and to extend financial aid to the same to carry out the purposes of the act; and (3) to set certain conditions for the granting of benefits, such as enactment by state and local erosion laws and the individual use of land.

In practice SCS's work is not so dissimilar to that of the Extension Service except in the fact that it focuses upon conservation practices rather than "farm and family living." Despite charges of overlapping and duplication, perhaps in part true, the two agencies do complement one another; and except for these charges, no important farm or related interest has ever opposed either program. And the structures of the two services are similar. SCS has organized an elaborate complex of soil conservation districts, which they like to think of as units of local government, each with its own elected farmer committee. Each individual farmer receives an acre-by-acre soil survey and a land-capability map designed according to SCS's philosophy that every acre must be treated according to its needs. Each farmer receives advice and guidance on practical alternatives for carrying out SCS recommendations, and he is given a hand in carrying out the plan as well as maintaining it. Seedlings are provided as well as machinery and other aid when available. Other special assistance is provided by SCS on watershed development. Until World War II farmers received considerable aid through the loan of CCC and WPA workers.

The most important contrast between SCS and the Extension Service is in the location of the center of administration. Extension is centered in the land-grant colleges and the state Extension Directors. SCS, despite a similar local structure, is centered in the SCS itself. Much is made of the conservation districts, but conservation agreements are actually made directly between SCS and the farmer: "The Soil Conservation Service is the very lifeblood of the districts."[5] The most important similarities between the two programs are that (1) both are purely supportive (no penalties are involved, and the only influences on alternatives are those aimed at increases in productivity); (2) the outputs of both are available to all farmers; (3) the units of output can be cumulated or divided with ease; and (4) each unit can be dispensed almost wholly without regard to how the other units are treated or who is receiving them.

7. The Forest Service, with all its peculiarities, deals essentially in distributive policies along with the two agencies covered immediately above. Its primary function is direct management of over 180 million acres of national forests. The Service becomes a typical line agency with typical exposure to the outside world through its power to cut trees

or to give or sell permits for cutting, to license grassland for pasture, to permit use of streams and waterways and the acquisition of rights of ways within its domain, and to develop recreational access and facilities. In addition to its direct activities as a "public enterprise"—Kaufman reports receipts of $137 million in fiscal 1956[6]—the Service is empowered to cooperate with and give assistance to private and state-local owners of commercial forests. In this latter respect, the Service looks like the SCS, except that the Forest Service may also sell as well as give its services to private owners.

Almost from the birth of the Forest Service control of commercial access to public lands rested upon the Secretary's power to issue licenses and permits—the granting or selling of permission to individuals to do what is otherwise prohibited. Within rather broad standards of conservation and "multiple use-sustained yield," Forest Rangers in their widely separated districts grant and sell these privileges on an individual basis, deciding between small and large herds, cattle and sheep, nearby and distant ranches and lumbering companies, amount of use, rights of way, replanting, and so on. The possibilities of discretion and of individual manipulation are infinite, and use of both discretion and manipulation is almost inevitable. "Whether [the Forest Service] cuts trees, builds dams, puts up hotels, or leaves the woods undeveloped, it would be hard indeed to hold the outcome to be legally in conflict with any congressional mandate."[7] While every effort is made to coordinate Ranger decisions with standards and plans laid down at the center, local Rangers are officially encouraged to participate in local affairs and to discuss their plans with local congressmen, officials, groups, and interested individuals.[8] As a result, relations between administrator and his clientele are likely to be even more intimate and supportive than those in SCS, approximating the "community-relations" approach of the Corps of Engineers.[9]

8. The Farmer Cooperative Service and its programs offer no particular problem of classification. Under Chapter 18 of the Agriculture title (Cooperative Marketing Act of 1926 as amended) the Cooperative Service is authorized to render service and assistance to all farmer cooperatives and to those state, local, college, and private agencies which are fostering co-ops. Later Acts (Chapter 12) exempt, with some limitations, farmer cooperatives from the antitrust laws. The research, marketing studies, and expertise of the agency are put to the service of creating as well as improving the co-ops. While not every farm organization sees the cooperative as the panacea, there is virtually unanimous support for the movement, which during the 1920s was at the very center of "farm bloc" interest. Like other distributive programs, cooperative service is available to all and can be administered on a highly individual, case-by-case basis. Other agencies, such as the Agricultural Marketing Service in effecting marketing orders, make use of the cooperative in carrying out their programs; but this is regulation of, not creation of and service to, the cooperatives. The latter is the job of the FCS.

Redistribution

All of the programs so far identified redistribute wealth toward agriculture from commerce, toward a poor industry from rich industries, and to a certain extent to poorer people from richer people. This is a real issue, and it is one that occasionally enters into controversy in Congress and the upper reaches of the Executive branch. In fact, the farm organizations themselves once sought to and, for a while, succeeded in defining the entire agriculture problem in the redistributive terms of getting for agriculture, and the poorer segment thereof, equal benefits of industrialization. The agrarian aspect of progressivism at the turn of the century sought redistribution largely through inflation, because all farmers but the rich ones constituted a debtor class. By the 1920s, with the founding of the last major farm groups, redistribution was still in the rhetoric, but the actual pressure campaign was for distributive policies epitomized by McNary-Haugenism and the movement for government aid to cooperatives. The solid front of agriculture, supported by the rhetoric of redistribution, finally broke over the issue of regulation of agriculture, touched upon earlier. But in the midst of all this, some strong redistributive goals remained and were eventually realized in public policy. The technique of inflation was almost totally abandoned, perhaps because debt had become as characteristic of the rich as the poor. The more selective technique of farm credit was hit upon. It is selective in that it can deal with individual farmers and specific regions and commodity areas on the basis of need. And it is selective in the sense that it can be used to draw market power directly from industry, commerce, and the financial institutions created for their services. Manipulation of the entire economy is not necessary.

9. The Farm Credit Administration (FCA), the largest single agency in this field, is not at present in the Department. Created in 1933 as an independent agency, it was made a part of the Department in 1939 and again made independent in 1953. Its authority extends back to the Federal Farm Loan Act of 1916, and was enlarged on many occasions since the 1920s. The 1933 Farm Credit Act consolidated all farm credit institutions and operations in FCA. In 1961 alone, $4.5 billion was borrowed from the various systems within FCA by farmers and cooperatives.

Actually, there are four distinct credit systems within FCA: (1) the 12 land banks for making mortgage loans, coordinated since 1953 by a 13-member Farm Credit Board in Washington; (2) the 12 intermediate credit banks for making (short-term) production and marketing loans; (3) the 13 banks for cooperatives; and (4) the 12 production credit corporations, which provide for a local mechanism to aid individual farmers to get access to the intermediate credit banks. For each system there is an elaborate structure of farmer representation. And for the latter three, membership is limited to those who actually own stock in the system, and a stock purchase up to 5 percent of the loan is required for the loan. The regional banks approve and supervise the loans, sell and discount the paper, guarantee mortgages, refinance mortgages, sell farm loan bonds on the open market, and so on. With favorable rates and protections, these systems directly channel capital away from commerce toward farming at a rather large yearly rate.

10. Assistance selectively to the small and subsistence farmer is furthered by still another program, carried out by the Farmers Home Administration. Its stated purpose is to provide "credit accompanied by technical farm and money management assistance to eligible farmers who cannot get the financing they need elsewhere at reasonable rates and terms."[10] Established by the Bankhead-Jones Farm Tenant Act of 1937, FHA was to be an instrument for converting tenancy into ownership, sub-marginal farms into subsistence farms, and subsistence farms into prosperous farms. Operating loans (7-year, renewable, up to $35,000), ownership loans (40-year, up to $60,000), and a brace of lesser types of credit are available. Following agriculture practice, local committees of farmers

determine applicant eligibility and review borrower progress. Rates, terms, guarantees, and the like are held measurably below those offered on the general capital market.

11. The general thrust of the Rural Electrification Administration (REA) is reflected in the fact of its creation under the Emergency Relief Appropriation Act of 1935. It was to be one of the several New Deal promotional and evangelistic programs. REA makes loans on the building and improvement of electric and telephone equipment in rural areas. Only 25 percent of the loan funds have been allocated to the states on the basis of the proportion of farmers not enjoying electricity or telephones; 75 percent of the funds have been within REA's discretion provided that no state received more than 25 percent of the total. The original statute gave REA full discretion on interest rates, allowing no-interest up to very low-interest loans. In 1944 the interest rate was set at 2 percent. Nearly $5 billion of loans have been made under the program. While it is impossible to say what proportion of this was a diversion of capital to agriculture that would otherwise have gone into other sectors, the low interest rates and the types of rural areas supplied with power and communications as a result suggest a rather large proportion.

The Areas of Governmental Activity: Definition and Classification

There is no rule of thumb method of classifying public policies according to the type of stakes involved in them. There are no simple indices the capture of which leads to the direct capture of the beast itself. Identifying policies for purposes of political analysis requires a careful reading of the origins of each policy—the statutes and basic interpretations—and a proper translation of the elements of the policy into relevant terms. All that can be done before the fact is to formulate some criteria by which each policy can be treated consistently. Thus, what *of political relevance* do all policies of a stated type have in common? The only general answers seem to lie in the direction of the impact or expected impact of the policies as adjudged over time by observation and assessment at any point in time of the techniques employed for implementation.

As I tried to make clear in the formal analysis above, distributive policies seem to be characterized by the ease with which they can be disaggregated and dispensed unit by unit, each unit more or less in isolation from other units and from any general rule. Congress lays down certain criteria for dispensation of services or funds, but in every case the leeway is enormous. Soil conservation services and assistance provided by several agencies, for example, are available for farmers who want to improve their lands in various ways. Up to a point the amount the farmer receives is up to him. Those farmers who are not receiving aid may get into the programs without competing with other farmers. Administrators can easily accommodate new entrants by making further subdivisions of their available funds. Funds are usually apportioned by states, but in every program a large proportion of the total can be administered at the discretion of the agency chief or the Secretary. This creates the extra slack from which state or regional conflicts among claimants can be reduced or avoided altogether. Few who are in any one program have any reason to oppose the program, for it works entirely by inducements. With inducements, easily "budgeted," farmers who oppose can be co-opted by further subdivisions of funds.

The regulatory activities of AMS and Agricultural Research Service (ARS) offer no problem of classification. But what general definition of regulation can be stated which will capture the common element of all regulation and at the same time distinguish it from other types of relationships between government and society? Robert Cushman has offered one of the few general definitions: "A commission is regulatory when it exercises governmental control or discipline over private conduct or property interests. This control may take different forms and use different methods, but there is always present an element of coercion. It is this coercion which distinguishes the regulatory Federal Trade Commission from the non-regulatory Reconstruction Finance Corporation (RFC)."[11] This is a good start and was certainly sufficient for Cushman's purpose, which was simply to distinguish between "regulation" and "non-regulation." But it can be argued that RFC, SCS, and other "non-regulatory" agencies influence conduct if only by holding out attractive inducements. And no one can question the fact that certain "non-regulatory activities," such as the open market operations of the Federal Reserve Board, or subsidized credit, or the income tax are both influential on conduct and coercive.

It seems to me, then, that to Cushman's definition must be added three characteristics: (1) there must be a specification of conduct to be prescribed or proscribed; (2) the control by government over this conduct must be direct and individual; and (3) specific controls must be applied in terms of general rules. In sum, *regulation is an attempt by government to exert a direct influence over the alternatives by the application of general rules to specified practices or types of conduct with the direct involvement (but not necessarily the use) of coercion.* Without doing any damage to the meaning of regulation, this formulation distinguishes it fairly clearly from the other two types of policy in the scheme. Redistribution involves coercion and definitely influences alternatives; but redistributive policies specify no particular conduct, and their influence over individual alternatives is through general market manipulation or some other type of long-run impact. Distributive policies also influence individual alternatives, but many do not follow from the application of general rules; and even when general rules are involved there is not in the strictest sense an influence on alternatives but simply an expansion of existing alternatives. This is why distributive policies can be broken down into isolated units and regulatory policies cannot. Regulatory decisions can be sustained only insofar as they can be shown to relate to other decisions (or precedents) and an applicable rule.

Finally, redistributive policies are characterized by the directness with which they divert resources from one broadly defined class to another, or by the directness with which they threaten to do so. Undoubtedly, as long as farmers as a class receive more in services than they pay in taxes, the policies called distributive actually do redistribute wealth or privilege in the long run. But it is the "long run" that makes so much difference. Such a distinction is not always an easy one to make even when policies and proposals are clearly understood. Furthermore, such a distinction involves a degree of tautology. But in definition some tautology is inescapable; it is legitimate, it seems to me, so long as it is the beginning rather than the end of the inquiry. The test of any definition, if it is the basis for a scheme of analysis, is how well it "cuts the ice." A definition is good or bad only insofar as it can expose and help explain similarities and variations in experience and data. All that is necessary here is for the author and the reader to understand the principle underlying the definitions (impact or expected impact) and, as concretely as possible, the definitions themselves.

It would not be possible, unless definition and classification were the only purpose of the book, to go into the elements of each existing program and major proposal. The Department of Agriculture was chosen as an instructive case because it comprehends several programs in each of the defined areas and because most agricultural activities of the federal government are so poorly understood by non-agriculturalists. Bureau or service units were chosen both as a convenient method of identifying and selecting policies and to emphasize the fact that issues and policies are realized only in administration. Particularly since the 1930s, virtually all major political issues have been simply amendments of greater or lesser scope to existing programs. The context of every issue is the existing program into which the issue and the outcome of the issue fit. It should be clear by now that one of the major assumptions of this study is that political structures form around ongoing or established governmental activities (programs) and that the political process of a given issue is determined to the largest extent by the program and structure most closely involved. All of this is what is hopefully implied by arena.

On the basis of the case of agriculture and the definitions, it should now be possible to classify all major domestic programs (in the sense given immediately above) in terms of the agencies in which they are housed. (See Table 8.1.) Only part of the following analysis will be focused upon administrative agencies, but the programs represented by them will never be very far from the surface. And it is unfortunate that each agency and its program cannot be described in detail so as to instruct the reader in the reasons why each has been so classified. Some of these programs will come in for such description when they are directly involved in the empirical work of later chapters. Those that are neglected will, I hope, lead readers to some policy analysis of their own. Those who need such instruction should be grateful for the opportunity.

Most of the independent agencies and commissions have been omitted from this listing. They have not been eliminated from later analysis, but they must be approached differently from the operating bureaus within Departments, which are listed here only because they are by and large unifunctional and, therefore, can more concretely "represent" the types of policies that are included in each of the larger categories of the scheme. The commissions are more like Departments in the sense that they comprehend many types of policy within a subject-matter area. As the case of the Department of Agriculture should have demonstrated, subject matter is no clue to the function or impact of policies. In the analysis of administrative structure, the commissions will be set aside. The kind of intensive research that would be required to identify the personnel performing the different functions goes too far beyond the limits of this study. And there are ample data in the bureaus and services for the purpose of testing the scheme as it applies to administrative structure. The commissions will come into play as policies under study effect them. Like Congress, the Departments, peak associations, or any other collegial or multifunctional decision-making unit, the internal structure and external relations of the commissions are likely to vary from one arena to another. Variations from one arena to another in the internal structure and external relations of political institutions constitute the primary focus of the study.

Table 8.1 Major Domestic Governmental Programs Classified by Agency and According to Area of Governmental Activity

Distribution	Regulation	Redistribution
1. Agriculture Agricultural Research Service (research divisions) Federal Extension Service Soil Conservation Service Forest Service Farmer Cooperative Service	1. Agriculture Agricultural Stabilization and Conservation Service Agricultural Marketing Service Commodity Exchange Authority Agricultural Research Service (regulatory division)	1. Agriculture Farm Credit Administration Farmers Home Administration Rural Electrification Administration
2. Commerce Area Redevelopment Administration Business and Defense Services Administration Bureau of International Commerce Maritime Administration Bureau of Public Roads	2. Commerce	2. Commerce
3. Labor Bureau of Apprenticeship and Training Bureau of Labor Standards	3. Labor Bureau of Veterans' Reemployment Rights Wage and Hour and Public Contracts Division	3. Labor Bureau of Employment Security
4. Interior Bureau of Commercial Fisheries Bureau of Sport Fisheries and Wildlife Bureau of Mines Geological Survey Bureau of Land Management National Park Service Bureau of Reclamation	4. Interior	4. Interior

(continues)

Table 8.1 (continued)

Distribution	Regulation	Redistribution
5. Health, Education and Welfare Bureau of Medical Services (PHS) Bureau of State Services (PHS) Office of Education	5. Health, Education and Welfare Food and Drug Administration	5. Health, Education and Welfare Social Security Administration Bureau of Family Services Children's Bureau Vocational Rehabilitation Administration
6. Treasury	6. Treasury Bureau of Narcotics Bureau of Customs	6. Treasury Internal Revenue Service Bureau of Public Debt
7. Justice[a]	7. Justice Antitrust Division Civil Rights Division Federal Bureau of Investigation	7. Justice
8. HHFA Community Facilities Administration Urban Renewal Administration Federal Housing Administration FNMA	8. HHFA	8. HHFA

Note: a. Other divisions or bureaus omitted for various reasons. Several are arms of the judiciary, serving as auxiliary or overhead agencies to other operating agencies. Others deal only in the federal domain.

Part IV

Economic Sectors and Collective Goods

Part IV applies the Arenas of Power model to a number of economic and social sectors to explore how the four policy types affect interest group influence, legislative processes, and administrative structures in different substantive areas. Sectoral issues and objectives seem to be an intuitive way to organize policy and political thinking. We naturally refer to agricultural policy, education policy, trade policy, or labor policy to define the goals of government action. Politics focuses on the problems of regions, interests, and classes—the problems of the farm belt, of cotton or corn farmers, and of the rural poor. Policy analysis typically uses the methodology of case studies—cases focused on clusters of issues defined by processes both within and outside the political process. Two competing intellectual traditions have attempted to integrate these diverse sectoral analyses into a general theory of power and policy: the pluralist approach focused on interest groups, and elitist theories. Lowi suggests that the power structure and political processes described in each of these competing theories are merely special cases and that sectoral politics are better understood through the analysis of the type of policy choices that are made.

The structure of economic interests, and the level of mobilization and organization of those interests, are indeed important variables. But it is the choice of policy type, Lowi argues, that will determine whether politics is pluralist or elitist, whether various types of interest groups can be effective, or where the balance of power lies within the U.S. constitutional structure. For example, distributive politics is pluralistic, favoring narrowly focused interests, and taking place below the public radar, in congressional committees. In contrast, redistributive politics tends to be elitist, favoring class-based peak organizations, and focusing on the executive branch.

In discussing agricultural interests in the U.S. political system, Lowi comments in passing that because the United States lacked a peasantry sharing common objective conditions, it was difficult for agriculture interests to move beyond distributive policies. This observation deserves greater attention. In those parts of the world where a peasantry exists, the pattern is large numbers of very small subsistence farms, often tenant farms, producing basic food crops. They are typically both socially and economically disadvantaged. Thus, by Lowi's reasoning they constitute a class—sharing common interests by the uniformity of their relationship to the economy, society, and political structure. But because they are geographically scattered in their farms and isolated from the national and global economy, and also politically and socially marginalized, these peasants are difficult, but not impossible, to mobilize and organize. This disadvantage is critical because large numbers and organization are essential to political power at the national level. However, once organized in a classic peasant uprising, it is not surprising that they associate themselves with powerful redistributive policies directed against landlords, urban elites, or foreign exploitation. These redistributive policies may or may not serve the longer-term interests of peasant farmers.

Yet, while granting the truth of that, it is also true that agriculture (or peasantry) as a class can remain an organized class interest only as long as their demands are redistributive. Lowi demonstrates in Chapter 9 that for a short while, late in the nineteenth century, American agriculture did operate as a class, through a Populist party and directly as a social movement, the beginning of Progressivism. The all-agriculture movement disaggregated into sectoral and commodity interest groups as regulatory and distributive policies returned to Congress's agenda.

This reasoning does not mean that policy necessarily determines group structure, but that the policy types do determine the conditions of political success in each policy arena. For example, Lowi explains that there are significant limitations on the capacity of distributive policies to aggregate interests to national scale and to mobilize the political will to address the basic issues of structural change. However, large farmers who are integrated into an increasingly national or global market might well support a regulatory policy directed toward the railroads, sanitary standards, or redistributive policies that manipulate foreign exchange rates or property rights, as they do in many countries. Lowi would not have been surprised, however, by a public lecture by Joseph Stiglitz in 2006 in which Stiglitz commented, in effect, that the North American Free Trade Agreement should have been a page long to be effective—declaring free trade. Instead, it is hundreds of pages long and, in Lowi's terms, is a distributive commodity-by-commodity tariff policy disguised as a redistributive free trade agreement.

The discussion in Part IV provides three important insights gained from the application of the Arenas of Power.

First, an adequate analytical tool must deal with the growing complexity and institutional differentiation of the American polity. Lowi's treatment of interest group interaction with policy arenas in this part needs to be read in the context of the nationalization of the U.S. economy and polity—a persistent force for institutional change for over 200 years—and the more recent impact of the explosion of globalization in the 1990s. After World War II, the United States stood at the threshold of an era of globalization with a distributive tariff policy that would take a half-century to work out of. As we will see in Chapter 11, the United States began in the post–World War II era to build a national and global economy, but with legislation and administrative structures in key economic sectors poorly suited to a complex and competitive modern economy. New structures had to be built around those of the 1930s and 1940s. In redistributive policy, for example, we still struggle without a viable national social safety net.

Lowi's analysis makes clear that since the watershed of the New Deal and the emergence of an American modern state, single policy types can seldom define political issues and sectoral politics. Rather, a basket of policies—distributive, regulatory, redistributive, and even constituent—will be necessary to deal with any sector, including agriculture, in the twenty-first century. Neither the policy mix nor the institutional arrangements can be as simple as they once were. Differentiation and increasing complexity in institutional arrangements challenge both policymaking and policy analysis.

Second, the nationalization, and even internationalization, of social and cultural issues threatens to increase conflict at the national level and undermine the capacity of logrolling and instrumental processes to resolve conflict. Lowi's arguments about the interaction of policy choices (arenas) and broad social and economic changes are reflected in his discussion of the burgeoning of national social policy in the 1960s and 1970s. Chapter 10, "Policy Choices and Political Consequences: The Case of Population Control," demonstrates the difficulties in dealing with the complex social problems of the late twentieth century. It shows the need to be clear not only about the goals but also about the type of policy choices made. Further, it builds on Lowi's analysis of the New Deal policies to urge caution about the impact of those choices on the polity. The characteristic inability of regulatory and redistributive policies to contain conflict becomes an issue of paramount importance in an area as sensitive as population policy, especially when policy moves from the local level and becomes national in scope.

Third, institutional arrangements, which include interest groups and bureaucracies that populate political arenas, can be very path dependent and persist well beyond their objective utility. Institutional change has both a demand and a supply function. Demand needs not only to reflect objective conditions but also organization to articulate it. The supply of institutional change requires resources, leadership, and an enabling policy environment. High transaction costs tend to make radical institutional changes rare. Political processes and administrative structures may be unable to produce the needed policy mix in a timely fashion and without conflict. Political systems tend to tackle new problems with the tools at hand and innovation tends to be incremental. And as Lowi so often emphasizes, distributive policies are most frequently tried first and when all other types of policy effort fail because they produce too much conflict. This is why he later replaced the "distributive" label with the more expressive synonym: "patronage policy."

"Interests, Politics, and the Variety of Group Experience" (Chapter 9) deals with the relationship between interest groups and policymaking. The structure and behavior of interest groups differ substantially across the four types of policy. In this chapter Lowi presents a brief history of legislative and interest group activity related to agriculture, labor, and social security policies during the thirty years surrounding the New Deal. The intent is not so much to describe the politics of these several areas of economic policy, although the treatment is rich in historical detail. Rather, the case studies collectively demonstrate how the structure of interest groups constrains the choice of policy arenas available to them and conversely how the policy choice shapes the political impact of interest group action however they are organized. That is to say that the structure, behavior, and influence of interest groups must differ substantially and consistently among distributive, regulatory, and redistributive policy arenas if they are to be effective.

Further, the role and influence of congressional committees, the executive branch, and the federal bureaucracy also vary systematically among the policy types. This is a basic tenet of the Arenas of Power model. Chapter 9 lays out Lowi's analysis that the political system contains multiple political processes and that the choice of policy type engenders the choice of a political process, not the other way around.

Lowi's analysis eventually led him to believe that the prevailing theories embraced by political scientists (pluralist, elitist, corporatist, libertarian, and so on) are shaped by type or types of policy (distributive, regulatory, redistribution, constituent) dominant at the time the scholars were living through and studying the policies. In a sense, then, the Arenas of Power model provides a megatheory that integrates much previous scholarship on public policy. (See also Chapter 5 on the four Roosevelts.) Much has changed in each of these policy areas since these chapters were originally written, but the significance of the period, in which New Deal politics were played out, is that it was then that the great expansion of national government occurred and the "modern state" appeared in the United States. During the 1960s and 1970s, politics at the national level began to differentiate into distinct policy arenas with distinct political processes, administrative structures, and configuration of interest groups, which shaped policy development for the next fifty years.

The key to the relationship between policy arena and interest group structure and activity lies in the primary tenet of the model—that policy choice is an independent variable that affects fundamentally the nature of the relationship between the state and its citizens. Different citizen-state relations, in turn, affect political strategies, transaction costs, and the distribution of spoils. Elements of group formation, such as the scale of interest aggregation and the level of group cohesion, are affected by the structure of the interests involved, macroeconomic factors such as the level of national integration, or the articulation of the issues, for example, as pragmatic incremental benefits or, alternatively, articles of faith and cultural survival. But the political success of group demands lies in whether its structure and internal politics are consistent with the requirements of different policy arenas.

"Policy Choices and Political Consequences: The Case of Population Control" (Chapter 10) provides an excellent example of how the Arenas of Power model can be used to inform policy choices by clarifying the nature of the policy choice and by providing predictive statements about both the political and administrative impact of policy choices. It suggests how the sequencing of types of policy choices and the interaction of different policy types can affect the outcomes of government action. The discussion also advises a certain caution in policy initiatives. Recognizing the high potential for unanticipated consequences, Lowi first calls for incremental policy decisions in combination with policies that permit easy adjustment in the light of experience. Second, he reminds us that high cost, large scale, and the potential for significant restructuring of the society or economy are all reasons for caution. But Lowi's third caution is perhaps the most interesting. Most policy analysis focuses on the desired outcomes within an issue area—in this case population growth. However, Lowi reminds us that for issue areas as momentous as population policy, there is great potential for restructuring the constitutional arrangements, the basic relationships between citizens and the state, and the expansion or diminution of citizen empowerment. None of these insights require the application of the Arenas of Power model, but the model greatly strengthens our ability to address such concerns.

The quote from David Hume at the beginning of Chapter 10 is also instructive. In effect, it says that policy choices can be differentiated by their transaction costs, both the costs of reaching a decision and, ultimately, the cost of implementing the policy and applying the sanctions implicit in the decision. Further, Lowi points out, these transaction costs, and the potential impact on the political system from major policy innovation, exist whether or not the policy actually has the anticipated impact.

Finally, the chapter provides a useful bridge between Lowi's historical analysis, discussed in Part II, and the analysis of mass movements that will be addressed in Part V. Our ability to anticipate the probable impact of policy choices on the political system can be derived from the policy types themselves. However, it is also clear that institutional arrangements exist in history and demonstrate some inertia. Thus, the insights Lowi offers depend greatly on the interaction of the model with our rich understanding of the U.S. political system, its institutional traditions, and political values. Conversely, the treatment of mass movements in Part V permits us to understand the potential that specific policies have for restructuring the political system in the guise of solving a social or economic problem. This chapter clearly demonstrates the model's utility for tracing macro and micro analytic linkages.

"The Perils of Patronage: Tendencies Toward Corporatism in the 'Clientele Agencies'" (Chapter 11) traces the development of distributive and regulatory policies in the areas of agriculture, labor, and commerce (all key components of the U.S. economy) in the era just before and after the New Deal. The policies and the administrative structures associated with them were designed to promote key economic interest groups through distributive policies, to which were added instruments of self-regulation that strengthened the market power of these interests in the national and global economy. Thus economic policy and administration in different sectors of the United States became a fragmented system of closed arenas.

The consequence of this, Lowi argues, has been that the complex interactions that characterize a modern national and global economy, and the conflicts inherent in this interaction, have been difficult or impossible to address through public policy. Incrementally, new policies and agencies have been created in response to emerging problems, but U.S. politics has lacked the capacity to address the conflicts, anticipate the problems, or exploit the interactions of the diverse policy types that populate U.S. economic policy. The result, Lowi suggests, has been the collapse of the pluralist political order. Within such a pluralistic system, it is impossible to negotiate global trade regimes that are rule based rather than interest based. It is difficult to reconcile the educational requirements of global competitiveness with local control of education and other social policies.

In this part, Lowi discusses the structures through which groups are mobilized to participate in modern, nation-state politics. In this process there is an interaction between the underlying social and economic structure that defines "interests" and the supply of policies to meet their demands. The application of the Arenas of Power model more broadly outside the United States requires that one address the fact that in much of the world today, fragile states are the rule. Poverty and weak state capacity do not necessarily limit policy choices but do limit policy implementation, when corrupt and unaccountable elites follow premodern traditions of rent-seeking regardless of the policy choice. In this setting, the Arenas of Power model would illuminate the policy choices urged on developing regimes.

—*Norman K. Nicholson*

Suggested Reading

There is a considerable literature on distributive politics in developing countries and its consequences.

E. L. Jones. *Growth Recurring: Economic Change in World History.* Ann Arbor: University of Michigan Press, 1988.
> Jones provides an excellent historical analysis of the politics of premodern predatory elites and attributes the scarcity of sustained intensive growth to the predominance of such regimes.

Nicolas van de Walle. *Overcoming Stagnation in Aid-Dependent Countries.* Washington, DC: Center for Global Development, 2005.
> Another outstanding analysis of the politics of predatory elites.

Robert Klitgaard. *Adjusting to Reality.* San Francisco: ICS Press, 1991.

Robert Klitgaard. *Topical Gangsters.* New York: Basic Books, 1991.

Robert Klitgaard. *Controlling Corruption.* Berkeley: University of California Press, 1991.
> Klitgaard has produced several volumes on institutionalized corruption in weak states.

Norman Nicholson. "The Factional Model and the Study of Politics." *Comparative Political Studies* 5, no. 3 (1972): 291–314.

Norman Nicholson. "Factionalism and Public Policy in India," pp. 161–192. In F. P. Belloni and D. C. Beller, eds. *Factional Politics: Political Parties and Factionalism in Comparative Perspective.* Santa Barbara: ABC-Clio, 1978.
> Nicholson's articles reflect Lowi's thesis that patronage or factional politics may indeed limit the development of a modern state.

Robert H. Bates and Anne O. Krueger. "Generalizations Arising from the Country Studies," ch. 10. In *Political and Economic Interactions in Economic Policy Reform.* Cambridge: Blackwell, 1993.
> In their conclusion to the volume they edited on the politics of structural adjustment in Latin America, Bates and Krueger observe that uncertainty regarding the impact of policy and institutional reform inhibits action in the first place and that interests that benefit from reform, and would therefore support it in an interest group model, seldom exist until well after the reforms have been implemented.

Stephan Haggard and Robert R. Kaufman. *The Politics of Economic Adjustment.* Princeton: Princeton University Press, 1992.

Haggard and Kaufman similarly concluded a volume they edited on the politics of structural adjustment (redistributive) policies occasioned by external economic shocks with the observation that the weaker the state, the more likely the adjustment policy was to be associated with regime change—with or without the desired reforms. This begins to address how to break out of the trap of weak state politics.

Jeffry A. Frieden. *Debt, Development, and Democracy: Modern Political Economy and Latin America, 1965–1985*. Princeton: Princeton University Press, 1991.

This collection comes to similar conclusions about the relationships among external shocks, redistributive structural change, and regime change.

CHAPTER 9

⚬⚬⚬

Interests, Politics, and the Variety
of Group Experience

For a substantial part of the second half of the twentieth century there were two prevailing theories of power in the social sciences: the elitist and the pluralist. But both were built on a fundamental fallacy, which was not readily revealed because measurement in the social sciences is so difficult. It has been described most forcibly by Keynes through Samuelson as "the fallacy of composition." Simply stated, "what is true of a part is, on that account alone, alleged to be also necessarily true of the whole."[1] Actually, there are three fallacies of composition—one that is shared by elitists and pluralists, the other two applying to one theory alone.

The common fallacy is the premise that the state (government and politics) is an epiphenomenon. For the elitist theory, the state "power structure" is an epiphenomenon of *economics*—the distribution of wealth and the relation of each person and group to the market. For the pluralist, the state and its politics are an epiphenomenon of *society*— the sum of associations and the parallelogram of forces among them.

The fallacy unique to the elitist theory is the mistaking of the resources of power for power itself. A million units of economic power translates, with no cost of transition, into a million units of political power, defined as control of the instrumentalities and command posts of the state. The emergence of an elite of wealth and status signals the existence of a class structure, with the dominant class constituting a directorate of class interests—whether a community power structure or a national power elite. C. Wright Mills added an element of neo-Marxist sophistication with his argument (inspired by Weber) that there are three domains in the American power elite—class, status, and power, which "tend to come together [through overlapping class and status upbringing] to form the power elite of America"—realized as standing at the top of government, business, and the military.[2]

Pluralism as a full-blown theory came in as a reaction to Marxist-elitist theory with a simple, devastating question: "What happens when members of the power elite disagree?" Conflict decentralizes and disperses power, creates uncertainties in outcomes, and makes necessary the extension of support through some kind of coalitional activity. In some consensus situations, resources may count directly; but in most consensus situations *access* is all that is really necessary. And in all conflict situations the problem of reaching agreement sufficient for making some kind of a decision is interposed between resources and power (as gauged by outcomes).

However, for all their sophistication regarding the problem of elites, pluralists fall into their own particular fallacy of construction. Pluralist political theory begins with the observation of an incontrovertible fact of American society: its plural and associational composition. The fallacy is the elevation of social pluralism directly into a theory of politics. Mills and others have correctly, if too extremely, argued that pluralist political theory has amounted to no more than the displacement of classical economics onto politics. This is why Mills refers to it as the "theory of balance."[3] Generally, it is a pattern of balancing among fairly clearly identified interests organized in relatively coherent groups. Pluralist students of local politics have managed to overcome some of these weaknesses. But even with the students of community power there remains the residue of balancing and grouping like an old favorite ideology.[4] At the national level these classic pluralist presumptions remain quite strong, and here we get to the crux of this chapter: What is the relation between private resources and public policy? How do the many interests find their way into public policy? Can wealthy interest groups transfer their economic power into equal units of political power?

If resources for political power do in actuality constitute power itself, then there would necessarily be a fairly permanent *structure* of power with an elite of power made up of the elites of all the values we hold most dear. If, on the other hand, the pluralist society places an indelible stamp on all its politics, then an altogether different array of attributes would be found in the data. "Pluralists," says Polsby, "are not surprised at the low priority Americans give to their class memberships as bases of social action.... [I]t is not only inefficient but usually unnecessary for entire classes to mobilize when the preferences of class members are pressed and often satisfied in piecemeal fashion."[5] Interests are narrower than classes. Fragmentation of government both reflects and ensures the continuation of these basic units of politics, the "interest groups," where interests are clear enough to provide the basis for organization in the first place. Representation lies in the specialization of interests; leadership is also able to shape *opinion*. The more specialized the interest, the more effective the group. These units provide the building blocks; policy is "the equilibrium reached in the group struggle at any given moment."[6]

Far apart as the two theories may be, there is at least one common factor, the presence of groups. This validates the social pluralism of the United States and most relatively free societies. Groups can be found in every kind of political struggle, whether the community power structure is elitist or pluralist. However, there are many important variations. A good theory will be one that recognizes those variations and accounts for them in a predictable manner.

There are at least three types of variation in the group pattern from one struggle to the next. One variation is by subject matter. Agricultural groups are active here but not there; business and labor here but not there. A second type of variation can be found in the differences in the makeup of groups, their size, composition, and internal structures, regardless of similarities or differences in subject matter base or interest. Some struggles activate only highly specialized groups; in other struggles the general interest groups or peak associations are cohesive; in others neither type seems to get anywhere but breaks up into components. Among strictly agricultural groups, as dealt with in Chapter 8, differences in size, base, structure, and cohesion are most interesting and rhetorically relevant. The third type of variation can be found in changes in external, or "intergroup," relations. Every group is more or less a part of an alliance, has more or less access to government, focuses attention more or less on a congressional committee or administrative agency, and so on, as conditions vary. Of the three types, questions regarding the latter two comprise the bulk of attention in this chapter.

Internal Structure and Dynamics

Some groups are cohesive, some are not. Some groups are cohesive sometimes and not at other times. Questions regarding the cohesiveness of groups and the conditions for cohesiveness are politically significant because cohesiveness is one of the vital links between resources and power. It is "of vital significance in the internal and external politics of groups,"[7] for no matter what the size of wealth or prestige or access of a group, its leadership should speak with one voice for its members or it might as well not speak at all. Any theory of politics would have to deal with questions regarding the conditions for group cohesion.

The search for conditions can go on in many directions. Within the Arenas of Power scheme, however, many opposing arguments about the determinants of group cohesion become less inconsistent, often mutually supportive. One of the best test cases can be found in the issue of overlapping membership and its relation to cohesion. Following directly from his definition of the group as a bundle of shared attitudes[8] is Truman's thesis that cohesion in any given group depends most mightily on the proportion of the individual's life and interests the group is able to absorb. Totalitarian ideological groups and religious cults are the limiting cases. "Complete stability within any interest group is a fiction," says Truman,[9] who continues:

> The internal political problems created by such influences [as the activities of other groups, the economic environment, and other external events] derive basically from a characteristic of group life that is particularly noticeable in complex modern society, namely, that no individual is wholly absorbed in any group to which he belongs. Only a fraction of his attitudes is expressed through any one such affiliation, though in many instances a major fraction.... [A]n individual generally belongs to several groups ... [and the] demands and standards of these various groups may and frequently do come into conflict with one another, a situation that is the primary source of the problem of internal group politics.[10]

But there is not necessarily universal agreement on Truman's very plausible point that overlapping membership is a source of conflict leading to reduction of cohesion. Bauer, Pool, and Dexter found that in tariff politics this very overlapping of membership has been a condition *for* cohesion: "unanimity (or cohesion) is maintained by the use of multiple group memberships for purposes which might produce conflict within a single given group."[11] The U.S. Chamber of Commerce supported lower tariffs in the 1950s, but in so very meek a form as to be ineffectual. The National Association of Manufacturers (NAM) in 1953 decided explicitly to remain without a tariff policy and stuck with that decision, as did specialized large associations, from the National Electrical Manufacturers Association to the CIO, along with many large and diversified individual corporations.[12] These organizations maintain a minimal level of cohesion not by leadership strategies, internal propaganda, or any other pattern of reaffirmation of goals, but rather by the fact of overlapping memberships itself. Most firms belong to more than one association, and "large firms belong to scores."[13] For example, a textiles firm may belong to the Textile Research Institute, the American Association of Textile Technology, and a variety of other service or research agencies. Then, depending on the fabrics the firm processes, it may also belong to the National Association of Wool Manufacturers, the Burlap Council, Lace Manufacturers, and others. As a producer, the firm may combine with dealers in an American Wool Council or American Cotton Council and beyond its own fabric in one or more textile "peak associations"[14] as well as general business peak associations. Then each of the smaller groups in which it holds memberships also is a member of one or more peak associations. Where agreement in any large organization cannot be reached, members are, when possible, allowed, and often even encouraged, to pursue their own goals through separate, even competing, organizations.

This suggests *there is no simple and direct relation between common attitudes and cohesion.* "Renegade Kautsky" of German Socialist fame might be taken as one universal syndrome, a type of inner group schisms that can result from shared attitudes. Overlapping is a form of specialization that can allow individual firms, or special constituent groups within larger associations, the freedom to pursue outside the association the goals that are contrary to other associated individuals, firms, or groups. Meanwhile, cohesion of the larger group is preserved for the goals about which there is no particular controversy.

Here are two opposing but equally plausible views of internal structure. One sees cohesion as dependent upon common attitudes, and sees groups handling differences by turning inward in a form of policymaking that might be considered a microcosm of the larger system itself. The other view finds that common attitudes matter less and sees groups handling internal differences by a kind of displacement upon the outside world, as though the life of one group depended critically upon the existence of other groups. This is group symbiosis rather than group combat.

The fact appears to be that both positions are correct but that they apply to or emerge out of entirely different situations. The different situations can be identified and dealt with meaningfully as part of the separate and distinct political processes of each arena. In fact, each of the factors that comprise the issue between Truman and Bauer, Pool, and Dexter are predictable from the Arenas of Power scheme. The argument should begin with reference to the relation between attitudes and cohesion and, as earlier observed, the lack of necessity for a positive correlation between them. The next step is to propose that some *types* of attitudes may be, while other types may not be, related to cohesion or any other aspect of internal group dynamics. Looking back at Table 1.2, especially columns 1–4, for each policy arena there appears to be a characteristic type of political relationship among units and members.

Distributive policy issues can engender cohesion among members who have quite uncommon interests. Why? Because distributive policies can be disaggregated into discrete units, creating an environment for logrolling; and logrolling has already been defined as a political relationship between two or more persons who have nothing at all in common. Thus, due to the unrelatedness of the elements that comprise a distributive issue, the activities of single participants can be specialized as the situation warrants. When a heterogeneous association faces a distributive issue, therefore, it need not take a formal stand on it, and there is no particular threat of having a decision forced upon the leadership by a faction. In other words, the Bauer, Pool, and Dexter findings here are stated as generalizations when they apply to groups in distributive policy but only distributive policy situations.

The natural interrelatedness of regulatory policy issues makes a different group pattern inevitable. Trade associations and other organized sectors of the economy achieve cohesion on the particular policies around which the group was formed, or they enjoy no cohesion at all. The interrelatedness of regulatory issues leads to the containment of all these "common interests" within the association and, therefore, to the dynamic situation erroneously ascribed by Truman to all groups and their internal processes under all situations. Regulatory issues bring out the common factor among constituents of any group, but they also can convert the group to a mass of brawling siblings. Constituents have little alternative but to fight against each other to shape through compromise and side payments the policy positions of that organization or actually to abandon the organization altogether.

Redistributive policy situations are a further extension of interrelatedness, but one which tends, superficially at least, to calm the waters. Class issues approach a level of generality that makes for a more peaceful relation among common interests. Interests such as antiwelfare state and antitax progressiveness are not likely to be in any organization with their opposites, except for ad hoc distributive politics where compatibility of interests is not required. The number of redistributive issues has been relatively small in U.S. history, but when a redistributive issue does emerge there will be high commonality, low internal conflict, *and* high cohesion. It's called class politics.

A look back over other studies will help to illustrate these points and to push the argument still further. First, how does the structure of a peak association alter from one type of issue (therefore one arena) to the next? Lane's data on the Manufacturers Association of Connecticut (MAC) provides an excellent opportunity to ask the question and to test the thesis.[15] The MAC is a large trade association claiming to "represent more than 95 percent of all industrial employees in Connecticut" as well as most public utilities.[16] In the ten-year period just before and after, but not including, the war years, the MAC represented its members in a variety of issues of national policy. In turning back to Table 1.1 we see a summary of how the MAC expressed itself during those years. Despite the fact that it is a trade association, the MAC did not concern itself equally with all federal matters affecting trade. Arranging Lane's data according to whether the policy was redistributive or regulative, the content analysis figures become particularly interesting because they fit the pattern predicted by the Arenas of Power scheme, and very strongly so. The MAC expressed itself overwhelmingly more frequently on redistributive than on regulative matters. This is true despite the fact that there were more policies of the latter type about which to express an opinion.[17] These differences are remarkable to those who take repetition as an index of intensity, but such an assumption, while tantalizing, is not necessary. It is less controversial and just as significant to assume (1) that a group expresses itself most frequently on matters closest to the center of its raison d'etre and (2) that among these the most frequent expressions will be a reflection of where the group can gain consensus.[18]

The data on total references become all the more interesting when seen in light of the other figures in the table. They add further meaning to pure and simple frequency. Note first the drastic contrast in the proportion of references that express approval. There are also clear differences in expressions of disapproval,[19] but more interesting still is the nature of the disapproval. When redistributive policies were denounced the one theme most often invoked was "coerciveness," the most damning of appellations in U.S. political rhetoric.[20] With the exception of the abstract "trade practices," there is a dramatic difference between the two categories of policy. For regulatory policies the reason most often given for disapproval was that the policy was confused and has failed to achieve its purpose.[21] And an almost equal proportion of negative responses regarding each regulatory policy were "residual" or "other" expressions too miscellaneous to warrant one or more additional categories. Even allowing for weaknesses in Lane's classification scheme, the figures in the residual category are extraordinary. Where high, they suggest a widespread lack of agreement as to the very meaning of the policy and how it could be defined for the members.

Data on the formal expressions of a group serve as manifestations of the internal processes of the group, in the above instance as an insight into the policy determinants of cohesion and integration. It is still better, however, if we can look into the little black box directly at the internal workings of groups. While it is not possible to reinterpret a mass of quantitative data like Lane's for these purposes, there are many case studies that can perform similarly in smaller numbers.

Intergroup Relations and the Arenas

Peak associations are to a great extent "holding companies" of groups with their own independent identities and organizations. Thus, much of what was said of the internal dynamics of peak associations is applicable also to questions of the external dynamics of more specialized groups *inside* the peak association. The variations from one policy arena to the next that are problems of *cohesion* from the standpoint of the association leadership are problems of *coalition* from the standpoint of group members. The peak association is obviously the result of a successful coalition of groups that lasts long enough to form a bureaucracy. Findings, therefore, about variations in cohesion contribute to the confirmation of hypotheses regarding coalitions and suggest a few new slants as well. The principle is that there are separate political processes in the three arenas that are shaped by and reflected in intergroup relations in a manner consistent with all other institutions and relations at all levels and stages of policymaking. The same factors that shape intragroup cohesion also influence the composition, breadth, and stability of external group relations, that is, coalitions. Thus the same questions of power and power structure apply to intragroup cohesion and to multigroup coalitions: Under what conditions are the separate resources of leaders additive when the leaders agree to coalesce? What are the limits on the size of coalitions? How long can resources remain combined, what separates them, and what sets limits on their uses? What consequences in political use of resources flow from different bases of coalition?

Once we know that a coalition has taken place and whether the coalition is unified, the questions on resource use are, of course, easier to answer. But, generally speaking, little attention has been given to the prior questions of what made the coalition possible. Treatment of this is usually by an inventory and discussion of the various techniques of coalition building—the How, not the Why, of the problem. Truman identifies two types of coalition—alliances and logrolling—and illustrates them with cases that suggest that there are fundamental differences of conditions for the two types. But they are treated as part of his inventory of group "techniques in the legislative process."[22] Lester Milbrath, following Truman, finds two main varieties of collaboration among Washington lobbyists, logrolling and "common interest";[23] but there is no suggestion at all as to the conditions for the one or the other type. Milbrath is aware that different consequences do flow from the one or the other, but in the absence of any data except those from his sample survey, his conclusions on collaboration verge on the truistic.[24] At one point, he does come close to a discussion of conditions, when he observes, "There seems to be an optimum level of problem generality suitable for collaboration; problems that are too specific or too general do not benefit much."[25] But he quickly falls back into the truistic and does not inquire into the "level of problem generality." And he offers nothing further on logrolling except the dubious suggestion that logrolling may not be effective because policymakers are skeptical of logrolling coalitions. But both authors do recognize that there are distinctions among coalitions, and where there is a distinction there might also be a difference.

Types of and Conditions for Coalition

The story of agricultural developments in politics ending in the 1930s, laid out in the next section, reveals certain vital conditions underlying group patterns. The ebb and flow of agriculture politics forces revision and sophistication of pluralist theory and helps in the discovery of limitations in its applicability. Agriculture politics began after the Civil War in alienated dispersion. Discovery of common irritants led to organization along various lines that by the beginning of World War I had brought agriculture to an improved political state of organized disunity. Various public policy solutions were pursued, but upon none was there a sufficient base for all-agriculture solidarity until the discovery of the tariff. When the all-agriculture coalition finally emerged, the distribution of power in the federal system was clearly altered. As the scope and variety of government intervention in agriculture expanded, the proportion of policies upon which an all-agriculture coalition is possible has gotten smaller and smaller. But the potential for unity remains as long as some policies can be logrolled. In the distributive arena, coalition building among agriculture interests has been possible, and it has insured a high degree of agriculture control—a kind of corporate self-regulation.

However, in the regulatory arena, agriculture groups outnumber all other groups where agriculture policy is concerned; yet there is no dominant coalition, and such seems impossible. Settlements have been unpredictable, centering in Congress. Redistributive issues in agriculture for the same reasons will be treated later in this chapter and in Chapters 7 and 10.

Judging from most of the cases reported in the group literature, it would be fair to say that all strategies are appropriate to all political games and that skill and chance determine which will be successful.[26] Since a single group or voting bloc can only rarely achieve its purposes it must extend its base of support through other groups and blocs. According to Truman, "the two principal forms of mutual assistance among interest groups are alliances and logrolling."[27] The Employment Act of 1946 is recognized as an alliance of an extraordinarily broad class base, with labor unions at the center, including many other spokespersons for "service-demanding," lower-income groups as well as the liberal intellectuals.[28] An alliance of an entirely different type is illustrated by the Fair Trade League, which combined the National Association of Retail Druggists with many organized retail groups for promoting resale price maintenance. For logrolling there is the familiar example of flood control and rivers and harbors development. (See especially Chapters 8 and 11.) But nowhere is it indicated that the success of a logroll or an alliance based on class interests (Employment Act) or on sector interests (fair trade) is limited to or in any way associated with the policies or with any other set of conditions. Truman suggests only that his two forms are "not always clearly separable and are normally supplementary,"[29] leaving the clear impression that the choice of strategy, therefore the question of how to relate to whom, is strictly up to the strategist.

Bertram Gross, second only to Truman in effective and influential use of group theory, seems to take a similar line of argument. His "campaign for support" involves friends, neutrals, and the opposition. There appear to be two types of friends, therefore, of support. *Vertical* support is support "within a given grouping," by which he can only mean a sector.[30] *Horizontal* support seems to be support among "friendly groups" without regard to the "vertical" dimension. His illustrations suggest that he means support within classes rather than sectors.[31] The appropriate pattern for getting support of neutrals and enemies is not suggested. In any case, Gross's "patterns of support" constitute only another inventory of the obvious steps available and necessary to participants. Gross's treatment of group relations is even less instructive than Truman's argument or analysis. Large coalitions beat small coalitions. Large coalitions are "a difficult task of social engineering";[32] just about anything is likely to be appropriate as long as it is within the very wide tolerance of the "rules of the game." Little wonder that power to a pluralist is so decentralized, fluid, and situational. There is just no differentiation.

A fresh look at some well-known aspects of U.S. political history, which comprises the bulk of this chapter, leads us to discount any assumption of the universality of any and all strategies or patterns of group relations. There is no need to argue in rebuttal that a certain policy "causes" a certain type of strategy or outcome in coalitions. It is just as significant for the theory and easier to support from the cases to argue that a policy determines the success of certain strategies over others, and that certain strategies bring about characteristic results in coalitions. Gross, Truman, and others are probably correct at one level in their implication that participants in the power struggle employ as many different strategies on as many different participants as their time and resources will allow. But if so, then it must also be said that some succeed and are further employed; others are dropped in failure. The result is a type of coalition characteristic of a type of strategy and, therefore, of a type of policy.

An interest leader would be foolish not to draft proposals so as to make them attractive to the most likely supporters. But it would be equally foolish to persist in this plan if the leader—say as representative of upper-middle-class independent department store owners—sought common company for "fair trade" laws with an equally upper-middle-class representative of discount store operators. Only certain kinds of proposals would in fact be attractive to others of this leader's own class if all other things were equal. But if the proposal was of that sort, there would probably be an existing class group ready to receive it or already working on it. Difficult as it is for Americans to accept, class interests are real interests; they are broad, perhaps diffuse, but no less real.[33] The peak associations, led by elements of Mills's power elite, have reality, but only in the redistributive arena, where the political structure is highly stabilized, virtually institutionalized. Interests are aggregated to the highest level possible in the group process—across broad classes. Only the legitimate institutions of government can aggregate interests any further. Thus, where peak associations are cohesive (and represent a coalition of groups of the same class) they are in fact functioning as major interest-aggregating structures in the polity. Resources are highly concentrated under these conditions, but they are concentrated on both sides of issues that almost always have only two sides. Impasse, or stable equilibrium, tends to be the result except in critical periods. For example, the bourgeoisie could not prevent establishment of the principle of government involvement in welfare, but the proletariat could not get more than a very mild element of real redistribution built into the programs. Liberals in the New Deal could get a Farm Credit Administration, but they could not for long maintain it as an instrument of Wallace's agriculture policy.[34] In the redistributive arena, then, the group structure is centralized toward a class. As a result of this pattern, the functioning of government agencies is distinctively different in the redistributive area of policy. In many respects the boards of directors of the peak associations perform functions in the redistributive arena that are performed by congressional committees in the distributive and by Congress in the regulatory. The role of administration, as will be seen, also varies accordingly.

In the distributive arena, the cases suggest that cohesion within organizations of single-firm members or highly specialized trade associations tends to be difficult to maintain; but fairly intense coalitions between and among these many small units tend to be fairly successful. It is for this reason necessary to insist that there is more than one basis of cohesion and type of coalition and that the differences are important. First, aggregation of interests along *class* lines fits established patterns of thought that are around long enough to be part of an ideology. *The existence of ideology both reflects a stable power structure and contributes to the maintenance of that structure by legitimizing it.* Second, at the farthest extreme, is the nature of relationships in *distributive* politics. A coalition is possible among virtually any set of interests, within or across classes, sectors, or regions. The result can be quite stable, like the Rivers and Harbors Congress, or relatively transitory, like the farm bloc. But either way this second aggregation process is not accurately described as interest articulation *or* aggregation. As in chemistry, *it should be called a suspension rather than a solution.* At the national level relations among interests dealing in distributive policies, as will be seen, have tended to find ultimate lodging in the congressional committee system. As Truman put it, "Logrolling is a form of trading operation for which access is the coin."[35] Ultimate access to patronage in policy had always been in the committees, and the interests enjoying access have conspired to keep it that way. In general, then, it is in the nature of relationships in distributive politics to perpetuate existing elites, because conflict can be either avoided altogether or bought off.[36]

The third—but not a middle between the two extremes—is the type of relationship to be found in the regulatory arena. Some elements of both of the above types can be found. And in fact, logrolling is the strategy of coalition that is sought, because it might avoid or finesse the conflict inherent in regulatory issues. But regulatory policy turns out to be an environment quite inhospitable to logrolling. A *regulatory* policy issue cannot be disaggregated into multiples of units that can be bargained over without having to enter into the substance of the issue. Thus, the contestants in regulatory policy issues have to confront each other over the merits, even to the point of having to rewrite and revise policy drafts in hopes of keeping a coalition close to a majority vote in the legislature, and to hold that coalition together just long enough to vote for passage. And the problem of keeping such a conflicted coalition together throughout the long legislative process involves very heavy transaction costs, but at the same time is highly creative. *This describes the pluralist's model exactly,* and its beauty as a model of "creative democracy" inspires belief among political scientists that this is the standard American model.

Chapter 5 demonstrates through the different characterizations of Franklin D. Roosevelt how markedly the policy caused the politics. Each biographer of Roosevelt characterized the real secret of FDR's leadership according to the policy lens through which FDR was seen. The account here builds upon the conclusions of Chapter 5. There is much more to follow in this chapter.

A Key Case: The Farm Bloc and Coalition Building

Ever since the takeoff of U.S. economic development, agriculture has been outside the mainstream. Agriculture remained decentralized and dispersed in the face of industrial concentration. Agriculture became part of the money economy through a transportation system not of its own making, in a market very much under the control of nonagricultural interests. Being out of joint with the economy, agriculture interests became organized relatively early and turned quickly to politics and government to get help in overcoming their disadvantages relative to the other forms of economic endeavor. Before the heyday of the organized pressure group a little organization went a long way. Basic agriculture needs were reflected first by Congress in land grant and homesteading acts, followed by a host of federal services such as research, productivity, and education. But these were only palliatives, not solutions. Further distress led to bolder organizing and bolder demands. One set of demands was for the redistribution of wealth toward agriculture. Cheap money and cheaper credit provided the basis for a vigorous farmer movement, first through groups such as the Grange and the much larger Farmers' Alliance, and later in local and state political parties. Unfortunately, no farmer movement could really be sustained on class issues because farmers were not a peasantry and therefore not a single class. The farmer-based Greenback party lasted eight years (1876–1884). The People's, or Populist, party was formed on the same principles between 1888 and 1890, and died in a short but splendid decade. It was swallowed up by one of the major political parties because only a major party could deal across an entire agricultural sector.

A second set of demands made equally vigorously by farmer spokesmen was for direct regulation of those economic forces identified as the cause of the agriculture problem: the grain dealers and other processors, the railroads, the banks, and the exchanges. Because these energies were easy to identify, the regulatory approach had the advantage of uniting farmer interests without regard to differences in wealth. But the forces of separation and division were stronger. In agriculture this meant the *commodity,* and the organization of commodity interests arose faster than the proposals and schemes for sectorwide regulation could be invented. From the 1890s onward, as more farmers were organized in more ways, the natural dispersion and diversity of interest in agriculture became more manifest. At the critical moment in recent agriculture history—the end of World War I—organization and fragmentation were both at their greatest extreme. For example, the corn interest alone was represented by at least the twenty major organizations that met later, in 1925, as the Grain Belt Federation of Farm Organizations (better known as the Corn Belt Committee).[37] Many of these were specifically corn organizations; others had a major interest in corn along with one or more commodities as well (which meant that some could not be "whole hog" on corn alone because of overlapping memberships). Many of the latter type were, in fact, the state affiliates of a national federation (the Grange, Farmers Union, and, most important, the Farm Bureau Federation); but within these, corn could not always come first. This list of separate corn-based organizations fairly represents the state of the agricultural union-without-unity on the eve of the McNary-Haugen era.

The so-called McNary-Haugen bills embodied a simple scheme for the realization of "parity," a new term for equality of income as between agriculture and industry. To the McNary-Haugenites, led by businessman George N. Peek, agriculture prices were out of line with industry because industry was able to control prices and agriculture was not. Industry could maintain high prices at home and protect itself with tariffs on lower priced goods from abroad. In contrast domestic agriculture prices were determined by world prices because of the infernal "surplus"; that is, if prices were pegged higher than the world price, not all of a commodity could clear the market at home or abroad. So, the solution was to "make the tariff work for agriculture."[38] At no time did Peek and his associates ever question protectionism. But also at no time did they consider acceptance of production control, the sine qua non of business price control. This meant a solution through a government-supported marketing device. An export corporation, capitalized at a large sum, would be created to purchase crops at a "parity" (1910–1914) price when an emergency was declared, and to sell abroad at whatever price the market would bear. A high tariff wall would be erected to prevent imports attracted by the high domestic prices. The export corporation would deal with each commodity in terms of the most favorable treatment it could get in the tariff schedules against the competitive imports. An "equalization fee," a tax, on farmers would pay for a proportion of the costs of administration.

The McNary-Haugen bill started with wheat, but the important factor was that it could be simultaneously particularized and universalized with no difficulty. At first the campaign was diffuse, spontaneous, and unorganized. Even so, the first attempt, in June 1924, received, in defeat, over 40 percent of the votes in the House. Following the first attempt, Peek managed to organize an American Council of Agriculture (ACA) to coordinate warring commodity and regional groups. Due to falling prices and an adjustment of the new proposal even closer to a purely tariff device, Peek was able to bring tobacco, corn, and hogs into the ACA.[39] Peek had never been happy about making the proposal a mere "wheat bill."[40] By early 1925 another association had been formed, the Corn Belt Committee, cited earlier, with Peek's American Council as an affiliate. By late 1925 there were All-Iowa, All-Kansas, and many other "All-State" federations of agricultural groups, many of which were supported by state banker and other local or state business associations. In early 1926, Peek turned from corn successes to cotton: "We told the cotton people to write their own ticket, change the proposal in any way they wanted to and that we would cooperate with them in getting what they wanted in return for their cooperation in helping us get what we want."[41] The adjustment removed almost every trace of regulation by deferring the so-called equalization fee for cotton and by providing for a special loan fund for co-ops. The second attempt at legislation was defeated the following June, but the increased Southern vote, while not militant, showed progress.

Two events of 1926 provided those last elements necessary for creation of a unified farm bloc. The first was a drop in cotton prices by more than one half of the 1925 price. This not only made militants out of the hitherto Southern cotton moderates but worked as a bandwagon effect on rice interests as well. The second event was the adding of a new device to the bill, designed to bring in the tobacco interests. This was the creation of a farmer council for each commodity in each federal land bank district where over 50 percent of the agricultural produce was in a particular commodity. Council consent would be required before the national marketing board could act.[42] This maximized the control of each commodity by the organized commodity groups. Starting with the Rice Farmers' Credit Association of Crowley, Louisiana, rice, cotton, and tobacco organizations joined in, one by one. All the leaders met in St. Louis on November 16, 1926, and adopted resolutions supporting a new but only slightly modified version of McNary-Haugen. The "farm bloc" was born.

McNary-Haugen never became law, but that makes no difference to the moral of our story: "It is doubtful if farm leaders in the United States had ever before demonstrated greater unanimity in their demands."[43] In February 1927, McNary-Haugen Number Four passed the Senate by a 47 to 39 vote, and the House by 214 to 178. Within the week President Coolidge returned the bill with a veto message unusually long and acrimonious for so reticent a man. One year later, McNary-Haugen Number Five was passed, vetoed, and failed of passage over veto by a scant four votes in the Senate. The farm bloc did not have a broad enough electoral base to capture the presidency (at least not in 1924 and 1928), but they had at least hit upon one mechanism for building up a unified farm movement and a congressional majority: logrolling.

Logrolling had made the farm bloc possible. Thus, the farm bloc is an excellent illustration of the "logrolling technique." But that is only part of the story, and, once said, a relatively obvious point. What makes the story significant is that it helps identify *the conditions under which disparate interests can use logrolling to unify their efforts and expand the influence of each member of the coalition.* The truth seems to be, then, that while logrolling made the farm bloc possible, the tariff made logrolling possible. It allowed for a fusion among groups that had tried and fallen short of fusion many times before. *Redistribution* of wealth had failed to provide a unifying focus during the many years of its popularity between the 1880s and 1912. *Regulation* of utilities and transportation was associated in cause and effect with the rise of militant commodity groups, but these developments were politically even more inconsistent with a broadly based farmer movement than were the redistributive foci of cheap money and cheap and secure credit. Only a policy like the traditional tariff could have brought about an all-agriculture coalition. Even at the end in 1927 some of the members of the bloc were still unhappy because the tariff mechanism was not ideal for them. Cotton, for example, was more favorable toward the co-ops and loans that would help restrict production to the demands of the domestic market (which later became a central feature of the Agricultural Adjustment Administration [AAA]). But crop regulation did not appeal to Midwest producers of foodstuffs. Only the tariff could be universalized.[44]

Tariff is not the only possible base for all-agriculture coalition formation and maintenance; and, as so often stressed in these pages, it is of a type that includes far from a majority of conceivable policies. Evidence for both parts of this contention can be found in the New Deal period and afterward. The farm bloc lasted through the 1928 and 1932 elections, but it quickly declined into dissolution as it became clear that its new patrons, the Democratic leaders, were not committed to McNary-Haugen principles. Because of his services in the Smith and Roosevelt campaigns, George Peek became an insider after 1932. But there was a bitter agriculture battle within the family, and it centered upon the difference between Peek's "making the tariff work for agriculture" and the Wallacite's production control (regulatory) formula. There was absolute continuity of goals; there remained almost total agreement that (1) government power should be used and (2) that it be used to manipulate prices.[45] But once the regulatory factor in the new parity program was introduced, the end of agriculture unity, so recently gained, was near. Peek, who represented agriculture unity, was made the first administrator of the Agricultural Adjustment Administration; but this was the wages of defeat rather than victory. It was Wallace's effort to create an impression of peace when real peace was no longer possible.[46] In the ensuing years, peace within organized agriculture was maintained not in a unified bloc but literally in a "separation of powers."[47] Interests represented early in the Farm Bureau leadership split off from the Democratic party. On redistributive policies such as easy farm credit, AFBF provides active opposition, far from being a "spokesman for agriculture." As the lineal descendant of the farm bloc of the 1920s, AFBF seems to be unified and at the center of agriculture consensus *only* upon the maintenance of the privileged sanctuaries of governmental services, the distributive policies.[48] This is not to suggest AFBF "control," but only a cohesive holding company of many farm coalitions. However, when unified it can obviously be a formidable creature. The "separation of powers" denotes the remnants and fragments of the farm bloc that enjoy access in other, separate programs. Commodity groups create a pluralist spectacle in the parity and other regulatory programs. Such associations as Farmers Union cut across commodity groups in their activity on behalf of (redistributive) tenancy and credit programs and provide a unified, opposing voice to AFBF and its nonfarm allies on these programs.

The Last Traditional Tariff: A Postscript

Preparations for what was to be the last traditional tariff were under way immediately following candidate Hoover's campaign promises for a special session on agricultural relief. Having vetoed a succession of McNary-Haugen bills, the Republicans had become vulnerable to charges that the tariff protected business at the expense of agriculture. The House Ways and Means Committee took this promise to mean full-dress revision of the 1922 tariff and announced the opening of hearings for January 7, 1929. The committee had less than three months of the lame duck Congress to complete the tariff bill and to present it to the special session in April.

The Ways and Means Committee gave general public notice that hearings were to be held. The committee specified the place and hour of the hearings, the procedure by which interested persons might apply for time, and the form for writing briefs. But it gave no specific guidance as to the aims of the hearings or to its schedule. In fact, there was no proposed bill to help give the hearings a focus or to provide a basis whereby the testimony of one witness might be related to that of other witnesses. The working bill was simply the Tariff of 1922, as amended; the eventual bill was to be a committee bill. Following the announcement of hearings, the committee simply waited for all interested parties to apply for time and present briefs. And as the hearings proceeded, the interested parties were left to themselves to find out what the committee was up to, what other witnesses were proposing, and how the proposals of each witness affected other interests.

Thus, the hearings were strictly a matter of the relationship of the committee to each one of the hundreds of separate witnesses and interests. The committee took up the tariff schedule by schedule and item by dutiable item, with each item and "basket clause" being considered on its own merits in total isolation from other items. Schattschneider is particularly impressed with the deference between committee and witness. The hearings seemed to amount to a survey of "What do you think?" "Would it suit you if there were a specific duty of eleven-and-a-half cents?" "Would you be satisfied if Congress should adopt this in principle?" In this manner, hundreds of witnesses were heard and over 11,000 pages of testimony were taken between January 7 and February 17. The cross-questioning revealed no effort to relate the testimony of one witness to that of any other, making it possible to take 64 witnesses on one day, 44 on another, and so on. Of equal importance was the fact that the committee relied almost totally upon the testimony of the tariff-seeking witnesses for the information upon which the specific tariff decisions were to be made. Estimates of the number of tariff items in the final bill range from 15,000 to over 100,000 depending upon how the "basket clauses" are handled. These, plus the 11,000 pages of testimony and supporting data, were reviewed and assessed by a committee staff of one clerk and two assistants.

Between the end of the lame duck session and the special session in late April, the fifteen Republican members of the Ways and Means Committee met in fifteen subcommittees of three members each (each member, therefore, getting service as a subcommittee chairman) and wrote the bill. At no time did the Democratic committee members take part. On May 7, 1929, a 200-page bill with a 2,700-page summary was introduced in the House by Chairman Hawley. On being read it was returned to the committee; officially the bill was now in the hands of the committee for the first time. The committee promptly reported the bill to the House, following a strict party vote. Under its traditional closed rule, the bill proceeded through the House without parliamentary mishap and was passed three weeks later exactly as it had come from committee.

In the Senate the bill ran into trouble. Hearings before the Finance Committee and the executive sessions of the committee were as friendly and secretive as they had been in the House. But the many commodity interests without access to the Republican committee members in either House found an opportunity on the Senate floor. Debate was bitter and sufficiently broad to delay passage until the 1930 regular session. Final success came not with revision of schedules or existing items, however; nor did it come as a result of any general revision of the "policy" of protection. Rather, *it came through the addition of many new items to the schedules.*

Traditional tariff-making is clearly not a case of pluralism in the strictest sense, nor is it a case of "power elite." The policy underlying the bill was never an issue; thus it was never an object of conflict and compromise. The policy of protection was purely and simply an accumulation of thousands of individual, isolated decisions that, after the fact, appear to be a policy of protection. There were no "interest groups" in the strictest sense. The peak associations were silent, but so were the special interest groups. Tariff-making has been a case of every man for himself and every firm for itself—practically every farm for itself. The Ways and Means Committee constituted an elite, and every participant was supportively related to the committee or was relatively easily co-opted at one stage or another. The role of debate on the floor of the House was minimal, as was the role of interest groups and coalitions forged out of compromises. If the committee-*qua*-elite had any trouble, it was on the Senate floor, but even here the *definition* of the policy, in terms of what general impact the act was to have, was never touched. The Senate was simply an additional route of access for individuals to the committee. The executive branch also had no role. The most outstanding features of tariff-making were as follows: the extreme fragmentation of the arena, the contrasting stability of the committee as a leadership group, and the absence of the classic interest group–Congress interplay. The most outstanding feature of tariff as a policy was the ease with which it could be disaggregated into separate, isolated units. The consequences of this kind of a policy, and therefore the relations among all participants that it brings about, are clear, compelling, and politically significant.

The Chamber of Commerce, the NAM, and the Group Process

The Chamber and the New Tariff: A Review

One of the most interesting test cases is the development of foreign trade policy in the 1950s and the consequent or associated changes in the group process around foreign trade politics. This section highlights the patterns first observed in Chapter 2. The traditional tariff was the classic case of distributive policy and politics. However, following World War II, U.S. relations with the rest of the world slowly brought about changes in the function of the tariff. As the function changed, so did its definition in the eyes of the policymakers and so did the nature of the threat to the organized participants. The traditional tariff was essentially a manipulation of international markets to suit domestic political and economic purposes. The traditional tariff was an ideal instrument of patronage because most burdens could be displaced abroad. Beginning with reciprocity in the 1930s, the tariff slowly, and not clearly until after World War II, underwent a redefinition. On becoming an instrument of foreign policy, with our assumption of world leadership, the tariff slowly became a means of regulating the domestic economy for foreign political and economic purposes. And the significant feature here is not the international aspect but the *regulatory* aspect of the redefinition. This process was slow, because the highly particularized traditional tariff schedules remained tariff law and, therefore, the basis of negotiations between outside interests and government. But by the mid-1950s, our having to deal with and having to be continually involved with whole countries and their total outputs in relation to ours was having its impact on tariff. It required a more consistent treatment of many dutiable items, perhaps even simultaneous treatment. It was becoming less and less possible for individual firms and combinations of firms around miniscule interests to carry on business as usual in politics. In other words, as the process of redefinition took place, a number of significant shifts in power relations took place as well, because the *nature* of the redefinition rendered no longer possible the treatment of each dutiable item totally in isolation from the others.[49] Redefinition culminated in the 1962 Trade Act, in which Smoot-Hawley was laid to rest and was replaced by a statute empowering the president to negotiate on broad categories of goods.

The Chamber of Commerce was one group whose response to changes in the nature of the tariff was clear. Like most heterogeneous groups the chamber had generally followed a policy of "quasi-unanimity" on the tariff in bygone years. In the 1930s the chamber's silence could be counted upon in tariff issues. In the early 1950s during the first post-Hull reciprocity crises the chamber supported the liberal position, but weakly enough to be considered still silent. Chamber affiliates, both local and industry, were free to pursue their respective individual courses very much without regard to U.S. Chamber of Commerce policy.

By 1962, however, the chamber faced a new tariff, and the tariff produced a new chamber. Once again the chamber leadership in its Foreign Commerce Committee endorsed the liberal position, the Kennedy program. This decision was upheld by the board of directors on the grounds that they were merely reaffirming the general resolutions accepted at past annual conventions. The legislative representatives so testified during the late winter and early spring of 1962. However, in May, at the fiftieth annual convention, solidarity was, to say the very least, shaken. No longer was peace preserved by the simple device of particularization. Controversy over tariff policy became fully contained within the chamber, and overlapping membership began to work according to the predictions of Truman rather than those of his critics. An unusual two-hour floor debate ensued, and an even more rare repudiation of the national leadership took place in the rejection of the official resolution. Much later, when many delegates had retired, a motion to reconsider was passed, saving the directors of a most ignominious defeat.[50] Long and short staple cotton and wool—production and processing—had become "textiles" for the first time where tariff is concerned. Coal, oil, and rails had come closer together within sectors. More importantly, it was impossible any longer to avoid confrontation among many if not all parties interested in tariff. Try as they did to avoid internal stresses, the Chamber of Commerce failed and became for the moment a tired but true functional equivalent of Congress. In interviews, one chamber official said, "We finally got a stand on the Trade Act, but it cost us thousands of dollars in memberships. The only way an organization like ours can exist is to be sure that policy positions flow from the bottom up. We don't speak otherwise." But it is not possible to be permissive on some issues. Permissiveness and logrolling are possible on highly individualized policies, such as the traditional tariff and the 1960s Area Redevelopment Administration (ARA), but not possible on most regulatory policies. Bottom-up strategies are not necessary in redistributive issues because there is *actual* rather than apparent unanimity.

NAM—Different Group, Same Problem

The same is true of NAM, which has been united around basic class issues throughout its life. And they have been basically the same issues, manifest in the same forms, treated by the same symbols.[51] There has always been unanimity in NAM on the general objectives of (1) reducing the relative advantages of organized labor and (2) reducing the tax and regulatory burdens on industry and industrial profits. And this cohesion based on agreed goals has been supported by public relations campaigns of fear regarding hostile economic and social groups, the "isms" from abroad, and loss of individual status.[52] Like the U.S. Chamber of Commerce, NAM develops policy appropriate for the day through the "bottoms-up" procedure. Policy positions are developed slowly through the fourteen policy committees that are served by full-time experts in each area. If adopted by one of the fourteen committees, the position must then be accepted by the board of directors by a two-thirds vote. On this basis, NAM was accustomed to taking no position on tariffs. NAM did not exist insofar as the traditional tariff was concerned. But by the 1950s even to remain silent on tariff became a critical decision. Strong postwar forces within NAM were pushing not only for a position but a liberal trade position at that. In 1953, facing the first Eisenhower renewal bill, a liberal proposal was pushed all the way up to the NAM Board of Directors. Only a resignation threat by some of the members could put the stop to the resolution and keep NAM silent and "quasi-unanimous." Thinking back over the 1962 Trade Act in 1964, one NAM official said of the membership, "A third are protectionist, a third are liberal and a third don't give a damn." With NAM, as with the chamber, the new kind of tariff made overlapping membership a problem rather than an advantage. On traditional tariffs (and other distributive policies) NAM is a sleeping giant, powerful only in the eyes of its adversaries. On redistributive policies it is a true peak association whose leaders constitute a stable, long-standing elite. On regulatory policies, NAM reveals the true heterogeneity and diversity of and capacity for conflict within the industrial community.

Where Were Groups in the Social Security Act?[53]

As the 1934 elections approached, pressures for social security began to mount and to focus on the national government. The Townsend Plan, the Lundeen Bill, Upton Sinclair's End Poverty in California (EPIC), Huey Long's "theory of democracy," and others were gathering widespread support. Tugwell and other insiders report that the president had already become enthusiastic for some permanent system of welfare as part of a "Second New Deal" step away from emergency measures. All of the popular proposals were severely redistributive, aiming to give all citizens access to government support as a matter of right.

In June 1934, the president created a Committee on Economic Security (CES) composed of top cabinet members, to be chaired by Secretary of Labor Perkins. The CES set up an elaborate advisory mechanism both to represent major interests and to carry out technical studies and drafting. A Technical Board was created to carry out the studies, but the members of this board assisted the CES in running the Advisory Council, the more "representative" body. The Advisory Council was composed mainly of expert spokesmen for industry and labor. The former were drawn largely from companies such as GE, Standard Oil, and Eastman, which had already experimented with insurance plans. Labor members were drawn from the Executive Council of AFL and from three state labor federations. The Technical Board, composed primarily of intellectuals and experts drawn from government agencies and universities, was the working component of the Committee on Economic Security.

In September 1934, the Technical Board began its "study phase." Massive studies were undertaken by board members, a host of staff experts, and members of expert advisory committees to the board on medicine, public health, child welfare, and the like. In addition, the board actually held hearings as well as an open conference of invited persons in Washington. During the fall of 1934, the Advisory Council as well as the Technical Board debated the reports and the policy recommendations in the reports. A number of the most significant controversies were settled at this stage (including the relationship between the national and state governments, which was embodied in the final act). Finally, on January 17, 1935, the Committee on Economic Security emerged with a *fully drafted bill*, which had been written entirely by the Technical Board. This is a very different kind of political process, mostly to be experienced in redistributive policymaking.

To this point the activity and "pressure" of interest groups were minor, particularly when one considers the importance of the issues involved. Except for the continuing agitation of the more radical groups, the debate was contained within the CES, its committees and boards, and the several tax and welfare bureaucracies. This apparent quiescence continued. Although the president now had an elaborate and well-studied bill, not all of the most important issues had been settled, and virtually all the unsettled ones had to do with how redistributive the social security system was to be. (For example, the Treasury feared that the tax schedule proposed for Old Age and Survivors Insurance [OASI] would by 1965 result in a large deficit that would have to be covered out of general revenues. More on this directly.) When the executive faces Congress without a unified position on a controversial proposal, the way is clear for free and open congressional and interest group access, and the legislative process is likely to be free, open, and protracted. The startling thing about the social security bill, with its vast importance and so many issues yet to be resolved, was that neither Congress nor the most interested groups seemed to be intensely involved.

The bill was introduced by Robert F. Wagner (NY) in the Senate and David Lewis (MD) and R. L. Doughton (GA) in the House. Immediately, jurisdictional conflicts arose in both chambers between the revenue committees and the labor committees. With support from the White House, the bill was assigned in short order to the more conservative Ways and Means and Finance Committees. In the Senate there was no opposition to assignment to the Finance Committee. In the House, members of the Education and Labor Committee bitterly objected to the Speaker's decision and later expressed their displeasure by reporting out the more liberal Lundeen bill.[54] But this was not the end of the "legislative struggle." Hearings on the House Ways and Means bill began on January 21, before the Senate Finance Committee on January 22, continuing until February 12 and 20 respectively. The hearings in both chambers were dominated by administration spokesmen and "government witnesses"—most of whom had been connected with CES. Other important witnesses were well-chosen business spokesmen. (For example, the National Retail Dry Goods Association spokesman vigorously supported the program.) NAM and various state manufacturers' associations appeared in opposition, but the most outspoken opposition came from the Left, not the Right, with Dr. Townsend (inventor of the Radical Townsend Plan) and Earl Browder (leader of the American Communist party) out front. Generally speaking, the Ways and Means hearings seem to have been simply part of a campaign to build up support for social security.

Nearly two months of executive sessions following the close of hearings produced one major and a few minor changes in the original bill. The major change was one proposed during the hearings by Secretary of the Treasury Morgenthau. This was a proposal to put the old age insurance on a strictly "self-supporting" basis (1) by providing smaller annuities to those who retired in the first thirty years, (2) by starting the rates of contribution at a higher level (1 percent each from employer and employee rather than half that amount), and (3) by scheduling the increase of rates to rise more rapidly to a maximum of 7 percent rather than to 5 percent. The minor changes, arising out of the committee itself, involved such things as exempting certain industries from coverage and exempting all employers of ten employees or less. Again these were aimed at expanding support of the bill, primarily among southerners. On the House floor, all amendments and substitutes were resoundingly defeated, and at the end of aimless debate the bill passed 371 to 33 in the form submitted by Ways and Means.

The only significant change contributed by the Senate was an amendment by Senator Joel Bennett Clark (MO) authorizing the substitution of private pension plans, with certain safeguards, for the OASI.

The Clark amendment brought about the only vigorous debate in the Senate. It was accepted 51 to 35. The bill with the Clark and some lesser amendments was passed, 76 to 6. In conference, the Clark amendment was eliminated after presidential pressure was exerted. To placate the Southern Democrats, extra flexibility was devolved to the states by the Senate version. In return, the Senate conferees yielded to the House on a vital administrative point by eliminating a provision added by the Finance Committee to place the Social Security Board in the Department of Labor. This was the final defeat of the liberal forces, the creation of an autonomous and independent welfare bureaucracy.

The legislative process was unusually quiet in the face of the first great "welfare state" decision. It was quiet because in all probability the real battles had been and were taking place on other arenas, essentially within the CES between Treasury and the Hopkins-Perkins bureaucracies. The major conservatizing amendments to the original proposals were those offered by Morgenthau and the Treasury Department. Most of the effective lobbying on the liberal side was done by or through the Department of Labor. For example, during the days when the Ways and Means Committee was in executive session, Secretary Perkins had the CES set up a meeting of prominent supporters to draft and sign a public statement.

Nothing epitomizes the nature of the struggle better than the issue of placement and control of the Social Security Board. At various times it was wholly within Labor, then parceled out among several agencies within the Department of Labor and the Federal Relief Administration, then all of a piece to Labor but without any powers granted to the Secretary, and finally, given independence and autonomy. Throughout all of this some public expressions could be heard from interest groups, but they were mainly confined to the roles played by their very upper-class spokesmen *within the quieter proceedings of the bureaucracies.* Congress's role seems largely to have been one of settling issues and ratifying agreements that arose out of the bureaucracies and between the bureaucrats and the representatives of the peak associations and other broad class interests. Many of the peak associations and "catalytic" groups—such as NAM, the American Medical Association (AMA), and religious and welfare organizations—devoted great energy to some of the specialized titles (aid to dependent children, child welfare services, maternal care). But here, too, the eventual compromises were worked out between these groups and the staff of the CES and Technical Board.

Out of this detailed case study arises a profoundly important distinction: *the move from agricultural and tariff politics to welfare politics is a move from particularistic, log-rolling pluralism to C. Wright Mills's power elite.*

Labor Policy and the Conditions of Labor Unity

In the passage of the Taft-Hartley Act one finds a third distinct political process and power structure: the *classic pluralistic* model. The legislative committees play a central role. But because in regulatory policies committees cannot contain all disagreement, debate and coalition building dominate policymaking. Even the executive is pluralized. And interest groups appear to speak as a single voice, as effective appliers of pressure. While there is a role for representatives of individual corporations, the trade associations and other special interest groups are more prominent. On the other hand, although the business elites and big peak associations play a more prominent role here in regulatory policy than in tariff and related struggles, they are far from uniformly cohesive or effective. Yet, the business peak associations were more cohesive than were AFL and CIO. Why? The answer helps clarify the distinction between the politics of redistributive policies and regulatory policies. For business the issue was one of redistribution—a general rollback of the Wagner Act. In contrast, AFL and CIO could maintain a general class position only as long as it could maintain a massive negative ("don't turn the clock back") position. But that strategy failed to hold labor together as a movement because such *regulatory* matters as jurisdictional strikes, secondary boycotts, the closed shop, and the new list of unfair labor practices hit each union in each sector of the economy in a different way. The labor peak associations were unable to find any positive positions around which all constituent groups could rally.

The Department of Labor and the National Labor Relations Board (NLRB), like labor itself, opposed the Taft-Hartley bill and favored the veto, but were not able to agree on a common argument to offer advice to the president as to how the veto message was to be constructed, along with what kind of an administration bill should be offered afterward. President Truman was left alone with his close White House staff, and even they were unable to agree on a unified position.[55]

There is diversity in labor, particularly organized labor, but the true extent of that diversity was masked until the legal position of organized labor was established and the social status of labor unions and labor spokesmen was substantially improved. In brief, AFL and CIO—merged or separate—are not, strictly speaking, trade associations but are better understood as peak associations. They have all the same problems and pathologies as business peak associations. And the conditions for cohesion are essentially the same. There is no study comparable to Lane's on union leader statements, but all available evidence points to similar patterns and stresses. Andrew Biemiller's observation, quoted earlier, bears repeating: as much as 80–90 percent of the formal expressions of his organization and a like amount of his own time were devoted to welfare policies and general rights of collective bargaining. Only occasionally does the central labor bureaucracy touch upon specific labor regulatory issues. Bauer, Pool, and Dexter noted that the big unions followed the pattern of "quasi-unanimity" on tariffs just as did big business.[56] In contrast, minimum wage is associated with quite high cohesion, despite regional and sector variations. Minimum wage has been so uniting, in fact, that there had been a special joint AFL-CIO committee on the subject long before merger. It was a factor in the success of the merger.

In 1935, when national labor was weak, the Wagner Act, the most important piece of labor legislation in U.S. history, was passed. In 1947, at the height of union membership, wealth, recognition, and access, the restrictive Taft-Hartley Act was passed. At the time, this was posed as a conundrum: "The Taft-Hartley example ... seems to contradict the adage that political power follows economic power."[57] Many explanations could be offered, post hoc. But one factor could have predicted it, a priori: the substance of the two bills as they were proposed and pushed through the policymaking process; Wagner was redistributive policy—to establish the laboring class as a legal and protected entity. Taft-Hartley, for organized labor, was regulatory policy, not "labor laws" but "labor *union* laws." For business it was redistributive, or we should say *re-redistributive.*[58]

As I have stressed before, whether a policy is distributive, regulatory, or redistributive is objective, a priori, to be known by reading proposals and understanding statutes and rules. It is not merely in the eye of the beholder. It is jurisprudence. When new issues arise, the participants have a share in shaping the very substance of the issue and also have some influence over how the issue will be understood. That may be the major function of interest groups. However, once the nature and substance of the issue are settled, then try as they may as a matter of strategy to extend their support, *leaders cannot for long define an issue as something it is not.* In 1935, management and labor defined the Wagner Act as a class issue; since it was in fact class legislation, the definition could provide the basis for broad, class-based relations. For labor, Wagner was redistributive. There were indeed some regulatory features, but these were, for labor, far outweighed by laws of recognition. The class factor was reaffirmed by the Supreme Court, in *NLRB v. Jones & Laughlin Steel Corp.* The regulatory part of Wagner was addressed exclusively to business, as a set of relatively severe "unfair labor practices." In contrast Taft-Hartley, for labor, was regulatory, its principal substance a list of "unfair practices" equivalent to those imposed on employers in Wagner.

Policy Decisions and Arenas of Power

To study the politics of policy and policy formulation without losing hold of the realities, the use of case studies cannot be avoided. Policies have to be initiated, squabbled over, resolved, enacted, and implemented. Each phase of a complex policy decision—the relation of each phase to the other phases, the identities and strategies of all participants—can be understood only in context. There are better and worse case studies. But either way, the case method, with all of the advantages it offers in capturing reality, suffers one debilitating problem: the problem of uniqueness. To what extent and in what manner do the patterns revealed in one case apply to all cases? Or, toward what class of cases does the single case apply?

Each of the cases reported throughout the book tends to support some aspect of theory. In fact, most case study authors either devote their conclusion to confirmation or refutation to an existing theory or will try to formulate a new theory of their own. All of that is to the good, but it just does not go far enough. It provides an escape from uniqueness, but toward what? Although each case may support one theory, it is an exception to all other theories. For example, my four arenas of power have brought together in logical relation four theories of power. If a case is confirmation of one of those theories, it is an exception three-fourths of the time. To put it another way, any theory will be very strong (almost a genuine predictive, scientific theory) for one-fourth of all the cases and wrong or very weak three-fourths of the time. In sum, *each theory of politics becomes a theory of just one arena.* The arena that develops around distributive policies is best captured by Schattschneider's generalizations about fragmentation, patronage, and party—though he never formalized his argument into a theory. (His generation of empiricists did not encourage or reward theory.) The regulatory arena has been elaborately if not exhaustively captured or confirmed by pluralist theory. The redistributive arena is quite satisfactorily captured, or at least solidly confirmed, by elitist, neo-Marxist theory.[59]

Two concluding points: First, the Arenas of Power model strengthens political theory by defining and delineating the limits of applicability of every generalization. No theory is mature until it can recognize the limits of its applicability. Second, the Arenas of Power scheme strengthens immensely the prospects of scientific, empirical validity of policymaking case studies by providing a method of logical classification of cases and other data according to the type of policy (or mission of the agency) at stake. This classification guides each case study toward the environment of policy within which it is taking place. The Arenas of Power scheme is a methodology for determining *what each case is a case of.*

CHAPTER 10

Policy Choices and Political Consequences

The Case of Population Control

It is the fate of government to deal with many problems for which there are no acceptable human solutions. Population growth may prove to be a case in point. Demographers can plot the curves and identify the correlates, but population pressure is at bottom a problem of political economy, and in this respect Malthus continues to have the last word.

Yet, even if there are few theoretic guidelines, future governments will probably experiment on a large scale with population growth policies. Modern man rejects being a mere creature of his environment. He often demands and rarely rejects the right of his government to make authoritative decisions about how he, and his neighbor, shall live. One of the first distinctly modern philosophers, David Hume, put the case this way:

> Two neighbors may agree to drain a meadow, which they possess in common: because it is easy for them to know each other's mind; and each must perceive, that the immediate consequence of his failing in his part, is the abandoning of the whole project. But it is very difficult, and indeed impossible, that a thousand persons should agree in any such action; ... each seeks a pretext to free himself of the trouble and expense, and would lay the whole burden on others. Political society easily remedies both these inconveniences.[1]

If, as is probable, the future brings a significant expansion of governmental policies to control population growth, these policies could have a serious impact upon the political system. And this is possible even if the policies failed to make a dent in the population growth profile itself. The impact of population growth policies on the American political system could be particularly significant for at least three reasons. First, the population field is more vast than any domestic sphere into which the Federal government has ever tried to introduce central controls. Second, many, if not most, of these policies would intrude into areas once defined as within that realm of civil liberties which lies beyond the reach of governmental power altogether. Third, without established theoretical guidelines, the numbers and types of such policies could become quite large, and both the political and fiscal costs of implementation and impact could be very high—even if the actual impact of these policies on population growth itself were negligible.

If any political impacts of these policies can be foreseen, the time is more than ripe to identify them—and to plan accordingly. For, if we can identify patterns of impact on the political system, these patterns could serve as criteria for defining good policy without interfering at all with the right of the people to have population growth policies if the majority so wills. For example, if two alternative population policies appear to experts to have about the same probability of significant impact on the growth profile, and if one of the alternatives could be shown to be more favorable to the maintenance of open, democratic policy-making, then the latter ought to be preferred. Or, if two policies are about equally likely to succeed, then the one shown to be more just (however that be defined) should be preferred to the other. Some policies, regardless of impact on society, may produce a more exciting polity, or a more flexible one. Some policies may produce more civic education than others; some may be conducive to a stronger Congress, or to stronger national parties. Thus, there may, in brief, be some side benefits for the political system on the way to the war on population pressure. The greater the uncertainty regarding ultimate societal impacts, the greater should be the concern for the side benefits as guides to developing public policy.

This chapter is concerned with those side benefits. The case for the desirability of population planning in the United States does not yet enjoy broad consensus. And the projected impact on society of each specific proposal for control of population growth remains at best unclear. Specialists in the various aspects of demography, biology, and medicine will continue to evaluate population programs from the standpoint of impact and acceptance. Evaluation of these same proposals should be taking place at the same time from the standpoint of their possible impact on the political system. If political science has any expertise to offer, it should include this kind of evaluation.

What Is "Population Policy"?

Such an evaluation requires a definition of the problem—or perhaps a redefinition—from the point of view of the political scientist rather than the demographer, biologist, or physician. And from this point of view, the most problematic concept is not *population* or *control*. It is *policy*. A proper definition and explication of this concept will shed a great deal of light on the other concepts and, it is hoped, on the substantive problem itself. At the outset, this involves identifying what policy is *not*.

First, policy is not merely a statement of the problem. Documentation does not speak for itself. Clearly stated cases of overpopulation and well-supported arguments of cause and effect are not policies. Nor is a policy an expression of sentiments about the problem. To summarize these two points quite concretely, a *whereas* covering the problem and its causes, followed by a *therefore* stating, for example, that we need zero population growth, is not a policy. At best, it is an assertion that a policy dealing with the problem at hand may be desirable.

Policy is also not an appropriation backing a sentiment. At least, that is not what we shall be calling policy here. Statements of fact, coupled with expressions of sentiment, and attached to an authorization for expenditure, are the three typical sections of American public policies. But these actions merely enable others to take actions on behalf of policy-makers. What this means is that some real policies are being made by obscure officials at lower levels of some specialized bureaucracy. Or, it means that some social movement has been bought off by being given the impression that serious actions are taking place when, typically, no real actions are taking place at all.

If these are pseudo-policies, what then does a *real* policy look like? *A policy is a general statement by some governmental authority defining an intention to influence the behavior of citizens by use of positive and negative sanctions.* A policy can influence behavior by use of monetary inducements, as in the case of the so-called farm parity programs. Or, a policy can seek to influence conduct by threat of punishment. A single decision, a specific issue, and a description of the activities of a public official all constitute the data by which we instruct ourselves about a policy. But these are not policies. A policy must possess the following three characteristics: (1) an official expression of intentions concerning desirable or undesirable conduct; (2) a provision for inducements, positive, negative, or both; and (3) some provision of means for implementing the intentions and applying the sanctions.

In light of this, analytic clarity will be enhanced if we eliminate the notion of "population policy" altogether and concentrate instead upon population *policies*. Population *policy* usually signifies a broadly stated sentiment that, at best, encourages serious consideration of specific proposals for population policies. But if our concern is for assessing impacts, the focus ought to cut through to the clearest cases of probable future public actions that intend to be effective. A statute or decree enunciating zero population growth as a goal would be nothing but an expression of sentiment. Setting up a department or independent commission on population would also be a pseudo-policy, until the agency itself generated some real policies. It is necessary to look carefully at each activity and proposal, to identify intentions, to assess sanctions, and after that, to look toward the likely impact—both upon the relevant demographic rate, and, for the political scientist, upon the political system.

Once real policies have been defined, proper assessment requires still another distinction—between those governmental activities which affect the population size or distribution without intending to, and those which explicitly adopt population impact as the goal. War is, for example, an important policy of governments, and war can have a profound effect on population size and composition. But it would be stretching a point to call the typical war a population policy. Other examples of population-relevant policies that are not actual population policies include expansion of hospital services, reduction of the price of wonder drugs, improvement of food stamp plans, improvement of sanitation and epidemiology in cities, development and dispensation of new vaccines, and so on. Except for war, most of these population-relevant governmental activities seem to have an upward effect on population growth rates. Expansion of new and serious policies aimed at reduction in population growth rates could, for example, easily counteract some of the positive goals of the most benevolent population-relevant welfare policies. This could pose a real dilemma of governance in the future.

In contrast, and still more ironically, many policies, especially at the local level, are coming to be seen as undesirable or even as downright unconstitutional. Examples include exclusive zoning, segregated public housing, and other housing, schooling, and service programs that maintain ghettoes and slums. Yet, if, as is likely, these local programs are invalidated by the county, population growth rates could increase among the families who have most to gain by the elimination of those undesirable laws and programs.

These are factors and paradoxes that have to be taken into account in any serious effort to develop a plan for population growth. Modern medicine, technology, and enlightened welfare policies tend—by reducing death rates without affecting birth rates to a similar degree—to make population growth rates upwardly flexible and downwardly sluggish. This could be comparable to the effect of organized labor on wages. Potentially, then, any intentional population policies will be extremely significant and politically divisive because they must cut across important existing welfare and urban policies which affect many and profound interests.

The closer one gets to the serious and intended population growth policies, the more one sees these and other ramifications. To have a planned and measurable effect on population growth, most population policies must be aimed at birth rates, because modern amenities keep pushing death rates, especially infant mortality, down. But such policies can hardly avoid class, ethnic, and racial bias. Even when equitably drafted and implemented, population control policies can be most burdensome among those least able to bear the burdens. To many, especially from an international perspective, population policies can be made to look like a white racist plot against the nonwhite populations of the world.

This special problem of the real and symbolic biases in so many population policies can surely, with careful consideration, be softened, if not altogether eliminated. Nevertheless, the problem itself helps to identify and emphasize the one common and unavoidable characteristic of all real public policies, including population policies. This characteristic is *coercion*. This will turn out to be the most important analytic characteristic. One might quibble over fine points and special definitions, but, as a general rule, it is wise to follow the proposition that it is impossible to have a government policy without having coercion. Coercion can be remote and indirect; for example, a recipient of government services may not be aware of the fact that the financing is based on a highly coercive revenue system. And coercion, as suggested before, can involve positive or negative sanctions, can be benevolent or malevolent, can coerce some in order to be of explicit assistance to others. But policy is no less coercive because there are different forms of it. This only means that governments have a choice among types of coercion, among types of persons to be coerced, and among the various sanctions to be employed. In fact, it is these very distinctions among types of coercion that will provide the basis for all the propositions about the different impacts that can be anticipated from the various efforts to control population growth rates.

A Scheme of Analysis

Classifying population policies, or any other policies, according to the type of coercion involved amounts to an attempt to define policies according to those elements most likely to have political implications. The possibility of being coerced or the prospect of coercing others must be highly motivating factors in political life; and if that is true, then a proper classification of policies in these terms could have a lot of predictive power in our effort to assess how these policies will shape political institutions and patterns in the decades to come.

To simplify matters as much as possible, let us substitute the word "statute" whenever the word "policy" crops up. In doing this, we give up a great deal of information about the policy in the real world; but we gain a great deal in clarity. And even from a partial and very formalized statement of policy in the statute, we can predict enough of the political consequences to provide a basis for judging the policy itself and determining whether it is one we would recommend adopting.

The predictive propositions we would like to be able to make can be indicated by the following questions:

1. Will the particular policy (statutory) effort favor executive power over legislative power?
2. Will the particular (statutory) effort be dominated by career bureaucrats, or will their activities be joined by nongovernmental specialists, opinion leaders, and groups; or will the effort be dominated by high-level officialdom?
3. Will the particular policy (statutory) effort enhance the power of Congressional committees, or will the effort tend to accentuate the parliamentary powers on the floor of the House and the Senate?
4. Will the politics of the effort in question ground itself in interest groups or in social movements—or neither?
5. What kinds of policies seem most frequently to be associated with party politics, and, among these, which ones tend to encourage central and national parties as opposed to local parties?

Obviously, there are other, more subtle behavior patterns that political scientists are interested in. But when a government is on the brink of committing itself to a vast new undertaking, it is most important to be able to anticipate gross developments in the large institutional aggregates.

Table 10.1 is an attempt to systematize the types of coercion available to governments as they seek to influence their environments (see also Table 2.1). It simply translates earlier observations about types of coercion into a more formal and exhaustive statement of logical possibilities.[2] The vertical dimension of the table suggests that, in a governmental context, coercion can be remote if the sanctions accompanying a given decision are mild or uncertain. Coercion can also be remote if it is indirect—as in the earlier illustration of a program based on services or subsidies where the coercion is displaced onto the general revenue system. When coercion is direct or immediate, however, it is usually quite easy to find in the statute.

The horizontal dimension is slightly less obvious, but no less important to the understanding of public policies. Some government decisions work by coming to bear specifically upon individual conduct. For example, there can be a general rule governing

Table 10.1 Types of Coercion and Types of Policy

	Applicability of coercion (works through)	
	Individual Conduct	Environment of Conduct
Likelihood of coercion: Remote	Distributive (e.g., 19th-century land policies, tariffs, subsidies)	Constituent (e.g., reapportionment, setting up a new agency, propaganda)
Likelihood of coercion: Immediate	Regulative (e.g., elimination of substandard goods, unfair competition, fraudulent advertising)	Redistributive (e.g., Federal Reserve controls of credit, progressive income tax, social security)

false and fraudulent advertising, but it is applicable to the conduct of individual advertisers. As noted previously, some public policies seek to influence conduct not by direct application of coercive measures on the individual, but rather by manipulating the environment of his conduct. For example, a minor change in the Federal Reserve discount rate can have a tremendous impact on my marginal propensity to invest, yet no government official need know of my existence.

In each of the four cells in Table 10.1, there is a label for a type of public policy. It is not necessary to provide elaborate definitions of each, since the essential aspect of each definition is implied in the cross-tabulation of the two dimensions of coercion. Distributive policies, for example, are best illustrated by the 19th century land grant programs. Modern examples include the work of such agencies as the Extension Service, Soil Conservation Service, Weather Bureau, Office of Education, or Corps of Engineers which work strictly from the perspective of benefits. One of the synonyms for this kind of policy is "patronage," not as a mere giving of jobs but in the generic sense of "to patronize."

Regulatory policies are also specific as regards individual conduct; but regulatory policies are very different along the other dimension, for here the likelihood of coercion is quite immediate. In the regulatory statute, one has no trouble finding the provision for sanctions. They can be inducements, as in the case of farm "parity" programs; or they can, more frequently, be punishments. Whatever type, these sanctions are associated with certain conducts that the statute seeks to encourage or discourage.

A constituent policy, such as establishing the Office of Management and Budget (OMB) or passing a reapportionment statute, may have profound effects on individual conduct; but the coerciveness of the government decision itself in either case follows from some basic change in the structure in which individuals operate. Or, the coerciveness may follow from decisions made by OMB but not *directly* from the statute setting it up. In contrast to this, a redistributive policy, such as the Federal Reserve rate mentioned above, or a basic change in the internal revenue structure, affects individuals through their environment; but in contrast to constituent policies, these are directly rather than indirectly coercive.

Table 10.2 attempts to capture a few of the political characteristics that a common-sense review of Table 10.1 ought to generate. [See also Table 2.1.] If the policy distinctions have any meaning at all, each category immediately suggests a regular and predictable association with its own distinct political process. In other words, if coercion comes in more than one form, so will politics.

Each of the characteristics of coercion seems to be associated with some fairly clear consequences for political behavior. For example, we know historically that logrolling, localized parties were very much associated with the 19th century federal government preference for subsidy policies.[3] But when the policies at issue are constituent, as in the 19th century when new states were admitted to the Union, a very different set of political characteristics prevailed. Party organizations dominated, but they were more nationalized, centralized, and ideological.[4] Distributive policies are likely to combine electoral and decentralizing political tendencies (the mixing of marginal characteristics (1) and (3) on Table 10.2) because the remoteness of coercion and the individualized focus allow each distributive decision to be made almost completely in isolation from other decisions. This is the essence of logrolling, and a logrolling politics is generally the most stable and usually, at low levels, out of public view. Constituent policies, on the other hand, tend to produce mixtures of political characteristics (2) and (3) precisely because efforts to change the structure of conduct involve central and historical (i.e., ideological) considerations that cannot be so stable or so covert as the mixture of characteristics (1) and (3). By the same pattern of reasoning, we can predict that political processes composed of characteristics (1) and (4) will tend to develop around regulatory policies, and that processes composed of mixtures of characteristics (2) and (4) will tend to develop around redistributive policies.

These have been the central hypotheses of a large-scale research project in policy processes beginning in 1962. It would be overly burdensome to present the tests and methods here.[5] It seems to be rather more useful to report a few of the findings that bear most clearly upon our present effort to make projections about the impact of population policies on political processes—i.e., findings that suggest patterns of institutional variation. For example, statistical analysis of the amending process reveals, as predicted, that distributive bills are dominated by congressional committees; regulative bills are dominated by the floor, with the executive being creatively involved; and redistributive bills are dominated by the executive, with a fairly pronounced role reserved for the open floor.[6] From a 20-year analysis of roll call votes, it can further be shown, again as predicted, that the behavior of members of Congress is dominated by party relationships in distributive issues; but, on redistributive issues, behavior tends to be ordered along nonparty, ideological lines. Legislative behavior on regulative issues is not ordered by any single factor at all; rather, it is here that coalitions tend to build virtually from the bottom up for each issue.[7]

Finally, extensive reanalysis of 17 major policy-making case studies produced confirming patterns in a variety of areas.[8] These detailed studies tended strongly to bear out statistical patterns and direct observations: The executive is the center of redis-

Table 10.2 Types of Coercion and Characteristics of Arenas

Applicability of coercion (works through)

Likelihood of coercion:	Individual Conduct	Environment of Conduct
Remote		• logrolling (3) • party (electoral organization)
Immediate		• bargaining (4) • interest organization
	• decentralized • disaggregated • local • interest • identity (person) (1)	• centralized • "systems" level • cosmopolitan • ideology • status (type of person) (2)

tributive politics; its groupings tend to be very large and stable, and their relations are quite strongly ideological. On the other hand, Congress is at the center of regulatory politics, and it operates largely as a terrain where groups, through shifting coalitions, make policy by sharing interests. Congressional committees, alone or in combination with low-level administrative agencies, dominate the distributive policy process, using the party and logrolling within party lines to get majority votes.

These distinctions will be pursued below. Their purpose here was to demonstrate the plausibility of the notion that policies determine politics, and that, therefore, the impact of policies on the political system can be predicted and planned for: The projected impact of policies on politics can be developed as a criterion of policy choice, a criterion that does not have to await the long-range impact of a policy on the society.

Population Policies and Their Politics

Evaluation of American population policies has hardly begun in earnest. Ehrlich, for example, devotes more than 90 percent of his book to an alarmist treatment of the problem calculated to produce a public opinion supportive of population planning.[9] Late in the book, Ehrlich proposes several policies which, if seriously drafted and implemented, would very probably cut the growth rate. But as an enthusiast, he leaves the job of evaluation to others.

Among the many kinds of evaluation now beginning to take place, perhaps the most difficult and controversial are the socioeconomic and political. One of the pioneering efforts in this area is Nash's evaluation of population growth policies from two important political perspectives. He categorizes proposals according to the degree to which they clash with basic American political norms ("Lockean norms") and according to their potential for mass acceptance.[10] The present effort jumps off from there in an effort to determine whether these various policies have any lasting effect on political patterns and institutions. The four categories employed here are not based upon projected divisiveness, as are Nash's; however, since divisiveness and its long-range consequences ought to be predictable from categories that are based upon type of coercion, the Nash and the Lowi categories are not incommensurate. On the contrary, they operate in large part as confirmations of the power of public policies to predict political patterns.[11]

Distributive Policies

Examples of distributive population policies are subsidies for research on birth control, subsidies for pharmaceutical houses to improve contraceptive chemicals and to reduce their prices, grants to wholesalers and retailers to encourage lower prices and more promotion, cash payments for women who accept intrauterine devices, subsidies for doctors and hospitals to encourage sterilization programs, and expansion of clinics to provide guidance and promotion in this field.

These kinds of policies most resemble Nash's first category—the least divisive, the least violative of traditional values.[12] Consequently, they are likely to be adopted earliest and in largest number. Whatever conflict does develop can be displaced among many interests—a pattern that has generally been called logrolling. These programs, once enacted, tend to enjoy a kind of consensus because access to them can be universalized—anyone who objects to the benefits someone else is getting can be included. Perhaps with each expansion of access everyone already included gets a little less, but everyone can get something. The colorful term pork barrel has developed to apply to the programs in this category that dispense material benefits. But the word applies equally well to the service programs in this category.

The voluntaristic appearance of these programs, with such an attraction of potential consensus (or perhaps because of such an attraction), has at least two consequences worth serious assessment. First, the distributive approach could minimize the desired impact on population growth rates. Many people, especially in cultures and subcultures that set high value on large families or male heirs, would turn to these programs only after having their second son, even if this required having a third or fourth child. To guard against that kind of abuse or manipulation of the spirit of these programs, governments might then seek to interpose certain standards between the person and the services. Such statutes could be revised so that they are no longer merely permissive and enabling statutes. For example, sections could be added that limit the discretion of the administrators, so that services would be rendered or cash would be paid "only if" the seeker had fulfilled certain standards. But—as suggested by the paradigm—the imposition of such standards changes the character and the politics of the programs in a fundamental way. The type of policy would have changed toward the regulatory quadrant, and the consensus politics would tend to be replaced by something more divisive.

The second consequence of distributive population policies flows over time from the very type of consensus these programs can purchase. The "power structure" around distributive policies tends to be highly resistant to change. If subsidy and permissive service policies in the population field even faintly come to resemble their counterparts in other fields (such as natural resources, defense procurement, the traditional tariff, and agricultural extension), we should expect that control would come to rest a considerable distance from politically responsible levels and would tend to resist being recentralized if and when a change is desired. Local elites have many resources when it comes to resistance. These include the local administrators of the program, the congressmen whose reelection may be tied to the maintenance of these benefits, and the congressional committees or subcommittees which often come to be dominated by those whose most outstanding interest is in the maintenance of the program.[13]

It should further be emphasized that all of the case studies of distributive policies discover that the committee or subcommittee system is the national center of distributive politics.[14] When Woodrow Wilson, in 1886, complained that "Congressional government is committee government,"[15] he was actually describing the pre-20th century Congress that dealt in almost nothing but distributive policies. Once the Federal government began to take on modern—that is, regulatory and redistributive—tasks, the centers of national politics began to shift. But even now, on those numerous occasions when subsidy or pork barrel policies are being adopted, the executive tends to be relegated to a lobby role at best, and the floor acts as a House of Commons; the Crown shifts according to whatever committee's distributive legislation is on the calendar.[16]

At first, one might consider that these political results are a worthy price to pay in order to get going on a large scale in this new and controversial area. But the trouble is, once a commitment is made to the distributive pattern of public policy and takes on elements of distributive politics, the agencies involved may join in opposing later changes aimed at making the whole program more effective. One good example of this is the vigor with which the Public Health Service avoided being shackled with the regulatory policies that flowed from their own findings and recommendations on the problems of air pollution.[17] Another example is the way in which the Office of Education has evaded responsibility for regulatory programs in the field of education standards or race discrimination in education.[18] Perhaps the most famous example is the way the Corps of Engineers has successfully avoided anything that breaks up their intimate relationship with the Public Works Committees of Congress, and both the Corps and the Committees have avoided any outside planning criteria in the development of water control and navigation.[19]

None of the case studies is concerned with population policies. However, if the political patterns described here are usually true whenever distributive policies prevail, it would seem wise to adopt these possibilities as criteria in any consideration of population policy proposals.

Constituent Policies

Included here are such policies as setting up a Department of Population Control, and vigorous programs of birth control education and propaganda. One of the big problems here, of course, is that many of these appeals are least effective where they are most needed. However, programs for effectiveness can be designed even for the least literate, most isolated communities in the United States or abroad. Information on the availability and desirability of birth control devices and medications can be provided for and received and understood by people of all races, classes, and religions. Appeals on the basis of a better life for children, attacks on the need for a male heir, and revisions of public attitudes on abortion can reach all levels of all cultures, especially if the campaigns have government sponsorship and if appeals can be made on the basis of patriotism.

If such policies were adopted on a large scale, the short-run political consequences could be profound, even if their impact on population growth rates were not felt for a very long time. As Nash's second category suggests—and his examples of policies here heavily overlap the constituent policy category—constituent policies do not directly force people to do anything.[20] Thus, they can be expected to be less intensely divisive and conflictive than policies that do directly coerce. However, a concerted effort to alert some people and actually to change the values of many others constitutes something of an assault on existing values and practices. The question is, therefore, not whether such policies will be divisive but how, and in what manner?

Almost so as to emphasize the divisiveness of constituent policies, proponents of population control policies are quite torn about whether an assault on traditional values will be divisive. Their response to the first systematic study of opinions on birth control suggests the degree of their concern as well as the probable character of the political pattern in this area of policy. Judith Blake's analysis of many opinion studies concluded that 29 percent of the non-Catholic wives in 1960 were against even such mild limitations as spacing pregnancies. Among lower-income Catholic wives, 48 percent expressed opposition to birth control. Blake also reported that 79 percent of all wives of grade school education in the sample already used contraceptives to varying extents, and that many of the remaining 21 percent were younger women not using contraceptives because they wanted pregnancy.[21] A year later, Bumpass and Westoff reported what was, in their estimation, a strongly conflicting set of figures.[22] They showed, for example, that almost 20 percent of recent births in the United States were "unwanted"; the proportion of "unwanted" births, they surmise, could have been greater among people in lower economic and education brackets and ethnic groups.

All of these figures are soft, and are susceptible to considerable manipulation by special pleaders on both sides of the population control issue. However, one line of argument seems supportable in both sets of studies. Appeals for family planning as a patriotic duty do more than put useful information before the public. They involve something of an assault on traditional values. Traditional values may not be held so strongly anymore, but the assault may indeed restore their strengths to many, while activating others who were previously passive on these matters. Moreover, if the appeals come to be seen as biased against special groups known to have large families, the possibilities for political divisiveness are not remote. And even as the proponents admit, the possibilities are for divisiveness along broad class, racial, and ethnic lines; the basis of appeal and interaction is broadly ideological; and the potential for militancy and partisanship is higher than one would at first have suspected.[23] As Nash puts it, this very intense and broad rhetoric about class and racial genocide will have nothing to do with the merits of the charges or with the motives of the planners.[24] According to our paradigm, such large aggregates of political division tend to be innate in constituent policies, whatever the subject or field.

These large divisions in constituent politics do not have to be intense, bordering on revolution and repression. For example, the long fight for the 18-years voting age amendment was large scale and divided but not particularly intense. Final ratification by the 38th state legislature surprised many people. While not intense, however, the divisions are very likely to be national and partisan, in some sense.[25]

Political patterns that have developed around other constituent policies suggest, therefore, that while reeducation and other propaganda approaches to birth control may not be involuntary, they will very probably be divisive on a large scale. Despite the controversy surrounding the Blake and Bumpass-Westoff studies, it is entirely possible, for example, that a future Democratic party, representing lower-income Catholics and blacks, could become the "conservative" voice on population policy, vis-à-vis a "liberal" Republican party of middle-class suburbia.[26]

This pattern of partisan cleavage could lend a strong sense of excitement and public choice to population issues, and much is to be gained from that. But on the other hand, proponents of population planning could lose everything as a result, if the opposition party happens to win elections on the explicit basis of their opposition to birth control propaganda. This could easily come to be the case if the opposition party goes on to develop supporting doctrines such as defense of the lower classes against the efforts of the upper classes to eliminate them. This possibility is not at all inconceivable, especially considering the large number of urban and conservative Catholics. A comparable case might be the flurry over state public school requirements to salute the flag in the early 1940s. There the issue was regulatory, but the purely propaganda aspect of the case was not taken lightly by Americanism groups or by civil liberties groups.[27]

All things considered, the constituent approach may be particularly attractive to policy-makers because it might produce a kind of national referendum on the whole question of whether the American people want any governmentally sponsored population planning. As a general rule, because the making of constituent policy tends to center in the parties, the judiciary, and top officialdom, it may be a good way to enter into a new venture in intervention whose legitimacy needs fully to be established.

Redistributive Policies

Examples of important redistributive policies all share one common characteristic: a positive and involuntary manipulation of the structure or environment in which people have families. If we change the Internal Revenue Code so as to tax rather than exempt each child, or all children beyond the second, we alter the privileges and rights of all, without judging the conduct of any. Others of the same would be to set family size as a condition of welfare eligibility, to support the dependent mother in absolute grants that are not adjusted if her family expands, or to shift tax advantages away from the married and back toward the single.

Redistributive policies are almost self-executing. A marginal change in tax, welfare, or credit rates can have considerable impact regardless of personal idiosyncrasies or values of the millions of individuals and families affected by the change. The swiftness of impact may be still greater due to the fact that the lower classes tend to bear the heaviest burden, yet are the least capable of organizing for effective political action.

The politics of redistributive policies, in general, is most often class-oriented and ideological;[28] its resemblance to constituent politics is rather superficial. Where constituent politics tends to be national and partisan, the cases suggest that a redistributive approach to population planning would more probably be national and executive centered. Thus, the president would find himself in direct interaction with mass publics and with (and against) the spokesmen for large, class-oriented groups. The cases also suggest that a large expansion of population controls through redistributive policies might produce upper class cohesion—a phenomenon we have seen little of in our 20th century system of federal government, complex economy, and pluralistic interest group structure.[29] But this also might be accompanied by moves in the opposite direction, toward effective organization of the proletariat, or spokesmen for the proletariat.[30]

Finally, once a redistributive program is established, the politics tend to center to a larger than average extent in the bureaucracies. But this is not a matter of local bureaucrats and local influentials enjoying a cozy communal relationship, as would tend to be the case for the implementation of the typical distributive policy. In contrast to that, the redistributive approach tends to perpetuate original conflicts throughout the life of the program. Often the bureaucracies in this area end up administering politics as much as money or services. Escalation tends to move up the agency hierarchy toward the department head rather than through local politicians or congressmen.[31]

Thus, although the political process of redistributive policies is more centralized and bureaucratic, and dominated by large groups more than by individuals and small groups, it is also more exposed to the public eye. In that sense, it is more responsible than distributive approaches to the same problems. Elites may be centralized, but there is greater likelihood of "counterelites." It is not a partisan politics, in contrast to the constituent arena, but it is focused on alternatives salient to individual voter preference.

However, the risks of redistributive policies are great, especially in the population field. First, redistributive policies increase the social movement potential in the society. Beyond that, redistributive policies increase the movement capacity of the lower economic and racial status groupings. These groupings are much more unstable and violence prone when mobilized outside party politics, for mobilization outside party organizations involves charismatic leadership and a grandiose (if not hostile) rhetoric that can destabilize the regime. Concomitantly, the movement potential of the better-off classes is enhanced, and population policy could easily be used by leaders of upper middle class movements as a mask for repression. Short of that extreme, it is all the more possible to anticipate enough consensus among the upper classes to be able to attach to population control an effective effort to eliminate the very mild redistribution of wealth the revenue system has managed, over a period of 40 years, to introduce. That is to say, population policies that work through redistributive techniques amount to a reredistribution of wealth. The rich and the poor alike must be punished for having too many children. Suspicions now held about "genocide" among many black and white spokesmen for the poor would begin to appear substantiated if and when the government effort shifted from mildly annoying propaganda to clearly involuntary tax and welfare punishment.

This pattern of severe reaction on a large scale is of course less probable in its fullest realization in the United States than in some already unstable country with runaway population growth. But the tendency does exist in the United States, and other mature countries, as we can see by the Townsend-type and Poujade-type economic movements of the United States and France and the more recent black and welfare rights movements of the 1960s in the United States.

Regulatory Approaches to Population

Regulatory policies are mainly the ones Professor Nash would reserve for his fourth category, the only category he would clearly label "involuntary."[32] These include marketable licenses to have children; permanent sterilization or required abortion after so many births; investigation of all parents and children concerning suspected genetic problems that might make sterilization advisable; requirements of elaborate reporting on the part of all hospitals and doctors in cases of genetic defects, exceeding some set birth limit, or births of illegitimate or welfare children; requirements placed on all doctors to perform prenatal inspection in relation to all genetic and welfare problems, and the number of children each mother has had. Such eugenic policies had been anticipated by such liberals as Huxley.[33] After all, it was Holmes, not Hitler, who, in supporting the validity of a state law requiring forceful sterilization of mentally retarded mothers, said, "Three generations of imbeciles are enough."[34]

Other, quite mild, policies include special regulation of businesses whose goods or services have some notable population impact. Drug companies could easily be required to use a significant proportion of their profits on birth control propaganda. Private (as well as public) adoption agencies could be regulated so as to make adoption and foster parentage more attractive to potential mothers and to unmarried females and males. To go to a further but still practicable extreme, health insurance companies could be regulated to adjust their maternity services in a way that encourages smaller families.

These types of policies, especially the most effective ones first listed, are least likely to expand significantly in the near future. The reasons for this say a lot about the political pattern of the regulatory approach. Regulatory politics is a great deal more decentralized and unstable than any other type of politics. It is the one arena that tends to be dominated by tightly organized interest groups. In fact, virtually all of the good things pluralists say about pluralism apply with particular accuracy here. This means that one of the significant power patterns will tend to be that new coalitions will form around each regulatory issue. A coalition that is effective in getting one regulatory bill through the legislature can find itself quite ineffective in getting the next regulatory bill passed. This is far less true of the political patterns in the other arenas. Interest groups are easier to form and are more effective than social movements or large peak associations like the Chamber of Commerce. But the very specialization of interest groups limits their continuity across issues or their capacity to maintain peaceful coalitions with other groups.

Problems arise when a dynamic interest group system is too stalemated to arrive at any appropriate policy decisions at all. Dynamic stalemate is not at all a pathological condition for a polity, but reactions to the stalemate can be. When the pressures for some kind of policy decision build to crisis proportion, at least three potentially dangerous reactions are possible. First there is repression—a decision by governing elites that they can no longer cope with the political situation. This was most clearly the case with the draft in the mid-1960s, where the inability to make it more equitable led first to militant protest and then to the use of the draft powers to remove the agitators.

A second reaction to stalemate is the emergence of a social movement and an eventual redefinition of the policy as a demand for a broad redistribution of power. The best illustration of this will be found after the Civil War when the inability of the states to deal with railroads and other monopolies led to agrarian movements that focused policy demands on a dismantling rather than a reforming of the capitalist system. Schattschneider refers to this political transformation as the expansion and socialization of conflict.[35] Such expansion has policy consequences: It is associated with extensive redistributive policies and pressure for change in the very structure of the system rather than for regulation of the specific evils. In the case of the railroads, this meant expansion of policy demands from attacks on price discrimination, rebating, gouging, and other monopolistic practices to efforts to eliminate monopolies per se, cheapen the dollar, and generally redistribute incomes and power.

The third reaction may be the worst, but it is also the most typical. Rather than have the stalemated regulatory issue transformed into redistributive policies and politics, politicians attempt to buy their way out of stalemate by giving the impression that a policy decision was made. This they do largely by passing statutes in which the real decisions are delegated down the line from Congress and president to lower and lower levels of the bureaucracy. When this happens, what started out to be regulatory policy turns out to be distributive, and the politics will change accordingly—toward local irresponsibility. The difference lies, as suggested by the paradigm and earlier discussion, in the degree to which the statute specifies or fails to specify criteria by which conduct is to be guided by clear rules and by sanctions. When effective criteria are involved (and conduct is regulated), the politics of passage and implementation will be dynamic. When policies are not intended to be clear and sanctioned, the politics will tend to come to rest in a reactionary, distributive pattern.[36]

Thus, regulatory policies may be most desirable for all the reasons that they are least likely to be adopted. They, among all population control methods, give the strongest appearance of placing the burdens on the rich as well as the poor. They are most likely to provide conditions for defense, retaliation, and reform on the part of those most heavily hit by a particular policy. And they are most likely to enhance the power of Congress over president and bureaucracy: Due to the intensity of specialized interest groups, and the resources of many of them, it is hard for the president to keep things coordinated or for committees to keep things contained. Most of the occasions in recent years when the floor of House and Senate seized the center of the political process have been regulatory.[37] That was even more clearly the case during the so-called strong presidency of FDR.[38]

There is no reason to expect otherwise in the population field. The interests involved in these regulatory policies, even the least extreme ones, are far from casual. And if the policies cut across various groups and sectors in different ways, the politics is likely to run along those lines, as it has in trade and labor regulation, and in the regulatory aspects of public health, communications, and securities.

Policy Impacts as Criteria for Policy Choice

The ultimate moral question, whether the United States should adopt any population control policies at all, is a question for which political science may have no more expertise than physiology, physics, or plumbing. However, if governments in the future are almost certain to adopt many policies to control population growth, it is already beyond the appropriate time to try to work out some criteria to guide governments and the people, whose approval will ultimately be sought.

We might begin this consideration with one of the few "categorical imperatives" in the American constitutional system: Civil liberties and personal privacy should be immune from government intervention, except in cases where overwhelmingly clear and compelling justification can be provided. Obviously, this requirement has not led to complete government inaction in abridging civil liberties. Total war has been sufficient as a justification. Large-scale natural disasters can provide justification. Rioting and other anarchic or frenzied behavior, when large-scale, may provide justification for abridging some aspect of individual freedom. In fact, the Supreme Court, though generally watchful of the First Amendment and other constitutional immunities, has used such doctrines as "clear and present danger" and the "balance between public need and private rights" to uphold many interventions that, if only by hindsight, were much too permissive.[39]

The original moral question turns out in this case, therefore, to be whether, or under what conditions, the "population problem" is sufficient to justify intervention. No area of human endeavor would seem to be more clearly within the realm of civil liberties and personal privacy than the decision to have children. Yet it is difficult to accept Professor Ehrlich's definition of the problem as a "population bomb." If his image came to be accepted, it would justify almost any number and kind of interventions. But there is probably no discrete moment in time when society reaches such a sudden, irreversible, explosive turn. This is not to deny the seriousness of the problem. The intention here is only to distinguish population growth from clearer cases of sudden disaster, in order to understand the special problem of intervention that can be involved in population policy. Population growth is not yet the "clear and present danger" that justifies government abridgment of civil liberties. In fact, population policy would be a means of heading off the danger. Wherever the danger is anticipatory rather than present, the burden of justification ought to be proportionately greater, if not overwhelming and prohibitive.

To be as pragmatic and permissive as possible, at least two basic political considerations would have to be involved in such a justification (political is being used here not in its contemporary sense of strategies calculated to influence, but classical): The first of these political considerations is constitutional. It is concerned not only with what government has the power to do, but with the ensemble of government powers and the gradations and shadings of coercive intervention among them. The second consideration has to do with the impact that these different approaches to government coercion may have on the capacity of people and their institutions to react and to put an end to overly repressive or unsuccessful interventions. Contemporaries would call this dimension of politics "political processes" or "power structures," but an older characterization, "regimes," might be more useful. These two dimensions—constitutional power and regimes, or gradients of legitimate coercion and variations in political processes—can, and should, be handled simultaneously, for the impact of the one upon the other is not only an empirical question, as this chapter has tried to pursue, but is also a source of criteria for making public choices among alternate routes toward a higher quality of life in America.

Following those guidelines, the first policies to be tried would be (1) those for which there is strongest constitutional authority and, simultaneously, (2) those whose impact on the American system would be minimal. These two criteria point to policies dealing with problems external to ourselves. No government action has stronger constitutional support than foreign policies, and surely actions controlling foreign phenomena have minimal internal impact. The United States could, therefore, begin a serious population planning program by adopting, and joining with other governments to adopt, policies to "quarantine the aggressor." Concretely, this means setting severe limitations on immigration, based upon the population growth rates of exporting countries rather than upon national origin, race, or the other limitations usually put upon immigration.

Although the figures on Table 10.3 are not all up to date or as accurate as one would prefer, they do indicate the wide range of rates of natural increase among countries and regions; they also suggest the basis upon which a quarantining policy could actually be formulated. The United States, as well as any other country concerned about world population, could take some measure such as its own average rate of natural increase in the past "n-years" as the height of the immigration barrier to be raised. Or, it could work out a quota system to discriminate in particular, either against the countries with the most extreme rates of natural increase or against those countries whose per capita impact upon environmental deterioration was the greatest. There is far greater justification in this method than in attaching birth control policies as a prerequisite to our foreign economic assistance. The latter constitutes a direct intervention into the internal affairs of the recipient countries, while the former only sets limits on the extent to which the recipient, or any other nation, can displace its population excesses on the rest of the world. Such an approach would be a direct contribution to world population control even as many separate countries' population growth rates are reaching explosive proportions.

Eventually, however, if not simultaneously, there will be sufficient pressure of reason and public clamor to adopt effective domestic policies to reduce our own rate of natural increase, and the question is what to do first, and why. The principle of judgment has already been established: Try policies involving the least coercion before adopting policies involving maximum coercion. With this principle, the claim to constitutionality will be strong, and the amount of impact on the political system might also be minimal.

This could mean adoption of distributive policies, because personal choice seems maximal and coercion minimal. However, if the earlier analysis is even fractionally confirmed, arguments against distributive policies, at first or at last, are overwhelming. These policies distribute valuable resources too much on the basis of privilege (which usually means whoever is lucky enough to be near the point of distribution), and the impact on the system tends toward privacy and inflexibility.

This points toward constituent policies, the second category of policy; and this means vigorous education and propaganda in favor of universal family planning. The rates of natural increase in the Western European countries suggest that government programs of family planning and birth control propaganda could, in many instances, be sufficient. This may be especially promising when we consider that many countries with low rates of natural increase are Catholic countries. An educational approach as a first approximation of population control is all the more desirable if, as earlier analysis has in part shown, education as a constituent policy encourages partisan and electoral activity. After all, this would also mean that population policies, after the first serious round, might derive more directly from referenda or from issue-oriented electoral campaigns. As frightening as tyranny of the majority may sound, it is nonetheless true

Table 10.3 Rates of Natural Increase: A Selection of Countries, Ranked by Rate of Births over Deaths

Country	Census Year	Births over Deaths per 1,000 Population	Country	Census Year	Births over Deaths per 1,000 Population
Hungary	1965	2.45	Canada	1964	15.74
Belgium	1963	4.57	USSR	est. 1959	17.75
Sweden	1965	5.77	Israel	Jewish pop. 1960	18.34
Austria	1964	6.20	China (mainland)	est. 1953	20.59
West Germany	1965	6.21	India	est. 1961	21.82
France	1965	6.58	Chile	1962	22.05
United Kingdom	1963	7.14	Puerto Rico	1965	23.58
Finland	1965	7.25	Thailand	1960	24.42
Czechoslovakia	1964	7.57	Pakistan	est. 1961	26.94
Denmark	1964	7.74	Ceylon	1962	26.99
Bulgaria	1964	8.16	China (Taiwan)	1965	27.22
Ireland	1960–1962	9.60	Egypt	1960	27.24
Greece	1965	9.85	Dominican Republic	1960	27.34
Italy	1964	10.09	Singapore	1962	28.48
United States	1965	10.18	Turkey	est. 1960	29.16
Japan	1963	10.31	El Salvador	1950	33.96
Spain	1963	12.42	Honduras	1963	34.70
Portugal	1965	12.47	Mexico	1959–1961	34.83
Netherlands	1963	12.88	Venezuela	1963	36.23

Source: Nathan Keyfitz and Wilhelm Flieger, *World Population* (Chicago: University of Chicago Press, 1968).

that the most legitimate of governmental interventions in private life are those that are based on broad electoral choice.

As effective as education-propaganda programs could be, they are nevertheless high in personal choice; and as a consequence, if they are ineffective, greater and more immediate effectiveness is likely to be sought. What would be the next step in the escalating war on population growth? And why? Part of the answer lies in our notions of constitutionality and preferred impact on the political system. We can apply these criteria to the next step by arguing that in matters of public choice collective or common faults should, wherever possible, be attacked prior to individual variations. For example, a family of 10 may ultimately be treated as a violation of a public regulation; however, if a whole community is having an effect on population, that should be dealt with first. In a sense, this is a domestic application of the principle underlying the international quarantine idea, for country birth-death ratios and world population movements are not the only spillover or neighborhood effects to be guarded against.

Because population policy should be concerned with "supportable population," it is not a question of absolute numbers or density. It is a matter of definition involving, to a great extent, the number of people who can be supported at a specified level of comfort in a given place. Therefore, it also involves the level of technology and the efficiency of social organization relative to the density and life patterns in each case.

However, defining the population problem as one of supportability in relation to technology and social organization casts a long shadow across the United States, for there are two kinds of highly probable spillover effects of the great American productive society. One of these is upon supportable world population, one is upon the supportable domestic population. Both of these are collective patterns of spin-off that justify internal controls taking the form of generalized policies before seriously attempting to introduce policies which would seek specifically to control individual family size.

Just as it is probable that countries with extremely high rates of natural population increase will tend to be aggressors by displacing their population excess on the rest of the world, so it is possible for the most materially productive nations to be aggressors in regard to the ecological effects of their productivity. It must be treated as significant that the United States produces more than 50 percent of the world's goods—and a still higher proportion of the war-related goods—because it is also likely that the pollution we displace upon the world is out of proportion to the goods we export. It is far more difficult to measure the displacement of industrial exhaust than it is to measure the exportation of excess population; but, as a consequence, it would be completely unjust to assume that the pollution and depletion of life supports by the industrial nations are irrelevant to the population problem.

Consequently, enlightened population control policy should step early into the ecology field to regulate the effects of corporate productivity on supportable world population. One important means of limiting the displacement of industrial exhaust is to lay a heavy tax, a regulatory tax, sufficiently burdensome to give corporations the incentive to keep their exhausts close to home. Another would be to require any corporation which exports goods and pollution to set aside a proportionate share of its voting stock for ownership abroad. If we would seek to quarantine excess producers of population, we must also be prepared to quarantine ourselves in regard to our possible aggressions against the world ecosystem. And it is not the sort of thing that can wait for full documentation before action. Just as we have to anticipate the population explosion before we are certain the statistical projections will actually be borne out, so we must anticipate those ecological developments most relevant to supportable population. In both instances, to wait for proof, as though population growth and pollution were like a new medicine for the market, is to be too late to do anything about either.

The second of these spillover effects of collective or community, rather than individual, behavior has to do with strictly domestic patterns that only affect supportable population inside the United States. To repeat the criterion, before government policy concerns itself with individual family size and individual population-relevant behaviors, it should concern itself with those aspects of community structure and organization that seem to be most relevant to population spillover effects. Let us take suburbanization as an example. Even if it cannot be shown that the suburbs produce too much of the natural increase in actual population, it might be shown that the pattern of suburban sprawl is a variable of tremendous significance in the overall question of supportable population. First of all, suburban sprawl, unless checked by rational planning, can affect the environment far beyond a suburb itself. The most obvious but not necessarily the most pressing aspect of this is, of course, the intimate relation between suburban sprawl and the automobile, which in turn affects the pollution levels and therefore the amount of supportable population—as opposed to the actual size or density of the population. Another, and perhaps still more important, aspect of suburban sprawl is the problem it poses for traditional social control and the provision of basic amenities. Adam Smith opened his classic *Wealth of Nations* with a disquisition on the division of labor, in which he recognized the basic need of concentrated populations for any rational economic endeavor. Jane Jacobs in her fundamental work, *The Death and Life of Great American Cities,* reaffirmed that proposition in her studies of "the need for concentration."[40]

The point of this is that there is a very great difference between density and overcrowding or "too much population." The question is, what *kind* of density? And one can see the problem quite clearly in relation to the American suburb. Suburban sprawl can never support the kind of population that can be supported by a rationally ordered city. As Jacobs observed, when large areas of any community go unoccupied for different parts of the day, as a result of their sparseness or of their functional specialization, these areas become very special problems for provision of services and social controls, as well as special producers of pollution due to the high rates of resource use just to provide basic needs.[41]

Thus, one of the most pressing questions of population policy is how to design urban structures that can take advantage of concentration, rather than how to design escape routes through which to spread smaller populations throughout larger territories. A government that has the rightful power to intervene between persons and progeny is certainly a government that has the legitimate power to set limits on community land use. It would be absolutely extraordinary to consider systematic regulation of family size prior to placing systematic regulatory limits on the extent to which communities squander the earth. Forceful land-use planning of this sort will have an immediate effect on supportable population. In contrast, while a governmental assault on family size may ultimately slow rates of growth, this is a very long-run proposition, and the results of such population policies cannot actually be assessed until it could be too late to adopt other strategies.

A further advantage to this approach is that its impact on the political system would be positive. These are regulatory measures and, thus, are likely to encourage the dynamic, organized politics described earlier. Moreover, since these regulations hit whole communities, large corporations, cities, counties, and their governments, the burden of the regulations would rest upon those most able to bear it; and, the thrust of political action would come from those already organized to provide it. In fact, federal regulations of this sort would make the whole American system more dynamic by pitting these organized interests against one another after so many years in which, thanks to distributive policies, they have worked out peaceful alliances with each other.[42]

Finally, if the rate of population explosion is already critical, governments in the United States and around the world are not likely to stop with educational approaches and quarantines on collectivities, even if they are rational enough to try these first. Already we can note plans in the direction of direct controls on individual population behavior; and if Mr. Huxley is correct, the world is already beyond its appropriate time for turning to eugenics as the new religion. Thus it becomes compelling to try to develop a priori criteria by which to guide such efforts, to maximize the impact of governmental programs while minimizing their worst effects. One important criterion that has had a great deal of consensus in the past century, even though often honored in the breach rather than the observance, is to try to place the public burdens on those best able to bear them. In operational terms, this means hit the rich before the poor.

Now it is patently obvious that the rich either have fewer children than the poor or can more easily and promptly respond to appeals to reduce their own birth patterns. It is also true that there are fewer rich than poor; therefore, the birth patterns of the rich are less meaningful while at the same time are, by virtue of wealth, more supportable. They do not become charges on the community. However, there are at least two very practical reasons why population policies should begin by distinguishing between rich and poor.

First, the rich have very great bearing on the size of supportable population, even if they are not responsible for the actual population growth profile. That is to say, while the rich are not numerous nor do they have the largest families, the rich set the conditions of population growth and of supportable population size. Suburban sprawl is primarily influenced by wealthy land developers and implemented by those who can afford to buy and live on suburbanized land. The corporate rich make suburban sprawl almost necessary by moving factories out to areas called industrial parks provided for them by the suburban land speculators. It is also the wealthy and not the poor who profit from converting concentrated city areas into overcrowded areas by allowing the properties to "slumify" and then charging the kinds of rentals that make double and triple family apartment occupancy a necessity. As long as there is profit from these patterns, there will be people who will continue to pursue them and, as a consequence, reduce the actual supportable population in the United States. It is an historic irony that the United States cannot contain a population that is small in relation to its continental land mass, despite its marvel of mechanism and the astonishing success of its productive apparatus. No governing elite is serious about population control until it is willing to control itself.

A second reason for distinguishing between rich and poor prior to entering into population programs involves the question of legitimacy. The highly sensitive and private business of birth and death requires, as earlier defined, compelling justification prior to intervention. But even with such justification there are strategies that would ultimately be self-defeating. A population strategy aimed primarily at birth rates could easily be taken as a form of suppression, as a preventive form of class and racial genocide. And indeed, if all of population policy were concentrated on birth patterns, exempting from its controls those whose operations and behaviors define the upper limits of supportable birth rates, this would be almost self-evidently a genocidal act of the rich against the poor, the white against the colored races, essentially the West against the East.

Policies that make a pretense of universality are usually hiding coercions that favor the rich over the poor. This amounts to a punitively regressive tax and, as a redistributive measure, would shape the polity in organized classes and movements, much as redistributive politics was earlier described. However, there can be bad as well as good redistributive politics; and the bad case could be one in which the question of legitimacy, rather than the mere shifting of burdens, is involved. Hidden regressiveness would ultimately be found out, especially in something as close to home as population control. Exposure of such deceits could spread and intensify redistributive policies until the very survival of the regime itself came into question. This alone would produce real population control, for violence and other chronic disorders exert strong downward pressure on birth. But if that is the kind of birth control we get, we may as well wait for it to happen without bothering with any population control policies at all. If such a public environment as that develops, James Thurber might have been our prophet when he observed: "You might as well fall flat on your face as lean over too far backwards."

If the government of the United States is going to enter this field in any significant way, it therefore should be guided by its own great tradition and by the errors it has made whenever it has disregarded that tradition. Constitutionalism means government by explicit rules of law, without deceit. Legitimacy means government by consent, and consent requires due attention to the forms of politics that are most likely to produce consent. Constitutionalism, legitimacy, and consent also require redress, and once again that leads to a concern for the political forms best designed to provide dynamic channels for redress. These linkages among American public norms and traditions all point to the reason why political criteria, as defined in this chapter, can and should be highly significant guides to good public policy in any field of endeavor.

CHAPTER 11

❧

The Perils of Patronage

Tendencies Toward Corporatism
in the "Clientele Agencies"

Liberal governments cannot plan. Planning requires the authoritative use of authority. Planning requires law, choice, priorities, moralities. Liberalism replaces planning with bargaining. Yet at bottom, power is unacceptable without planning.

Application of pluralist principles in the construction of liberal government has made it possible for government to expand its efforts but not to assemble them. We can invent ingenious devices like the Executive Budget, the Executive Office of the President, Legislative Clearance, Program Budgeting, and Computerized Routines, but we do not use them to overcome the separatist tendencies and self-defeating proclivities of the independent functions. Liberal government seems to be flexible only on the first round of a response to political need. It allows for a certain expansion of functions to take place and then militates against any redistribution of those functions as needs change. New needs therefore result in expansions, never in planning. James Madison could have been writing for our times when he observed that government control and government self-control go together. The lack of rationale in our modern government has tended to vitiate its potential for good by sapping the strength and impairing the legitimacy of its authority.

Nowhere are the consequences of pluralist principles better seen than in those agencies in which the principles were first applied. Agriculture policy set the pattern of organizing the government along pluralist lines. Its influence spread far and wide, most notably to the Departments of Commerce and Labor, when these were created. Together the three provide the limiting extremes by which other programs and agencies can be analyzed. With these three departments one can begin to appreciate the extent to which the alienation of public authority has taken place, why it has taken place, and how this is reducing the capacity of modern government to govern responsibly, flexibly, and determinatively. The pattern will be established through observations on the practices of the Democratic 1960s, with side glances at a few antecedents. It will then be tested for continuity against the Republican 1970s.

Agriculture: The New Feudalism

Agriculture is that field of American government where the distinction between public and private has come closest to being completely eliminated. This has been accomplished not by public expropriation of private domain—as would be true of the nationalization that Americans fear—but by private expropriation of public authority. That is the feudal pattern: fusion of all statuses and functions and governing through rigid but personalized fealties. In modern European dress, that was the corporativistic way; it is also the pluralist way, the way of contemporary liberalism in the United States. However, the best definition is one that puts the reader in the very presence of the thing.

The Present Estate of Agriculture

On December 18, 1963, President Lyndon Johnson summoned a conference of the leaders of major agriculture interests and interest groups. These representatives were asked to formulate a program by which they and their supporters could be served and regulated. The president's call for an agriculture congress was followed on January 31 with a Farm Message. In the message the president proposed the establishment of a bipartisan commission to investigate the concentration of power in the food industry and "how this greatly increased concentration of power is affecting farmers, handlers and consumers." Such investigations are always popular in farm states in helping spread the blame for high prices despite large subsidies. As one Administration spokesman explained, "We're not making a whipping boy out of anybody, but we're receiving repeated charges that certain retailers are setting market prices and it is clear that some chains do have large concentrations of market power." In the same message the president also called for new legislation to strengthen farmer cooperatives, to encourage their expansion through merger and acquisition, and to provide them with further exemptions from the antitrust laws.

The summoning of an agriculture congress was a call to agriculture to decide for itself what it wants from government. The president's attack in his Farm Message on concentration of market power, coupled with his proposals for expanded and stronger farm cooperatives, was obviously not an attack so much on concentration itself as on the intervention of nonagricultural power into strictly agricultural affairs.

Origin and First Consequences of Pluralistic Government

That agricultural affairs should be handled strictly within the agricultural community is a basic political principle established before the turn of the century and maintained since then without serious reexamination. As a result, agriculture has become neither public nor private enterprise. It has been a system of self-government in which each leading farm interest controls a segment of agriculture through a delegation of national sovereignty. Agriculture has emerged as a largely self-governing federal estate within the federal structure of the United States.

President Johnson recognized these facts within three weeks of his accession when he summoned the conference of agricultural leaders. The resulting concession to agriculture's self-government was the wheat-cotton bill of 1964. Because cotton supports were too high, the cotton interests wrote a bill providing for a subsidy to mills of six to eight cents a pound in order to keep them competitive with foreign cotton and domestic rayon without touching the price supports. On the other hand, wheat supports were too low because wheat farmers in the 1963 referendum had overwhelmingly rejected President John Kennedy's plan to provide some federal regulation along with supports. The wheat section of the new act called for a program whereby wheat farmers would voluntarily comply with acreage reduction for subsidies of up to seventy cents a bushel but without the federal supply regulations. The press called this a major legislative victory for Mr. Johnson. But the victory really belonged to organized cotton and wheat and testified to the total acceptance by the president, press, and public of the principle that private agriculture interests alone govern agriculture. It is a sturdy principle; its inheritance by President Johnson was through a line unbroken by personality or party in the White House. For example, in one of President Kennedy's earliest major program messages to Congress, on March 16, 1961, he proposed:

> The Soil Conservation and Domestic Allotment Act … should be amended to provide for the establishment of national farmer advisory committees for every commodity or group of related commodities for which a new supply adjustment program is planned [as proposed in the same message]. Members of the committees would be elected by the producers of the commodities involved or their appropriate representatives. In consultation with the Secretary of Agriculture, they could be charged with the responsibility for considering and recommending individual commodity programs….
>
> In order to insure effective farmer participation in the administration of farm programs on the local level, the Secretary of Agriculture is directed to revitalize the county and local farmer committee system and to recommend such amendments as may be necessary to safeguard such farmer participation.

Origins in Economics and Tactics

The reasons for agricultural self-government are deep-rooted, and the lessons to be drawn from it are vital. For a century agriculture has been out of joint with American economic development. Occasional fat years have only created unreal expectations, making the more typical lean years less bearable. As industries concentrated and discovered the economies of scale and how to control their markets, agriculture remained decentralized and subject to the market. As industries showed increasing capacity to absorb technology and to use it to increase profit, agriculture took on technology only with net debt. Profit from increased productivity was either neutralized with lower prices or absorbed by the processing, distributing, and transporting industries interposed between agriculture and its markets. After the Civil War America's largest and most basic industry was never for long out of trouble. At the beginning of World War I, for example, net farm income was $3.6 billion. By 1919, it was $9.3 billion; but two years later it was back down to $3.7 billion. It rose slowly to $6.1 billion in 1920–30 and had fallen off to $1.9 billion by 1932. At a higher level, these fluctuations have beset agriculture since World War II as well. The only things stable about agriculture have been (1) its declining relative importance in the census and in the economy, (2) the reverence it enjoys in the American mythology, and (3) the political power it possesses despite (1) and largely because of (2).

As observed elsewhere in this book, agriculture was early to discover the value of political power. The land-grant and homesteading acts were followed by governmental services in research, quarantine, and education. But continuing distress despite governmental support led to bolder demands. First the movement was for a redistribution of wealth and power toward agriculture. As a debtor class, farmers saw inflation as the solution; William Jennings Bryan was one of many spokesmen for cheaper money and easier credit. Farmers also sought government regulation of those economic forces they had identified as the causes of their problems. The monopolies, the railroads, the grain merchants and other processors, the banks, and the brokers were to be deprived of market power by dissolution or by severe restraints upon the use of that power. Finally farmers sought solutions by emulating the business system. Almost simultaneously they hit upon the cooperative to restrain domestic trade, and international dumping over high tariff walls to restrain international trade.

All these mechanisms failed the farmers. The blunderbuss—inflation of the whole economy—failed both for want of enough legislation and because more and more of the national debt was held by the industrial rich. Regulation of industry failed for want of will and power to administer it; a governing elite opposed to inflating the business system could not be expected to dismantle it. International dumping never was given the test; Coolidge and Hoover vetoed the Smoot-Hawley tariff bills that would "make the tariff work for agriculture." The cooperative movement did not fail; it simply did not succeed on a large enough scale.

By a process of elimination, organized agriculture turned then to another way: the *regulation of itself.* In the Democratic Party of 1930 and the Democratic Party philosophy, to be called the New Deal, agriculture found an eager handmaiden. And in the modest government assistance programs of the pre–New Deal period the appropriate instrumentalities and precedents were found. After the 1932 election all that remained was to ratify in legislation the agreements already reached. The system created then has remained with only a few marginal additions and alterations. Bitter political conflicts within the agriculture community have been fought out over the margins, but on the system itself there is almost total consensus among the knowledgeable minority and total apathy and ignorance among the nonagricultural majority.

The principle of self-regulation might have taken several forms, the most likely one being a national system of farm representation within a farmer's type of National Recovery Administration (NRA). Instead, a more elaborate and complicated system of "cooperation" or local self-government developed largely for constitutional reasons. There was already experience with local districts in the Extension Service that had become a proven way for the federal government to get around the special constitutional problem of regulating agriculture. Agriculture was the most "local" of the manufactures the government was attempting to reach. The appearance if not the reality of decentralizing federal programs through local, farmer-elected committees helped to avoid straining the Interstate Commerce Clause and to escape the political charge of regimentation.

Eventually, many separate programs were created within the government-agriculture complex. Each constituted a system in and of itself. The programs were independently administered and often had conflicting results. But underneath all the complexity of parity, forestry, conservation, electrification, education, extension, and credit there was a simple principle: It amounted to the loan of governmental sovereignty to the leadership of a private sector to accomplish what other sectors could accomplish privately. Agriculture was so decentralized and dispersed that private, voluntary agreements to manipulate markets were obviously too difficult to reach and impossible to sustain. Therefore it was not going to be possible to emulate business. So, in a travesty of the Declaration of Independence, to secure these rights governments were instituted among farmers. Administrative agencies were created to facilitate agreements, and, once reached, public authority was expected to be employed where necessary to sustain them.

The System: Building on Local Committees[1]

The prototype, the Federal Extension Service, is "cooperative" in the sense that it shares the expense of farm improvement with the states, the land-grant colleges, the county governments, and the local associations of farmers. As observed elsewhere, local chambers of commerce were enlisted but were replaced with a "farm bureau" of the chamber of commerce. The county agent was employed by the county association, as required by law. In order to coordinate local activities and to make more effective claims for additional outside assistance, these farm bureaus were organized into state farm bureau federations. The American Farm Bureau Federation, formed at the Agriculture College of Cornell University in 1919, was the offshoot. A filial relationship between farm bureau, land-grant college, and the Extension Service continues to this day. This transformation of an administrative arrangement into a political system has been repeated in almost all agriculture programs since that time. The Extension Service exercises few sanctions over the states and colleges, which in turn leave the localities alone. All are quick to scream "Federal encroachment!" at the mere suggestion that the Department of Agriculture should increase supervision or investigation, or that it should attempt to coordinate extension programs with other federal activities.

As other agriculture programs came along, most were similarly organized. Any inconsistency of purpose or impact among programs has been treated as nonexistent or beyond the jurisdiction of any one agency. The Soil Conservation Service operates through its soil conservation districts, of which there were 2,936 in 1963 and 2,950 in 1976, involving over 90 percent of the nation's farms. These districts are actually considered units of local government, and each is in fact controlled by its own farmer-elected committee, which is not to be confused with other farmer associations or committees. Agreements between the farmer and the service for acre-by-acre soil surveys, for assistance in instituting soil-conserving practices, and for improving productivity are actually made between the farmer and the district committee. Enforcement of the agreements is handled also by the district committee.

Additional aid to the farmer channels through the cooperatives, which are in turn controlled by farmer-elected boards. Four out of five farmers belong to at least one co-op. The Farmer Cooperative Service touches the farmer only through the boards of directors of the cooperatives as the boards see fit.

When the stakes get larger, the pattern of local self-government remains the same. Price support, the parity program, is run by the thousands of farmer-elected county committees of farmers, which function alongside but quite independently of the other local committees. Acreage allotments to bring supply down and prices up are apportioned among the states by the Agricultural Stabilization and Conservation Service (ASCS). (The ASCS is the lineal descendant, thrice removed, of the Agricultural Adjustment Act [AAA].) State committees of farmers apportion the allotment among the counties. The farmer-elected county Stabilization and Conservation Committees receive the county allotment. The county committees made the original acreage allotments among individual farmers back in the 1930s, and they now make new allotments, bring about any adjustments and review complaints regarding allotments, determine whether quotas have been complied with, inspect and approve storage facilities, and act as the court of original jurisdiction on violations of price-support rules and on eligibility for parity payments. The committees are also vitally important in campaigning for the two-thirds vote acceptance of high price-support referenda. Congress determines the general level of support, and the Secretary of Agriculture proclaims the national acreage quotas for adjusting supply to guaranteed price. But the locally elected committees stand between the farmer and the Congress, the Secretary, the ASCS, and the Commodity Credit Corporation.

In agriculture credit, local self-government is found in even greater complexity. The Farmers Home Administration (FHA, but not to be confused with Federal Housing Administration) and the Farm Credit Administration are, in essence, banks; and as banks they are unique. Credit extended by the FHA is almost entirely controlled by local FHA farmer committees. There is one per county, and again these are not to be confused with the other committees. The much larger Farm Credit Administration, an independent agency since 1953, was within the Department of Agriculture from 1938 until 1953 and was autonomous before that. But its departmental status is irrelevant, because it also operates through local farmer control. There is not one but three bodies politic within the FCA.

1. Membership in the mortgage loan body politic requires the purchase of stock in a local land-bank association. Broad participation is so strongly desired that it has been made mandatory. The farmer borrower must purchase an amount of voting stock equal to 5 percent of his loan in one of the 750 land-bank associations.

2. In the short-term loan body politic, 487 separate production credit associations own virtually all the stock, and the farmer-owners or their representatives pass upon all requests for loans within their respective districts. It is a point of pride in the FCA that ownership and control of these banks have passed from government to local, private hands.

3. The third body politic within the FCA is the cooperative system, controlled by elected farmer-directors and operated by credit available from the FCA's Central Bank for Cooperatives and its 12 district Banks for Cooperatives.

The Ten Systems and Politics

Taking all the agriculture programs, there are as many as ten separate, autonomous, self-governing systems—each with its own local constituencies, private support groups, and participation routines that give it consensus and legitimacy, and help maintain its separation from the others and from the department and the White House. In fiscal year 1962, $5.6 billion of the total $6.7 billion Department of Agriculture budget were accounted for by these self-governing systems. An additional $5.8 billion in loans were handled by these systems. In fiscal year 1976, because of a cyclical drop in price-support payments, $6 billion of a $15 billion budget went through these same systems, essentially unchanged 13 years after the first visit. Loans administered through these systems (mainly through the Commodity Credit Corporation, the Farmers Home Administration, and the Farm Credit Administration) amounted to $25 billion in fiscal year 1976. A better sense of the continuing importance of these self-governing systems can be conveyed by subtracting from the total expenditure budget the $7.5 billion food stamp program because this is basically part of the welfare system ancillary to Aid to Families of Dependent Children (AFDC) and other welfare programs (see Chapter 8). This means that 80 percent of agriculture policy was still lodged in these systems. They are the state of agriculture.

Due to the special intimacy between federal agriculture programs and private agriculture, each administrative organization becomes a potent political instrumentality. Each of the self-governing local units becomes one important point in a definable political system which both administers a program and maintains the autonomy of that program in face of all other political forces emanating from other agriculture systems, from antagonistic farm and nonfarm interests, from Congress, from the secretary, and from the president.

The politics of each of these self-governing programs is comprised of a triangular trading pattern, with each point complementing and supporting the other two. The three points are: the central agency, a congressional committee or subcommittee, and the local or district farmer committees. The latter are also usually the grassroots element of a national interest group.

The classic case is Extension. The Extension Service at the center of this system is supported in Congress by the long-tenure Farm Bureau members of the agriculture committees, particularly in the Senate. The grassroots segment is composed of the Farm Bureau Federation and the local extension committees around which the Farm Bureau was originally organized and to which the Bureau continues to contribute assistance. Further interest group support comes from two intimately related organizations, the Association of Land-Grant Colleges and Universities and its tributary, the National Association of County Agricultural Agents.

Another such triangle unites the Soil Conservation Service (SCS) with Congress primarily through the Subcommittee on Agriculture of the House Committee on

Appropriations, through which SCS managed to double its appropriations between 1940 and the early postwar years while severely limiting the related activities of the FHA and the old AAA and its successors. The third point is the local soil-conservation districts, which speak individually to the local congressman and nationally to Congress and the president through the very energetic National Association of Soil Conservation Districts. The SCS draws further support from the Soil Conservation Society of America (mainly professionals) and the Izaak Walton League of America (formerly Friends of the Land, mainly urban well-wishers).

Similar but much more complex forms characterize the price-support system. The Agriculture Stabilization and Conservation Service ties into Congress through the eight (formerly ten) commodity subcommittees of the House Agriculture Committee and the dozens of separately organized interest groups representing each of the single commodities. (Examples: National Cotton Council, American Wool Growers Association, American Cranberry Growers Association.) These in turn draw from the local price-support committees.

As in geometry and engineering, so in politics the triangle seems to be the most stable type of structure. There is an immense capacity in each agriculture system, once created, to maintain itself and to resist any type of representation except its own. These self-governing agriculture systems have such institutional legitimacy that they have become practically insulated from the three central sources of democratic political responsibility: (1) Within the Executive Branch they are autonomous. Secretaries of agriculture have tried and failed to consolidate or even to coordinate related programs. (2) Within Congress, they are sufficiently powerful within their own domain to be able to exercise an effective veto or to create stalemate. (3) Agriculture activities and agencies are almost totally removed from the view of the general public. Upon becoming the exclusive province of those who are most directly interested in them, programs are first split off from general elective political responsibility. (Rarely has there been more than one urban member on the House Committee on Agriculture, sometimes not even one.) After specialization there is total submersion.

The Corporate State

Important cases illustrate the consequences. In fact, in even a casual reading of the history of agriculture policy such cases are impossible to avoid.

Case 1

In 1947, Secretary of Agriculture Clinton P. Anderson proposed a consolidation of all soil-conservation, price-support, and FHA programs into one committee system with a direct line from the committees to the secretary. Bills were prepared providing for consolidation within the price-support committees. Contrary bills were produced providing for consolidation under soil conservation districts. Stalemate, 1947. In 1948, a leading farm senator proposed consolidation of the whole effort under the local associations of the Extension Service. Immediately a House farm leader introduced a bill diametrically opposed. The result, continuing stalemate.

Case 2

In Waco, Texas, on October 14, 1952, presidential candidate Dwight Eisenhower said, "I would like to see in every county all federal farm agencies under the same roof." Pursuant to this promise, Secretary of Agriculture Ezra Taft Benson issued a series of orders during early 1953 attempting to bring about consolidation of local units as well as unification at the top, mainly by appointing some professional agriculture employees to membership in local committees. Finally, amid cries of "sneak attack" and "agricat," Benson proclaimed that "any work on the further consolidation of county and state offices ... shall be suspended."

Case 3

From the very beginning, Secretary Benson sought to abandon rigid price supports and bring actual supports closer to market prices. In 1954, as he was beginning to succeed, Congress enacted a commodity set-aside by which $2.5 billion of surplus commodities already held by the government were declared to be a "frozen reserve" for national defense. Since the secretary's power to cut price supports depends heavily upon the amount of government-owned surplus carried over from previous years, the commodity set-aside was a way of freezing parity as well as reserves. Benson eventually succeeded in reducing supports on the few commodities over which he had authority. But thanks to the set-aside, Congress, between fiscal 1952 and 1957, helped increase the value of commodities held by the government from $1.1 billion to $5.3 billion. What appeared, therefore, to be a real Republican policy shift amounted to no more than giving back with one hand what had been taken away by the other.

Case 4

President Eisenhower's first budget sought to abolish farm home-building and improvement loans by eliminating the budgetary request and by further requesting that the 1949 authorization law be allowed to expire. Congress overrode his request in 1953 and each succeeding year, and the president answered Congress with a year-by-year refusal to implement the farm housing program. In 1956, when the president asked again explicitly for elimination of the program, he was rebuffed. The Subcommittee on Housing of the House Banking and Currency Committee added to the president's omnibus housing bill a renewal of the farm housing program, plus an authorization for $500 million in loans over a five-year period, and the bill passed with a congressional mandate to use the funds. They were used thereafter at a rate of about $75 million a year.

Case 5

On March 16, 1961, President Kennedy introduced a "radically different" farm program in a special message to Congress. For the first time in the history of price supports, the bill called for surplus control through quotas placed on bushels, tons, or other units, rather than on acreage. An acreage allotment allows the farmer to produce as much as he can on the reduced acreage in cultivation. For example, in the first ten years or so of acreage control, acreage under cultivation dropped by about 4 percent, while actual production rose by 15 percent. The Kennedy proposal called for national committees of farmers to be elected to work out the actual program. This more stringent type of control was eliminated from the omnibus bill in the Agriculture Committees of both chambers and there were no attempts to restore them during floor debate. Last-minute efforts by Secretary Orville L. Freeman to up the ante, offering to raise wheat supports from $1.79 to $2.00, were useless. Persistence by the Administration led eventually to rejection by wheat farmers in 1963 of all high price supports and acreage controls.

The politics of this rejected referendum is of general significance. Despite all the blandishments and inducements of the Administration, the farmer had had his way. The local price-support committees had usually campaigned in these referenda for the Department of Agriculture, but this time they did not. And thousands of small farmers, eligible to vote for the first time, joined with the local leadership to help defeat the referendum. It is not so odd that wheat farmers would reject a proposal that aimed to regulate them more strictly than before. What is odd is that only wheat farmers were allowed to decide the matter. It seems that in agriculture, as in many other fields, the regulators are powerless without the consent of the regulated.

Economic Policy for Industrial Society: The Empty Houses

The Departments of Commerce and Labor, along with Agriculture, are very special units of government. From the very beginning, these departments were founded upon their dependence, not their independence. Widely known as clientele departments, they are organized around an identifiable sector of the economy and are legally obliged to develop and maintain an orientation toward the interests that comprise this sector. While there are other governmental agencies of the same type, these are the only three of Cabinet status and scope. All other departments of Cabinet rank are organized around some governmental process or function rather than around a set of persons legally identified as desirable.

As clientele agencies the Departments of Commerce and Labor are not meant to be governing agencies except in some marginal way. They are and were meant to be agencies of representation. They were, in other words, set up not to govern but to be governed. In a manner not unlike the early German and Italian Councils of Corporations, these departments provide functional representation, to be contrasted to the geographical representation provided for in Congress under the Constitution. With Agriculture, these departments are three Economic Parliaments; they constitute a true Fourth Estate in our governing order. Since Agriculture possesses many powers along with its representation function, largely because it represents the class in retreat, Commerce and Labor are left as the pure cases of functional representation.

The Departments of Commerce and Labor were founded simultaneously in 1903 as a single Department of Commerce and Labor "to foster, promote, and develop the foreign and domestic commerce, the mining, manufacturing, shipping, and fishing industries, and the transportation facilities of the United States." But this arrangement was not at all satisfactory to the newly organizing AFL, which rightly saw itself as the poor relative in the family. Labor had been seeking representation in a Cabinet department for many years. They had taken only minor satisfaction in the Bureau of Labor, established in the Department of Interior in 1884; and no improvement was seen in making that bureau an independent but non-Cabinet agency in 1888.

Labor was not to get its full representation until 1913, when the separate Department of Labor was created to "foster, promote, and develop the welfare of the wage earners of the United States, to improve their working conditions, and to advance their opportunities for profitable employment."

Merged or separate, however, the entire history of Commerce and Labor attests to their special character and function in the governmental scheme. From the beginning they were both feedback agencies. Both were charged with any and all research and statistical work necessary to make certain that the problems and needs of their clients were known at every turn. The original Bureau of Labor, a research agency, was the core of the new department, and long after Cabinet elevation, references were frequently made to the Department of Labor Statistics. Commerce always housed our census, geographical surveys, weights and measures, domestic and international business surveys, and other research activities essential to commercial enterprise.

While the pattern of development has not been exactly the same in the two departments, neither has departed from its original responsibility for being an official collectivity of unofficial economic interests.

As the national government grew in size and power, these two departments grew also, but consistently in a way reflecting their special legal and political character: They grew through expansion of services and promotional activities. Neither department took on more than one or two of the functions involved in the new relationships between government and the economy. The revolution of the modern state bypassed them almost completely.[2]

Commerce: Government Italian Style

Functional representation in the Department of Commerce quickly expanded after 1903 in response to business needs. To its research activities was very early added the mission of encouraging business representation in government through one of the most significant of business institutions, the trade association. Trade associations, which were just beginning to form in significant numbers after 1903, are essentially legalized restraints of trade. Each serves its members and helps regularize relations among competitors by sharing information, eliminating cutthroat competition, standardizing products, pooling advertising, and so on.

The Department of Commerce fostered the trade associations where they already existed and helped organize them where they did not yet exist. Thus the department took the initiative in founding the U.S. Chamber of Commerce. Without official endorsement in 1912, the fusion of local chambers into one national business association would more than likely never have taken place. Most of the negotiating sessions among local leaders, the National Association of Manufacturers, and others were arranged by, and took place in, the office of the Secretary of Commerce and Labor. The final organization charter was written there.

The practice of official recognition and representation of trade associations in the inner processes of policy formulation was established, very much in a manner to anticipate NRA, during the war years of the Wilson Administration. This was fostered and given doctrinal support in the 1920s, primarily by Secretary of Commerce Herbert Hoover. In 1924, Secretary Hoover observed, "Legislative action is always clumsy—it is incapable of adjustment to shifting needs ... Three years of study and intimate contact with associations of economic groups convince me that there lies within them a great moving impulse toward betterment."[3] Even then the vision was one of codes of business practice formulated by trade-association processes and promulgated by the Department of Commerce. This Hoover saw as "the strong beginning of a new force in the business world."[4]

These relationships were further formalized early in the New Deal when Roosevelt's first Secretary of Commerce organized the Business Advisory Council to guide the department on "matters affecting the relations of the Department and business." This group, under the Kennedy name of Business Council, remained central to the modus operandi in the department. During the 1950s a new agency, the Business and Defense Services Administration (BDSA), was set up around a vast network of specialized business advisory committees to determine cold war industrial policies.

Labor: Little Sir Echo

Although growth in the Department of Labor produced a different pattern, it fulfilled the same purpose of bringing private interests into the interior processes of government. Here it did not take the form of fostering a trade association movement because, ironically, labor was more laissez-faire than business. Labor unions lacked status, but they had their Magna Carta in the Clayton Act and were, following Samuel Gompers, officially opposed to government intervention in the affairs of collective bargaining.

As a consequence, the department remained quite small, and the primary addition to statistics in its functional representation was the evolution of the office of the secretary itself. During the first twenty years, that Cabinet post was filled with people taken directly from the leadership ranks of organized labor. The appointments of Frances Perkins, Louis Schwellenbach, and Maurice Tobin during the New Deal–Fair Deal period did not really constitute a change from this tradition since labor representation continued to be lodged in the office of the secretary. And the contemporary role of the secretary in intervening in disputes, settling strikes, and helping with guidelines is a natural result of the department's evolution.

Commerce, Labor, and the Mainstream

The histories of these two departments present a stunning contrast to the history of American government. The 20th century political revolution has erected an enormous apparatus for public control of economic life, and the end is apparently not in sight. Yet, the Departments of Commerce and Labor have been bypassed almost altogether. As clientele agencies they are simply not to be entrusted by anyone with significant direct powers over persons and property. The existence of functional representation meant that the growth of new functions of government would almost have to take place outside the Cabinet and, therefore, in a piecemeal and uncoordinated fashion.

The original Department of Commerce and Labor included a Bureau of Corporations, armed with power to make the Sherman Antitrust Act more effective. Within a decade this had become the core of an independent Federal Trade Commission, and its removal took from Commerce the only significant regulatory and planning powers it was ever to have. One by one, and with increasing frequency, new powers and agencies of public power over business were created outside the department and outside the Cabinet. Regulation of railroads in the Interstate Commerce Commission (ICC) predated Commerce by 16 years. However, positive planning for a national railway system, a function not necessarily consistent with rate regulation, also passed to ICC when the rails were returned to private ownership after 1920. For 46 years this anomalous situation continued, until the new Transportation Department was created—outside Commerce, independent of and equal to Commerce, larger than Commerce, too late to influence the shape of transportation.

Radio communication, from the beginning a part of commerce near the very center of public domain, was also from the beginning made the responsibility of a new agency—outside and independent of Commerce. Commerce got a small piece of civil aeronautics control under the 1934 act, but by 1938 even this had been lost to the semiautonomous Civil Aeronautics Administration and then to the fully autonomous Federal Aviation Agency. The entire realm of securities, credit, banking, and currency are outside Commerce. The power industry, including civilian atomic development, got its own, non-Cabinet agencies.

True, Commerce did get the Maritime Administration in 1950, but this is a semiautonomous subsidizing agency with an altogether independent tradition and constituency. The Bureau of Public Roads was Commerce's only significant traditional exercise of commerce power, and it is clear that the secretary's authority over the bureau was almost nonexistent. For example, the April 8, 1967, release of $1.1 billion in highway construction funds was authorized by the president and the budget director without any reference whatsoever to the Secretary of Commerce.

Governmental responses to the civil rights revolution also bypassed Commerce, despite the deep involvement of civil rights laws in business decisions. The only part of the historic 1964 Civil Rights Act going to Commerce was the Community Relations Service, which is essentially a center for communications, conciliation, and conference holding. The only part of the New Frontier–Great Society in which Commerce participated was the Area Redevelopment Administration, an important but relatively declining feature of the new social legislation which, by 1965, as the Economic Development Administration, had become essentially a public works program. The Appalachia Program was developed in Commerce but immediately became the property of the Appalachian states. In sum, almost every significant commerce power of the federal government has been lodged somewhere other than in Commerce.

The Department of Labor is a pint-sized version of the same story. On the eve of the Roosevelt revolution, Labor was a microscopic Cabinet department whose only significant governing activity was the Immigration and Naturalization Service. (This unusual responsibility for controlling the noncitizen competitors for jobs comprised 80 percent of the department's budget.) During the 1930s, government expanded its relation to the laboring man in many ways, but little of this involved the laboring man's department. On the contrary, the department declined relative to virtually every other sector of public activity.

Over the protest of Frances Perkins, almost all New Deal labor programs escaped her department. The 1934 railway labor legislation came early in her incumbency and set the tone for what was to follow. A board was set up with 36 representatives, outside Labor, to deal with railway labor disputes in a gray area somewhere between private arbitration and public adjudication. The National Labor Relations Board became an independent commission. All but one of the Social Security programs, the least important one, were organized outside the Department of Labor. The National Bituminous Coal Commission, with its many labor responsibilities, escaped both Labor and Commerce.

The only major governmental responsibilities entrusted to Labor by Roosevelt were the regulatory programs under the Walsh-Healy and Fair Labor Standards Acts, now administered by the one Wages and Hours and Public Contracts Division. But while Labor was gaining those tasks, it was losing still more. Of its four original core jurisdictions—labor statistics, immigration, conciliation, and children—Labor lost as follows: Immigration went to the Department of Justice in 1940; the Children's Bureau went to the Federal Security Agency (now the Department of Health, Education and Welfare) in 1946; the Federal Mediation and Conciliation Service was converted by the Taft-Hartley Act into an independent agency. Labor even lost the Bureau of Employment Security in 1939, regaining it in 1950 only after a long struggle.

In general, Labor participated almost as little as Commerce in the social revolution of the 1960s. This includes almost all the most significant features of the New Frontier–Great Society programs. The Office of Economic Opportunity (OEO), VISTA, and the antidiscrimination provisions of the civil rights and antipoverty legislation are in the labor field but not in the Labor Department. About half of the manpower training program of 1962 comprises all of Labor's share of the government explosion of the 1960s.

Pluralistic Power and Pluralistic Government

In 1967 President Johnson made a serious but vain proposal to merge once again the Departments of Commerce and Labor, just over half a century after their original union was dissolved. Some types of merger can be significant. Merger of the National Guard with the Reserve would be significant. Merger of Nassau County with New York City would be significant. The very insignificance of the proposed Commerce-Labor merger raises all sorts of fundamental questions about the politics and administration of economic policy in the national government of the United States.

Nothing possible could have been changed by making a duplex out of the House of Labor and the House of Commerce. Nothing would have been subtracted except one voice from Cabinet meetings. Nothing would have been added except frustrated expectations. No additional order, coordination, purpose, or policy could have come out of the merger *because the really important controls over economic life would not have been involved.*

This only barely suggests the state of things. The insignificance of the Commerce and Labor Departments is a monument to the overwhelming innocence of the liberal spirit in America, which has justified the tangle of government controls as necessary for maximum flexibility, maximum expertise, and maximum insurance for keeping control out of politics. The real economic powers of government are nonpolitical if Humpty-Dumpty is your lexicographer. They seem flexible only because they are numerous. They seem rational only because they are specialized. Control over the American economic system is split up among the Treasury, the Office of Management and Budget, the Council of Economic Advisers through the president, the Joint Committee on Internal Revenue Taxation, the Federal Reserve Board, the Social Security System, the ten or more agriculture systems, the many specialized regulatory agencies, the Office of the Secretary of Defense—and others. All of them exist separately and independently. There is hardly a scintilla of central control, because no such control could ever be entrusted to any one of them. No governing institution possesses central control, because in the liberal state a virtue is made of its absence.

Commerce and Labor are on the periphery still further because they were captured by too narrow a range of interests. As a consequence their very existence works a positive harm. They have done little more than help prevent expansion of the Cabinet toward an attempt at central control. And the two departments not only helped prevent development of an integrated and rational economic policy establishment; the harm goes further. The processes of functional representation in Labor and Commerce have helped to blind national leadership to the need for integration by creating and reporting business consensus and labor solidarity when the only consensus was that among the very special interests established therein. Merger of Commerce and Labor would have created false hopes and expectations. A bold approach to economic policy can be begun only with their abolition.

There will also be little rationality to national economic policy until somehow agriculture is integrated, and this is an even more difficult problem, because the Department of Agriculture administers real government programs and therefore cannot simply be abolished. Political responsibility and the prospect of planning were destroyed when agriculture policy-making was parceled out to the most interested parties. No progress toward correcting that situation can be made until it is fully realized that over $10 billion of government-agriculture intimacy per year is too much agriculture policy to be entrusted to agriculturalists.

Reversing the situation in agriculture is made still more difficult by the fact that the autonomy of agriculture is grounded in the still more legitimated local committees. To attack them is to chip away at idols. This legitimacy reinforces the very considerable political power of agriculture interests, the source of which is often misunderstood. The problem of rural versus urban political power was never really one of simply poor legislative apportionment. Rural interests hold sway because of the specialization of their concerns and the homogeneity of interests within each agriculture system. Rural congressmen and state assemblymen, for example, are recruited by and owe their elections to the same forces that operate the quasi-public committees, and each level of activity reinforces the other. Mere legislative reapportionment is not likely to change this as long as there is no direct confrontation between agriculture interests and nonagriculture interests.

This confrontation could not take place as long as interest group liberal values prevailed. The cases of Agriculture, Commerce, and Labor suggest that weakened national efficacy and impaired political responsibility—the incapacity to plan—are not recent developments. However, special responsibility rests with the Eisenhower, Kennedy, and Johnson Administrations. Pluralistic solutions may have been thrust upon the New Deal due to the seriously weakened state of public confidence and public finance. The weakened state of the presidency and the Democratic Party under Truman made fresh departures in domestic affairs close to impossible.[5] But after 1952 there was peace, confidence, and efficacy. In Europe and the United States in the 1930s pluralist solutions were turned to out of weakness. The state was forced to share its sovereignty in return for support. *In the 1960s pluralist solutions were not forced upon national leaders but were voluntarily pursued as the highest expression of their ideology.* This must change before the pattern will change.

Republican Succession: No Change, More of the Same Thing

Yet, during the late 1960s the character of the clientele departments was further confirmed. Their extreme resistance to change seems to have succeeded beyond merely the avoidance of change. Despite the rumors that agriculture power had been waning or that union and corporate power were being fragmented by stagflation, the pattern of the 1970s seems to have been no change *and* more of the same thing. In the country at large, even in the rhetoric of the Nixon Administration, there was a vast preoccupation with poverty, hunger, and a variety of specific ills for which a Department of Agriculture, a Department of Labor, a Department of Commerce, and other related clientele departments might have been a focus for appropriate action. It probably comes as a surprise to few that no such actions came from or through those departments.

The State of Agriculture

Let us examine the Department of Agriculture. The 1969 bill of the Nixon Administration, although touted as an Omnibus Farm Bill, extended the basic features of the legislation of previous Democratic administrations. As enacted in 1970, the Nixon Administration program actually added a few reinforcing twists of its own. The only sign that the class and racial turmoils of the 1960s had been recognized at all in the Agriculture Department or related congressional committees or in the White House was the ceiling of $55,000 on the price-support payments the government could make to any one farmer. (Title I. This was lowered to $20,000 in 1973.) Although this ceiling may have established a principle of fundamental reform for the future, and although the principle was to come up for debate again and again in succeeding years, the realities of 1970–73 produced so many loopholes that the principle was virtually overturned. And these loopholes are consistent with the established interest group liberal pattern in the field of agricultural policy. For example, the law permits farmers to sell or lease part of their acreage allotment (the number of acres on which any farmer can raise a surplus crop) and to receive income from that sale or lease without counting that income against the government price-support payments. This means that a large farmer, who has acreage allotments on which he can receive no further price-support payments, can sell or lease the allotments for further income while the purchaser or lessee of those allotments can either grow the crop or himself receive price-support payments—up to the ceiling. Meanwhile, the original farmer, having shed the unneeded allotment, can grow certain alternate (nonsurplus) crops and again not have to count the income received from those crops against the total price permissible for support payments.

The rest of the Republican formula for agriculture was wholly consistent with approaches of the 1960s. Title II continued federal milk marketing orders. Title III extended the National Wool Act for three more years, retaining the high "incentive price" for wool growers. Title IV continued the price-support structure for wheat and in fact liberalized the supports by suspending acreage quotas through 1973. The Eisenhower soil-bank approach to acreage reduction was extended under a new name, set-asides. And the elaborate committee system described earlier was left completely untouched.

Another indication of the continuation of established patterns of policy and government in agriculture was the posture of the 1970 act toward government sponsorship of private interests. The act went further than merely continuing the Cotton Board established during the Johnson administration (affectionately called Cotton Inc.); it actually authorized the Commodity Credit Corporation (CCC) to pay Cotton Inc. up to $10 million per year to enable it to "enter into agreements with [a contracting organization] for the conduct of domestic and foreign markets, of market development, research or sales promotion programs, and programs to aid in the development of new and additional markets" (section 610). The only proviso in this section of the act was that none of these funds could be used to try to influence future agriculture legislation. Cotton Inc. brought on a clamor of demands for equivalent promotional programs for other commodities. One was for funds to pay for advertising and promotion for milk; another was for funds for the promotion of apples and papayas. Two demands succeeded extremely well: Late in 1970 Congress passed the Potato Research Promotion Act creating a National Potato Promotion Board to engage in potato research, development, advertising, and promotion. It was to be financed by an assessment of up to 1 percent per hundredweight of potatoes produced commercially in the United States. The act also added tomatoes to the list of commodities for which the Agriculture Department could run paid advertisements. (Others on the list, going as far back as 1937, were peanuts and cotton.)

In 1974, Congress established the Egg Board to accomplish these same purposes for the egg producers. The official legislative history on this act explicitly recognized that government sponsorship was necessary because the egg producing industry has been unable to organize itself independently for [these] purposes. A basic impediment has been the wide variation in the size of the nation's egg producers.... The bill is specifically designed for the participation of only commercial egg producers with laying flocks of more than 3,000. Even though small producers will not participate, ... benefits from the program will accrue to all egg producers.[6]

In the grand tradition, membership on these new boards was to be composed of representatives of producers designated by the Secretary of Agriculture from nominations made by producers in a manner prescribed by the Secretary.

The 1973 Agricultural and Consumer Protection Act continued most of the existing 1970 and pre-1970 provisions, despite the context of extremely high domestic and world demand for agricultural products. The government took no significant steps to bring agriculture prices down; in fact, agriculture price increases were not brought within the wage-and-price-control system established after 1970 for virtually all nonagricultural commodities during that period. The important innovation in the 1973 legislation was the adding of target prices against which to compare actual prices paid to the farmer. The difference between the two would be made up for by direct government support payments for farmers participating in the set-aside program. This is reminiscent of the very generous Brannan Plan of the late 1940s, and the Republicans were lucky enough to be saved from its full budgetary implications by the high world demand for U.S. produce. And although in greatest part this high demand was natural, part of it was artificially induced by still another, purely interest group liberal victory, the famous 1972 trade agreement providing for the sale of over $1 billion of American grain to the Russians through low-interest credit plus a heavily subsidized per bushel price. This story is related in detail (in Chapter 6 of *The End of Liberalism*) as part of the analysis of the Republican approach to foreign policy.

One other significant piece of legislation during the Republican period was the creation of the Commodity Futures Trading Commission, which consolidated government control over speculation in agricultural products and their prices. This effort to enhance and clarify regulatory power was in no way a sign of political defeat for agriculture but rather was a reaction to the explosive growth of commodity trading and a blow against the many exploiters of instability in agriculture prices working in the major exchanges in the large cities. What is really significant politically about this act is the fact that the new Commodity Futures Trading Commission, which was established to take over all authority of the Commodity Exchange Commission, was withdrawn from the Department of Agriculture and made into an independent regulatory commission.

Interest Group Liberalism in Labor and Commerce

The Republican administration was not at all reluctant to intervene in matters affecting the nation's commercial life. Although President Nixon had not wanted wage and price control, he utilized this authority with vigor not very long after it was handed to him by Congress through the Economic Stabilization Act of 1970. Characteristically, this most important single government intervention of the decade—possibly any decade before or since the 1930s—was formulated and implemented outside the Departments of Labor and Commerce. Nixon's Ash Commission (the President's Advisory Council on Executive Organization) recognized the lack of utility of these departments by proposing their abolition through reorganizing their constituent agencies into a new superdepartment. Although the Watergate crisis killed any chance of serious departmental reorganization, the Nixon and Ford Administrations continued to view the Departments of Labor and Commerce as nothing more than the channels for interest accommodation they had always been. Revenue sharing not only bypassed the departments but weakened them still further by reducing the needs of local governments to seek their specific assistance.

The Commerce Department had the most barren record of all departments in the 1970s. By Executive Orders in 1969 and 1971, President Nixon established the Office of Minority Business Enterprise (OMBE). Its job is to coordinate federal efforts to strengthen minority business. But the agency has no direct authority over other agencies in the federal government or over the activities of local agencies receiving federal assistance. Thus the only White House moves of any importance in matters affecting commerce or the Commerce Department were the Rail Passenger Service Act in 1970 and the Consumer Product Safety Act of 1972. The former created Amtrak (the National Railroad Passenger Corporation). The latter created the Consumer Product Safety Commission. Both were made almost completely independent of the Commerce Department. The Consumer Product Safety Commission is a classic independent regulatory commission. Amtrak is an independent enterprise attempting to bail out and operate the nation's passenger rail service. It is independent of the Department of Commerce and the Department of Transportation. Its board of directors is composed of nine public members appointed by the president without need of Senate approval and three members actually selected by the various railroad companies which own Amtrak stock.[7]

The Labor Department got a bit more attention during the 1970s, not because it received any authority to implement wage-and-price controls—which it did not—but because of two particular programs—OSHA and CETA. OSHA (Occupational Safety and Health Administration) is a rare instance of a regulatory program housed in a regular departmental agency rather than set up as or within an independent commission. OSHA has also been one of the more maligned and caricatured government agencies (not without justification—for example, one OSHA regulation uses several pages to define a safe ladder; another regulation requires steel workers to wear life jackets even when building bridges over dry riverbeds in the Southwest). However, what is most significant about OSHA—and what may explain why it was housed as a regular agency within the Department of Labor—is its authority under the 1970 act to adopt "national consensus standards." The act states explicitly that a

> national consensus standard [is] any occupational safety and health standard or modification which (1) has been adopted and promulgated by a nationally recognized standards-producing organization under procedures whereby it can be determined by the Secretary that persons affected have reached substantial agreement on its adoption; (2) and formulated after an opportunity for consideration of diverse views; (3) and designated as such a standard by the Secretary, after consultation with other appropriate Federal agencies.[8]

CETA (Comprehensive Employment and Training Act of 1973) is even more an indication of the continuity of values from Democrats to Republicans, because it was a legislative culmination of a four-year effort by the Nixon Administration. Although CETA probably did clarify the lines of administrative authority among manpower programs, the CETA legislation, long and detailed as it was, failed to set any guidelines or limits on the decisions of its newly created Office of Comprehensive Employment Development Programs (OCED). CETA defined OCED's authority in terms that were completely open-ended: "Comprehensive manpower services may include, *but shall not be limited to.*" The act then went on to identify at least two dozen things the OCED might do, but in any case this was in the context of the opening clause that the OCED was not limited to just these things.[9] Therefore, for almost any purposes within the judgment of the agency, OCED could make grants to states or units of local government on the basis of applications made by those state and local units to OCED. OCED was to have no plan but was obliged (sections 104–5) to consider only those applications based upon (1) a "comprehensive manpower plan produced by the applying unit and (2) a local planning council consisting, to the extent practicable, of members who are representative of the client community and the community-based organization, the employment service, educational and training agencies and institutions, business, labor and, where appropriate, agriculture." Some critics, especially congressional Democrats, accused President Nixon of hiding a drastic reduction of manpower dollars behind a bid for rational administration. Possibly so; nevertheless, Nixon's method of cutting down the budget could hardly have been more consistent with Democratic ways and means of using government.

CETA may best be understood as part of Nixon's general plan as expressed in revenue sharing to push more federal activities down to local levels. As discussed elsewhere, General Revenue Sharing, provided for in the State and Local Fiscal Assistance Act of 1972, went a step further than the Democrats but in exactly their direction. This is true regardless of the inclination of Republicans to spend less or to consolidate, reduce, or terminate some programs. For example, despite, or through, a few programs like CETA, Nixon did cut back drastically on "categoric aid" (federal grants that are given to state and local governments on condition that the money be spent only in the prescribed subject matter area, such as grants-in-aid or soil conservation, education, vocational rehabilitation, and so forth). But rather than cut further, Nixon diverted the remaining federal assistance and grants-in-aid to revenue sharing. This meant that Nixon was removing the remaining limits on the discretion of administrative agencies to make policy as they saw fit. Under categoric aid programs, there were already no explicit standards to delimit or guide administrative decision-making. Yet, there is a bit of limitation on discretion inherent in the subject matter categories themselves. Under General Revenue Sharing, even these limitations were abolished. When a local government gets money under revenue sharing, it can choose almost without any constraint whether to spend that money to pay the interest on its local bonds or to spend that money to buy a General Sherman tank. Thus, here again Nixon's New Federalism turned out to be no change, more of the same thing. Republicans in the 1970s were simply more niggardly interest group liberals.

It is quite misleading to try to explain the politics of the Departments of Agriculture, Commerce, Labor, and, for that matter, the other clientele departments such as Interior and Transportation, in terms of the power of the respective groups or sectors of the economy. First of all, power begs the question. Having seen results that look like success—access, favorable policies, appropriations, holding actions—observers then use *power* as the ancient scientist used phlogiston to explain combustion: "Something must have been present. Let's give it a name." In the second place, power implies an exercise of some kind of influence or force by the outside interest upon the agency or legislature. It is probably closer to the truth to deny altogether the role of influence *upon* the government and to look instead for the influence that is *within* the policy-maker. What we see mostly in the policies and in the administrative practices of a whole succession of administrations and their agencies and support blocs in Congress is a congruence of values and ideologies. And this is by far the most insidious of types of influence, especially when the influence is so internalized and all-inclusive as to go unrecognized as ideology and be accepted as a natural phenomenon—indeed accepted not merely as the truth (in the sense of a confirmed hypothesis) but actually as something that is inherent in the system itself. Political scientists and practitioners call what they see the political process without recognizing that *process* brings unfair and misleading connotations from its use in biology. Politics may be natural, but particular forms are artificial. They can be made and remade.

Few who are familiar with the United States are surprised to learn that agribusiness, with 5 percent of the population, determines whether the other 95 percent will eat and how much they will have to pay for the privilege. Few will be surprised with the assertion that a tiny minority of workers—those organized in a few of the larger unions—call the tune on labor and employment legislation. Most knowledgeable observers will also shrug off as truistic any reports that all the procedural and most of the policy decisions toward commerce and industry are precleared with the National Association of Manufacturers (NAM) and related business interests. What is likely to surprise and disturb most observers is the mere contention that none of this is natural or inherent. Few have stopped even to ask whether *process* is fair terminology in society, especially in government. Pluralistic politics, as observed in these programs of the Departments of Agriculture, Labor, and Commerce, is not a process at all, if this is meant to imply something natural and inevitable. What we have seen is the result of actual government sponsorship of pluralism. It is not natural; it is simply repeated, through a succession of Democratic and Republican administrations. Pluralism as we can observe it in the actual conduct of American government is nothing but an artifact, an expression of widely shared ideology. It is the furthest thing from a natural and inevitable expression of capitalism; it is not even a necessary expression of what could be called pluralist democracy. It is simply one pathological expression of pluralist democracy. The fact that Democratic patterns are picked up and repeated by as partisan an anti-Democrat as Richard Nixon proves not that the observed patterns are inherent but only that they have become institutionalized. And if they are artificial patterns rather than natural processes, these patterns can be changed. If the supportive ideology of interest group liberalism can be changed, then the pattern it supports will also change. However, it must be admitted that changing the ideology and the patterns will be more difficult after the 1970s than it appeared to be at the end of the 1960s. Succession from partisan Democrats to partisan Republicans nails the pattern down more firmly in the heads and habits, and eventually in the mores, of American leaders, American active publics, and the ordinary American citizen. Indeed, it is all so well established in our minds and in our legitimized and government-sponsored power patterns that we are obliged to call it the Second Republic. Consequently, only a radical, organized constitutional revolt will succeed now where once a sustained intellectual attack might have been sufficient.

Part V

**Outside the Box,
Outside the Mainstream**

The Politics of Movements, Radicalism,
and Morality in Comparative Perspective

Part V begins to test the application of the Arenas of Power model in political processes and regimes that are outside the mainstream of the stable modern state. The implicit question is whether the model is specific to the relatively stable nation-state structures that prevailed in Western Europe and North America from the mid-nineteenth century to the mid-twentieth century, or whether it can also provide valuable insights in conditions where mass movements, emerging states, and recurrent conflict prevail—a good deal of today's world. Lowi's ability to fit this model to the United States as both an emerging state in the eighteenth century and an emerging global power in the twentieth would appear to justify serious consideration of the model's broader applicability. Chapter 12 and Chapter 13 focus on the politics of radical social movements that seek to alter significantly the structure of policy and power and to redefine the relationship of the citizen to the state. In Chapter 14, Lowi addresses yet a different set of potentially disruptive political and economic forces that could largely be ignored in exploring mainstream U.S. politics of past eras—globalization. The chapter addresses inherently important questions in U.S. politics. But these questions are even more important analytically because they set the stage for the application of the Arenas of Power model to environments other than those in the United States.

These questions about the potential explanatory power of the Arenas of Power model are critical, for example, to understanding the politics of less developed countries. Developing countries typically have distinct political institutions, great volatility and fragility, and regimes trying not only to adapt to a global political economy but to define themselves as a nation. They are attempting to consolidate the power to govern in the face of enormous fissiparous tendencies and competitive sources of legitimate authority. Poor countries with minimal economic growth and minimal revenues generally also have minimal governance capacity.

Without revenues, distributive policies that could minimize conflict and tie citizens to the state cannot be maintained. For the same reason, redistributive policies are equally difficult to sustain. Threats to the government in a poor country are, therefore, common, which convinces fragile regimes to invest heavily in the police power of the state that frequently translates into a preference for regulatory policies. But many of these regimes cannot even meet the recurrent costs of paying their public servants, including the police and military. What evolves is a combination of ineffective regulation combined with distributive policies based on indulgences and patronage—exemptions from regulations.

In this environment, the political economy becomes dependent on foreign aid. Aid makes distributive policies possible (medical services, food, and infrastructure) without serious redistributive implications. It appears to mirror some nineteenth-century U.S. policies Lowi describes, such as the federal land grants. This set of distributive policies is the key to the political economy of the UN Millennium Development Goals, through which the international donor community makes government possible by subsidizing some of the fundamental welfare functions of the modern state—but generally only through distributive policies and often through intermediaries such as nongovernmental organizations. It is interesting that many advocates of the Millennium Development Goals explicitly criticize previous redistributive policies associated with macroeconomic reform as failures. Lowi's model may indeed offer insights as to why this might be the case.

For those countries with important extractive industries, external resource flows can also sustain distributive policies. Diamonds, oil, and timber, for example, finance patronage and the maintenance of minimal police functions. However, this source of revenue, unlike foreign aid, does not seem to be associated with broad-based distributive policies. Rather, there is a high correlation between extractive industries in fragile states and recurrent civil war and violence that seem to suggest that distributive policies do not invariably reduce conflict. Further, regimes where institutions become specialized in patronage politics find it difficult to make the structural changes in the economy that make growth and integration into the global economy possible. The powerful have no interest in a competitive economy and the weak that would be helped by one are either unorganized (farmers) or do not exist (manufacturing).

Thus, stepping outside mainstream politics, as this part does, invites us to explore how the four policy types interact with diverse constitutional environments, as well as great variation in institutional capacity and institutional incentives. It may also broaden our set of cases, which may help us to explain how, for example, distributive policies may sometimes be highly stabilizing, but alternatively may produce either stagnation or conflict. Such analysis may also help us to understand both the supply and demand for institutional and policy change and the factors that facilitate or inhibit major structural changes in the political economy of a country.

"Prospects of Conquest: With Liberty and Justice for Some" (Chapter 12) departs from most of the other material in this book, and in Theodore Lowi's work generally, by addressing the historical traditions of violence and protest in the United States that repudiate both existing laws and the political processes that create them. These traditions, he suggests, are much more frequent than students of U.S. politics usually admit.

Protest is rooted in the fact that the most basic characteristic of government is coercion. He questions the idea that public policy, even in a democracy, actually reflects a consensual political will of the populace. There are always winners and losers resulting from less than perfect compromises. Transaction costs multiply. By their nature, institutions respond slowly to inevitable changes in the environment, yielding increasingly unsatisfactory results. Nor can the misuse of power and tyranny be discounted as a source of discontent. Conversely, new interests emerge, or become self-conscious, but may lack the skill, organization, or access to play within the existing rules. In short, consensus is a possible but not a necessary or stable condition of the political system.

Dissidence, mild or severe, is a function of the degree of stress on the system, the options open to dissidents, and the capacity of the state to provide and implement effective policy options. Lowi considers the last point to be crucial. The modern state, he argues, has vastly more opportunities to respond to dissidence than its predecessors did. The modernization of the American state in the post–World War II era has produced a sea change in the frequency, depth, and determination of the federal government's response to dissidence and violence, not always efficacious.

Lowi distinguishes three types of dissidence—withdrawal, revolution, and rebellion. The last, he suggests, is the most common form of dissent in the United States. Rebellion, he argues, is direct and conscious effort to change *the behavior* of the regime through extralegal and extraconstitutional action, but, unlike revolution, rebellion does not seek to change the regime. He recounts a history of rebellion in the United States that includes the American Revolution, various agrarian rebellions, the southern white rebellion (Civil War), labor violence, and urban protest (both white and black).

This line of argument is central to the themes of Part V. At some level, rebellion is a catalyst for policy and institutional changes. Up until the New Deal most of the rebellious activity took place at the state level and was addressed there. The national government was hyperstable—thanks to the predominance of distributive policies. But as we have seen (Chapter 6), with the "Europeanization" of U.S. politics in the 1960s, the federal government began to expand both its regulatory and redistributive policies and, in consequence, played an ever larger role in response to dissidence as the national government became the focus of protest. National politics must now address the contradictions between freedom and control that were well understood by the drafters of the U.S. Constitution, but largely driven to the state level by the federal Constitution.

"New Dimensions in Policy and Politics" (Chapter 13) extends the argument in the previous chapter and provides suggestions for treating radical politics within the framework of the Arenas of Power scheme. It is part of the definition of radicalism that political goals are pursued outside the institutions and politics of the mainstream. Nevertheless, within the categories of the previous chapter, radical politics (rebellions) are still attempting to influence the behavior of the existing regime, which means that they are trying to shape policy. That being the case, Lowi argues, there are still only four types of policy—four ways the coercive power of the state can be employed—so even radical politics can be seen within the Arenas of Power framework.

This chapter served as an introduction to a collection of studies of social movements from which the authors concluded that the Lowi Arenas of Power model required a fifth category titled "social regulatory policy," which at a minimum would have threatened the symmetry and elegance of the original model. Lowi accepts that the existing model focused on the policies emanating from mainstream and stable politics. Once radicalism is taken within the purview of analysis, it is evident that Lowi's work generally focuses on the center of the possible distribution of political goals and practice and not the multiplicity of extremes. Within his model political goals are instrumental, not absolute. Their political modality is defined by compromise and incrementalism. For the mainstream, bad policy is simply in error. But for the radicals, bad policy is "sin." When radicals add morality to the set of instrumental goals, Lowi concludes, each of the four policy types is transformed fundamentally. Policymaking at the margin of the political system is not new in U.S. politics, but as we saw in Chapter 12, it is new to federal politics.

In expanding the model in Figure 13.1 and Table 13.1, Lowi suggests that there are, engendered in policy choice, predictable characteristics of the radical dimensions. Regulation of bad conduct becomes the elimination of immoral conduct. The instrumental value of public education and public health, with access determined by equal protection of the law, becomes a rights-based approach to social benefits defined in terms of an absolute standard. One can interpret this extension as either a threshold that a policy type crosses and is then transformed, or as a third dimension of the two-dimensional model. Either interpretation will explain the fact that politics within that dimension or beyond that threshold is significantly changed, but still retains many predictable components that can be deduced from the Arenas of Power model itself. But the really interesting question is, if there is one additional dimension or threshold, cannot one imagine a third, or more? For example, the internationalizing of regulatory policy beyond the U.S. political system through treaty, or the recognition that the type of good or service being produced by public policy (private, public, or mixed goods) fundamentally alters citizen incentives and transaction costs, and would both imply additional dimensions to the analysis. Likewise, for political systems that are inherently unstable or fragile and in which the state has no monopoly on coercion, informal systems of power predominate and the center of political gravity may well be outside mainstream politics.

"Our Millennium: Political Science Confronts the Global Corporate Economy" (Chapter 14) argues that the essence of globalization is a global market economy, operating in a context of laissez faire policies in which the social and political controls of local and national governments are consistently eroded in the name of market efficiency. However, Lowi argues, markets cannot provide the efficiencies of reduced transaction costs and adjusting supply and demand absent well-known institutional foundations that require the action of the state. It is now widely accepted that good markets require good governance. These government-supplied institutional arrangements include law and order, property, standards, contracts, and other mechanisms for dealing with market failure (or reducing risk and uncertainty). Clearly, there are historic and even current examples of all of these institutional arrangements being provided by nongovernmental collective action, but scale, predictability, and lower transaction costs seem to give government a comparative advantage. In short there is no economy without political economy.

The difficulty is that globalization engenders global markets without global governance. Further, Lowi suggests, the intellectual culture of globalization is one that is highly antagonistic toward government interventions in markets. Thus, issues of equity, rights, risks, inclusion, community, and self-determination—all of which are the stuff of social cohesion, individual worth and expression, and community identity—are endangered.

Lowi argues that these issues can be clarified by recognizing that there are three separate layers of political economy, each affected differently by globalization. The macrolevel deals with global institutional arrangements that are characterized by constitutive or redistributive policies. The second is a mesolevel that focuses on the adjustment of national institutional arrangements and policies to the economic forces generated by a global economy. The third, the microlevel, deals with the reaction of communities to the erosion of control over their own lives and the maintenance of community values.

What we see in this chapter is an analog to the impact of a national economy or vastly greater scale on local politics and state-level governance at the end of the nineteenth century and into the twentieth century. Increasing differentiation, interdependency, and scale transform both the economy and the polity. Along with these trends goes the need to aggregate problems and demands within these expanded boundaries. It is not only markets that have become global. Information, culture, disease, crime, terror, and pollution have all acquired global dimensions. There are, for example, serious attempts to turn a distributive foreign aid program into a redistributive rights-based approach.

Chapter 14 presents a basic tension between the liberal, antigovernment tendencies inherent in economic expansion and globalization and the statist, self-preserving policy and institutional changes that emerge from affected societies. Lowi's observations are fully consistent with a growing consensus that ineffective governance is the key constraint to the economic integration of poor countries into the global economy—calling for government-led microeconomic and institutional reform as the answer to persistent poverty. The interaction of policy types with institutional arrangements and the broader economic and social context is the key to understanding the great changes in political history. The historical watersheds are associated with dramatic changes in the use of state power—the westward expansion of the United States, the New Deal and the Great Society that established a modern state, and, finally, a growing global order.

—*Norman K. Nicholson*

Suggested Reading

The international community has been forced to increasingly come to terms with fragile states as famine, terrorism, civil wars, and predatory elites combine to defeat international development efforts and destabilize strategically important regions of the world. The application of the Arenas of Power model to political processes that are outside mainstream politics may be helpful as we move beyond attempts to explain the origins of violence and protest to understanding government policy in an unstable setting. In this context readers may wish to refer to the growing volume of works on fragile states, including:

Engaging with Fragile States: An IEG Review of World Bank Support to Low-Income Countries Under Stress. Washington, DC: World Bank, 2006.

> The sources of fragility are many, but regardless of the cause, fragile states require special development assistance strategies.

Paul Collier. *Breaking the Conflict Trap: Civil War and Development Policy.* Washington, DC: World Bank, 2003.

> Collier has done groundbreaking work on the sources, conditions, and prospects of conflict-prone states. This particular study is a good overview of his findings.

Stephan J. Flannagan, Ellen Frost, and Richard L. Kugler. *Challenges for the Global Century.* Washington, DC: Institute for National Strategic Studies, National Defense University, 2001.

> This study charts the expanding number of fragile states and their association with terrorism, and suggests dramatic changes in U.S. security strategies in this context.

Minerals and Conflict. Washington, DC: USAID, 2005.

> The paper is part of a series of studies that relate extractive industries, in conjunction with fragile states, to recurring conflict, corruption, and increasingly fragile regimes.

Chapter 14 places the Arenas of Power model in a context of the rapidly expanding globalization of the 1990s. The interaction of national sovereignty with global institutions and problems, the relationship of local politics with global movements and global forces, and the question of whether governance at the national level is possible without new forms of governance at the global level are important in the twenty-first century. In this context, it is valuable to compare the insights provided by the Arenas of Power to an existing body of scholarship on these issues. The following deserve close attention:

Robert O. Keohane and Elinor Ostrom, eds. *Local Commons and Global Interdependence.* London: Sage, 1995.

> Focusing on natural resource exploitation as a special case of the problem of common pool resources, this collection explores institutional arrangements for governing the commons at the local level and the international level—both levels without sovereign governments.

Robert O. Keohane and Joseph S. Nye. *Power and Interdependence,* 3rd ed. New York: Longman, 2001.

> This has become a classic in the study of global governance institutions.

Peter M. Hass, Robert O. Keohane, and Marc A. Levy. *Institutions for the Earth.* Cambridge: MIT Press, 1993.

> This book provides further insights into global institutions for environmental management—a subset of the problem of global public goods management.

Andreas Hasenclever, Peter Mayer, and Volker Rittberger. *Theories of International Regimes.* Princeton, NJ: Princeton University Press, 1992.

> This volume provides an excellent summary of approaches to the study of transnational regimes.

Joseph E. Stiglitz. *Making Globalization Work.* New York: W.W. Norton, 2006.

> This book from an economist who has provided valuable criticism and analysis of the risks of globalization is noteworthy for suggesting the institutional requirements in various sectors for making globalization viable.

Stephen D. Krasner. *Sovereignty: Organized Hypocrisy.* Princeton, NJ: Princeton University Press, 1999.

This study of sovereignty in a global world is a useful complement to Lowi's treatment of globalization in this part.

One is tempted to suggest that the coalition of actors around the Millennium Development Goals, a coalition that includes bilateral and multilateral aid organizations, nongovernmental organizations, and private firms and foundations, begins to approach a global governance network pursuing a global distributive policy. The scale of this effort perhaps deserves some attention in the context of the Lowi model. Readers might refer to the United Nations Millennium Development Goals website and particularly,

Investing in Development. UN Millennium Project. New York: UNDP, 2005.

In addition, Jeffrey Sachs has launched a major international debate about global distributive policies.

Jeffrey Sachs et al. "Ending Africa's Poverty Trap." *Brookings Papers on Economic Activity.* No. 2 (2004): 117–216.

Michel Clemens and Todd Moss. *What's Wrong with the Millennium Development Goals?* Center for Global Development Brief. Washington, DC: Center for Global Development, 2005.

William Easterly. *Reliving the '50s: The Big Push, Poverty Traps, and Takeoffs in Economic Development.* Working Paper No. 65. Washington, DC: Center for Global Development, 2005.

CHAPTER 12

⚭

Prospects of Conquest

With Liberty and Justice for Some

The inevitable is seldom what anybody expected.

—*Barrington Moore, 1973*

It is impossible to look into the future of the United States without seeing a much larger national government using more coercive power on larger and larger numbers of people. The national government is growing because there are no longer any constitutional barriers against its growth. It will continue to grow because so many individuals feel that, as a condition of their own freedom, they need to support government control over others while trying to displace it from themselves.

Control by the national government will increase also because more and more individuals and corporations will seek governmental controls upon *themselves*. Economic stability seems often to be possible only if private contracts are enforced by government agencies rather than courts, through such arrangements as the licensing of commercial airlines by the Civil Aeronautics Board or the regulation of competition by the Federal Trade Commission.

Wide popular support for more government tends to produce an impression of natural harmony between government and the private sphere. Nevertheless, the notion that natural harmony prevails is a myth, and a dangerous myth at that. It encourages acceptance of unfavorable terms of conquest. Those who are willing to accept the idea of government as a friendly force are much more prone to give unconditionally their consent to be governed; they are much more willing to accept administrators who give orders without authority and who claim authority without warrant.

Most modern politicians foster the myth of natural harmony precisely because it encourages consent. When Republicans are in power, they are likely to speak of "business-government partnership and cooperation." When Democrats are in power, they tend to say the same thing with a slightly different stress. One of the favorite comments during the two Democratic administrations of the 1960s was "Antitrust is probusiness."[1] Nevertheless, harmony is a myth, and it has enormous potency because it has some basis in fact. Many programs receive little vocal opposition, especially where the actual burden or cost of the program is unclear. Nevertheless, some segment of society is always bearing the brunt of the controls or paying the main share of the costs. At the very least, claims to harmony and partnership between government and private individuals should always be suspect.

Suspicion about the myth of harmony is not merely the mark of conservatism, or of laissez-faire orthodoxy, or of a defense of entrenched interests. In fact, entrenched interests usually have the most to gain from the myth of harmony. Skepticism about harmony is derived from a definition of government as conquest; if government by definition means control—conquest updated—then also by definition government will always involve the reduction of somebody's freedom. This does not mean that government expansion is never supportable. It simply means that the expansion has to be justified.

Skepticism gives rise to a belief in the natural *dis*harmony of relationships between government and the individual. This too is a myth, but it has the advantage of encouraging vigilance. Skepticism about harmony is more likely to force a proper accounting of the costs along with the gains of control. Although resistant to the expansion of government, skepticism is at the same time a safeguard against disappointment. In the long run, legitimacy is very sensitive to a false picture of government and to falsely high expectations of government. Abraham Lincoln must have had something like this in mind when he observed:

> You can fool some of the people all of the time;
> You can fool all of the people some of the time;
> But you cannot fool all of the people all of the time.

To this we should add:

> You can control all of the people some of the time;
> You can control some of the people all of the time;
> But you cannot control all of the people all of the time.

Reactions to Being Conquered: The Meanings of Political Violence

What, then, of the rest of the people the rest of the time? How do people react when the terms of conquest seem permanently antagonistic to them? Most of us are so well conquered that we obey nevertheless, hoping perhaps that someday the balance of advantages will shift favorably. But no matter how successfully we are socialized to obey, obedience cannot always be a comfortable or a permanent condition. Dissidence is a fact of life, and although most dissident minorities obey most of the time, their dissidence is a factor of fundamental importance to the state.

All countries are organized to deal with dissidence. For example, Great Britain's newspapers are controlled far more strictly than newspapers in the United States.[2] French television and news reporters are accustomed to "news management." Most European countries require all adults to carry a government identity card, which helps the large national police forces keep track of political dissidents.

Indignation over revelations of FBI surveillance and illegal domestic spying activities by the CIA and the army, expressed by so many millions of Americans during the 1970s, is a very healthy reaction. But it also reveals massive ignorance of the fact that our own government does have regular policies to control dissidence despite the absolute prohibition against such policies in the First Amendment. In fact, the Supreme Court doctrine of "clear and present danger" was developed as an escape hatch from that absolute prohibition, giving the courts a means of allowing government agencies to censor and restrain dissidents whenever their words or actions, in the opinion of an official, tend to disrupt public life.[3]

Politics in the Extreme: Three Models of Reaction to Conquest

Leaving aside muttering in the marketplace and ordinary crimes against persons and property, dissidence can be appreciated as a reaction against being conquered—a reaction against the state, its authority, its symbols, and its apparatus. But dissidence is not a single phenomenon; there are several forms of it. Three distinct models of extreme reaction require special attention. The first is extreme but nonviolent—the *withdrawal model*. The other two are both extreme and violent, because they involve deliberate disobedience. One is the *revolution model;* the other is the *rebellion model.*

The Withdrawal Model

Withdrawal has not been strong in the American tradition of political extremism. A few thousand have decided to return to their homelands after immigrating to the United States. A few hundred citizens may trickle away each year to new countries or new frontiers beyond the authority of the United States. A few thousand American youths of draft age chose to emigrate each year rather than be part of the Vietnam War during the 1960s. Other persons withdraw into themselves by forming communes, by taking refuge in drugs, or by embracing some separate ethnic or religious community. Still others withdraw by rejecting active participation in politics. Since participation is a technique of conquest—a technique much needed by politicians who believe in consent—withdrawing participation on an organized scale can have a profound effect, because it amounts to withdrawal of support for the regime. This form of withdrawal could increase in significance if Americans ever discover that participation is a favor citizens do for politicians.

All of these various styles of withdrawal can obviously have a deep effect on political authority. Yet, government agencies can do very little about withdrawal, either to reduce it or to control its political effects. Withdrawal into oneself or into separate ethnic or religious communities cannot be punished as long as those who withdraw do not violate a law along the way, giving the authorities pretext. Emigration to another country can be controlled by the state, but this is very risky. If would-be emigrants are prevented from leaving the country, their dissatisfactions could curdle into more active and antisocial forms. If they are allowed to leave, their leaving can be a terrible reflection upon established authority.

American leaders have been very outspoken in the international sphere about the rights of citizens of other countries to immigrate to the United States. During the 1970s Congress publicly pressured the Soviet Union to change its policy against emigration of Soviet Jews. However, those same American authorities look very differently upon American emigration. The actual number of persons who emigrated from the United States during the Vietnam War has very probably been suppressed. Of perhaps greater significance is the fact that the *Statistical Abstract of the United States,* an official government document, publishes ample statistics on immigration into the United States but none whatsoever on outward migration or repatriation.

The Revolution Model

Revolution is the most particular, the most fundamental, the most radical of extreme reactions against conquest. Far from withdrawal, revolution involves disobedience. It is an organized effort to change *by force* the regime, the rules by which the regime operates, and the social class and social values that prevail in the regime. Organized radical activity should be called revolutionary only if the clear intent and theory of the group are revolutionary. To paraphrase Lenin, there is no revolutionary party without a revolutionary theory.

Because some of the important revolutionary parties in Europe have been relatively quiet and obedient in recent years, some observers have been led to speculate upon the "twilight of revolution." For example, the French and Italian Communist parties, largest in the West, have for many years been cooperating with the more conventional political parties. The French Communist Party even went so far as to oppose the revolutionary agitation of 1968, and both the French and the Italian parties have been trying to reassure their countries that they are ready to participate as a conventional party in a conventional democratic government.

But it is equally possible that their cooperativeness is a matter of self-conscious strategy. The revolutionary model usually calls for patience, warning against "adventurism." Sometimes it is better to wait for things to get worse before seizing the initiative. The point here is that the extremist following the revolutionary model is loyal to a system that does not yet exist.[4]

When revolution is defined fairly strictly as a deliberate effort to change the entire course of history in a country,[5] or "an insurrection, an act of violence by which one class overthrows another,"[6] or an "internal war ... designed to overthrow the regime or dissolve the state ... by extensive violence,"[7] the observer is immediately struck by the notable lack of such experience in the history of the United States. This absence of revolutionary tradition has been explained largely on the basis of the assumption that, for the most part, America was born "free and equal" and did not have to tear down an old feudal society to achieve that status.[8] I am aware of no better general explanation for why the revolutionary tradition was not brought over from Europe to the United States.[9]

However, two features of the American experience have to be added to this thesis. First, totally aside from the absence of a feudal tradition, the United States was extremely slow to develop a large central government. In European terms, we had a "weak state." Second, although it is true that we have had little *revolutionary* experience, it is distinctly not true that we have lived all those generations in conditions of social peace and political consensus. There is much violence in the history of the United States, and it cannot be explained away as exceptional. While it is not revolutionary violence, it is still violence; and we need another name for it: *rebellion*.

The Rebellion Model

Rebellion, like revolution, is an extreme reaction to authority. Rebellion also involves disobedience, and it is a violent political activity. But rebellion is not revolution. Rather than using violence to displace one regime with another and one dominant class and dominant set of rules with another, rebellion seeks to use violence and disobedience to *change the behavior of the existing regime*. If a rebellious group or movement has a theory at all, that theory will be aimed at bringing behavior into closer proximity with existing rules rather than changing those rules entirely; it will be oriented toward joining the ruling class rather than displacing it.

Civil disobedience is the classic example of rebellious action. It virtually defines itself as deliberate violation of law in order to shock authorities into appreciating the anomaly or the injustice of the law. The purpose of the action is not to avoid application of the law but to make a political cause out of the law. Sometimes the appeal is in terms of an abstract moral principle, such as the attack on British property called the Boston Tea Party, which was based upon the standard of "no taxation without representation." At other times civil disobedience is based on the claim that a local or state law is in violation of the Constitution or in conflict with other state or federal laws. This would have been true of much of the civil disobedience of blacks in the South during the 1950s and 1960s.

Some people disobey for personal gain—for example, by not paying their taxes for fun and profit. This is not a political act. Nonpayment of taxes becomes a political act—an act of rebellion—when its aim is to protest the tax burden, to object to a war in which the taxes are being used, or to fight against expansion of public education. The whole purpose of civil disobedience as an act of rebellion is spoiled unless the disobedience is public and carried out in a way calculated for maximum effect. If the act is not public, not organized, and not eventually punished, it is unlikely to draw the attention of the public or bring the appropriate response from the authorities. America's most famous proponent of civil disobedience, Henry David Thoreau, engaged in acts of civil disobedience as well as writing about them. However, his acts gained far less attention than his writings, because he tried to have a political effect as one peaceful malcontent.

Rebellion is at its very basis organized political violence. Either the rebellious group will use violence in its disobedient action against the state, or the government will use violence to suppress and punish the disobedience. The more political the explicit motivation of the rebellion, the more likely the government will use violence against it. In fact, governments have a way of converting a haphazard riot into a movement of political significance by treating it as though it were a politically significant action. For example, the race riots of 1917, 1919, and 1943 all seem to have begun as direct and nonpolitical confrontations of white and black *individuals* in some public place, such as a bathing area. In many instances the authorities did not even try to intervene until blacks organized themselves to retaliate against whites.[10]

Not all rebellious acts warrant being called civil disobedience. In the 1960s when blacks burned homes and businesses in their own neighborhoods in the urban ghettos, they were clearly engaging in rebellious acts, but their aims were a good deal more vague and general than is implied by civil disobedience. In these instances, "the rebellion becomes a community event; for once, the ghetto is united, and people feel they're acting together in a way they rarely can.... As in all rebellions throughout history, eventually agitators and professional revolutionaries come into the picture, but only after the ordinary and usually law-abiding ghetto residents have begun the rebellion."[11]

Revolutions and rebellions are both imbued with hope and optimism. Each operates under the banner of some utopian goal. But there the similarity ends. Revolution holds no hope for the existing political order; it is optimistic only in its belief that the organized actions of the revolutionary movement can eliminate injustice and create new institutions within a short (revolutionary) span of time. Revolutionaries may look for the worst only because the worst provides the opportunity to strike out for the best. Revolutionaries have a tremendous tolerance for contemporary injustices and inconveniences, because these are a sign for opportunities to come. In contrast, rebellion accepts the existing political order. Its optimism is its belief that rulers are redeemable and institutions are reformable. The violence committed by or in the name of a rebellion is virtually a result of the belief that the existing system can be everything it claims to be.

Extreme Reactions to Conquest, in the American Tradition

The student revolts of the 1960s in France and the United States provide a good case study of the difference between the tradition of revolution and the tradition of rebellion. In France, the explicit purpose of the student movements was to bring down the Fifth Republic in the name of one fundamental critique or another. Their strategies included nightly demonstrations in the important public places, provocation (barricades) to test the police and to encourage the police to make mistakes, exhortation of unions to join them in strikes, and many disobedient actions aimed at disrupting life in Paris (and eventually in other cities) to such an extent that it would be impossible for the regime to conduct public business. President de Gaulle ultimately did fall, and the regime came closer to falling than anyone let on at the time. Even though the protests may have been on new issues, the strategy of disruption aimed at overthrow was very much a part of the French tradition.

Although there has been only one major revolution in France, there have been many lesser revolutions and organized revolutionary efforts. It is no coincidence that the label for lesser revolutions, coup d'état, is a French term. Since the Revolution of 1789, French regimes have had an average life of only 12 years. In 1968, the Fifth Republic was in its tenth year. It did not fall, but French political activists in the 1960s must have been aware of the pattern and of the tradition.[12] Although there are also many examples of rebellion in the history of France, the revolutionary model is clearly available and is obviously thought to be a rational, if extreme, reaction against political authority.[13]

American student movements of the 1960s were in many ways more dramatic than the French. Public manifestations were frequent, and acts of disobedience involved far more injury and death in the United States than in France. But the great distinction between the French and American movements of the 1960s was not in the greater number of injuries and deaths in the United States but in the fact that American students were by and large not committed to revolutionary theory—in fact, most were virtually unaware of revolutionary ideas.

The most self-consciously committed part of the student movement of the 1960s, the Students for a Democratic Society (SDS), had many leaders whose ideas were intensely revolutionary, but these ideas did not become a central part of the SDS strategy until rather late in the history of the organization. During most of the 1960s, its members followed an almost pure strategy of rebellion, attempting to use campus obstruction to activate the larger society toward changes in foreign policy, military involvement, the draft, and race and labor relations.[14]

At no point did the student actions seek to overturn the national government or to rewrite the rules for selecting elites. Most student actions were aimed at specific and programmatic goals and took place far from Washington. At the most general level, students were seeking to redeem the American system, to take actions, however shocking, that might bring American leaders to policies more in keeping with an ideal standard. Here again, we find that the student demands virtually defined the nature of rebellion—to redeem the system, not to bring it down. Only a few at the fringe spoke of and organized for revolution in the classical sense.

H. Rap Brown, an early leader of the Student Nonviolent Coordinating Committee (SNCC, pronounced "snick"), made the widely quoted observation that "violence is as American as cherry pie." Brown's observation is more than confirmed by the history of labor in the United States, which has been "the bloodiest and most violent . . . of any industrial nation in the world."[15] Major instances of organized political violence in our country have been catalogued and studied by historians and sociologists. These will be reviewed here, in the context of two major hypotheses: (1) Some of the most important changes in American history were brought about by violent political action, not by normal or consensus politics; and (2) radicalism and political violence in the United States belong to the *tradition of rebellion*.

The American Revolution

Our own so-called revolution was itself a rebellion and was so understood by the British and the American loyalists. Acts of rebellion preceding the Declaration of Independence were aimed largely at pushing Parliament toward important reforms in the British system and its relation to its colonies. And although the war itself resulted in a new and independent nation, the American leaders moved rather steadfastly toward the reconstitution of the United States on the British model. The patriots were not concerned with the British system, except to adopt parts of it for their own. This is the basis of Edmund Burke's famous distinction between the American and the French Revolution, leading him to support the former and bitterly oppose the latter.[16]

Agrarian Rebellion

Farmer rebellions also preceded independence but did not disappear afterwards. Many were given names, such as the Whiskey Rebellion in Pennsylvania. Although no single farmer rebellion rates as a historic moment, this series of early rebellions probably created the conditions or experiences for far more important nonviolent farmer movements after the Civil War. Farmers could be radicalized, and were. The pitchfork was one of the great symbols of agrarian radicalism; it beautifully combined the ideas of sword *and* ploughshare. But in most of the cases of farmer action—violent and nonviolent— the primary goals were redemption and reform, not revolution. Although some of the Populists in the nineteenth century dreamed of fending off or transforming the capitalist system, most of the actual farmer movements made demands for basic reforms of the system in order to make it work better for agriculture.[17]

Southern White Rebellion

For the South, the Civil War, ending in military occupation, was in many respects a repeat of the Revolutionary War. The South conducted the Civil War against actions and tendencies of the national government that were thought to be intolerable. The northern states treated secession, quite properly, as rebellion. President Lincoln tried desperately to treat the situation as a state of "insurrection" by trying to frame concessions that would prevent the South from going to war or would end the war quickly and maintain the Union. For example, in Lincoln's second State of the Union Address, in January of 1862, he proposed a scheme of "compensated emancipation," by which the national government would indemnify each slave owner in a manner very much comparable to acquisition through eminent domain.

In its turn, the South would have been satisfied either with drastic changes in national policies or with secession to form a new entity. There were no plans to win the war in order to remake the entire United States. Victory for the South would have meant the establishment of a separate nation-state, leaving the United States as a smaller, nonslave nation-state with the system of government it already had. Defeat did not turn southern whites away from rebellion and from the causes of the original rebellion. For example, the Ku Klux Klan, founded immediately after the surrender, was a significant type of rebellion, aimed at reversing, if not terminating, Reconstruction policies and the military government. The Klan's violent actions were part of a larger effort of guerrilla action aimed at reform, not at any goals comparable to the guerrilla actions of the Viet Cong during the 1960s.

The Labor Movement

In the context of twentieth century trade unions in the U.S., the notions of either rebellion *or* revolution seem terribly remote. However, given the laws and attitudes of American leaders and governments in the nineteenth century, most efforts to improve the condition of labor involved disobedience. The main question was, of course, what kind of disobedience. The revolutionary model was tried briefly as a means of violently changing the policies of state governments and the actions of state and local police. However, nonrevolutionary political action became dominant long before the situation had developed into nonviolent, ordinary politics.[18] Even after the Soviet Revolution there is no indication that revolutionaries made much headway inside American labor.

The only element of political violence left in the labor movement is the strike, and it provides us with telling evidence of the importance of the rebellion model. In Europe, the strike is frequently used as a broad political weapon, a class-conscious act by workers against the state. In the United States, the strike is a specialized weapon of momentary obstruction aimed at altering management behavior at the bargaining table. The strike in the United States assumes the persistence of the existing power structure. Even when it has been used as a political weapon in the United States, the purpose has been to extract specific concessions from the government. These actions have included laws providing for shorter hours, better conditions, the right to organize, and expansion of welfare legislation. The strike, or threat of it, has almost always followed a rebellion model in the United States.[19]

Urban Protest

Violence in American cities seems to have followed the rebellion model for at least the past century. Many white urban riots and gang wars were violent actions by a nativist or older ethnic group to oppose the advance of some newer ethnic group, without public intervention at all—a form of "private self-government" or direct-action politics, as described in Chapter 3.[20] Other radical urban actions were aimed at getting the local police and other government officials to intervene more forcefully against encroachment by new immigrants.[21]

Violent action by blacks in the cities has also followed the rebellion model. Many of the most spontaneous uprisings have developed into collective protests, despite the spontaneity of their origins. Protests which started as a reaction to an arrest of a single individual may have grown into widespread attacks against white landlords and merchants and eventually have been drawn up by a few articulate leaders into a protest against the injustices throughout the system. "Hence," observes Fogelson, "the riots were meant to alert America, not to overturn it.... For the great majority of Negroes, the American dream, tarnished though it has been for centuries, is still the ultimate aspiration."[22] Another expert observer of civil strife notes that:

> With few exceptions, the demands or apparent objectives of participants in civil strife in the United States have been limited ones. Civil rights demonstrators have asked for integration and remedial governmental action on Negro problems; they have not agitated for class or racial warfare. Peace marchers vehemently oppose American foreign policy and some of the men who conduct it; none of them have attempted to overthrow the political system. Black militants talk of revolutionary warfare; such sentiments are rarely voiced by

those who participate in ghetto riots. By the testimony of most of their words and actions, they have been retaliating against the accumulated burden of specific grievances.... The United States has experienced chronic conspiratorial violence in the past decade, but it has been almost entirely defensive.[23]

Conquest and Public Morality: The Obligation to Justify

The rebellion model is so much a part of our experience that some of our wisest observers have taken it as the definition of the entire phenomenon of political radicalism. For example, in one of the best available treatments, political violence is defined as acts of disruption whose purpose is to "modify the behavior of others in a bargaining situation."[24] While this is the essence of the rebellion model, there is at least one other type of political violence—the revolutionary model, which is oriented toward replacement of the bargainers as well as the bargaining table.

A model operates as a guide. When people are radicalized by their exasperation with the regime, they tend to imitate the past. There is a form to extreme action just as there is a form to conventional action. Rebellion tends to take place some distance from the political center, out where the specific grievances and the specific symbols exist.[25] The demands of the rebellious leaders tend to be demands that can be met, in whole or in part, by the authorities. In fact, one of the great self-designated American radicals, Saul Alinsky, laid down as one of the cardinal rules of radical action that the behaviors ought to be extreme but the demands ought to be concrete and achievable.[26]

The rebellion model guides rulers as well as dissidents. Since extreme action violates the law, or threatens to violate the law, state intervention is usually unavoidable. But extreme action must be perceived and defined by the authorities: How dangerous are the dissidents? How much force is needed, and when and where? Acts that are defined as rebellions will almost certainly be treated in the United States less violently than acts defined as revolutionary. Unquestionably, rebellion does threaten public authority; and the police feel themselves implicated even when their own position is not directly attacked—all the more so because they tend to be drawn from the same social classes as the rebels.[27]

However, when a revolutionary group turns to violent action, the heat of official reaction is disproportionately greater. For example, the Black Panthers, who were never more than a few dozen members, became the object of nationwide surveillance and suppression, not merely because they had threatened to use weaponry, but because the Panthers had developed an eclectic but nevertheless explicit revolutionary theory to accompany their local actions. The elimination of the Panthers was carried out by a carefully planned and heavily armed police detachment led by the state's attorney in Chicago. Yet, "with all in the perspective of American history, the Panthers were less violent than white minorities had been as they fought their way up the social and economic scale."[28]

Even when quiescent and conventional, a group with a revolutionary theory in the United States is badly off, subject to infiltration, surveillance, discrimination. Let it just hint at intellectual espousal of direct action, and the official reaction is disproportionately swift and severe. The revolutionary model is apparently so unusual in the American tradition that revolutionaries are treated almost by definition as foreigners.

Actually, since there are inevitably going to be occasional outbreaks of political violence in any country, an elite should count itself fortunate if its dissidents tend naturally to pattern their behavior on the rebellion model. The demands of a rebellious movement can almost always be met. Although it is the inevitable urge of the officials to suppress, they usually end up making substantial concessions; and in the process of doing so, they tend to co-opt the movement—satisfying many of the members even if not entirely placating all of the rebellious leaders. Either way, in the wake of rebellion, the regime tends to be reinforced.

Our tradition of rebellion seems also to have saved us from radical action of one segment of our elite against another. It is unimaginable that the stakes of a dispute between two segments of the American corporate elite were never high enough to warrant an attempted coup d'état. Yet, there is no record of so much as a plan of this sort. Why, for example, did Richard Nixon not attempt to suspend the Constitution in 1974 as Indira Gandhi did in India in 1975? The record shows that President Nixon never hesitated violating the law to suppress the opposition and to concentrate power in his own hands. Yet, when it became certain he was doomed to go down in disgrace, he yielded rather than try to overturn the legal situation or suspend constitutional procedures.

Nixon's chief of staff was a high-ranking and highly respected military officer, who went on to become the commanding officer of NATO. Nixon's own standing with the military and with the "civilian hawks" was very high. He was respected by most conservatives, revered by many. It is useless to suggest that we are such a diverse nation and so love our Constitution that the president would never have succeeded. Perhaps that is true, but why did he not try? By July 1974, he had so little to lose by attempting to remain in power through extraconstitutional means.

Perhaps the answer is that such a course of action would probably never have occurred to President Nixon. Or if it had occurred to him, *he would not have known how to behave.* Revolution, even a small palace revolution, is so far outside American experience that there is no scenario for it. Who should be called in first? What kinds of deals ought to be made? What are the contingencies?

In a very important sense, rebellion has become part of the institutionalized politics of the United States. Most of the time the political process works through elections, bargaining, secret deals, legislative action, and consensus. Competition is between two unprogrammatic parties on the same side of property, industry, employment, and poverty. Change usually takes place at the margins of the existing system, and when there is violence, they are simply extended until the rebellion is placated or palliated.

However, traditions can change. If our tradition of violence is explained by the absence of an old aristocracy and the weakness of the state, what will happen to that tradition if one of those conditions changes? There is no old aristocracy to reemerge, but the state can be "Europeanized" and become a strong center of national life. How far can the state go in responding to the demands for more conquest without becoming the kind of force and symbol that confirms the revolutionary critique and converts rebellious leaders into revolutionaries? The very optimism of American leaders toward the capacity of the national government has brought the country some distance already along this route.

Note, for example, how far we have come toward the nationalization of response to local disorders. During the nineteenth century there were of course occasions when the president called out the militia to deal with a local rebellion. President Washington sent 12,950 troops drawn from four states to meet the Whiskey Rebellion.[29] However, these instances were few and far between until the 1960s, especially the late 1960s. In the 20 years between September 1945 and August 1965, federal intervention by the use of the national guard and other military troops became a regular occurrence. Eighty-three callups involving 44,927 troops have been identified during that period of time. Then, in the three and one-half years between August 1965 and December 31, 1968, there were 179 callups involving 184,133 federal troops.[30]

One response to these statistics might be that the years of the late 1960s were unusual because of the culmination of war opposition and of civil rights militancy. Nevertheless, the significant feature during that time is the regularity of federal response to local disorder. The national government seems to have become a regular party to each and every rebellion anywhere in the country. Local disorder has been nationalized. The national government has not only used federal troops on a regular basis, it has also got into the business of regular surveillance and infiltration of local organizations. Revelations during the Watergate investigations showed not only that the CIA and the FBI were engaged in local surveillance during the Nixon administration but that these activities, including civilian surveillance by the army, had been going on at least since 1965.[31]

It is too early to assess precisely the extent to which the nationalization of response to local disorder indicates a basic change in our system. However, it is not too soon to view this development with alarm. When the state makes itself a party to all disputes, it must prepare itself for the consequences. There are great advantages to a national approach, as, for example, in the matter of civil rights. But as the national government moves out of its nineteenth century conception of weak-centered federalism, it must enrich its appreciation of control and must concern itself increasingly with the requisites of justifying control at every turn. And now that our modernized and sophisticated citizenry no longer responds to appeals to obedience based upon God or nature, community, or tradition, a stronger central government must search for ever stronger justification for its control.

One of the great tragedies is that human beings must be conquered and governed at all. But if this is to be our lot, let us resolve to be conquered only by a good argument and to be governed only by ample justification. The requirement of justification is the only dependable defense the powerless have against the powerful.

Equally tragic is the requirement that rulers must rule. But if they must, let us teach them to justify their actions. The obligation to justify can only make them better rulers. Nothing will make them good rulers, since rulers must coerce, and coercion can never be absolutely good. Rulers deal in necessity, and the best they can do with necessity is to justify it within the forms of governing provided for them long before they ever took power.

If the American system has any claim to greatness, do not look for it in the goodness of its rulers but rather in its forms and how proportionately these forms deal with everlasting contradictions between control and freedom, control and representation, control and justification—between conquest and incomplete conquest.

Few governments in all history have coped any better with the contradictions inherent in incomplete conquest. Through two centuries we have persisted as a system of government while perhaps making some modest strides toward the advancement of individual dignity. Yet, persistence proves nothing, except that human beings will strive for progress despite inhuman odds, despite the certainty that for the everlasting problems of government there are no lasting solutions.

> Do I contradict myself?
> Very well then I contradict myself;
> (I am large, I contain multitudes.)
>
> *—Walt Whitman, 1855*

> It is my fate … to swing constantly from optimism to pessimism and back, but so is it the fate of anyone who writes or speaks of anything in America—the most contradictory, the most depressing, the most stirring, of any land in the world today.
>
> *—Sinclair Lewis, 1930*

Chapter 13

❧❧❧

New Dimensions in Policy and Politics

Public policy can be defined simply as an officially expressed intention backed by a sanction. Although synonymous with law, rule, statute, edict, and regulation, public policy is the term of preference today probably because it conveys more of an impression of flexibility and compassion than the other terms. But no citizen, especially a student of political science, should ever forget that *policy* and *police* have common origins. Both come from "polis" and "polity," which refer to the political community itself and to the "monopoly of legal coercion" by which government itself has been defined. Consequently, all public policies must be understood as coercive. They may be motivated by the best and most beneficent of intentions, and they may be implemented with utmost care for justice and mercy. But that makes them no less coercive.

There are multitudes of public policies because there are multitudes of social arrangements and conduct that people feel ought to be controlled by coercive means if public order is to be maintained and people are to be able to pursue their private satisfactions in peace. Consequently, some kind of categorization is necessary if meaningful policy analysis is to take place. [If Raymond Tatalovich and Byron W. Daynes, editors of *Social Regulatory Policy: Moral Controversies in American Politics,* the volume in which this chapter originally appeared as the foreword,] had a particular reason for inviting me to participagte in their important project, it was probably because I was young and foolish enough 25 years ago to attempt to provide a categorization of public policies and, somewhat later, to describe the logic underlying the categories. If there had been a second reason for involving me it was probably because they found the scheme uncomfortable as well as useful. In brief, I began the categorization with a simple question: If all policies are coercive, is it possible that we can develop a meaningful, small set of policy categories by asking a prior question of jurisprudence: How many kinds of coercion are there? Leaving aside the fine points of definition, I identified four logically distinguishable ways that government can coerce, and I then attempted to demonstrate, with some degree of acceptance in the field, that each of these types of coercion underlies a type of identifiable public policy. The source of each type of policy was, therefore, so close to state power itself that each, I reasoned, should be located in history and that each would, over time, tend to develop its own distinctive political structure. I was attempting to turn political science on its head (or back on its feet) by arguing that "policy causes politics."

The four categories were given the most appropriate names I could contrive at the time: Distributive Policy (or as I have come more recently to call it, Patronage Policy), Regulatory Policy, Redistributive (and Welfare) Policy, and Constituent Policy. (Table 2.1 is the fourfold formulation.) Lately I have grown accustomed to a modification of the names of the categories in order to emphasize the intimacy of the historical association between the type of policy and the type of politics that tends to be associated with it: the Distributive (or Patronage) State, the Regulatory State, the Redistributive (or Welfare) State, and the State Within the State.

During the very decade (roughly 1964–1974) that these categories were being developed, the national government was going through a virtual second New Deal. There was an explosion of new regulatory and welfare programs. Although most of these new policies fit comfortably enough into the fourfold scheme, there *was* something new about many of them that was not being captured by the scheme. Every scheme of categorization (of anything) sacrifices informational detail and nuance in order to gain analytic power, but is there a point where the sacrifice is too great? Students of these 1960s and 1970s policies referred to them as "new regulation," "social policy," and "social regulation" in order to convey an emerging sense that there is indeed something about these policies that does not fit comfortably into existing categories. Tatalovich, Daynes, and associates do a valiant job of trying to catch the meaning of the "new" and the "social" and why these policies somehow don't fit into any preexisting scheme. In the opinion of these authors, the only way to preserve the fourfold scheme is to add, in effect, a fifth category, which they call "social regulatory policy."

There is no need to take issue directly with the definition of this fifth category. I will try instead to *subsume* it. I recognize at the outset that there is something special about the cases being dealt with in Tatalovich and Dayne's book. They are cases of regulatory policy in my terms; if they don't seem to fit comfortably it is because the *politics* of the "new" or "social" regulation looks a lot more like what is to be expected with the politics of redistributive policy. The authors discover in their cases that the observed political behavior is more ideological, more moral, more directly derived from fundamental values, more intense, less utilitarian, more polarized, and less prone to compromise.

However, while granting these authors their empirical findings, I hesitate to create a new category to fit the findings until all ways of maintaining the fourfold scheme have been exhausted. This position is one part ego but at least four parts bona fide concern not to destroy the simplicity and, more importantly, the logic of the analysis. For one cannot solve the problem by merely adding a new category. Addition of a category weakens the logic altogether. The fifth category won't work entirely until its logic has been worked out and until a probable sixth is coupled with it to give the new scheme a reasonable symmetry.

In the spirit of trying to preserve the fourfold scheme and at the same time trying to give the new findings their due, I will try an alternative. Some people will agree with me that it is a way to preserve the fourfold scheme. Others will say that I am being too accommodating and will destroy the fourfold scheme by turning it not merely into a six- or eightfold scheme but in fact into a twelvefold scheme. Either way, the effort will enhance and dramatize the value of the case materials presented in this volume.

For several years I have shared with these authors a concern for how to make sense of the "new politics" of the public interest groups on the left and the right in the United States and in Europe. Although these groups seem to be seeking policies that could be categorized as (largely) regulatory or redistributive, they refused to join what most of us would consider mainstream political processes, insisting instead on trying to convert political issues into moral polarities, claims into rights, legislation into litigation, grays into blacks and whites, and campaigns into causes and crusades. If there is confusion among analysts about all this, it is because there is an obvious, age-old fact that we have all been overlooking: that for every type of mainstream politics there is a *radical politics*. Policies can remain the same, insofar as the type of coercion involved is regulatory, or redistributive, or whatever. But just as some mainstream strategies will pay off and some will not (giving each policy type its political distinctiveness) so will radicalization as a strategy sometimes pay off and sometimes not pay off. When it does pay off, there is likely to be an intensification of all the political elements without necessarily transforming the patterns altogether. And, to repeat, the policy at issue can remain in the same category even as its politics is being radicalized.

Figure 13.1, a first step toward a new scheme, is an attempt to define radical in relation to mainstream in politics. The *Oxford English Dictionary* defines radical as "of or pertaining to a root or roots." That is also the meaning in mathematics and the origin of the term in politics. It is associated with extremes precisely because people who insist on getting to the root of things are likely to express themselves intensely, rejecting the rules and procedures designed to produce compromise—in other words, rejecting mainstream or ordinary politics. However, as soon as the two dimensions, radical and mainstream, are put side by side it becomes obvious that they are not a simple dichotomy because it is in the nature of radical politics to be so much more ideological that radicalism is at least dichotomous within itself. (I say "at least" because a full-scale analysis of radicalism would require more distinctions than the simple two needed here.) Ideology is not absent in mainstream politics, but lower intensity permits mainstream politicians to practice their skill, which is to obtain practical consensus on goals and to reduce differences to a point where political conflict becomes political competition, strategy becomes tactic, and compromise is possible because the stakes are incremental. To the radical, mainstream means trivialization, and that is absolutely true. Figure 13.1 attempts to capture this evaluation for the mainstream by placing relevant ideologies on a continuum, with the concentration of positions toward the center, where the frontier between left and right is very fuzzy.

This is precisely where radicalism differs most: What is a rather fuzzy frontier for the mainstream is a formalized border between radicals of the left and the right. Intensity of commitment demands an underlying logic, and logic demands some degree of consistency, reinforced by a conscious affiliation. Positions are distributed accordingly, in what can best be illustrated in Figure 13.1 as a bimodal distribution. So consistently is radical politics polarized that this distribution has to be maintained in any diagrammatic analysis.

Table 13.1 moves the analysis one step further by attempting to specify the general substantive orientations of the two dimensions. The basic four policy categories are maintained (across the top and extending through both Mainstream and Radical di-

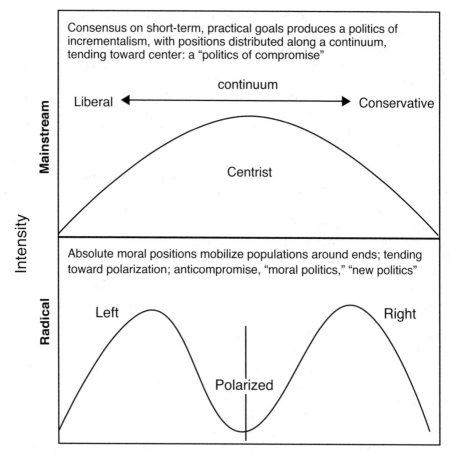

Figure 13.1 Public Philosophy: Mainstream and Radical

mensions). The cells contain brief descriptions of the general political orientation for each of the eight resulting patterns. In this diagram, the left-right direction of ideology is disregarded for the sake of simplicity, based on the assumption that even radicals can, in the words of Carl Friedrich, "agree on what to disagree about." A word of explanation is needed mainly for the concepts in boldface. These were the best available words to connote the general orientation; the prose in each box is an effort to spell that out. Note, for example, the distinction between ERROR and SIN; this is an antinomy, which is intended to suggest how differently the two types view the same regulatory issue. The mainstream approach to regulation is as close to instrumental as human beings can get. Mainstream political actors avoid taking a moral posture toward the conduct to be regulated; conduct is to be regulated only because *it is injurious in its consequences.* Though privately the mainstreamer may consider prostitution immoral, the mainstream *public* position would be that prostitution should be regulated as to its potential for disease or its association with drugs and abduction. The radical would

Table 13.1 How Policy Problems Are Defined in Mainstream and Radical Politics

	Regulative (Policy toward conduct)	Distributive (Policy toward facilities)	Redistributive (Policy toward status)	Constituent (Policy toward structures)
Mainstream	Control the *consequences* of conduct, consequences defined in purely instrumental terms. Orientation of the discourse is:	Goals defined instrumentally or denotatively, without a governing rule. Orientation of the discourse is:	Class and status relations are specified but redistributive effect minimized by spreading benefits upward and obligations downward. Exclusiveness softened with equities. Orientation of discourse is:	A process definition of the Constitution and rights; a representation definition of government; the good administrator is neutral, obedient to elected officials; decision by competition. Orientation of discourse is:
	Error	Utility	Entitlement	Accountability
Radical	Control of conduct as good or bad *in itself*; consequences defined in moral absolutes; stress particularly on bad conduct. The orientation of discourse is:	Goals defined in terms of consequences but moral consequences, such as improvement of character (right) or defense against capitalism (left). The orientation of discourse is:	Class and status relations are exclusive, imbedded in absolutes that transcend policy. Property rights (right) and welfare rights (left); social definitions of rights (left), individualist definitions of rights (right). Orientation of discourse is:	A substantive definition of the Constitution. Good government is commitment to a substantive definition of justice. The good administrator is committed to the program (left) or to good moral character (right). The orientation of discourse is:
	Sin	Civic Virtue	Rights	Commitment

define the conduct moralistically; i.e., for the radical, conduct is to be regulated because *it is good or bad in itself.* From the radical left, prostitution is a sinful product of a sinful economic system; for the radical right it is a sinful expression of bad character. But radicals take a moral posture toward it while mainstreamers can take it as a conduct in need of modification. Regulation is itself a mainstream word, coming from the French, *règle* (rule), so that *règlementation* means "to impose rules upon" or to regularize. From the radical, moralistic standpoint, something like elimination would be a more accurate description.

There is no need to treat the three remaining categories too extensively, since the phenomenon of concern [here] is regulation. Suffice it to say that the concepts in each of the categories (on Tables 13.1 and 13.2) were also selected as antinomies that distinguish most clearly between mainstream and radical discourse, with radicals of both sides agreeing with each other on what to disagree about. Thus, even on something as commonplace as distributive policy (patronage), radicals can be quite moralistic: Railroads should be public corporations because capitalism is bad; museums should be built because art is good. In contrast, for mainstreamers, the whole point of resorting to patronage policy is its UTILITY, its complete *a*morality; patronage policy is a way to displace conflict, not confront it. For redistributive policy, the near antinomy between ENTITLEMENT and RIGHTS should be close to self-evident. Description in the boxes might help marginally. The constituent policy categories may cause a bit more of a problem, but that need not be a burden for us here. The best way to think about this category is through the history of American approaches to the "good administrator." The mainstream ideal was the "common man"; the modern version of this is the individual trained in the appropriate skills but loyal to majority rule and to the elected representatives of that majority, presumably whatever the "goal." To the radical, majorities and skills are not irrelevant, but they are subordinate to character. Administrators are good if they are committed to virtue (on the right) or "program" (on the left).

We can now turn to Table 13.2, the main point and purpose of this enterprise. Table 13.2 combines features of Table 2.1, Figure 13.1, and Table 13.1 and joins them to actual policy examples. The antinomies from Table 13.1 are repeated to evoke a sense of the political patterns to be expected.

Table 13.2 is a variation on an earlier effort to make sense of environmental policies, which are so rich in "new politics."[1] The Regulatory column is most relevant (therefore put first), but the comprehensive (and I hope exhaustive) presentation in the table makes a productive linkage to the findings in this book and puts these findings in an inherently comparative context.

I like this format, as revised, not merely because it might preserve my scheme. It confirms my own confidence that policy categorization (not necessarily mine) will in the long run be the route to the new political theory because it arises out of some fundamental political truths: (1) that there are inherent limits to the ways a state can control society, no matter how powerful that state may be; (2) that each of these ways is so fundamental that it has enough of a history and a regularity to become in itself a kind of regime; and (3) that every regime tends to produce a politics consonant with itself. This particular effort has perhaps added a fourth truth: that political leaders can radicalize politics by adding a moral dimension to policy. Radicalizing the policy (i.e.,

Table 13.2 Policies and Politics in Two Dimensions

Dimension of Politics	Policy Type							
	1 Regulatory		2 Distributive		3 Redistributive		4 Constituent	
Mainstream	Error		Utility		Entitlement		Accountability	
	Standards of conduct		Public works		"Social costs"		"Causal theory"	
	Economic sector regulation		Defense installations and stockpiling		Income taxation		Liberal, value-free education	
	Regulation to maintain competition		R & D		Economic policy through the tax system ("tax expenditure")		Policies restricting state action	
	Regulatory taxes		Sales of public property or access to it		Social security		Administrative reform for neutral, scientific decisionmaking	
	Licensing to enforce standards		Unconditional licensing		Monetary policies			
	Sin		Civic Virtue		Rights		Moral Government	
	Left	Right	Left	Right	Left	Right	Left	Right
Radical	Right to results of regulation (suits to force regulation)	Right to public order and self-defense	Public ownership of essential service	Public works for private market	Progressive income taxation exclusively	Sales taxes and other regressive taxes exclusively	"Class theory"	"Obligation theory"
	Cost-oblivious economic regulation	Regulation for moral guidance	Displacement of corporate power	Subsidies to industry for the public good	Anti-wealth taxes (estate, luxuries, etc.)	Punitive taxes ("sin" taxes to discourage alcohol, tobacco, etc.)	Socialization education	Moral education
	Affirmative action	Victimless crimes	Planning for national use of resources	Convert distributive to moral regulation	Welfare as a right	Welfare as a moral lesson	Bill of Rights (complete nationalization)	State rights
	Capitalism as morally suspect	Capitalism as a moral good	Convert distributive to redistributive				Participatory democracy (judicially enforced)	Republicanism ("rightly understood")
							Programmatic administrator	Good administrator
							Party executive	Commander-in-chief executive

adding the moral dimension) will almost certainly change the political patterns, but even radicalized political patterns will probably vary according to the particular policy category (regime) in question.

Since Tatalovich, Daynes, and associates concentrated on the regulatory category [in their volume], I will hold my elaboration of this now two-dimensional scheme to the regulatory quadrant alone. But this should not mask the fact that if we had cases here of radicalized policies in, say, the redistributive category, the political pattern, though radicalized, would probably differ from the pattern observed in the radicalized regulatory cases.

Virtually all regulatory policy, as we know it from the familiar economic regulatory programs of the national government, approaches conduct in an almost purely instrumental way. It arises largely out of concern for conduct deemed good or bad *only in its consequences.* (See Table 13.2, upper left corner.) The very term *regulation* or *regulatory policy,* as suggested above, became the term of choice by lawyers, economists, and policymakers because the goal of most of these policies is not so much to eliminate the conduct in question but to reduce it, channel it, or otherwise constrain it so that the conduct might persist but with fewer of the injuries (or in some instances, more of the benefits) attributed to it. But there is another whole reality of regulatory policies, and those policies are concerned with conduct *deemed good or bad in itself* (lower left corner in table). Call the first C_1 and the second C_2. The first type, instrumental regulation, will be abbreviated as C_1. The second, moral regulation, will be referred to as C_2. Most C_2 regulation in the United States has escaped the recent attention of most political scientists (until the Tatalovich and Daynes volume) because it has been the province of state government. Examples include the criminal law, all the sex and morality laws, most family and divorce laws, the basic compulsory education laws, and the fundamental property laws. The intrinsic moral orientation of this kind of policy accounts also for the fact that state politics in the nineteenth century (when most of these policies were being enacted as a matter of positive, statute law) was far more radical, often violent, than the politics of regulation at the national level. But note well, the descriptions of state politics will reveal that they were dominated not by political parties but by interest groups and movements. Some of those interest groups engaged in mainstream politics—lobbying, bargaining, and compromise like the interest group patterns we associate with the national government. But those groups engaged in "direct action politics," "single-issue politics," and "social movement politics" to a far greater extent than is found at the national level, except during the epoch of what we now are calling "new politics."

In contrast, the regulatory policies at the national level have not only been quite recent (most of them dating from the New Deal) but have been almost exclusively of the C_1 type. To repeat, the politics is mainstream—dominated by organized interest groups and engaging in lobbying and all the patterns associated with pluralism— and, in a word, regulatory. However, it is an obvious point, though made significant within the context of the cases and Table 13.2, that this standard type of national regulatory policy *can be radicalized by the addition of moral (C_2) considerations.*

An example of radicalization by degree would be elements of the 1964 Civil Rights Act. Most of the titles were by and large of the C_1 type. Following the spirit of *Brown v. Board of Education,* Congress reasoned that separate schools and public facilities and separate criteria of employment were inherently unequal in their consequences, unconstitutional because they gave minorities a badge of inferiority and tended to render minority individuals in actual fact unequal in their ability as well as their opportunity to enjoy what society had to offer. People who have never read *Brown* would be surprised at how instrumental and nonmoral (i.e., how mainstream liberal) the Supreme Court's argument was. Although this same utilitarian, C_1 rationale was sufficient to win a congressional majority in favor of the historic 1964 Act, it was far from the full argument the civil rights movement itself was making. Happy as the movement was to have such a historic law, the leaders of the movement had good reason to be frustrated by the public debates and by the modesty of the message and the sanctions in the regulatory provisions of the Act. The *moral* case against all forms of discrimination was overwhelming, and there was equally strong moral justification not only for far stronger and more unilateral sanctions eliminating all discrimination but also for more direct compensatory policies to overcome the effects of past discrimination—in other words, affirmative action. This amounts, as the critics say, to positive and group discrimination that contradicts the individualist definition of rights as comprehended by the Constitution and also contradicts the explicit wish of Congress, as expressed, for example, in the following passage from the employment provisions (Title VII) prohibiting "preferential treatment to any individual or group ... on account of an imbalance which may exist with respect to the total or percentage of persons of any race, color, religion, sex, or national origin." The civil rights movement (note the form: a movement) sought what amounted to a radicalization of the civil rights laws and, if not the laws, the implementation of the laws by the agencies and courts. To the extent that civil rights policy embodied a moral dimension, it both reflected and contributed to a "new politics"—the politics of morality, of movements, of polarization, and of what the authors in the Tatalovich and Daynes volume call "social regulatory policymaking."

Many of the same persons who have decried what I have described here as the radicalization of civil rights share responsibility not only for radicalizing the opposition to civil rights but also for radicalizing other important policies in other subject matter areas. Although the list is longer than the cases in the Tatalovich and Daynes volume, all the cases here belong to such a list. And note well the several following characteristics of these cases:

1. Each C_2 policy had once been the almost exclusive province of state government power;
2. Each policy experienced radical politics almost any time the issue got on state policy agendas, in the nineteenth or the twentieth century;
3. All but gun control were removed altogether or in substantial part from state jurisdiction by the Supreme Court;
4. Each in recent years was then nationalized altogether or in substantial part.

Thus, none of the politics flowing from these issues was "new." The policies and the politics were relatively new merely to the *national* government. All of the laws and proposals in these cases qualify as "social" in that their focus and preoccupation were not on economic activities as such, even when companies and employers were the main objects of regulation. But now we can get a better sense of what people have been trying to convey by calling policies new or social. If people only meant that these policies were noneconomic, that would not add much to our understanding of policies *or* politics. But if we take *social* to indicate that the policy is aiming at the moral base of conduct, then we have opened an entirely new dimension or have put an old dimension into a new and more useful context. That is at least what I intend to convey by the concept of radicalization. George Will, a self-defined man of the right, provides the distinction between mainstream and radical that I am striving for here: "In a famous opinion in a famous case ... Justice Felix Frankfurter wrote: 'Law is concerned with external behavior and not with the inner life of man.' I am not sure what Frankfurter meant. I am sure what he said cannot be true. The purpose of this book is to say why that proposition is radically wrong."[2] Taken in moderation, Will's position may be mainstream, simply toward the far right of the mainstream continuum. But embraced to the fullest extent, by our taking Will literally on the desirability of using law to reach "the inner life of man," the continuum becomes a circle, turning downward toward the radical half of Figure 13.1, Table 13.1, or Table 13.2. But note well that moral, C_2, considerations can also be introduced from the left, pushing the left side of the continuum in a circular turn downward toward radicalization. In the world of morality and radicalization, the left and the right are a unity of opposites, together as one, logically and empirically apart from the mainstream.

This formulation will, I hope, make a contribution to theory in political science in at least three ways. First, it may make cases more interesting and significant by rendering their findings more cumulative, due to their demonstrated membership in a common framework. Second, introduction of a second dimension of policy may contribute to overcoming a long-standing embarrassment in political science: our difficulty in dealing with political radicalism in U.S. history except as something exceptional, sporadic, and temporary. Radical politics is as regular as mainstream, even if less frequent. Some policies are radical from the start, but any area of policy can be radicalized. It depends upon the way the policy or policy proposal is constructed and the severity of the sanctions provided.

Third, success on the first two points would be good for theory in political science. But my hopes expressed in this third point are even more ambitious. Taking away the "new" from the so-called new politics could lead to a richer sense of the historic relation between society and the state in the United States. Radical elements are inevitable in a society as dynamic as ours, and society would be less healthy and less productive without the radical. The question for study of political development is how radicalized forces interact with governmental institutions, whether they are channeled into progressive changes, and how they make a place for themselves within the constitutional structure. Was the U.S. system lucky or successful in the great transition through the New Deal to the "Second Republic"?[3] Everyone will agree that the Depression had radicalized an unusually large segment of U.S. society. Yet, it is clear from this analysis that most of the New Deal policies were of the C_1 type. Imagine, if possible, what the outcome would have been if the radicalized groups and movements of the 1930s had succeeded in radicalizing the policies. If there had been in the 1930s a large number of cases at the national level like the cases in the Tatalovich and Daynes volume, we would not be talking here about the political system as it is today.

Tatalovich, Daynes, and their colleagues have given us not only cases and findings, but more. They have provided an agenda for a new policy analysis appropriate to the new politics.

CHAPTER 14

Our Millennium

Political Science Confronts
the Global Corporate Economy

When the old Chinese prophet said "May you live in interesting times," he intended it as a curse. There is a curse hovering over political science, and it is the possibility of being excluded from the struggle to define precisely what *is* interesting in our millennium. All teachers and debaters know that whoever sets the terms of discourse will almost always determine the outcome. Naming the game is the name of the game, and admission to this contest is controlled by gatekeepers who see little if anything to be gained from recognizing political science as a major player. We must speak truth to power, but is power willing to listen?

The cold war is over, and political science may have more to celebrate than any other discipline because the cold war was a war of ideas, in which the stated goals were freedom over slavery, democracy over dictatorship, and human rights for all human beings. These are *political* goals, and the principal means for their pursuit were free speech, free elections, free inquiry, and free enterprise.

Yet over the past two decades, political science has been losing the struggle for the definition of goals to a new hegemonic paradigm: an economic theory of democracy in which free enterprise alone is sufficient to accomplish all the other goals.

This economic theory of democracy is not economic science, for which we have admiration bordering on adoration. The economic theory of democracy is not science but ideology, which we should fear. It gains its credibility from economic science and from anecdotal evidence about how capitalism vanquished authoritarianism, while ignoring contrary and unsupportive anecdotes.

The point is that the free market does not make free all those who enter it, nor does it emerge or prosper without the substantial support of the state. Yet, for the past two decades, there has been a strong and dangerous tendency to denigrate the state—and therefore the political—as the primary source of irrationality in the world. The economy is assumed to be a closed and self-generating, self-perfecting system which works through its own internal dynamics. As Wesley Mitchell put it eighty years ago, the recurrence of business cycles is a working out of an "inner mechanism" in which one phase of the cycle generates the next, with each period of the cycle containing the seeds that inevitably flower and produce the next phase. This is the modern transformation of Adam Smith's *invisible* hand into Alfred Chandler's *visible* hand—an empirical phenomenon with working parts.[1]

Closely connected to this self-regulating mechanism is the assumption of equilibrium, which is the springboard to a claim far larger than mere economic theory. Let me put this in the mouth of one of the world's most successful capitalists, George Soros: "The concept of equilibrium is very useful, but it can also be deceptive. It has the aura of something empirical. That is not the case. Equilibrium itself has rarely been observed in real life."[2]

Soros refers to equilibrium as an aspect of "market fundamentalism [which] plays a crucial role in the global capitalist system [by providing] the ideology that not only motivates many of the most successful participants but also drives policy."[3] On the springboard of equilibrium, supported by firm data about the behavior of particular markets under certain strict conditions, and supported further by impressive equations, economics made a gigantic leap of faith to incorporate not only economic thought but social and political thought. This is precisely why economic theory has to be appreciated as ideology.

And this is where political science comes in. Political science is the discipline which studies most of the institutional phenomena that economics assumes away. It is through examination of these assumptions that we can gain the capacity to put economics in its place. And that should be our goal in this era of globalization: to advance an understanding of the institutions of government and the practices of politics that can actually improve the prospects for salvaging more democracy from the tyrant—whether that tyrant be repressive rule by malevolent political elites or repressive rule by mechanisms that recognize no law except the law of the market place.

Character of Economic Globalization

Linkage to the political in our millennium must begin with a close examination of the key concept, *globalization*. First of all, note that it is a *-tion* word; *-tion* is a suffix indicating a process of becoming. It is a matter of degree. Thus, although globalization is ordinarily thought of as "borderless trade," in the real world it is a moving target. Better still, several moving targets. For example, globalization can be operationally defined as a share of foreign capital in domestic investment; or it can be measured fairly precisely in terms of cross-border flows of investment in proportion to GDP, or cross-border flows of goods as a percentage of GDP, or cross-border flows of people as a percentage of the recipient population. And so on.

This brief characterization alone produces some fairly powerful insights. First of all, it forces us to recognize that ours is not the first epoch of globalization. Ours is Globalization II; Globalization I extended roughly from 1880 to 1914. That great libertarian magazine the *Economist* is a good authority on the subject: "By most important measures the world was more closely integrated before 1914 than it is now—in some [respects] much more so."[4]

Having thus encountered Globalization I, what can it tell us about Globalization II? It helps at the outset to recognize that 1914 is the date of termination for Globalization I. Although this opens up all sorts of questions of cause and effect, pursuing those would only belabor the obvious, and worse, would amount to a diversion from a much more intriguing inquiry: within the 1914 context, globalization reveals itself as at least a three-dimensional phenomenon, each with its own developmental track. Track 1 is the *macro* level; track 2 is, for lack of a better term, the *meso* level; track 3 is the *micro* level.

Track 1

The macro level is defined by those economic matters that are most globalized—that is, closest to complete borderless trade. It is the financial markets—international financial or capital transactions. This level also most closely approximates to the pure market as a self-regulating system. Annual turnover in global capital exchanges rose from an estimated $188 billion in 1986 to $1.2 trillion in 1995, and is still rising.[5] Cross-border capital transactions in the G7 countries rose tenfold in that period, but more striking is involvement of the developing world outside G7. The biggest capital importers between 1990 and 1995 were, in descending order, China, Mexico, Brazil, South Korea, Malaysia, Argentina, Thailand, and Indonesia, and significant major newcomers are Bolivia, Poland, Russia, India, and Vietnam.

Although the macro economy gets about as close as possible to the ideal of the self-regulating market system, it is not without an institutional structure. The International Monetary Fund and the GATT (now WTO) have been an effective framework. The IMF managed the system of fixed exchange from the end of World War II until rates were set loose by President Nixon in the 1970s. The IMF continued to contribute to world economic stability as a lender of last resort while using its lending power to leverage countries into membership in the global capitalist club. The IMF with the World Bank aided recovery of war-torn countries and then helped bring along newly developing countries. The IMF, World Bank, and GATT (WTO) have also helped prevent the world from fragmenting into hostile trading blocs euphemistically called free trade associations while at the same time leveraging the less developed and former Soviet satellite countries into domestic practices meriting membership in the global economy. Thus, the expansion of the genuinely macro market system was neither entirely economic nor spontaneous. This is *political economy*.[6]

Track 2

The meso level is the level of the major players, the key traders and dealers in the global economy. And already very early in Globalization I, they were not what they had been historically. *Homo economicus* was originally the rational actor, a human being using units of work and wealth to enhance satisfaction by making exchanges with others. The main actor then became the firm, and the simple firm gave way—or was completely overshadowed—by the incorporated firm. The corporation became the key player, first because markets are not simple acts or single decisions but are repetitive behaviors, and the corporation—being an eternal person—is the only engine that can sustain the market as a process. In the second place, the corporate form dominated because it was capable of vertical integration, capital concentration, and market organization and management on a scale that can make an international, global economy and then meet its demands. As Chandler put it, corporations were uniquely able "to *internalize* several processes of production and distribution and the market transactions between them within a single enterprise. Such internalization permitted the *visible hand* of administrative coordination to make more intensive use of the resources invested in these processes of production and distribution than could the *invisible hand* of market coordination."[7]

According to Chandler, most American industries had acquired their modern structure by the end of World War I, and this structure has remained the same ever since (ibid.). However, what Chandler does not say is that these corporations, including those that came to be called multinational corporations (MNCs), were then and are now far more dependent on state-provided frameworks than any previous form of enterprise. The following are a few telling examples. Space permits only a skeletal treatment, but it should be patently obvious to any serious observer how important each of these is to the life of the corporation. What I am calling frameworks, sociologists would call "functional prerequisites." The six identified here do not pretend to exhaust the possibilities.

Provisions for Law and Order
Predictability in human affairs obviously precedes everything else. But the social order is more than the order imposed by military means, important as that is. The market requires what Max Weber called "calculable law."[8]

Provisions for Property
Property is a legal fiction. It is a synthesis word for all the laws against trespass. Through this process, law renders highly probable that we can enjoy real dominion over that which we claim as our own. "The market" can come only after that.

Provisions for Contract Enforcement
It is impossible to imagine transactions today without contracts, and it is also impossible to imagine contracts without virtually absolute assurance that some source of authority *outside* the market and *prior* to the market will make breaches of contract more expensive than observance.

Provisions for Exchange
There are still other matters that lie behind contract, making contract itself possible. In brief, there has to be *standardization* of the language by which contracts are written. Standardization is of two kinds: the *legal* language and the specific *technical* or *substantive* language; both precede the contract and thus precede the market.

Provisions for Public Goods
Time and technology can transform an existing public good into a normal marketable commodity. But in any epoch there will be some functions that individual market players cannot provide for themselves without providing them free for others. There is, according to Hume (through Olson), an inherent *dis*incentive for one or more neighbors to empty the nearby swamp when they are aware that "free riders" can enjoy the result. And there is an inherent disincentive for a Microsoft to teach all of its employees to read, write, and calculate and then see them go, free of charge, to other employers.

Provisions for Allocation of Responsibility for Injury
No sane person would enter a market conscientiously if all responsibility for their initiative were personal and if there were no limit to that responsibility as their products or services pass through the economy. Tort law is one of the dominant examples in most capitalist environments. Another example is the corporation itself. One of the most valuable incentives for organizing economic activity in a corporation is that the liability of the owners is normally limited to their share of the ownership of the corporation.

The first conclusion to be drawn from these framework provisions is that in the real world of economic players there is no such thing as an economy. There is only *political* economy. Second, all the functional prerequisites of the market economy are met entirely or in largest part by deliberate, institutionalized governmental activity—laws, public policies, programs, statutes, and other official instruments. Some laws or policies have been in operation for so long that they are no longer recognized as deliberate contrivances developed by courts or adopted by legislatures or heads of state and their councils.

A third conclusion will be applied first only to the United States, but it leads to a larger conclusion applying to "the state" anywhere. Since the U.S. Constitution relegated to the state governments virtually all the authority to pass the laws that meet the prerequisites of the market economy, the absence of national provisions made it possible for Americans to believe they had once enjoyed free, laissez-faire enterprise which was eventually corrupted by government interference. The states continue to provide virtually all the legal support systems of American capitalism, despite the constitutional revolution of the 1930s. Even in countries with classical European-type states, a similar legal support structure is provided. In other words, all corporations, regardless of their size or their multinational character, have their legal feet on the ground in some particular locality and are supported by public policies there.

Track 3

The micro level is the dimension of community and local institutions. One reason why a causal analysis of 1914 is so tempting is because economic expansion acts on this micro level and produces antagonistic reactions as well as the supportive legal arrangements outlined above. The Europe of 1914 called it Balkanization because that is where local reaction was intense enough to provide the spark that lit the August fire. Balkanization became a generic term applying to any efforts at tribal, ethnic, communal, linguistic, racial, or other bases of self-determination. Balkanization also implied war, given the tendency of one tribe or ethnic or other population group to perceive as threatening the self-determination efforts of others of its neighbors.

Globalization has played a major hand in this Balkanization process because capitalism was the most revolutionary force in the previous millennium and promises to be the same in this one. Capitalism must be credited with (or blamed for) the transformation of the peasantry and the making of the working class, the creation of labor as a commodity, the conversion of all property into liquid/commodity form, the commercialization of agriculture, and so on. From the standpoint of local elites, traditional leaders, and established powers, capitalism and industrialization had to be seen as hostile because they were destabilizing—agents of change coming in from the outside.

Robert Reich put it rather neatly in his foreword to the mass-circulation *World Almanac and Book of Facts 2000:*

> Beyond the obvious, specific hazards ahead (such as global warming, excessive population growth, and nuclear proliferation), a more universal drama will play itself out in the coming century. Two great, opposing forces are likely to grow stronger, and the contest between them may well determine the fate of humankind. The first force is technology. The second is tribalism.[9]

But there is a great deal missing from this picture. First, he speaks of this antinomy between technology and tribalism as a force shaping the future when in fact it was already a force shaping the past and the present. Second, although capitalist expansion is and will be seen as hostile to local traditions and elites and power structures, Track 3 (the micro level) is absolutely essential to capitalism, for no matter how big corporations get and no matter how far-flung and multinational they spread, all corporations have their legal feet on somebody's ground, and they will daily, weekly, and annually need legal life supports; that is why these are called functional prerequisites. Whether the local arrangements are adopted by national governments (European style) or primarily by state governments (American federal style), implementation is ultimately local or localized. An old American political sage once observed that "all politics is local." He failed to add the explanation, "because all social control is local."

Still another factor is missing in Reich's picture, but is implied by his use of tribalism to epitomize local and community bonding: this is that micro level governments are inherently conservative. But this will have to wait until the politics of Track 3 in the next section.

Toward a Politics of Globalization

Disaggregation of globalization into separate dimensions or tracks has opened the economic definition of reality to question—or I should say, to political questions that might indeed produce a whole new discourse. It turned out to be impossible to deal with any of the levels or tracks without recognizing the deep and systematic involvement of the state: legal arrangements that use authority—legitimized coercion—to serve, to support, and to regulate conduct in a way that provides the structure within which economic processes work. To repeat an earlier contention, political science as a profession is capable of confronting virtually all the factors that economics assumes or assumes away. Political analysis extends beyond the structure, moreover, to ideology and ethics: beliefs and arguments based on beliefs that justify given sets of arrangements and existing structures of power. It is time to go back over each track and to highlight its political character: What are the goals at issue? Who plays? Who gets what? And why? That of course is an ideal agenda. No claim will be made that justice is done to each question.

The Politics of Track 1

It is not difficult to identify two primary goals that are at issue in the macro dimension: (1) constitutional transformation, and (2) redistribution of social obligations or, more accurately for our time, *re*-redistribution. The first goal, constitutional transformation, may sound dry and academic, but nothing is further from the truth. Globalization and its discourse seek a drastic restructuring of government and government authority, thereby raising the threshold of membership in the global economy club. Specific policy demands for constitutional restructuring have become dry by repetition: decentralization, de-concentration, devolution, deregulation. The alliteration is not accidental or contrived. As -*tion* is a key suffix indicating a process of becoming, *de*- is a key prefix indicating downward, away from, toward the bottom, reversing, undoing, exhausting.

When you get down to the specifics of policy at the macro level, the patent purpose is the same as that of Adam Smith: to deprive states of the authority to adopt any restraints against free trade. This is the constitutional transformation the macro economic paradigm supports, on the assumption that without state-erected barriers, the laissez-faire economy would grow and prosper.

But if free trade were the only goal, the policy would be the easiest thing in the world to draft and implement: "establishing free trade … could have been written on one page—a simple treaty to eliminate tariffs." In actuality, free trade treaties involve hundreds of pages of effort to impose obligations on member states to weaken or eliminate the social obligations and entitlements that were established and expanded during the preglobalization, postwar, social democratic years. Those obligations and entitlements have been redefined as "mercantilistic" interference with capital flow.[10] These are the reredistributive policies at the macro level.

In examining the political process of establishing and reaching goals at the macro level, it is notable that the most prominent players in the politics of constitutional and reredistributive policies are not the corporate elites and their interest groups but major economic theorists in universities and think tanks and high-ranking experts and technocrats occupying command posts in a few central state banks and a few international agencies, such as the IMF, World Bank, ITC, and WTO, and such regional agencies as EU and NAFTA. And so on. MNCs may have most to gain or lose, but neither their voices nor their clout has been prominent in the public discourse at the macro level. Peter Johnson reports on the basis of his book-length study of the U.S. Federal Reserve and the Deutsche Bundesbank during the 1970s and 1980s that the curtain on Globalization II at the macro level was raised by the victory of the

Friedmanites over the Keynesians—the "fresh water economists" over the "salt water economists." Once the ideological/theoretical debate was won, the new international monetary policy and monetary structure virtually fell into place.[11] Johnson goes on to observe that monetary policy is so comprehensive and immediate in its impact that policy makers at the macro level "must attempt to limit or exclude such claims [of losers and winners].... [T]his has increasingly fostered *the subordination of normal patterns of political representation* (party politics, interest groups, etc.) ... by recruiting economic expertise and incorporating it *into the policymaking process.*"[12] Macro level politics is distinctly unpluralistic.

There is an analog, which may be a companion and could possibly be the most concrete rendering of the politics of the entire macro domain: the government of the Internet. It consists of four (so far) institutions, specialized around certain tasks. World Wide Web Consortium (w3c) is the main Internet standards (or standardization) body. The Internet Engineer Task Force (IETF) develops consensual tech standards and has its own steering group (IESG) to coordinate them. The Internet Corporation for Assigned Names & Numbers (ICANN) oversees domain names such as .com and .org. All these bodies were spontaneously created, are self-governing, and are open to any and all as members. There is deliberation within each, but "We reject kings, presidents and voting." Consensus is the rule. However, the individuals most widely respected for their expertise are accepted as "benevolent dictators" to create a consensus. They sit atop a "meritocratic online 'community,'" comprising thousands of volunteers, "like-minded individuals."[13] This meritocratic, technocratic paradise is no myth. It is a reality just one step beyond the less pure technocracy we can already see and appreciate in the politics of the macro level, especially of the structure of world capital transfers.

Ideology (or theory) has also been the key attribute of the macro politics of re-redistributive policies, whose goal is "to shred the social contract."[14] It is amazing how parties of the left—all over Europe, from social democratic to labour to socialist and even former communist—have so readily swallowed the theory that "global free trade would eventually make everyone better off, even if some people would suffer in the short term."[15/16] Stigmatization of government is itself a major policy—as an ideological policy or a propaganda policy—to help guarantee that future leftist party governments won't dare try to reregulate, recentralize, or redistribute. "Government" has become the socialism against which we fought the cold war. If Ronald Reagan had been running for office in 1920 instead of 1980, he could have been imprisoned along with Sacco and Vanzetti for his criminally anarchic proclamation that "Government is not the solution; it is the problem."

Only time will tell if stigmatization went too far to be moderated. But we will never get nearer to an answer if we permit no discourse that can raise the question and keep raising it.

The Politics of Track 2

Meso politics is quite another matter. The goals at issue are different. The players are different. The "power structure" is different. The discourse itself is significantly different. Yet it is all part of the global phenomenon, giving rise to the question of how economic thinking can live with globalization as a unitary concept, without ever attempting to unpack it. Virtually all the meso politics is masked by the aggregate data on the macro "global market."

The goals sought by the players at the meso level are to a large extent coextensive with the list of "functional prerequisites" given above, because however old and established many of the fundamental promarket policies are, they are constantly in need of revision and amendment, especially when the pace of economic expansion or contraction is intense. Some of the newer policy issues arise out of technological innovation, generally called intellectual property rights. And the Microsoft case is only the tip of the iceberg of new issues in what had been treated as settled categories of policy, such as merger and strategic alliances, pricing and marketing agreements, revision of labor laws and civil rights laws, environmental protection standards, and so on. Each nation-state must make laws in these areas to meet their own needs, yet international standardization is more pressing than ever.

Even more interesting at the meso level of politics are the regional free trade associations, which have to make policy decisions for their own members. The two most important so far are the EU and NAFTA but there are already three more fledgling regional associations (Mercosur, Apec, and Asean), with more surely to come in the near future. These regional associations, like traditional nation-states, are "free trade" only among their member units but not with regard to nonmembers. To put it crassly, the regional associations by nature discriminate against nonmembers.

Since the EU is the most advanced and already has a fairly stable political process, it is worth a closer look. And it only takes a brief encounter with the EU to see that its political process is as pluralistic as the macro political process was seen to be elitist, hierarchical, and technocratic. The leading students of the politics within the EU, Wolfgang Streeck and Philippe Schmitter, are, after a decade of close study, unable to decide whether "Europe's would-be polity" is a classic American-style pluralistic system or a version of the older European corporatism variant of pluralism. But they are confident in their treatment of that political process as one dominated by interest group formation engaged in a bargaining process driven by "professional leaders of organized interest groups."[17/18] These organized interest groups include some MNCs themselves as well as trade associations which represent corporate members. Unions and professional associations are included, but they are far outnumbered by associations of business interests. In the formal EU policy processes, functional representation competes with parliamentary representation; and, with the encouragement of the formal EU governing bodies, the number of interest groups represented on advisory committees, expert groups, and consultative bodies has mushroomed.[19]

Regional associations, like nation-states, are very much a part of globalization, but they are amply capable of resistance to the macro economy. Cross-border exchanges between and among their members do contribute to the aggregate level of globalization, but that should not be allowed to mask the potential for conflict, indeed violent conflict. Regional associations, like traditional nation-states, modern multinational corporations, and old-fashioned cartels, are all groups composed of memberships willing to give up a certain amount of sovereignty and freedom of action in return for lower risk, higher short-term profit, or both.

OPEC, a cartel that combines common interests of several regions, is a dramatic case in point. Another case is a large nation-state like China, which is proving capable of forcing itself into WTO without having officially given an inch on human rights or environmental standards. Emerging regional associations will soon discover (just as subnational regional associations discover when confronting their national government's policies) that there are certain goals so fundamentally shared by employer and worker and rich and poor within the region that they can pursue their goals together despite global competition, WTO, and even IMF pressures. And finally, as a consequence of the dramatic merger movement, MNCs in the industrialized nations have internalized so much of what used to be regulated and coordinated by classic market mechanisms that they are the functional equivalent of dozens of new regional free trade associations or cartels. Thomas Friedman and other true believers in the free trade religion may sincerely embrace in their catechism that no two capitalist countries or no two countries with McDonald franchises will ever go to war with each other. But economically driven violent conflicts over wage slavery, spillover pollution, or illegal immigration are forms of "competition" that neither scientific economic theory nor free market ideology should claim it can handle.

If Globalization I has any relevance at all, there are Globalization II developments whose consequences are worth watching closely. And they are developments which defy systematic, quantitative economic science.[20] In fact, a lot of those quantifiable data cry out for a more disaggregated, *less* macro economic conceptualization. A recent report by one of the world's leading students of the relation between international trade and international development, Jeffrey Sachs, demonstrates that the providers of nearly all of the world's technological innovation, the "high-tech innovators," are distributed in just four regions—North America, Western Europe, Japan/Korea, and Australia. "Technological adopters" comprise only five more regions—Mexico, the Argentina/Chile half of South America, the European periphery, the South- and East-Asian periphery, and South Africa. All the other regions comprise the "technologically excluded."[21/22] One might argue that India and China, among others, should be added to the "technology adopters" list and there are numerous developing countries that are successfully adapting technology to the production, processing, and marketing of primary products. That said, we need not specify just how fundamentally different are the interests of each of these technologically defined regions.

The Politics of Track 3

The micro level is the *local* but might more meaningfully be called the *parochial* level—that is, parochial meaning local and "of the parish." This is indicative of the great distance between the character of the politics of Track 3 and the character of politics of Track 1 and Track 2. The earlier proposition, that micro level governments are inherently conservative, serves well as an entrée into the special character of Track 3 politics.

By conservative I mean genuinely conservative. Classical or laissez-faire, "neoliberal" ideology became defined as right of center because the litmus test of left vs. right in Europe is the attitude toward capitalism. But while that is not without validity as an indication of "right of center," conservatism is a poor and misleading label for it. Conservatism should be, and will here be, limited to what now has to be referred to as "social conservatism." Genuine conservatism takes a moral position toward individual conduct and social and community ties. A genuinely conservative policy would be oriented toward conduct "deemed good or evil in itself"; that is, conduct is consonant with some moral code or it is not. Research beyond reading relevant sacred sources is unnecessary; it is not difficult to know what is permitted or forbidden. In contrast, all forms of liberalism, including neoliberalism, are purely instrumental. Liberalism addresses conduct deemed "harmful in its consequences." Societies and communities are not moral entities or the source of virtue but are, to liberals, human contrivances subject to deliberate as well as spontaneous change. Research into causes and consequences is essential to liberal policy-making.

A false impression has prevailed for a long time in the United States and elsewhere that cities are the liberal, leftward, indeed revolutionary, components of a society. While there may be some truth to that in the cultural and aesthetic realms, such urbane values rarely prevail in local governance. By local I mean both state and local government (in federal) and regional and local (in unitary) systems.

Local governments are particularly conservative in the United States because they are not only responsible for adapting and implementing the policies passed by state legislatures to regulate "the health, safety and morals of the community" (the very definition of "police power" in English constitutional history). That built-in conservatism is reinforced by the local tax base, which is primarily the property tax. But regardless of country and regardless of the pluralist or elitist power distribution in cities, and regardless of how dynamic is their posture toward culture or economic development, all localities are strictly observant about their obligation to social order.

It is indeed true that federalism and other genuine devolutions of power to lower levels of government permit variation in policy from one principality to another. For example, in the United States, capital punishment is provided by law in 37 states and not provided at all in the other 13 states. Punishment for possession of drugs varies from slight to draconian. Contemporary social policies can also vary from quite left-leaning generosity to highly conservative paternalistic assistance that is coupled with severe restraints on eligibility and obedience. But much of this is transitory and a great deal of it is illusory. From the nineteenth century literally until the 1960s, charitable assistance by local governments in the United States was severely conservative. In the nineteenth-century United States there was a great deal of private charitable assistance and at least some signs of expanding public assistance for the elderly and the dependent. But the assistance was very closely tied to police functions, stressing research into whether applicants were deserving or undeserving. And, in direct violation of the First Amendment, even when local services were relatively generous, they were to a very large extent a cooperative venture between the local government and a church-based charitable organization heavily financed by the local government. One of the largest items in the New York City budgets in the early 1900s was "grants to eleemosynary institutions." The generosity and services we associate with local governments throughout the industrialized countries are largely a product or an artifact of the social democratic post–World War II epoch, and even then there was a great deal more surveillance and moral regulation by local social service workers over their clientele than is generally understood. And in the 1990s globalization cycle, surveillance and regulation intensified. Again taking the lead, the United States in 1996 abolished public assistance as an "entitlement" and virtually converted local social welfare workers into a welfare police.[23] Social order means keeping classes, races, ethnic groups, genders, and life-style groups in their places. Keeping people in their places is mainly achieved by segregation, which usually is given the more respectable name of community.

Communities in the United States are often given special racial and ethnic designations—Chinatown, Little Italy, Jewtown, Harlem (which in New York City had been a Jewish quarter before it became black); and Hoovertown and Shanty Town for the recently impoverished. Although in the United States "ghetto" was adapted for use in designating all distinct forms of segregation, the term was of course brought over from European usage as a designation for separate Jewish communities.

But it would be quite wrong to imagine that Jews were the only population grouping in non-U.S. cities subjected to local social policies of segregation. Two thousand years ago a Chinese philosopher advised his lord that "the scholar-official, the peasant, the craftsman and the merchant ... should not mix with one another, for it would inevitably lead to conflict and divergence of opinions and thus complicate things unnecessarily." This was echoed in 1910 by a Viennese architect who wrote, "We may consider it axiomatic that the administration of a great city ... demands its division into wards [which] form the foundation of the systematized regulation of the great city."[24]

This social regulatory attitude is so deep in the history and values of cities that it is even expressed in their architecture. Next to defense, it is what city planning was all about. Pre-nineteenth-century Paris was a city of *quartiers*, neighborhoods segregated along class, occupational, and cultural lines. Haussmann's nineteenth-century Paris, although known for its *grands boulevards* and magnificent vistas, was designed to segregate and resegregate the city distinctly. The boulevards also served to prevent "dangerous classes" (including students in 1968) from erecting barricades to prevent the passage of troops. *Grève*, the French word for strike, had its origin in a little piece of geography in front of what became the Hôtel de Ville where barges on the Seine were loaded and unloaded. As workers, who lived near where they worked in "a vile neighborhood,"[25] began to agitate by demonstrating in the Place de Grève, Haussmann moved them out of the central city into working class suburbs.

Signs of the conservatism of cities are not limited to architectural design and city planning. Braudel reports that Marseilles in the sixteenth century not only restricted citizenship but had a requirement that a period of ten years of domicile was necessary to possess property or to marry a local resident. "This limited conception of citizenship was the general rule everywhere."[26] City governments cooperated with the major craft guilds to control work opportunities in cities, including opportunities to start new businesses or create new trades.[27] And the great guild halls shared the central city squares and plazas with two other corporate sources of authority—the government and the church.[28]

Modern cities are not appreciably different. In the United States, the misleading impression about the leftward egalitarian progressivism of urban centers was strengthened during the 1950s–1970s epoch of federal urban policies. Generous grants-in-aid from the national government loosened the ties of cities to their property tax base and imposed an obligation on the cities to use the federal money in a more redistributive way. But the precise implementation of these national urban programs was devolved to the discretion of the city governments, and as a consequence, American cities were more segregated after the urban policy revolution than before.

Meanwhile, Gaullist France adopted a similar devolution policy in the 1970s, and this was embraced and strengthened by the socialist government elected in 1981. The Mitterrand government, calling it "functional decentralization," adopted an important decentralization law in 1982 and another in 1987, establishing a new system of regional government, authorizing them to use a maximum of discretion. The stated purpose of these laws was "to reduce the scope of national *tutelle*."[29] In order to emphasize this decentralization, the Mitterrand government actually abolished the revered office of prefect. Five years later, in 1987, as the socialist government was adjusting to globalization, the office of prefect was restored, but the devolution of discretion down to departmental and local levels was not reversed. This was the bellwether of the rightward movement of socialist governments throughout Europe.[30]

National governments had become untouchable. Stigmatization took on many forms, but classical economic theory's attack on national government and its policies as socialist interference was the leading strategy. Political corruption was another. Political corruption is a given, even in stable democracies; it, along with taxes, is "the price we pay for civilization." This is not to condone it but only to say, "Why now?" Why are so many politicians, especially so many high-ranking and well respected members of the political class, being discredited now? Why so much political turnover by means other than election?[31] It has to be considered part of the campaign to discredit democratic politics, indeed part of the still larger strategy of stigmatizing democratic government. And it served a dual purpose. First to delegitimize national government, because, as earlier observed, that helps guarantee no electoral politician would dare propose new national policies of trade regulation (any other interference). Since parties of the left tend to favor nationalization of authority precisely because that's the only way to establish common standards of human rights—mainly through redistributive policies—*any* embrace of devolution is a large rightward step. All that talk about local government being "closer to the people" is household noise. But it's popular noise, so popular that it was music to Clinton's New Democrats, Blair's Third Way, and to all their epigones among parties of the left and center-left all over Europe. This was the answer, as manna from heaven, to the question of how to go right and stay left: give power to the people while easing the burden imposed on trade by the entitlements and safety nets established by left-leaning national governments between the 1930s and the 1970s.

The key here is to recognize that globalization, whatever its benefits, is deeply problematic. Economics may drive and guide globalization; it is left to *politics* to confront the problems and pick up the pieces. And what are the pieces? In brief, they are virtually all the things that rational choosers do not include in their rational choice, cost-benefit calculations.

Conclusions, Reflections, Proposals

Toward a Global Political Science

I will conclude with a few observations that are not systematically linked but are all aimed at establishing some kind of linkage toward the political and away from the economic. The first is the most general proposition. The other propositions can be thought of as subsidiary to it. The most compelling conclusion arising out of this effort has already been articulated, and, to the best of my ability, established: there is no such thing as an economy; there is only political economy. The rest of this chapter is a lawyerly brief in its favor.

Another general conclusion of value to the purpose here is that a state that can make markets can unmake them. This is a superior cousin to Marx's thesis that capitalism is a system imposed through the state by ruling interests. The truth as I see it here is that, quite beyond Marx, capitalism did not need to be imposed, only facilitated. And not all state actions are facilitative. That's the story of political economy, and the opening to the agenda of a global political science.

To tease out this agenda for a global political science, I have chosen three problems of political significance that have been moved from fundamental to critical by global economic expansion: citizenship, wealth, and environmental externalities. But this is not exactly a research agenda, although more research is always better. It is my contention that political science does not need more research before we confront economic theory with a competitive discourse. All we need to do is to apply more passionately what we already know. Vigorous engagement in the discourse will in fact be the best way to find out just what research we really need. And in the process, we can expose the economist as that wily Wizard of Oz.

Citizenship

A political perspective requires that citizenship be unpacked into at least two dimensions. First, there is corporate citizenship, for, after all, corporations are legal persons. Then there is the normally understood individual or human citizenship. At the corporate level, a highly competitive market is the enemy of good citizenship. This is simply another way of saying that one of the greatest virtues of a laissez-faire system is also one of its greatest problems. As competition spreads and intensifies, prices are reduced toward marginal cost. If that is so, and there is no reason to believe it isn't, then no individual competitors can be virtuous citizens and choose to raise wages or to improve the work environment or recycle waste products, because the added cost would force them out of the market.

Citizenship—both corporate and individual—means membership in the city, in the polity. Citizenship means, above everything else, having a few rights in regard to matters essential to personal integrity, collective security, and public order. Citizenship is defined by rights, not obligations; obligations can only be imposed by specific laws, usually called "the rule of law." Rights are claims to a remedy of so high an order of need that the remedy can be denied only by an extraordinary authority, plus an extraordinary decision process specified in advance. The authority sufficient to dispose of rights is usually lodged in something we have come to call a state, and that state must have a credible theory of itself, not an abstract philosophy of right but a specification of rights and a decision process for disposition of rights claims beyond the convenience of the participants.

That is the essence of a constitution, but this in turn points to a fact difficult to dispense with—that rights are inconceivable without a state or some "moral equivalent of a state." Leaving the market alone (laissez-faire) to perfect its own solutions to claims of right, as part of the self-perfecting mechanisms of an economic system, would amount to allowing each corporation to be a judge in its own cause. And that is where corporate citizenship ends. Either the corporation is a citizen with rights claims on the state *or* it is its own state—a state within a state or a state without a state—with authority to dispose of rights claims made on it by its human members. But of course, no corporation known to us as yet has a theory of itself, especially one that defines its members, their rights, and the process by which those rights can be satisfied or denied. The corporation in economic theory is a mere behavioral unit. Where, except for political theory, will this other corporation come from?

In this context, "globalization" today is nothing more than a new feudalism, an escape from citizenship into labor and consumer serfdom, depending upon the good will of the corporate lord. Some political scientists are beginning to recognize this kind of tendency in the globalizing context, but are trying to help the economists out by formulating hopeful but quite illusory communitarian and voluntaristic arrangements, such as "participatory governance," as though citizenship and rights can be handled on an entirely voluntaristic basis within the spontaneous—or apparently spontaneous—corporate market place.[32] But if political science has any integrity at all, it seems to me that its discourse must recognize and must emphasize to the top of our voices that a voluntarism that depends upon consensus leading to the involvement of umpires to implement whatever consensus has determined is either phony or is preliminary to reinventing the state. From the standpoint of rights alone, can the state be allowed to wither?

Wealth

Globalization produces competition, and competition produces wealth. Who would be foolish enough today to question that? But the problematic worthy of discourse begins with the recognition that wealth also seems to produce poverty. Or, to follow one of the very few great American political economists, Henry George, there is a direct relationship between progress and poverty. George recognized this very early in Globalization I and he tried his best to emphasize the urgent political consequences of this relationship: "This association of poverty with progress is the great enigma of our times ... [and the] reaction must come.... To educate men who must be condemned to poverty, is but to make them restive; to base on a state of most glaring social inequality political institutions under which men are theoretically equal, is to stand a pyramid on its apex."[33] But just when does the level of unequal distribution become a public wrong? When do *meso* and *micro* politics begin to generate social movements? And when does redistributive state policy become justifiable?

One of the leading members of the laissez-faire college of cardinals, the editorial board of the *Economist,* would offer us the following solution: "As long as the boom continues, most Americans can subsume their envy in the thought that they themselves are better off."[34] The thought back of this is not limited to Americans. Thus, in any expanding country, progress and poverty can live together in equilibrium as long as there is enough hope and faith among those less well off to "subsume their envy." This is an economic theory of psychology at its most absurd.

I will give that problem to the psychologists and will concentrate on how we can take wealth inequality away from economists with a credible politics of economics. Policy analysis will have to be nudged away from costs and benefits to a new juris-prudence, with categories of rights and policies that confront differences of culture, tradition, and status. For example, why are there no developed approaches to the market value of home care and mother work? Why is poverty so highly and increasingly feminized? More generally, why does the market tend to denigrate the value of jobs traditionally dominated by females and lower-status ethnic and racial groups? At what points and with what status groupings does support for existing political processes begin to break down? These are political questions, and they point, among other things, to new uses of sample surveys. Methods might remain the same but hypotheses would be tested in groupings or categories, cumulatively around fundamental values in different culture contexts, rather than one micro-hypothesis at a time. Comparative, *global* behavioral research around political values needs less stress on causal analysis and more stress on consequential analysis. One outstanding example would be the work of Hans-Dieter Klingemann and associates on the consequences of political reforms in European postcommunist countries, coupled with the fact that the political reforms preceded the economic reforms.[35] A second example would be Seymour Martin Lipset and William Schneider's *The Confidence Gap* (1987), especially if it became the model for comparing questions of legitimacy in all the democratizing countries.

There is still another aspect of wealth distribution, the widening gap between rich and poor nations. But this can best be dealt with in the context of the third agenda item: environmental externalities.

Environmental Externalities

Unregulated markets in natural resources and production based upon the untamed exploitation of degradable natural resources wiped out forests, rain forests, wetlands, grasslands, water tables, and the atmosphere in vast areas of what became the developed capitalist countries. As long as the entrepreneur could disregard the spillover effects and could move on to new territory when the resources were exhausted, the savings were passed on to consumers and offered as evidence of the benefits of competition. The true cost of production has never figured in the free market, and, *ceteris paribus* (to use a favorite laissez-faire expression), the true cost of production will never be figured in. But now that the window of externalization is closing, late-comers to industrialization want to keep the window open, to use the same methods as their predecessors. Other things are not going to be equal.

Regulation seems inevitable. Environmental pollution and the use of nonrenewable resources are like any public goods: there is a *dis*incentive among all players (especially if they are competitors in a competitive market) to do the right thing because others could share in their contribution without paying, and worse, the added cost of doing the right thing—whether it is cleaning exhaust gases or paying above subsistence wages— would force the good guys out of the market. Regulation imposing a higher standard on all the players makes all the players good citizens and improves the public space by raising the field of competition while keeping it level.

Unfortunately, however, regulation is an inherently limited approach. Even on a national scale, regulatory policies are the most difficult ones on which to gain majority support, not to speak of consensus. It can only be more difficult on an international scale, because even if adopted by all the major governments, and WTO or some other international body were given impressive resources to implement them, regulatory policies would still be especially difficult to implement internationally for at least two very concrete reasons: internalization and blackmail.

First, the big multinational corporations can hide the conduct to be regulated by internalizing their transactions through mergers. It seems ironic but it is true that regulations that seek to limit the freedom of corporations to externalize their costs can be foiled by internalizing their transactions in dealing with their own subsidiaries. Capitalism preaches transparency; corporate mergers produce the opposite. The second method is blackmail—the threat to export companies, jobs, and capital to a more hospitable country. There will always be rogue countries that will not or cannot restrain exploitation of their nonrenewable resources, which are then usable on a scale that the world can no longer tolerate.

A second policy alternative is in many respects the reverse of regulation—a multinational system of purchasing environmental restraint. This could also become a key method of world redistribution of wealth. All poor countries have one thing in common: they are poor in capital, but they are very rich in something that all the other countries value enormously—they are rich in natural resources or in already polluted but localized resources (such as piles of radioactive materials) which if, through untamed use, they are unleashed upon the world would be crippling even to the richest of countries and peoples. Elsewhere associates of mine and I refer to this as "negative capital":

> Negative capital exists everywhere. It can be defined as situations, events, or environmental conditions which have externalities that degrade or threaten to degrade the standard of living or life expectancy of great numbers of persons, including those living in wealthy nations. It is capital because its presence, or more precisely the mitigation or elimination of it, is potentially of great value to the rich.[36]

Negative capital has not as yet been monetized or commoditized, but it can be and will be because it is as integral to the market as any other form of capital. Now some will call this another form of blackmail, where owners of degradable or dangerous resources threaten to harm all others by abusing or unleashing it, unless they are paid some kind of tribute. But this entire matter can be quickly redefined and made quite manageable as negative capital, because it has value and that value can be enhanced by its *non*utilization. This in fact can be compared to Abraham Lincoln's first approach to emancipation, nearly a year before the Emancipation Proclamation. Lincoln's proposal was not for freeing the slaves unconditionally but was for "compensated emancipation," whereby each and every slave would be purchased at a fair price from the owner, just as any private property would be purchased, through a process akin to normal *eminent domain* whereby any property can be acquired for a public purpose if properly compensated.

The vast, remaining nonrenewable natural resources of the earth and the substantial radioactive resources still sitting as time bombs in various countries have to be treated as capital, and the wealthy industrial countries are going to have to pay dearly for the acquisition of that capital in whatever form. This will require policies that are innately redistributive. Taxation will be required. Already in the public domain are proposals for millage taxes on international transactions. As small a tax as one-tenth of one percent could be imposed on every dollar transferred between international banks.[37] E-commerce is going to be taxed eventually. And all of the richer countries could then also provide from their own internal revenue sources additional funds to be made available for investment in negative capital. This could be done by the same means employed by the Marshall Plan, whereby accounts were opened at major private banks to be drawn upon by qualified owners and sellers of negative capital. Standards could be attached to the sale, indicating that the capital transferred, by gift or loan, has been put to use in productive (and sustainable and nonpolluting) ways. The actual carrying out of these plans could be monitored by the banks themselves, whose officers would have a stake in the honest fulfillment of these contracts. Moreover, by putting this on an open, transparent, and honest basis, the probability of bribery and corruption would be greatly reduced, if not eliminated.

It is not enough to confront individual and world inequalities (including the inequality of the public's health) with throwaway lines like how those who are less well-off can "subsume their envy" in hopes that economic expansion will make them better off. That is very flimsy political mooring for the gigantic, self-regulating, self-perfecting economic system. It is also insincere, since envy is an aspect of greed, and greed is absolutely essential in the profit-seeking that makes the rest of the economic wheels go round.

Permit me to conclude with the language of business: the bottom line. An international political science ought to be a science of political economy, and this should be the grounds on which we confront economics in a genuine competition. This puts us almost where the political sciences and economics were exactly a century ago, just before they split into two separate disciplines. Neither would have to abandon current objectives or methods of research. Both, however, would have to reinvent their terms of discourse, because this is a new world. And on that point, Alexis de Tocqueville[38] had the right question and the right answer.

His question: Can it be believed that the democracy which has overthrown the feudal system and vanquished kings will retreat before tradesmen and capitalists?

His answer: A new science of politics is needed for a new world.

Notes

Notes for the Introduction

1. Richard Merelman, *Pluralism at Yale: The Culture of Political Science in America* (Madison: University of Wisconsin Press, 2003).

2. Wallace Sayre and Herbert Kaufman, *Governing New York City: Politics in the Metropolis* (New York: Russell Sage Foundation, 1960).

3. Nelson Polsby, *Community Power and Political Theory* (New Haven: Yale University Press, 1963), p. 8, fn. 12.

4. Quotes from Sayre and Kaufman, *Governing New York City,* Preface, p. 1.

5. Harold Lasswell et al., *The Comparative Study of Elites* (Palo Alto, CA: Stanford University Press, 1952), p. 1. This passage is quoted in full in Lowi, *At the Pleasure of the Mayor—Patronage and Power in New York City, 1898–1958* (Glencoe: Free Press, 1964), p. 26, fn. 24.

6. Merton, *Social Theory and Social Structure* (Glencoe: Free Press, 1957), pp. 12, 104.

7. Some of the biographical data came from the Municipal Reference Library, but, by far, most of the data came from the *New York Times* obituary page. The daily *Times* was then and still is fully indexed, and no local political official, however obscure, dies without a detailed *Times* obituary. Eventually I became the world's foremost expert on New York City necrology.

8. Actually, during the first two administrations, party recruitment was 100 percent of all those on whom information was available (for about 8 percent information was not available).

9. In fact, the last traditional Tammany boss, Carmine deSapio, had been ousted by a reform chairman of the New York County Democratic party, and Mayor Wagner was in danger of having to fight for renomination by his own party for a third term. An account of this historically significant mayoral election of 1961 and the formation of a "new machine" in the bureaucracy itself, is provided in Lowi, "Machine Politics—Old and New," *The Public Interest* 9 (Fall 1967): 83–92.

10. Merelman, *Pluralism at Yale,* p. 161.

11. The items in quotes are to be encountered in a great many case studies and general pluralist interpretations.

12. Unlike the departments in the national government, which are multifunctional "holding companies," city departments are basically unifunctional, more like the agency or bureau level in Washington.

13. This was almost certainly a factor in the effort of the Republican party to deprive LaGuardia of renomination for a second term for mayor in 1937.

14. Harold Lasswell and Abraham Kaplan, *Power and Society: A Framework for Political Inquiry* (New Haven: Yale University Press, 1950), pp. 77–78 and 252–254.

15. For my purposes this meant the organic statute as amended.

16. For a discussion of the relation of law and policy see Lowi, "Law v. Public Policy: A Critical Exploration," keynote speech delivered at the Cornell Journal of Law and Public Policy Fall 2002 Symposium, November 1. *Cornell Journal of Law and Public Policy* 12, no. 3 (Summer 2003): 493–501.

17. Robert A. Pastor, *Congress and the Politics of U.S. Foreign Economic Policy, 1929–1996* (Berkeley: University of California Press, 1982), p. 44. The quoted passages are from Bauer, Pool, and Dexter, *American Business and Public Policy* (Chicago: Alden-Atherton, 1963 and 1972), p. 47 in the 1972 edition.

18. Theodore J. Lowi, "American Business, Public Policy, Case Studies, and Political Theory," *World Politics* (1964): 677–715. Morton Kaplan, one of the anonymous peer reviewers, took the piece to his colleagues at the University of Chicago, which triggered an offer for me to leave Cornell for Chicago. Kaplan later told me that this was the only review essay that had been sent to *World Politics* "over the transom," and it was the only piece that was not, strictly speaking, on foreign policy or international relations.

19. The "inputs" category in New York City was folded into distributive policy, because the principal source of revenue in New York and other cities was property taxation, with jurisdiction over the hundreds of thousands of units of real estate, with each plot being assessed and taxed on its own. That is the "disaggregability" factor that helped keep this category within party control. At the national level, personal income taxation is another matter altogether—patently redistributive.

20. Charles Hardin, *The Politics of Agriculture* (Glencoe: Free Press, 1952) and Grant McConnell, *The Decline of American Democracy* (Berkeley: University of California Press, 1953). There is also labor policy, industrial policy, monetary policy, civil rights policy, small business policy, and the list goes on ad nauseum. Are we to be stuck with a particular theory for each of these subject-matter categories?

21. "How Farmers Get What They Want," *Reporter* (May 1964). After the article was accepted, publisher and editor Max Ascoli, an Italian-born Jew, invited me to visit him in New York, and we talked at length about our perilous resemblance to 1930s Europe, Italy in particular. He urged me, however, to stick to the story and preserve the broader application for another piece. He even prevailed on me to change the original title, "Large Estates from Little Acres Grow." This argument was endorsed by my department chair Mario Einaudi, another Italian refugee, whose father, Luigi, served as the first postwar president of Italy. Mario then asked me to take over one of his long-standing courses, Government and the Economy, which set me on my career of writing what I teach and teaching what I write.

22. I had published a more or less autobiographical piece on Iron City in 1962, "Southern Jews: The Two Communities," *Jewish Journal of Sociology* (November 1964); and then I used Iron City again in a chapter in *The End of Liberalism* as a case study on how "policy without law" had provided cities resources that would enable them to segregate the races far beyond the segregation before the "urban policy" era.

23. If my life had been well ordered, *The End of Liberalism* would have been Volume 3. Volume 1 should have been *The Politics of Disorder* (1971), because it delved into the question that precedes both of the other books: It is an inquiry into how interests form, how they survive, and how they die. It was an examination of the "social pluralism" of the United States through the lens of social movements. I developed a theory of stages of development that never got the attention it deserved. Volume 2 should have been *Arenas of Power*.

24. Lowi, "Party, Policy and Constitution," in William Nesbit Chambers and Walter Dean Burnham, eds., *The American Party Systems* (New York: Oxford University Press, 1967; 2nd ed. 1975).

25. David Collier, dear friend and former student at the University of Chicago, is to be thanked for connecting "property space" back to Allen Barton in a paper published in 1955, "The Concept of Property-Space in Social Research," in Paul Lazarsfeld and Morris Rosenberg, eds., *A Reader in the Methodology of Social Research* (Glencoe, IL: Free Press, 1955), pp. 40–53. However, it was "in the air" in Lasswell's 1955–1956 graduate seminar at Yale. Although Lasswell was not a participant in Barton's presentation, Lasswell had been closely associated with Lazarsfeld and Bernard Berelson, in the late 1930s and early 1940s. In fact, Barton and Berelson credit Lasswell as being virtually the founder of political content analysis. And Lasswell makes more extensive use of the cross-tabulation of concepts with resulting property spaces, in Harold Lasswell and Abraham Kaplan, *Power and Society: A Framework for Political Inquiry* (New Haven: Yale University Press, 1950), see especially Chapters 4 and 5.

26.   H.L.A. Hart, *The Concept of Law* (New York: Oxford University Press, 1961), p. 6. See also p. 23 for "orders backed by threats." Hart's critique is focused on John Austin's book, *The Province of Jurisprudence Determined* (1832), in which Austin's argument is credited as "the key to the science of jurisprudence." Hart, p. 6.

Notes for Chapter 1

1.   For similar questions and a critique, see Herbert Kaufman, "The Next Step in Case Studies," *Public Administration Review* 18 (Winter 1958): 52–59.

2.   David Truman's rather weak and diffuse "potential interest group" is a doff of the hat in this direction, but this concept is so nondirective and nonobservable as to be disregarded even by its creator.

3.   The best critiques and analyses of all the various currents of thought are found in Nelson W. Polsby, *Community Power and Political Theory* (New Haven 1963); Daniel Bell, "The Power Elite—Revisited," *American Journal of Sociology* 54 (November 1958): 238–250; Robert A. Dahl, "Critique of the Ruling Elite Model," *American Political Science Review* 52 (June 1958): 463–469; and Raymond Wolfinger, "Reputation and Reality in the Study of Community Power," *American Sociological Review* 25 (October 1960): 636–644.

4.   *Politics, Pressures and the Tariff*, p. 88. The fact that Schattschneider holds his generalizations to the particular policy in question should be noted *here* as a point central to my later arguments.

5.   There are four approaches here if the "social stratification" school is kept separate from the "power elite" school. While both make the same kinds of errors, each leads to different kinds of propositions. In some hands they are, of course, indistinguishable and, for good reason, Polsby in *Community Power and Political Theory* treats the two as one. Since the distinction, once made, is not important here, I will more or less follow Polsby's lead.

6.   Milton Gordon, quoted in Polsby, p. 103.

7.   Cf. C. Wright Mills, *The Power Elite* (New York 1956), p. 245: "The political analyst is generally on the middle levels of power himself. He knows the top only by gossip; the bottom, if at all, only by 'research.'" Thus, Mills continues, the professor and free-lance intellectual are "at home with the leaders of the middle level, and ... focus upon the middle levels and their balances because they are closer to them."

8.   Thus, with no major decline in the numbers of industries and groups with a self-interest in protection—indeed, with the defection of virtually the entire South from the free-trade cause—liberal trade lost consistently until 1962. But in 1962 it won because tariff had finally lost its traditional definition. Lest it be concluded that the administration won merely because of its

use of traditional logrolling strategies in its textile concessions, note that on the crucial votes in both Houses most of the Democratic protectionist vote was Southern: In the House vote on the Mason motion for recommittal, 37 of the 44 protectionist Democrats were Southern, mainly from the textile and oil states of North and South Carolina, Texas, and Oklahoma. Kennedy's strategy probably got him only Georgia's votes. In the Senate, the crucial vote was on the "peril point," with the Southerners splitting 10 to 10. Despite Kennedy's concessions, the defectors included two from Georgia, South Carolina, Mississippi, and Virginia and one from North Carolina.

9. I obtain from this and other propositions in the book a conclusion not reached by the authors but strongly supported by their findings: There are probably *several* kinds of coalitions (rather than "a politics of coalition" where all coalitions are equivalent in every way except size and value of resources). Each type of coalition is appropriate for certain types of issues and each has extreme significance for outcomes, perhaps as much as cohesion and access. More on this presently.

10. Again suggesting that a distinct kind of coalition is involved here, the authors say "neither the interest of the New England textile manufacturers in supporting oil imports nor that of the Eastern railroads in opposing these imports was in any way self-evident. Offered the proper coalition, they both might well have been persuaded that their interest was in the opposite direction" (p. 398).

11. Access to and information about Congress and congressmen was so poor that the liberal CNTP's list of congressmen's positions was almost a third incorrect for both Houses in the case of those whose positions had been identified at all. Nearly 15 percent of the members of Congress were listed as "undecided," and in most cases this meant no contact at all had been made. Many pluralist writers before Bauer, Pool, and Dexter have recognized the "service bureau" role, but rather than reexamine their premises, they usually catalogue this as a "form of influence."

12. Aaron Wildavsky, *Dixon-Yates: A Study in Power Politics* (New Haven, 1962), p. 311.

13. "*Inter alia*, the transactional analysis here employed makes the concept of 'power' and 'pressure' in the ordinary political science sense of the terms somewhat more difficult to employ; Arthur F. Bentley himself pointed out to one of us in 1936 that he had long since abandoned these notions as not useful for systematic analysis" (p. 460). See also p. 456.

14. The first formulation, developed for urban politics, appears in my study, *At the Pleasure of the Mayor* (New York, 1964), Chapters 6 and 7. The scheme for national politics which is presented in this chapter is an adaptation of the national Arenas of Power model.

15. Their study is of further interest because they are dealing with a type of policy which made a transition from one of my "arenas" to another between 1930 and 1962. That the politics of tariff changed accordingly is the best test I have yet found for my scheme. The very differences they find between 1950s patterns and those reported so exceedingly well by Schattschneider— and which are branded by Bauer, Pool, and Dexter as inconsistent with Schattschneider or as due vaguely to the "changing times"—were both consistent with and anticipated by my scheme.

16. Dahl, *Who Governs?* and Polsby, *Community Power*, especially Chapter 6.

17. Foreign policy, for which no appropriate "-tion" word has been found, is obviously a fourth category. It is not dealt with here for two reasons. First, it overly extends the analysis. Second, and of greater importance, it is in many ways not part of the same universe, because in foreign policy-making America is only a subsystem. Winston Churchill, among other foreigners, has consistently participated in our foreign policy decisions. Of course, those aspects of foreign and military policy that have direct domestic implications are included in my scheme.

18. A "sector" refers to any set of common or substitutable commodities or services or any other form of established economic interaction. Sectors therefore vary in size because of natural

economic forces and because of the different ways they are identified by economists or business-men. They vary in size also because they are sometimes defined a priori by the observer's assess-ment of what constitutes a common product and at other times are defined a posteriori by the trade associations that represent the identification of a sector by economic actors themselves.

19. *Politics, Pressures*, 85.

20. Ibid., 88.

21. Ibid., 135–136.

22. The stable, intimate interlocking of congressional committeemen and their support groups in the Rivers and Harbors Congress and the Corps of Engineers has been made famous by Arthur Maass; see *Muddy Waters: The Army Engineers and the Nation's Rivers* (Cambridge, MA, 1951), and especially "Congress and Water Resources," *American Political Science Review* 54 (September, 1950): 576–592, reprinted in my reader, *Legislative Politics USA* (Boston, 1962). Cited widely as an example of interest group strategy and access, this case has not until now, as far as I know, been given its proper significance. That significance comes clear within my scheme. The pattern approaches that of the tariff but not of regulatory situations.

23. Schattschneider, in his more recent book *The Semi-Sovereign People* (New York, 1960), offers some fascinating propositions about the "scope of conflict" which can easily be subsumed within the scheme offered here.

24. I was surprised and pleased on rereading Truman's *The Governmental Process* (New York, 1951), after completing the first draft of this chapter, to find that he identified two types of "mutual assistance," alliances and logrolling (pp. 362–368). In my scheme, as will soon be clear, there are two types of "alliance," tangential interest and ideology. But what is of interest here is that Truman supports his distinction with examples perfectly congruent with my theory. His case of the alliance is the aggregation of interests around the 1946 Employment Act (redis-tribution, even if a peculiar "law"). The typical logrolling situation he identifies with rivers and harbors appropriations (distribution). The difference between us is that my scheme considers these patterns of coalition as revealing fundamental political relations that are limited to certain types of issues, while Truman implies that they are two strategies in an inventory of strategies more or less appropriate to any issue.

25. Sam Rayburn made one of his rare trips from rostrum to floor to support the closed rule and the integrity of Ways and Means: "Only once in the history of the House, in forty-two years in my memory, has a bill of this kind and character been considered except under a closed rule" (p. 64, emphasis added). It was on the following morning that Rayburn expressed his now-famous warning to the fresh: "If you want to get along, go along" (p. 64).

26. The facts and events are taken from Paul H. Douglas, *Social Security in the United States* (New York, 1936); Edwin E. Witte, *The Development of the Social Security Act* (Madison, WI, 1962); Committee on Economic Security, *Report to the President* (Washington, GPO, 1935); and Frances Perkins, *The Roosevelt I Knew* (New York, 1946).

27. Stanley S. Surrey, "The Congress and the Tax Lobbyist: How Special Tax Provisions Get Enacted," *Harvard Law Review* 70 (May 1957): 1145–1182.

28. "Involve" may appear to be a weasel word, but it is used advisedly. As I argued earlier when defining redistribution, it is not the actual outcomes but the expectations as to what the outcomes can be that shape the issues and determine their politics. One of the important strategies in any controversial issue is to attempt to define it in redistributive terms in order to broaden the base of opposition or support.

29. In personal conversations, Andrew Biemiller of AFL-CIO has observed that this is true even of his group. He estimates that perhaps from 80 to 90 percent of their formal policy expres-sions deal with welfare and general rights of collective bargaining and that only occasionally does the central board touch specific regulatory issues.

30. Robert E. Lane, *The Regulation of Businessmen* (New Haven, 1953), pp. 38ff.

31. Note also in the table the fairly drastic contrast in the proportion of references that expressed approval. Similarly drastic differences are revealed in Lane's figures on the reasons given for expressing disapproval. On those issues I call redistributive, the overwhelmingly most important reason is "coerciveness." In contrast, this reason was given for about 10 percent of general trade regulation and antitrust references, 3 percent of the basing-point negative references, and not once when Miller-Tydings and Robinson-Patman were denounced. For regulatory issues, the reason for disapproval given most frequently was that the policy was confused and that it failed to achieve its purposes. And there were equally high percentages of residual or "other" responses, suggesting a widespread lack of agreement as to the very meaning of the policy.

Notes for Chapter 2

1. Robert Cushman, President's Committee on Administrative Management, *Report with Special Studies* (Washington, DC: U.S. Government Printing Office, 1937); and Cushman, *The Independent Regulatory Commissions* (London: Oxford University Press, 1941), p. 3.

2. Theodore Lowi, "American Business and Public Policy, Case Studies and Political Theory," *World Politics* (July 1964); and Lowi, "Decision Making vs. Policy Making: Toward an Antidote for Technocracy," *Public Administration Review* (May–June 1970).

3. To visualize the analysis best, the reader should substitute "statute" for "policy." This gives up a great deal of information about policies in the real world, but clarity is gained by having a clear and common unit to classify. Moreover, even from this partial and formalized operational definition of policy, there is a great deal of predictive and ethical value in the classification scheme.

4. Leonard White, *The Republican Era* (New York: Free Press, 1958); and W. Binkley, *President and Congress* (New York: Vintage, 1962), pp. 215ff.

5. See especially Binkley, op. cit., pp. 217–218.

6. Quoted in ibid., p. 217. The essence of Wilson's treatment will be found in *Congressional Government* (New York: Meridian Edition, n.d.), pp. 58–81.

7. This goes a long way toward explaining the Huntington paradox, the spectacle of a highly dynamic economy developing in the context of a stable, "undeveloping" policy. See Samuel P. Huntington, "Political Modernization: America vs. Europe," *World Politics* (April 1966): 378–414.

8. Earlier instances, such as the Fugitive Slave Act of 1850, are dealt with elsewhere.

9. Binkley, op. cit., pp. 225, 217, 227.

10. Leuchtenberg, *Franklin D. Roosevelt and the New Deal, 1932–1940* (1963), pp. 87–94, esp. 90.

11. Binkley, op. cit., pp. 296–298.

12. Landis's own account has been republished in Lowi, *Legislative Politics USA* (Boston: Little, Brown, 1965), pp. 143ff; see also Chamberlain, *The President, Congress, and Legislation* (New York: Columbia University Press, 1946), pp. 58ff.

13. Ibid., p. 72.

14. Leuchtenberg, op. cit., pp. 150ff; and compare James MacGregor Burns, *The Lion and the Fox* (New York: Harcourt, 1956): "Quite unwittingly the new President acted as midwife in the rebirth of labor action" (p. 215). "Neither Roosevelt nor Miss Perkins had much to do with this provision (Sec. 7A, NRA). Framed mainly by the congressmen and labor leaders, it was simply part of a bargain under which labor joined the NRA's great 'concert of interest'" (pp. 215–216).

"Roosevelt failed to see the potentialities of an enlarged labor movement" (p. 216). The Wagner Act: "was the most radical legislation passed during the New Deal ... yet ... he threw his weight behind the measure only at the last moment, when it was due to pass anyway" (p. 219). These are not the portrait of a lion *or* a fox, but only of a man running hard to keep up with history.

15. Bailey and Samuel, cited in the bibliography accompanying the summary [of cases at the end of the chapter text].

16. Schattschneider, and also Bauer, et al., cited in the bibliography.

17. See David B. Truman, *The Governmental Process* (New York: Knopf, 1951), especially his notes on sources in Chapters 11–15, dealing with policy formulation; see also Earl Latham, *The Group Theory of Politics* (Ithaca, NY: Cornell University Press, 1952), whose opening theoretical chapter generalized on a pattern developed in the rest of his book, a case study of the federal attempt to regulate basing points practices in the cement industry and elsewhere. This case is very frequently cited in Truman.

18. Eighteen additional cases have been given the same treatment, but they are not yet ready for the same presentation. The pattern is about the same, although a few surprise exceptions bear checking out or explaining.

19. Each category of amending activity was dichotomized, so that the action on each bill and for each type of amendment could be scored 0 or 1—then multiplied by the difficulty weights, as described above. For example, if two or more significant amendments were added to a bill despite the objections of the sponsor, that was scored 1 and multiplied by 8. (If fewer than two such amendments passed, it was then scored 0 and did not increase the score.) These scores were then cumulated for all bills in each policy category, and the average shown on the table was the result of dividing by each of the Ns.

20. Some of these variations can be captured in the fourth category, constituent or system maintenance policy. These are not dealt with in this chapter because of many considerations too complicating for this first effort at reanalyzing cases. However, I have dealt with some of these patterns elsewhere, and have argued at length that the so-called foreign policy area actually breaks down into the four types captured in the paradigm. The break comes when one asks about the kinds of disciplines governments place upon their own populations in order to carry out foreign influence. For example, setting up a Marshall Plan is not the same kind of policy as actions revising our relations with Red China. Foreign policy is no more of a single piece than agriculture policy or any other conventional, subject matter designation. And, as shown with the different types of agriculture policy, the politics of each type of foreign policy will vary accordingly. See my chapter in James Rosenau (ed.), *The Domestic Sources of Foreign Policy* (New York: Free Press, 1967).

21. A more elaborate argument, with many more illustrations, will be found in my companion paper, "Population Policies and the Political System," mimeo., 1971.

22. Cf. Hannah Arendt, *The Human Condition*, Chapter 2 and pp. 193–199, especially her treatment of the Greek concept of lawmaking as akin to architecture in that laws define a space entirely restricted to citizens.

23. Obviously a distinction is being made here when a continuum is involved. There are degrees of vagueness, degrees to which a rule of law is present. However, any rule, no matter how vague, begins to transform distributive into regulatory patterns. For example, adding a vague and very mild antidiscrimination provision to an education subsidy statute can turn established distributive patterns literally inside out. On the other hand, it should be added that very broad delegations of regulatory authority to an agency can lead in the long run to a decline into an all too stable and private politics. Thus, the rule of law criterion is a good one that is often not provided in quantity sufficient to produce the predicted results. Cf. my *The End of the Liberalism* (New York: Norton, 1969), esp. Chapters 5 and 10.

Notes for Chapter 3

1. Leonard D. White, *The Federalist* (New York: Macmillan, 1956), pp. 507–508.

2. White, op. cit.; Margaret C. Myers, *A Financial History of the United States* (New York: Cornell University Press, 1970), pp. 54–74.

3. The best treatment of the fiscal and monetary aspects of the new government will be found in J. W. Hurst, *A Legal History of Money in the United States, 1774–1970* (Lincoln: University of Nebraska Press, 1973), pp. 3–61.

4. Ibid., p. 34.

5. Alfred H. Kelly and Winfred A. Harbison, *The American Constitution—Its Origins and Development* (New York: W. W. Norton, 1976), pp. 170–171.

6. Carl B. Swisher, *American Constitutional Development* (Boston: Houghton Mifflin, 1941), pp. 74–75; and Kelly and Harbison, op. cit., pp. 170–171.

7. Cf. Hurst, op. cit., pp. 8–10 and 36–38.

8. William N. Chambers, *Political Parties in a New Nation* (New York: Oxford University Press, 1968), pp. 43–44 and 88ff. See also Joseph Charles, *The Origins the American Party System* (New York: Harper, Torch Book Edition, 1961), pp. 96 and *passim*.

9. James Jackson of Georgia, quoted in op. cit., p. 67.

10. Cf. Joseph Charles, op. cit., on Hamilton and Adams; see Swisher, op cit., pp. 75ff, on the impact of taxation; see Chambers, op. cit., pp. 135ff, and E. E. Schattschneider, *Party Government* (New York: Rinehart, 1942), pp. 47ff, on various class-oriented party strategies, particularly those of Jefferson.

11. Hamilton had anticipated that most of the national debt would eventually be held by a new class of capitalists, and he was far-sighted enough to provide for the protection of these creditors against the possibility that the government would someday refinance the debt in order to take advantage of lower interest rates, etc. Hamilton provided for a funding procedure in 1790 that would limit the government's right to retire these new securities to a fraction of the total annually. See E. James Ferguson, *The Power of the Purse* (Chapel Hill: University of North Carolina Press, 1961), pp. 289–305.

12. White, *The Jeffersonians,* op. cit., pp. 12–15.

13. Quoted in White, *The Jeffersonians,* op. cit., p. 15.

14. Quoted in Lewis H. Kimmel, *Federal Budget and Fiscal Policy, 1789–1958* (Washington: Brookings Institution, 1959), p. 29.

15. Ibid., p. 21; see also Andrews C. McLaughlin, *A Constitutional History of the United States* (New York: Appleton, 1935), pp. 416–419.

16. For further descriptions of these policies, see especially Kimmel, op. cit., pp. 29–37; Frank W. Taussig, *The Tariff History of the United States* (New York: Putnam, 1931), pp. 7, 18, 24, 167, and *passim;* and White, *The Republican Era* (New York: Macmillan, 1958), Chapter 10.

17. For an excellent brief treatment of these developments in land policy, see Paul W. Gates, "The Homestead Act, 1862," in Daniel Boorstin, ed., *An American Primer* (Chicago: University of Chicago Press, 1966), pp. 386–392; and Herbert Agar, *The Price of Union* (Boston: Houghton Mifflin, 1950), pp. 169–170 and 190–191.

18. E. E. Schattschneider, *Politics, Pressures and the Tariff* (Englewood Cliffs: Prentice-Hall, 1935).

19. The Jeffersonians, op. cit., p. 15.

20. Richard P. McCormick, "Political Development and the Second Party System," in William Chambers and Walter Dean Burnham, eds., *The American Party Systems* (New York: Oxford University Press, 1967), p. 112.

21. Ibid., p. 112. McCormick also cites Ostrogorski, one of the most important foreign observers, who saw American parties as empty of program but full of ritual. This for him was probably the essence of the new democracy. Ibid., pp. 108–109.

22. Herbert Agar, *The Price of Union* (Boston: Houghton Mifflin, 1950), especially Chapters XIII and XIV.

23. Samuel H. Beer, "The Modernization of Americal Federalism," *Publius*, 3, No. 2 (Autumn 1973).

24. Woodrow Wilson, *Congressional Government: A Study in American Politics* (Boston: Houghton Mifflin, 1895).

25. Turner & Schneier, *Pressures on Congress*, full citation to be provided.

26. This paradox is identified and described in a classic article by Samuel P. Huntington, "Political Modernization: America vs. Europe," *World Politics*, 18 (1965–66), pp. 378–414.

27. Kelly and Harbison, *The American Constitution—Its Origins and Development*, op. cit., p. 514.

28. *Wabash, St. Louis and Pacific Railway Co. v. Illinois*, 118 U.S. 557.

29. *Civil Rights Case*, 109 US 3 (1883).

30. Reported in Lawrence Friedman, *A History of American Law*, op. cit., p. 404.

31. Valuable coverage of many of the regulatory efforts in this period will be found in Gabriel Kolko, *Railroads and Regulation, 1877–1916* (New York: W. W. Norton, 1970), pp. 57–80; see also Friedman, op. cit., pp. 384–408.

32. His most important act of presidential leadership, repeal of the Silver Purchase Act, is in the redistributive category. The important thing here is that president-Congress relationships were beginning to take on a pattern that was new and rarely associated with distributive policies.

33. Wilfred Binkley, *President and Congress* (New York: Random House, Vintage Edition, 1962), p. 225.

34. Quoted in Randall B. Ripley, *Congress: Process and Policy* (New York: W. W. Norton, 1975), p. 41, along with several other related descriptions of the unevenness and disorderliness of the parliamentary process in the House and in the Senate.

35. Cf. Binkley, op. cit., pp. 217–227; also George B. Galloway, *History of the House of Representatives* (New York: Crow, 1962); Samuel P. Huntington, "Congressional Responses in the 20th Century," in David Truman, ed., *The Congress and America's Future* (Englewood Cliffs: Prentice-Hall, 1965), pp. 5ff; and Ripley, op. cit., pp. 41ff, including a number of very important monographic studies cited in the footnotes of Ripley's treatment, especially those of Polsby, Hinckley, and Price.

36. For the House, see Nelson Polsby et al., "The Growth of Seniority System in the U.S. House of Representatives," *American Political Science Review* 63 (1969): 792ff. For the Senate and for a general discussion of these data in both chambers, see Ripley, op. cit., pp. 45ff.

37. The Lowell data and other important data on congressional roll-call voting will be found in Julius Turner and Edward V. Schneier, *Party and Constituency: Pressures on Congress* (Baltimore: Johns Hopkins Press, 1970 ed., revised by Schneier).

38. The same holds true for redistributive policies, but the three policies (fiscal/monetary, health and welfare, housing) were not as clearly distinguishable as the other two. Nevertheless, the average Indexes of Likeness were 42.3 for 1921–44 and 49.8 for 1948–64.

39. Samuel P. Hays, *The Response to Industrialism, 1885–1914* (Chicago: University of Chicago Press, 1957), pp. 55–56.

40. Thomas C. Cochran, *The American Business System—An Historical Perspective, 1900–55* (New York: Harper Torch Books, 1957), pp. 61–62. Also Donald C. Blaisdell, *American Democracy Under Pressure* (New York: The Ronald Press, 1957), Chapter 5, especially pp. 71–81; and

Merle Fainsod et al., *Government and the American Economy* (New York: W. W. Norton, 1959), pp. 449–460.

41. Murray R. Benedict, *Farm Policies of the United States 1790–1950* (New York: Twentieth Century Fund, 1963), p. 221n. For the best survey of groups in all the major sectors, see V. O. Key, *Politics, Parties, Pressure Groups* (New York: Crowell, 1964), pp. 20ff (on agriculture), Chapter 3 (on workers), and 4 (on business and business groups).

42. For more on interest groups as administrative agencies, see Lowi, *The Politics of Disorder* (New York: Basic Books, 1971), Chapter 3.

43. Almost all of the fiscal-monetary, or redistributive, policies of the federal government in the late 19th century were war-related—how to deal with the debt, how to deal with greenbacks, how to reduce the total amount of dollars in circulation—handled directly by the Treasury with few efforts to intervene, and even fewer actual interventions by Congress. Cf. Myers, op. cit., Chapter 8. This pattern of executive bureaucracy dominance of redistributive policy persists today.

44. Congress levied an income tax during the Civil War that was allowed to lapse in 1872.

45. One possible exception is the Reconstruction Finance Corporation (RFC), established by Congress in January of 1932, on the model of the War Finance Corporation. RFC was set up to make loans to bank and other financial institutions and eventually to states and localities to help bail out failing corporations. But this was actually passed by a Democratic Congress under the Lame Duck Hoover Administration and deserves actually to be counted as New Deal legislation.

46. Not many accounts of the Roosevelt period are thorough on questions of public policy. There is greater fascination with the man and his strategies and of the political causes and repercussions of the New Deal. Aside from actual bills and statutes themselves, the best guides have been: Herbert Stein, *The Fiscal Revolution in America* (Chicago: University of Chicago Press, 1969); Lewis H. Kimmel, op. cit.; and William E. Leuchtenburg, *Franklin D. Roosevelt and the New Deal* (New York: Harper Torch Book, 1963).

47. For a review and an assessment of the significance of government investment insurance, see Lowi, *The End of Liberalism* (New York: W. W. Norton, 1979, 2nd ed.), Chapter 10.

48. Details of the Act and its passage will be found in Myers, op. cit., pp. 215–222.

49. Binckley, op. cit., pp. 217ff; Wilson, p. 217.

50. Myers, op. cit., 216. Myers reports that Cleveland was bitterly criticized for making the deal but that it probably saved the Treasury from bankruptcy, at a time when Congress did not appear to be willing to make provisions for repayment of the bonds in gold.

51. See especially Kelly and Harbison, op. cit., pp. 604–608; and Alexander L. George and Juliette L. George, *Woodrow Wilson and Colonel House: A Personality Study* (Dover, 1964).

52. Grant McConell, *The Decline of Agrarian Democracy* (Berkeley: University of California Press, 1953).

53. Robert E. Lane, *The Regulation of Businessmen* (New Haven: Yale University Press, 1953), pp. 38ff.

54. Op. cit., p. 215.

55. Ibid., pp. 220–221.

56. Hurst, *A Legal History of Money in the United States, 1774–1970*, op. cit., p. 64.

Notes for Chapter 4

1. John F. Dillon, *Commentaries on the Law of Municipal Corporations*, 5th ed. (Boston: Little, Brown, 1911), Vol. 1, Sec. 237.

2. Op. cit.

3. In Chambers and Burnham, eds., *The American Party Systems,* op. cit., p. 109.

4. V. O. Key, *American State Politics,* op. cit., pp. 20ff; and Key, *Southern Politics* (New York: Alfred Knopf, 1949), *passim.* See also E. E. Schattschneider, *The Semi-Sovereign People* (New York: Holt, Rinehart, and Winston, 1960).

5. Samuel Hays, *The Response to Industrialism, 1885–1914,* p. 189.

6. More on this will be drawn on Schattschneider.

7. Key, *American State Politics,* op. cit., pp. 221–222.

8. Key, *American State Politics,* op. cit., p. 55.

9. Ibid., p. 52.

10. Bernard L. Hyink, Seyom Brown, and Ernest Thacker, *Politics and Government in California,* 9th ed. (New York: Crowell, 1975), p. 60. For a sophisticated treatment of California and its relation to the history of parties in the United States, see Martin Shefter, full citation to be provided.

11. Philip Taft and Philip Ross, "American Labor Violence: Its Causes, Character, and Outcome," in *The History of Violence in America,* Hugh Davis Graham and Ted Robert Gurr, eds. (New York: Bantam Books, 1969), p. 281.

12. A good, brief discussion of vigilantism and its purposes will be found in Lawrence Friedman, *A History of American Law* (New York: Simon and Schuster, 1973), pp. 318–322.

13. See, for example, Frances Fox Piven and Richard A. Cloward, *Poor People's Movements* (New York: Pantheon, 1977), esp. Chapter 2.

14. Cf. Robert Fogelson, "Violence as Protest," in *Proceedings of the Academy of Political Science* (Vol. 29, No. 1, 1968), pp. 25–41; and Herbert Gans, "The Ghetto Rebellions and Urban Class Conflict," in ibid., pp. 43–44.

15. Reported in Piven and Cloward, op. cit., p. 103. They also cite observations based on an international study of unionism by Lewis Lorwin, "in no other Western country have employers been so much aided in their opposition to unions by civil authorities, the armed forces of government, and their courts" (p. 105). Even where local police forces existed and entered the scene, the policy of union opposition and the authorization to intervene with impunity, with or without violence, came from the state governments.

16. Shefter, op. cit., pp. v–15.

17. Ibid., pp. v–32; and Williams, op. cit., pp. 61–62.

18. Cf. Williams, op. cit., who observed that workingmen's parties made headway in 40 of the state's 52 counties and achieved a number of victories in municipal elections. At the same time, in the context of state politics, the rhetoric indicated quite a different reality. Take one quote from a speech by Denis Kearney, "The people are about to take their own affairs into their own hands, and they will not be stayed by vigilantes, state militia, nor United States troops" (p. 16).

19. Lawrence Friedman, *A History of American Law,* op. cit., p. 303.

20. Ibid., p. 303.

21. Friedman, pp. 302–318; and Williams, *The Democratic Party in California Politics,* op. cit., pp. 16–27. States were constantly being pulled into local politics because of the intense lobbying of cities for more resources or more powers from the state legislature. One urban historian speaks of "urban rivalry" occurring during the 19th century where several localities bitterly fought it out against each other for railroad and canal routings, franchises to rival companies, land grants, and many other valuable resources for "internal improvements." Harry Schecter, "Urban Rivalry and Internal Improvements in the Old Northwest, 1820–1860," reprinted from *Ohio History* in Alexander Callow, ed., *American Urban History* (New York: Oxford, 1973), pp. 135–146.

22. Fiorello LaGuardia, New York's best mayor, tried and failed to get a Democratic or ALP nomination for the U.S. Senate in the late 1930s, and he spent his last, and dying year, in 1945 as head of UNRRA. His successor, William O'Dwyer, resigned from the mayoralty barely ahead of a scandal (in 1949) to accept President Truman's offer to serve as Ambassador to Mexico. All of the other mayors moved from City Hall almost directly and immediately into political obscurity.

23. Joseph Schlesinger, *How They Became Governor—A Study of Comparative State Politics, 1870–1950* (East Lansing, MI: Governmental Research Bureau, Michigan State University, 1957), pp. 9–19. Compare those figures to the 200 who went directly from the state legislature to a governorship, the 162 who went directly from law enforcement agencies to the governorship, and the 136 who went directly from state administrative agencies to the governorship.

24. Leonard White, *Introduction to the Study of Public Administration*, 4th ed. (New York: Macmillan, 1955).

25. Cf. Lowi, *The End of Liberalism*, op. cit., Chapter 7.

26. John J. Harrigan, *Political Change in the Metropolis* (Boston: Little, Brown, 1976), pp. 140–146.

27. Marshall Langberg, unpublished doctoral dissertation, University of Chicago. See also Martin Myerson and Edward Banfield, *Politics, Planning, and the Public Interest* (Glencoe, IL: Free Press, 1955).

Notes for Chapter 5

1. Mario Einaudi, *The Roosevelt Revolution* (New York: Harcourt, 1959), pp. vi, vii.

2. James MacGregor Burns, *Roosevelt: The Lion and the Fox* (New York: Harcourt, 1956), p. 486.

3. Einaudi, *Roosevelt Revolution*, p. 59.

4. Burns, *Roosevelt*, pp. 215–219.

5. William Leuchtenberg, *Franklin D. Roosevelt and the New Deal* (New York: Harper Torch Books, 1963), pp. 87–94.

6. Wilfred Binkley, *President and Congress* (New York: Random House, Vintage Books, 1962), pp. 296–298.

7. See Robert A. Brady, *Business as a System of Power* (New York: Columbia University Press, 1943). See also Grant McConnell, *Private Power and American Democracy* (New York: Knopf, 1966), esp. Chapters 7–8.

8. Einaudi, *Roosevelt Revolution*, p. 83.

9. Paul H. Douglas, *Social Security in the United States* (New York: Whittlesey House, 1936), pp. 185–196 and *passim*.

10. Richard Hofstadter, *The American Political Tradition* (New York: Knopf, 1948), pp. 334–335.

11. James Landis, "The Legislative History of the Securities Act of 1933," *George Washington Law Review* 28 (1959): 29–49. A full tabulation of the many Roosevelts can be found in Laurence Chamberlain, *The President, Congress, and Legislation* (New York: Columbia University Press, 1946), p. 58.

12. Compare Herman Pritchett, *The American Constitution*, 3rd ed. (New York: McGraw-Hill, 1977), pp. 180–181.

13. See for each subject, respectively, Theodore J. Lowi, *The Personal President* (Ithaca: Cornell University Press, 1985); "Party, Policy, and the Constitution," in William Chambers and Walter Dean Burnham, eds., *The American Party Systems* (New York: Oxford University Press,

1967), Chapter 9; and *The End of Liberalism: The Second Republic of the United States,* 2nd ed. (New York: W. W. Norton, 1979).

14. The title of this section is drawn from an admirable work by Stephen Skowronek, *Building the New American State* (Cambridge: Cambridge University Press, 1982).

15. Sources of figures: Herbert Stein, *The Fiscal Revolution in America* (Chicago: University of Chicago Press, 1969), pp. 69–72; and *Report of the Secretary of the Treasury,* Statistical Appendix (Washington, DC: Government Printing Office, 1972), pp. 12–13. Some of the prose is taken from Lowi, *Personal President,* pp. 44–45.

16. See esp. *Wickard v. Filburn,* 3317 US 111 (1942). The court validated the Agricultural Adjustment Act (AAA) in a case in which Filburn was allotted 11.1 acres for the growing of wheat but, in violation of the Act, put in 23 acres. In his defense, Filburn argued that he was too small a producer to have an effect on interstate commerce, and, besides, his wheat was intended not for trade but for use on his own farm to feed his livestock. A Supreme Court ruling agreed he was small and that his wheat was not intended for market but stated that he came within the AAA because the wheat he grew for his own consumption represented wheat he did *not* purchase from the market!

17. *Katzenbach v. McClung,* 379 US 294 (1964).

18. See in particular *Schechter Poultry Corp. v. United States,* 295 US 495 (1935), invalidating the National Industrial Recovery Act.

19. See Lowi, *Personal President.*

20. Samuel Huntington, *Political Order in Changing Societies* (New Haven: Yale University Press, 1968), p. 93. Huntington is of course not alone in his appreciation of the general significance of differentiation. See, e.g., the great Italian political theorist Gaetano Mosca, *The Ruling Class* (New York: McGraw-Hill, 1959).

21. Quoted in Burns, *Roosevelt,* pp. 341–342.

22. Quoted in Einaudi, *Roosevelt Revolution,* p. 100.

23. For a political assessment of the TVA, see Philip Selznick, *TVA and the Grass Roots* (Berkeley: University of California Press, 1949).

24. Einaudi, *Roosevelt Revolution,* pp. 337–340.

25. Ibid., p. 340.

26. Ibid., pp. 338, 341.

27. Andrew Shonfield, *Modern Capitalism* (New York: Oxford University Press, 1965), p. 298.

28. For a discussion of why liberalism is considered left of center in the United States and right of center everywhere else in the world, see Theodore J. Lowi, "Avantpropos," in *La Deuxième République des Etats-Unis* (Paris: PUF, 1987).

29. For an inventory of people and ideas in their "return-to-the-state" movement, see Peter B. Evans, Dietrick Rueschemeyer, and Theda Skocpol, eds., *Bringing the State Back In* (New York: Cambridge University Press, 1985).

30. Einaudi, *Roosevelt Revolution,* p. 60.

Notes for Chapter 6

1. J. Vincent and Vee Burke, *Nixon's Good Deed* (New York: Columbia University Press, 1974), 1.

2. The sentence immediately following was: "He would have been doubly mad if the prophet had also forecast that during the heat of the 1972 campaign, Nixon's Democratic rival for the presidency would delete help for the working poor from his own welfare platform."

3. For example, the Federal Deposit Insurance Corporation (FDIC) insures deposits up to $40,000 in the member banks of the Federal Reserve, and the Federal Savings and Loan Insurance Corporation (FSLIC) performs the same function for its member banks. In 1975 insured deposits were in the neighborhood of $520,300,000,000 and $278,774,000,000, respectively. Many of the Social Security titles are also nondiscretionary, while the other titles are discretionary but are not insurance. The latter titles are particularly important in the present context because, even though they are not as large, fiscally, as the other Social Security titles, they contribute with the other programs in Table 6.3 to the ability of the federal government to cement its ties to still another segment of the society—in this case the poor and dependent.

4. There is one other very important aspect of investment guarantee policies which is relegated to a note only because it is tangential to the present argument. Investment guarantees are completely "out-budget." Since there is no direct transfer of funds, there is no Treasury, OMB, or congressional clearance. Once Congress has set up the authorizing legislation, including a ceiling on the total commitments the insuring agency can extend, there is no further clearance activity until there are defaults to be liquidated. But this comes later, long after the initial commitment. Thus, an investment guarantee is "out-budget" at the beginning and "mandatory at the end."

5. Yale Commencement Address, Yale University, 1962.

6. Adam Yarmolinsky, *The Military Establishment* (New York: Harper and Row, 1971), pp. 154, 162–163.

7. Cf. Victor Navasky, *Kennedy Justice* (New York: Atheneum, 1971).

Notes for Chapter 7

1. Lawrence M. Friedman and Stewart Macaulay, *Law and the Behavioral Sciences,* 2nd ed. (Indianapolis: Bobbs-Merrill, 1977), p. 855.

2. Ibid.

3. Laurence Tribe, *American Constitutional Law* (Mineola, NY: Foundation Press, 1978), Chapter 18.

4. Lester Thurow, *The Zero-Sum Society* (New York: Basic Books, 1980).

5. R. Wilson, "Analyzing the Daily Risks of Life," *Technology Review* 81 (1979): 40–46.

6. Roger G. Noll, "What Is Regulation?" Social Science Working Paper 324 (Pasadena: California Institute of Technology, 1980).

7. Robert Summers and Charles G. Howard, *Law: Its Nature, Function and Limits* (Englewood Cliffs, NJ: Prentice-Hall, 1972).

8. H.L.A. Hart, *The Concept of Law* (New York: Oxford University Press, 1961).

9. Theodore J. Lowi, "Four Systems of Policy, Politics and Choice," *Public Administration Review* 32 (1972): 298–310.

10. Robert J. Spitzer, "The Presidency and Public Policy: A Preliminary Inquiry," *Presidential Studies Quarterly* 9 (1979): 441–456.

11. Theodore J. Lowi, *The End of Liberalism,* 2nd ed. (New York: W. W. Norton, 1979).

12. John Corson and R. S. Paul, *Men Near the Top* (Baltimore: Johns Hopkins University Press, 1966).

13. A. Darbel and D. Schnapper, *Les Agents du système politique* (Paris: Mouton, 1969) and *Le Système administratif* (Paris: Ecole Pratique des Hautes Etudes, 1972).

14. Darbel and Schnapper (1969), p. 126. Consensus does not exist on the definition of *corps.* For example, Sulieman defines *grands corps* to include major technical corps and the prefectoral corps. Without judging the merits of the differences, I am following Darbel-Schnapper because

their data are being used. Ezra Sulieman, *Politics, Power and Bureaucracy* (Princeton: Princeton University Press, 1974).

15. Note in Table 7.5 that in France redistributive agencies outrank regulatory agencies on unit differentiation. This could be true, but it is likely to disappear when agency size is controlled for. Since regulatory agencies tend to be smaller, the ratio of units to members is likely to be a great deal larger.

Notes for Chapter 8

1. Charles Hardin, *The Politics of Agriculture* (New York: The Free Press, 1952). "The study of a single phase of agriculture politics—such as soil conservation—will illuminate the whole" (p. 14).

2. Here lies the most divisive issue within the ranks of organized agriculture. The Farm Bureau–George Peek "conservatives" who produced and supported McNary-Haugenism were unalterably opposed to any form of agriculture regulation. Production controls they saw as leading to ultimate defeat before industry, leading to the creation of a smaller agricultural community unable to fight off the development of a permanent peasantry. On the other hand, there has never been any strong internal disagreement about such other programs as soil conservation and extension services (distribution) or farm credit (redistribution).

3. Charles Hardin, op. cit., p. 30.

4. Leverett S. Lyon, et al., *Government and Economic Life* (Washington: The Brookings Institution, 1940), Vol. II, pp. 874–875.

5. E. C. McArthur, first president of the National Association of Soil Conservation Districts, quoted in Hardin, op. cit., p. 57.

6. Herbert Kaufman, *The Forest Ranger* (Baltimore: Johns Hopkins Press, 1959), p. 30.

7. Charles A. Reich, *Bureaucracy and the Forests,* an occasional paper published by the Center for the Study of Democratic Institutions, Santa Barbara, 1962, p. 4. See also for example "Management of Public Land Resources," *Yale Law Journal* 60, no. 3: 455, where it is reported that while the Forest Service awards timber contracts by bidding, it can reject the highest bidder or all bids if in the Ranger's judgment the bidder has a bad reputation or if acceptance could lead toward a monopoly. For grazing, the Ranger may use any number of criteria for deciding on access, and he may alter the privilege in any way at any time. Ibid., p. 465.

8. Ibid., p. 4. Kaufman, op. cit., agrees and further emphasizes the practice by noting the policy of frequent rotation of foresters, employed to prevent too great a personal involvement (pp. 176–183). Kaufman is impressed with the degree to which the Rangers carry on actual negotiations (p. 192), and he shows at length how quickly a Ranger gets involved with the affairs and the interests of a new district (pp. 194–195).

9. See especially Arthur Maass, "Congress and Water Resources," *APSR* 49, no. 3 (1950).

10. *Government Organization Manual,* 1962–63, p. 265.

11. Robert E. Cushman, *The Independent Regulatory Commissions* (London: Oxford, 1941), p. 3.

Notes for Chapter 9

1. Paul A. Samuelson, *Economics,* 9th ed. (New York: McGraw-Hill, 1973), p. 14. For another view by a historian, see David H. Fischer, *Historians' Fallacies—Toward a Logic of Historical Thought* (New York: Harper Perennial, 1970), Chapter 8.

2. C. Wright Mills, *The Power Elite* (New York: Oxford, 1956), p. 9.

3. Ibid. The theory of balance, says Mills, "is mightily supported by the notion of an automatic economy in which the problem of power is solved for the economic elite by denying its existence. No one has enough power to make a real difference; events are the results of an anonymous balance. For the political elite too, the model of balance solves the problem of power. Parallel to the market economy, there is the leaderless democracy in which no one is responsible for anything and everyone is responsible for everything; the will of men acts only through the impersonal workings of the electoral process" (p. 17n). This is confirmed and expanded in *The End of Liberalism*, Chapters 2 and 3.

4. For example: "Pluralists ... see American society as fractured into a congeries of hundreds of small special interest groups.... In the decision-making of fragmented government ... the claims of small, intense minorities are usually attended to.... The empirical evidence supporting this pluralist doctrine is overwhelming." Polsby, *Community Power and Political Theory*, p. 118. In context this was an argument against Marxian assumptions about class as a base for social actions, but it reveals some pretty shaky assumptions of its own.

5. Ibid.

6. Quoted in P. H. Odegard, "The Group Basis of Politics: A New Name for an Ancient Myth," *Western Political Quarterly* (September 1958): 696.

7. Truman, *The Governmental Process*, p. 155. See also pp. 159–160.

8. Ibid., p. 24 and Chapter 2.

9. Ibid., p. 156.

10. Ibid., p. 157.

11. Raymond A. Bauer, Ithiel de Sola Pool, and Lewis Anthony Dexter, *American Business and Public Policy: The Politics of Foreign Trade* (Chicago: Aldine-Atherton, 1972), p. 332n.

12. Ibid., pp. 333–338.

13. Ibid., p. 338.

14. A peak association is an association of associations. It is an interest group whose members are other interest groups rather than individuals or individual firms. Peak associations are often called federations. Key examples include the National Association of Manufacturers, National Federation of Independent Business (NFIB), American Federation of Labor (AFL), and American Farm Bureau Federation (AFBF).

15. Robert E. Lane, *The Regulation of Businessmen* (New Haven, CT: Yale University Press, 1953), pp. 38ff. Lane's content analyzed the MAC's monthly magazine, *Connecticut Industry*, looking primarily for patterns of response over time to government programs. Lane tabulated responses on nine issues. Of these, the Office of Price Administration (OPA), a wartime agency, was eliminated because it was tabulated only for the two postwar years. All the others are treated for the entire ten-year period.

16. "Organized to Serve Industry," a pamphlet published by MAC, p. 1.

17. Thus, on a "per-issue" basis, redistributive expressions outnumbered regulative 251 to 51. Note also that there were no expressions at all on anything resembling distributive policies, such as tariffs and public works. This could be due to Lane's desire to focus on only those policies he deemed "regulation of businessmen." But judging from the problems such groups have had in these matters in recent years, it is possible that in fact MAC made no references at all to distributive issues.

18. Andy Biemiller—former member of Congress, a long-term lobbyist for AFL-CIO and a professor at Cornell—observed in an interview at Cornell that AFL-CIO conventions always discuss, debate, and pass strong policy positions on welfare, Social Security, and wages, but rarely debate and adopt strong policy positions "on Landrum-Griffin and reform of Taft-Hartley because we can't take a position that a large majority of delegates could enthusiastically endorse!"

19. The two columns do not add up to 100 percent because of a third category, "instrumental" or "neutral" expressions that advise the members, as a good trade association should.

20. Lane identified eight themes. The others were: "poor personnel," "red tape," "expensive," "political, biased," "confused of purpose," "makes uncertainty," and "too extensive."

21. The figures for this response are: trade practices, 31.2 percent; Robinson-Patman, 41.5 percent; antitrust, 35.0 percent; basing points, 32.2 percent; and fair trade, 46.0 percent.

22. Truman, *The Governmental Process*, pp. 362–364. The cases Truman uses are consistent with the Arenas of Power scheme, although there are three rather than two types of relation possible in the arenas of power. See also below.

23. Lester W. Milbrath, *The Washington Lobbyists* (Chicago: Rand McNally, 1963), p. 170.

24. Ibid., pp. 169–174. A good example is his final summarizing sentence: "Collaboration is useful only in certain settings and ... it is unwise where the conditions are not appropriate" (p. 174).

25. Ibid., p. 171.

26. Generally, "strategy" is defined as the basic campaign plan. Applied here it refers more specifically to (1) the types of people and interests a given leader seeks to associate with and (2) the type of relationship or association the leader seeks to establish as his means of gaining support.

27. Truman, *The Governmental Process*, p. 362 and *passim*.

28. Ibid.

29. Ibid., p. 363.

30. Bertram M. Gross, *The Legislative Struggle* (New York: McGraw-Hill, 1953), p. 233. Illustrations are AMA organization of the medical profession; liquor industry use of its salesmen, its union leaders, its retail outlets; union leader campaigning for rank and file support; Secretary of Agriculture Charles F. Brannan's attempts to mobilize agriculture for his plan.

31. Ibid., p. 234. "One of the chief functions of the 'peak' associations in the business community is to develop unified action among the thousands of separate business groupings. The key to effective campaigning by a labor movement which is organizationally divided is the development of broad support among the rival labor organizations for identical objectives."

32. Ibid., p. 238.

33. Carl J. Friedrich, *Constitutional Government and Democracy* (Boston: Ginn, 1947), pp. 297–298.

34. See Chapter 6.

35. Truman, *The Governmental Process*, p. 363.

36. Repeating Schattschneider on the tariff: "a policy that is so hospitable and catholic ... disorganizes the opposition," *Politics, Pressures, and the Tariff*, p. 88. It is also interesting to note that at the local level it is only in the distributive arena that the party machine has been able to maintain its control. Over 90 percent of the top appointees in such agencies had been party functionaries prior to appointment. In contrast, the average is closer to 20 percent among commissioners of 1790–1950 (New York: Twentieth Century Fund, 1953), p. 221n.

37. Representatives of the following organizations participated in the formation of the Corn Belt Committee: Missouri Farmers Association, National Producers Alliance, Farmers' Educational and Cooperative Union of America, National Corn Growers Association, Iowa Farm Bureau Federation, American Council of Agriculture, North Dakota Producers Alliance, Farmers' National Union of America, Equity Cooperative Exchange, Kansas Farmers Union, Iowa Farmers Union, South Dakota Farmers Union, Nebraska Farmers Union, Illinois Farmers Union, Nebraska Farm Bureau Federation, Minnesota Farm Bureau Federation, Iowa State

Grange, Chicago Milk Producers' Federation, Ottumwa Dairy Marketing Association, South Dakota Producers Alliance, Iowa Cooperative Creamery Association, Farmers Elevator Association of Iowa, and Minnesota Farmers Union.

38. See, for example, Gilbert C. Fite, *George Peek and the Fight for Farm Parity* (Norman: University of Oklahoma Press, 1954), p. 54. Most of the facts of this section come from this excellent biography and from Charles Hardin, *The Politics of Agriculture*; Wesley McCune, *The Farm Bloc* (Garden City: Doubleday, 1943); and Murray R. Benedict, *Farm Policies of the United States, 1790–1950.*

39. First, the coverage was expanded to include at least these three. But also, the pricing formula was now tied completely to the tariff by shifting from fixed ratio parity to a "world price plus the tariff." After an initial period, it was also understood that the co-ops would play the major role in distribution, so that there would be no chance of nonfarmer control.

40. Fite, *George Peek,* p. 68.

41. In a letter from Peek to Frank O. Lowden, March 24, 1926. Quoted in ibid., p. 152.

42. There were actually two formal means provided to insure commodity control of the board's decisions. The board could not act unless approved by the advisory councils composed of representatives of farm organizations dealing in the commodity; and it could not act unless the board members representing the districts where the majority of a crop was grown consented. See Fite, *George Peek,* p. 174.

43. Ibid., p. 171.

44. The general manager of the American Cotton Growers Exchange in 1927 put it this way. Noting that the Midwestern group would support nothing but the tariff, he explained to a friend, "Of course, in cotton we have no such views. We only want to take off the market temporarily unneeded surpluses.... However, we are in this difficult position ... that nothing will help wheat except an effective tariff added to the world price.... They do not want a loan bill and say it will not serve their purpose—we cannot get anything less without their approval and the support of their legislative representatives." (Quoted in ibid., p. 189.) Only the tariff could accommodate both wheat *and* cotton.

45. Arguments over whether this manipulation should be for price-raising or simply for price stabilization seem really merely arguments over proper rhetoric.

46. See, e.g., Fite, *George Peek,* Chapter 15. Peek resigned at the end of seven months.

47. There are at least ten separate, self-governing systems in the government-agriculture complex. See my "How Farmers Get What They Want," *The Reporter,* May 21, 1964; and *The End of Liberalism,* Chapter 4.

48. See ibid.

49. This section will only deal with internal dynamics. Concomitant changes in intergroup relations and in legislative process will be dealt with at the appropriate time.

50. Facts on the 1962 imbroglio taken from Bauer, Pool, and Dexter, *American Business and Public Policy,* pp. 333–334, and interviews with two legislative representatives of the U.S. Chamber of Commerce in Washington, April 1964. However, as usual the responsibility for interpretation rests with me.

51. See Alfred S. Cleveland, "NAM: Spokesmen for Industry?" *Harvard Business Review* 26, no. 3 (May 1948), and compare p. 356 and Appendixes A and B.

52. Cf. ibid., p. 361.

53. The facts and events are drawn from: Edwin E. Witte, *The Development of the Social Security Act* (Madison: University of Wisconsin Press, 1962); Paul H. Douglas, *Social Security in the United States* (New York: McGraw-Hill, 1936); Report to the President, Committee on Economic Security (GPO, 1935); and Frances Perkins, *The Roosevelt I Knew* (New York: Viking Press, 1946), pp. 279–301.

54. On the floor, both the Lundeen bill and the Townsend plan were offered as substitutes for the administration bill. Both received about 50 votes, and most of these were the votes of conservatives who hoped thereby to kill Social Security altogether.

55. Stephen Bailey, *Congress at Work* (New York: Holt, 1952), pp. 414–441; Seymour V. Mann, "Policy-Making in the Executive Branch," *Western Political Quarterly* (1960): 597–608; and Alonzo Hamby, *Beyond the New Deal: Harry S Truman and American Liberalism* (New York: Columbia University Press, 1973), pp. 180–185.

56. "A variant of avoiding internal friction is for a parent body to have a policy but not to enforce it on its members. The best example of this was the labor movement," p. 338. While AFL-CIO, UAW, and so on held actively to a policy of silence, unions in the bicycle, coal, textiles, glassware, chemicals, and other industries pressured in protectionist alliance with management organizations in those industries.

57. Avery Leiserson, "Organized Labor as a Pressure Group," *Annals of the American Academy of Political and Social Science* 274 (March 1951): 108.

58. Cf. Harry A. Millis and R. E. Montgomery, *Organized Labor* (New York: McGraw-Hill, 1945), pp. 761–762; and Harry A. Millis and Emily Clark Brown, *From the Wagner Act to Taft-Hartley* (Chicago: University of Chicago Press, 1950), pp. 76ff.

59. The theory of a fourth arena was not embraced until after the materials of Chapter 9 were developed. But it emerged quickly and distinctively once "constituent" was recognized as a type of policy and closed off the logic of the classification scheme. Its politics or power structure is as elitist as the redistributive arena, but not the same elite. It is best understood in comparison to the Grand Corps in France and the Senior Civil Service in Britain. Our constituent arena is an internal elite of career bureaucrats and career technicians whose power rests on control of information, the rules and procedures, precedents, and administrative integrity. [Editor's note, 2006.]

Notes for Chapter 10

1. David Hume, *A Treatise of Human Nature* (London: J. M. Dent, 1952, Everyman ed.), Vol. II, p. 239.

2. See also Theodore J. Lowi, "Decision Making vs. Policy Making: Toward an Antidote for Technocracy," *Public Administration Review* (May–June 1970): 320.

3. Compare Herbert Agar, *The Price of Union* (Boston: Houghton Mifflin, 1950), especially Chapters XII and XIV.

4. Ibid., and also Richard P. McCormick, "The Imperfect Union" (unpublished paper, Department of History, Rutgers University, 1971).

5. Some preliminary results of the study can be found in Lowi, "Decision Making," op. cit.; "Parallels of Policy and Politics: The Political Theory in American History," paper delivered to the Organization of American Historians, New Orleans, April 1971; and "The Four Systems of American Politics: How They Look from the Center," paper delivered to the Center for the Study of Democratic Institutions, Santa Barbara, July 1971. The entire study will be reported in *Arenas of Power.*

6. Lowi, "Decision Making," op. cit.

7. See, for example, Duncan MacRae, *Issues and Parties in Legislative Voting* (New York: Harper & Row, 1970), especially Chapters 3, 7, and 8.

8. Reported in Lowi, "The Four Systems of American Politics," op. cit.

9. Paul Ehrlich, *The Population Bomb* (New York: Ballantine, 1968).

10. A. E. Keir Nash, "Going Beyond John Locke? Influencing American Population Growth," *Milbank Memorial Fund Quarterly* XLIX, no. 1(January 1971): 3–31.

11. Some surface inconsistencies between the two schemes are due largely to the fact that the stress and purpose of the categorizations are not the same. This is not merely a semantic difference; nevertheless, with further discussion, the differences could be resolved in such a way as to produce a third scheme that is better than both for predicting and assessing the political consequences of political decisions. See ibid., p. 16.

12. Ibid., p. 15.

13. See, for example, Arthur Maass, "Congress and Water Resources," *American Political Science Review,* 1950; Maass, *Muddy Waters* (Cambridge: Harvard University Press, 1951); Grant McConnel, *Private Power and American Democracy* (New York: Knopf, 1966), especially Chapter 7; Philip O. Foss, *Politics and Grass* (Seattle: University of Washington Press, 1960); Lewis A. Dexter, "Congress and the Making of Military Policy," *New Perspectives on the House of Representatives,* Peabody and Polsby, eds. (Chicago: Rand McNally, 1969), Chapter VIII; and R. H. Dawson, "Congressional Innovation and Intervention in Defense Policy: Legislative Authorization of Weapons Systems," *American Political Science Review,* 1962.

14. See all of the above, especially Maass; also Stephen K. Bailey and Howard D. Samuel, *Congress at Work* (Hamden, CT: Shoe String Press, 1952), especially Chapters 5, 6, and 13; and Charles Hardin, *The Politics of Agriculture* (New York: Free Press, 1952).

15. Woodrow Wilson, *Congressional Government* (New York: Meridian, n.d.) especially pp. 58–81, where he fully describes and indicts "the imperious authority of the Standing Committees"; for a general historical review of the policies of that and other periods, see Lowi, "Parallels of Policy and Politics," op. cit.

16. A systematic analysis of a variety of distributive policies in different subject matter areas will be found in Lowi, "The Four Systems of American Politics," op. cit.

17. Randall Ripley, "Congress and Clean Air," *Congress and Urban Problems,* F. N. Cleaveland, ed. (Washington: The Brookings Institution, 1969).

18. Gary Orfield, *The Reconstruction of Southern Education* (New York: John Wiley, 1969).

19. Arthur Maass, "Congress and Water Resources," op. cit.

20. Nash, op. cit.

21. Judith Blake, "Population Policy for Americans: Is the Government Being Misled?" *Science* 164 (May 1969): 524–527.

22. Larry Bumpass and Charles F. Westoff, "The 'Perfect Contraceptive' Population," *Science* 169 (September 1970): 1177–1182, quoted with approval in Nash, op. cit., p. 18.

23. See, for example, Nash, op. cit., p. 18, who, despite considerable optimism regarding this second category of policies, admits the possible emergence of "the militants' charge that such schemes are—given the coincidence of minority racial status and poverty—sugar-coated genocide pills." See also the studies reported and evaluated in the *Wall Street Journal,* August 9, 1971, p. 1, which said that William A. Darity, head of the Department of Public Health at the University of Massachusetts, found that almost half of all black men under 30 in one New England city believed that encouraging birth control "is comparable to trying to eliminate [blacks] from society." This belief about genocide was held despite the fact that about 70 percent of the women the government expects to reach are white—according to the assessment of this article of the provisions of the "Tydings Act," passed in December 1970.

24. Nash, op. cit., p. 18.

25. Perhaps the best studies in constituent politics are of judicial structure and judicial reform, because here we find party dominance despite the sacred position of the judiciary. See, for example, Wallace Sayre and Herbert Kaufman, *Governing New York City* (New York: Russell Sage, 1960), Chapter XIV; see also Richard Harris, "Annals of Politics," *New Yorker,* December 5, 1970, pp. 60ff, and December 12, 1970, pp. 53ff. Historically, constituent policies played the

strongest role in the origin and shaping of our party system: See Joseph Charles, *The Origins of the American Party System* (New York: Harper and Row, 1961). For the pattern in organizational and procedural matters in Congress, see L. A. Froman and Randall Ripley, "Conditions for Party Leadership: The Case of the House Democrats," *American Political Science Review* (March 1965).

26. One might even say that this kind of controversy between Blake and Bumpass-Westoff over how to interpret statistical data is a solid foundation for partisan cleavage among scientists. There will be ample support for honest disagreement.

27. See David R. Manwaring, "The Flag-Salute Case," *The Third Branch of Government*, C. H. Pritchett and A. F. Westin, eds. (New York: Harcourt, 1963), Chapter 1.

28. See Theodore Marmor, *The Politics of Medicare* (London: Kegan Paul, 1970); Frank J. Munger and Richard Fenno, *National Politics in Federal Aid to Education* (Syracuse: Syracuse University Press, 1962); and Bailey and Samuel, op. cit., Chapter 12.

29. For example, compare the divisions among the rich and powerful in Raymond Bauer et al., *American Business and Public Policy* (New York: Atherton, 1963), with cohesiveness of business and their peak groups in Marmor, op. cit.

30. Labor is never as cohesive on labor-management regulation or on trade as it is on welfare and tax legislation. Compare Bauer, op. cit., and Alan McAdams, *Power and Politics in Labor Legislation* (New York: Columbia University Press, 1964) on Landrum-Griffin, with Marmor, op. cit., on Medicare-tax issues. For an assessment of how very special these redistributive issues are, even from the viewpoint of the presidency under Roosevelt, see Lowi, "The Four Systems of American Politics," op. cit.

31. Because redistributive agencies have longer histories in local government, the best cases will be found there. See, for example, Lowi, *At the Pleasure of the Mayor* (New York: Free Press, 1964), Chapters 6 and 7; also David Rogers, *110 Livingston Street* (New York: Random House, 1968). At the national level, the best view of this would be through Treasury or Federal Reserve. See Stanley Surrey, "The Congress and the Tax Lobbyist," *Harvard Law Review* 70 (1957): 1145ff.

32. See Nash, op. cit., p. 16.

33. See, for example, Julian Huxley, *Man in the Modern World* (New York: Mentor Books, 1948), pp. 28ff.

34. *Buck v. Bell*, 274 US 200 (1927).

35. Elmer E. Schattschneider, *The Semisovereign People* (New York: Holt, 1960), Chapters I and II.

36. See Lowi, *The End of Liberalism* (New York: W. W. Norton, 1969), *passim*, where this pattern is called "policy-without-law."

37. See, for example, the *Congressional Record* on Taft-Hartley or Landrum-Griffin.

38. For example, J. McGregor Burns's treatment in *Roosevelt: The Lion and the Fox* (New York: Harcourt, 1956): "Quite unwittingly the new President acted as midwife in the rebirth of labor action" (p. 215); "Neither Roosevelt nor Miss Perkins had much to do with this provision (Sec. 7a, NRA). Framed mainly by Congressmen and labor leaders, it was simply part of a bargain under which labor joined the NRA's great 'concert of interests'" (pp. 215–216); "Roosevelt failed to see the potentialities of an enlarged labor movement" (p. 216); The Wagner Act "was the most radical legislation passed during the New Deal ... [yet Roosevelt] ... threw his weight behind the measure only at the last moment, when it was due to pass anyway" (p. 219).

39. And the Court is always troubled by each abridgement it has validated. See, for example, its headaches and reversals in the Flag Salute Cases in Manwaring, op. cit. Or note its backward and forward motions and reluctance to issue leading opinions in the area of criminal justice and the area of the investigatory powers of congressional committees, in Philip Kurland, *The Warren Court and the Constitution* (Chicago: University of Chicago Press, 1970).

40. Jane Jacobs, *The Death and Life of Great American Cities* (New York: Vintage Books, 1963), especially Part Two.

41. See ibid., *passim,* for her general treatment of the problems inherent in all specialized land use.

42. Compare Lowi, *The End of Liberalism,* op. cit., and Grant McConnell, *Private Power and American Democracy* (New York: Knopf, 1966), especially Chapters 6–10.

Notes for Chapter 11

1. The following studies were invaluable in locating the several separate agriculture systems, although none of the authors necessarily shares my treatment of the cases or the conclusions I have drawn: Grant McConnell, *The Decline of Agrarian Democracy* (Berkeley: University of California Press, 1953); M. R. Benedict, *Farm Policies of the United States, 1790–1950* (New York: Twentieth Century Fund, 1953); Charles Hardin, *The Politics of Agriculture* (Glencoe: Free Press, 1952). However, the most important source was the U.S. Code. The secret of agriculture success, as well as the significance of interest group liberalism, lies in the extent to which pluralism is written into the statutes. No specific citations are made in the chapter because each system was pieced together from elements of all of the above sources.

2. See, for example, Chapter 5, in Lowi, *The End of Liberalism.*

3. Quoted in Grant McConnell, *Private Power and American Democracy* (New York: Knopf, 1966); see also Peri Arnold, "Herbert Hoover and the Continuity of American Public Policy," *Public Policy* (Autumn 1972): 525.

4. McConnell, p. 66.

5. Despite this weakness, the Fair Deal may have been less pluralistic than the programs of Eisenhower, Kennedy, and Johnson.

6. U.S. Code, *Congressional and Administration News* (1974): 5418–5419.

7. The railroad companies continue to own the tracks and to maintain the trains, for a fee paid to them by Amtrak. Legislation allowed the railroads either to receive Amtrak's stock for their fees or to treat their payment as a cost and take a tax write-off. Most chose the latter option, but four, who were in such bad shape they could not get an advantage from a tax write-off, chose to take stock. These four troubled companies became Amtrak's only shareholders. (The four were the Burlington Northern, Penn Central, Milwaukee, and Grand Trunk Western.) They also became the companies authorized to elect the three railroad representatives to the Amtrak board. Several of the so-called public members of the Amtrak board are also railroad or affiliated executives. See *Fortune,* May 1974, pp. 272–290. More on Consumer Products Safety will be found in Chapter 5.

8. *U.S. Code,* Vol. 3 (1970), pp. 5, 202–203. This means that many of the health and safety standards in this industry-wide safety program were to be those already developed and agreed upon by leading members of a trade association. To add insurance that standards would be acceptable to each industry, the law provided for a three-member Occupational Safety and Health Review Commission, an independent, quasi-judicial agency with power to review and set aside OSHA actions. The act also set up a National Institute for Occupational Safety and Health in the Department of Health, Education and Welfare to serve as a source of information on industry health standards. For further references to OSHA, see Chapter 5. For a reinforcing interpretation of OSHA see James E. Anderson, *Public Policy-Making* (New York: Praeger, 1975), pp. 116, 129–30.

9. *U.S. Code,* Vol. 42 (1973), section 101 and part A of Title III and Title IV. (Emphasis added.)

Notes for Chapter 12

1. For example, Robert F. Kennedy, *The Pursuit of Justice*, Theodore J. Lowi, ed. (New York: Harper & Row, 1964); Hobart Rowen, *The Free Enterprisers* (New York: Putnam, 1964); and Jim Heath, *JFK and the Business Community* (Chicago: University of Chicago Press, 1969).

2. For an excellent review of British practices and problems, see Anthony Lewis, "Edited by Lawyers," *New York Times,* July 31, 1975. As Lewis puts it, "American editors and publishers are rightly sensitive to anything that looks like an infringement of their freedom. But before their next speech about the First Amendment, some of them would do well to visit Britain.... Editing a newspaper in this country is a bit like walking through a minefield."

3. See also Henry Abraham, *Freedom and the Court,* 2nd ed. (New York: Oxford University Press, 1972), pp. 190–205.

4. For a worthwhile statement on these phenomena, see Octavio Paz, "Twilight of Revolution?" *Dissent* (Winter 1974): 56–62.

5. Hannah Arendt, *On Revolution* (New York: Viking Press, 1963), p. 21. This definition and several others are identified and compared in an excellent study: David V. J. Bell, *Resistance and Revolution* (Boston: Houghton Mifflin, 1973), pp. 7–13.

6. Mao Tse-tung, *Quotations from Chairman Mao* (Peking: Foreign Language Press, 1967), p. 7. Quoted in Bell, *Resistance and Revolution*, p. 8.

7. Ted R. Gurr, *Why Men Rebel* (Princeton: Princeton University Press, 1970), p. 11, assessed in Bell, *Resistance and Revolution*, p. 9.

8. See especially Louis Hartz, *The Liberal Tradition in America* (New York: Harcourt, Brace, 1955), Chapter 1.

9. For the best brief review, see Charles Tilly, "Collective Violence in European Perspective," in *The History of Violence in America*, Hugh Davis Graham and Ted Robert Gurr, eds. (New York: Bantam Books, 1969), Chapter I, p. 41.

10. For a comparison of earlier race riots to the ghetto protests and rebellions of the 1960s, see Robert M. Fogelson, "Violence as Protest," in *Proceedings of the Academy of Political Science* 29, no. 1 (1968): 25–41.

11. Herbert Gans, "The Ghetto Rebellions and Urban Class Conflict," in *Proceedings of the Academy of Political Science* 29, no. 1 (1968): 43–44.

12. Compare with Stanley Hoffmann, "Protest in Modern France," in *The Revolution in World Politics*, Morton Kaplan, ed. (New York: Wiley, 1962), p. 72.

13. The best brief review of this history will be found in Tilly, "Collective Violence in European Perspective."

14. See, for example, Irwin Unger, *The Movement—A History of the American New Left, 1959–1972* (New York: Dodd, Mead, 1974), especially pp. 101–116.

15. Philip Taft and Philip Ross, "American Labor Violence: Its Causes, Character, and Outcome," in *The History of Violence in America*, p. 281. See also Richard Rubenstein, *Rebels in Eden* (Boston: Little, Brown, 1970), p. 81.

16. Edmund Burke, *Reflections on the Revolution in France* (London, 1790).

17. See, for example, M. R. Benedict, *Farm Policies of the United States, 1790–1950* (New York: Twentieth Century Fund, 1953); and Grant McConnell, *The Decline of Agrarian Democracy* (Berkeley: University of California Press, 1953), especially his treatment of the rise and decline of the most radicalized segment of agriculture in the late nineteenth century, the People's Party.

18. J. David Greenstone, *Labor in American Politics* (New York: Knopf, 1969).

19. Compare with Daniel Bell, *The End of Ideology* (New York: Free Press, 1960), pp. 212–215.

20. See also Fogelson, "Violence as Protest," especially pp. 28–31.

21. For example, see Rubenstein, *Rebels in Eden*, p. 31.

22. Fogelson, "Violence as Protest," p. 35.

23. Ted Robert Gurr. "A Comparative Study of Civil Strife," in *The History of Violence in America*, Chapter 17, p. 587.

24. H. L. Nieburg, *Political Violence* (New York: St. Martin's Press, 1969), p. 13.

25. Compare with Allan Silver, "Official Interpretations of Racial Riots," *Proceedings of the Academy of Political Science* 29, no. 1 (1968): 146.

26. Saul Alinsky, *Reveille for Radicals* (Chicago: University of Chicago Press, 1946). See also Charles F. Levine, "The Political and Organizational Theory of Saul Alinsky" (Ph.D. dissertation, Stanford University, 1976).

27. Gans, "The Ghetto Rebellions and Urban Class Conflict," pp. 42–51.

28. Alexander Kendrick, *The Wound Within* (Boston: Little, Brown, 1974), p. 263.

29. Adam Yarmolinsky, *The Military Establishment* (New York: Harper & Row, 1971), p. 154.

30. Ibid., pp. 162–163.

31. Ibid., p. 374; Christopher H. Pyle, "CONUS Intelligence: The Army Watches Civilian Politics," in *Blowing the Whistle*, Charles Peters and Taylor Branch, eds. (New York, 1972), pp. 44–76; and Victor Navasky, *Kennedy Justice* (New York: Atheneum, 1971).

Notes for Chapter 13

1. Theodore J. Lowi, "The Welfare State, the New Regulation and the Rule of Law," in Allan Schnaiberg et al., *Distributional Conflicts in Environmental Resource Policy* (London: Gower, 1986), p. 113. My thanks to Schnaiberg for suggesting, albeit for different purposes, the first antinomy between error and sin.

2. George Will, *Statecraft as Soulcraft* (New York: Simon and Schuster, 1983), p. 20.

3. A formulation of mine in *The End of Liberalism* (New York: W. W. Norton, 1979).

Notes for Chapter 14

1. A. Chandler, *The Visible Hand* (Cambridge, MA: Harvard University Press, 1997), p. 364 (emphasis added).

2. George Soros, *The Crisis of Global Capitalism: Open Society Endangered* (New York: Perseus Books, 1998), p. 36.

3. Ibid., p. 128.

4. C. Crook, "The World Economy," *Economist*, September 20, 1997, p. 37.

5. B. Eichengreen, "The Tyranny of the Financial Markets," *Current History* 96 (1997): 377–382; P. Hirst, "The Global Economy: Myths and Realities," *International Affairs* 73, no. 3 (1997): 409–425.

6. J. Judis, "Fix It or Nix It," *American Prospect*, May 22, 2000, pp. 14–15.

7. An earlier passage in Chandler's important book emphasizes still further the capacity of the corporation to displace market mechanisms by internalization: "The first proposition is that modern multiunit business enterprise replaced small traditional enterprise when administrative coordination permitted greater productivity, lower cost, and higher profits *than coordination by market mechanisms*." Ibid., p. 6.

8. Max Weber, *General Economic History* (New Brunswick, NJ: Transaction Publishers, 1981), p. 277.

9. R. Reich, "Foreword," *The World Almanac and Book of Facts 2000* (Mahwah, NJ: Primedia Reference, 1999), p. 33.

10. J. Faux, "Whose Rules for Globalization?" *American Prospect,* June 5, 2000, p. 14.

11. Peter Johnson, *The Government of Money* (Ithaca, NY: Cornell University Press, 1998), Chapter 1.

12. Ibid., p. 6 (emphasis added).

13. "Regulating the Internet," *Economist,* June 10, 2000, pp. 73–79.

14. J. Faux, ibid.

15. T. Friedman, "The Datsun and the Shoe Tree," *American Prospect,* May 22, 2000, pp. 13, A23.

16. Friedman, no relation to Milton, is generally a left-leaning columnist, but on the macro economy he is a *gauleiter* of free trade. For example, to raise any objection or to fight for any amendment to the agreement to admit China to the WTO "is to speak utter nonsense," a "head-in-the-sand protectionism." T. Friedman, "Complete and Utter Nonsense," *New York Times,* May 16, 2000.

17. Wolfgang Streeck and Philippe Schmitter, "From National Corporatism to Transnational Pluralism: Organized Interests in the Single European Market," *Politics and Society* 19, no. 2 (1991): 133–164.

18. For a complementary treatment, see S. Mazey and J. Richardson, "Interest Groups in the European Community," *Pressure Groups,* Q. Richardson, ed. (Oxford: Oxford University Press, 1993), Chapter 13. Although they differ with Streeck and Schmitter on their bottom-line classification of the type of pluralism, they do indeed agree that it is a pluralistic, group-dominated process. For a more recent and more complex but consonant treatment of the same, see Richardson (1996).

19. Wolfgang Streeck and Philippe Schmitter, ibid., pp. 133–164; S. Mazey and J. Richardson, "Interest Groups in the European Community," *Pressure Groups,* Q. Richardson, ed. (Oxford: Oxford University Press, 1993), Chapter 13; J. Richardson, ed., *European Union: Power and Policy-Making* (London: Routledge, 1996), especially Chapters 1 and 11.

20. William Keller and Louis Pauly, "Globalization at Bay," *Current History* (November 1997): 370–376. This is an enlightening treatment of the continuing role of the nation-state in the "pluralistic" process of regulating market behavior in what appear superficially to be global markets.

21. Jeffrey Sachs, "Sachs on Globalization: A New Map of the World," *Economist,* June 24, 2000, pp. 81–83.

22. Sachs (2000): High tech innovation = ten patents or more per million population. Adopters = high-tech exports of at least 2 percent of GDP.

23. See especially Gwendolyn Mink, *Welfare's End* (Ithaca, NY: Cornell University Press, 1998).

24. S. Kostof, *The City Assembled* (Boston: Little, Brown, 1992), pp. 102–103. See also pp. 102–121 for a wealth of illustrations of what Kostof calls "keeping apart."

25. D. P. Jordan, *Transforming Paris* (New York: Free Press, 1995), p. 105.

26. F. Braudel, *The Structure of Everyday Life* (New York: Harper and Row, 1981), p. 518.

27. Ibid.

28. "The fundamental aim of the public place is to ensconce community and to arbitrate social conflict." S. Kostof, *The City Assembled* (Boston: Little, Brown, 1992), p. 124.

29. William Safran, *The French Polity,* 3rd ed. (New York: Longman, 1991), p. 217.

30. Ibid., pp. 217–218, 236.

31. Benjamin Ginsberg and Martin Shefter, *Politics by Other Means,* 2nd ed. (New York: W. W. Norton, 1999).

32. Philippe Schmitter, "Achieving Sustainable and Innovative Policies Through Participatory Governance in a Multilevel Context," introduction to the debate at a conference in Florence, 2000, unpublished.

33. H. George, *Progress and Poverty,* 50th anniversary ed. (New York: Robert Schalkenbach Foundation, 1948), p. 10.

34. Editorial, *Economist,* September 18, 1999, p. 31.

35. Hans-Dieter Klingemann and R. I. Hofferbert, "The Capacity of New Party Systems to Channel Discontent: A Comparison of 17 Formerly Communist Polities," in *Zur Zukunft der Demokratie,* H.-D. Klingemann and F. Neidhardt, eds. (Berlin: Sigma, 2000).

36. William Keller, Theodore Lowi, and Gerry Gendlin, "Negative Capital and the Wealth of Nations," *International Studies Perspectives* 1 (2000): 76.

37. Ibid., p. 22.

38. Alexis de Tocqueville, "Author's Preface to the Twelfth Edition," *Democracy in America* (New York: Knopf, 1945), p. 7.

Key Publications
by Theodore J. Lowi

1962. *Legislative Politics, U.S.A.* (ed.). Boston: Little, Brown; 2nd ed., 1965; 3rd ed., with Randall Ripley, 1973.

1964. *At the Pleasure of the Mayor: Patronage and Power in New York City, 1898–1958.* New York: Free Press.

1964. With Robert F. Kennedy. *The Pursuit of Justice.* New York: Harper and Row; Spanish edition, 1967; German edition, 1969.

1968. *Private Life and Public Order* (ed.). New York: W. W. Norton.

1969. *The End of Liberalism: The Second Republic of the United States.* New York: W. W. Norton; 2nd ed., 1979; Japanese edition, 1982; French edition, 1987.

1971. *The Politics of Disorder.* New York: Basic Books; 2nd ed., Norton Library, 1974.

1975. With Benjamin Ginsberg, Elliott J. Feldman, Gregory J. Nigosian, Jonathan Pool, Allen Rosenbaum, Carlyn Rottsolk, Margaret Stapleton, Judith Van Herik, Julia Vitullo-Martin, and Thomas Vitullo-Martin. *Poliscide: Scientists, the Giant Accelerator, and the Metropolis.* New York: Macmillan; 2nd ed., University Press of America, 1990.

1976. *American Government: Incomplete Conquest.* New York: Holt, Rinehart and Winston; 2nd ed., 1981, retitled *Incomplete Conquest: Governing America.*

1977. *American Government: Incomplete Conquest,* brief edition. Hinsdale, IL: Dryden Press.

1978. Coeditor and contributor. *Nationalizing Government: Public Policies in America.* Beverly Hills, CA: Sage.

1985. *The Personal President: Power Invested, Promise Unfulfilled.* Ithaca, NY: Cornell University Press; Spanish edition, 1993.

1990. *American Government: Power and Purpose,* with Benjamin Ginsberg and Kenneth A. Shepsle. New York: W. W. Norton; 10th edition, 2008.

1994. *Democrats Return to Power: Politics and Policy in the Clinton Era,* with Benjamin Ginsberg. New York: W. W. Norton.

1994. *Embattled Democracy: Politics and Policy in the Clinton Era,* with Benjamin Ginsberg. New York: W. W. Norton, 1995.

1995. *The End of the Republican Era.* Norman: University of Oklahoma Press; paperback edition, 1996; reissued with new afterword, 2006.

1997. *We the People,* with Benjamin Ginsberg and Margaret Weir. New York: W. W. Norton; 6th edition, 2007.

1998. *A Republic of Parties? Debating the Two-Party System,* with Joseph Romance. Lanham, MD: Rowman and Littlefield.

1999. *La scienza delle politiche.* Bologna: Società editrice il Mulino.
2002. *Essentials of American Politics,* with Robert J. Spitzer, Benjamin Ginsberg and Margaret Weir. New York: W. W. Norton; 2nd edition, 2006.
2008. *American Political Thought: A Norton Anthology,* with Isaac Kramnick. New York: W. W. Norton.
2008. *Arenas of Power,* edited and introduced by Norman K. Nicholson. Boulder, CO: Paradigm Publishers.

Index

Credits

Permission to reprint chapters from the following sources is gratefully acknowledged.

Chapter 1 reprinted from "American Business, Public Policy, Case Studies and Political Theory," *World Politics* 16, no. 4 (July 1964): 677–715.

Chapter 2 reprinted from "Four Systems of Policy, Politics, and Choice," paper delivered to Center for the Study of Democratic Institutions, July 1971; reprinted in *Public Administration Review* (July–August 1972): 298–310.

Chapter 5 reprinted from Theodore J. Lowi, "The Roosevelt Revolution and the New American State," from *Comparative Theory and Political Experience: Mario Einaudi and the Liberal Tradition,* edited by Peter J. Katzenstein, Theodore Lowi, and Sidney Tarrow. Copyright © 1990 by Cornell University. Used by permission of the publisher, Cornell University Press.

Chapter 6 reprinted from "Europeanization of America? From United States to United State," reprinted from Chapter 1 of Theodore Lowi and Alan Stone, eds., *Nationalizing Government: Public Policies in America* (Beverly Hills, CA: Sage Publications, 1978).

Chapter 7 reprinted from "The State in Politics: The Relation Between Policy and Administration," in Roger G. Noll, ed., *Regulatory Policy and the Social Sciences* (Berkeley: University of California Press, 1985), pp. 67–96.

Chapter 10 reprinted from "Population Policies and the American Political System," in A. E. Keir Nash, ed., *Governance and Population: The Governmental Implications of Population Change,* Research Reports Vol. 4 (Washington, DC: Commission on Population Growth and the American Future; Government Printing Office, 1972), pp. 283–300.

Chapter 11 reprinted from "The Perils of Patronage: Tendencies Toward Corporatism in the 'Clientele Agencies,'" Chapter 4 in Theodore Lowi, *The End of Liberalism,* 2nd ed. (New York: W. W. Norton, 1979), pp. 67–91.

Chapter 12 reprinted from "Prospects of Conquest: With Liberty and Justice for Some," Chapter 16 in Theodore Lowi, *American Government: Incomplete Conquest* (Hinsdale, IL: Dryden Press, 1976), pp. 691–707.

Chapter 13 reprinted from "New Dimensions in Policy and Politics," Foreword in Raymond Tatalovich and Byron W. Daynes, eds., *Social Regulatory Policy: Moral Controversies in American Politics* (Boulder, CO: Westview Press, 1988), pp. x–xxi.

Chapter 14 reprinted from "Our Millennium: Political Science Confronts the Global Corporate Economy," *International Political Science Review* 22, no. 2 (April 2001): 131–150.

About the Author

Theodore Lowi has been the John L. Senior Professor of American Institutions at Cornell University since 1972. He received his doctorate at Yale in 1961, and served on the Cornell faculty from 1959 to 1965, and on the political science faculty at the University of Chicago between 1965 and 1972. His primary fields are American government, political institutions, and public policy.

Elected to the American Academy of Arts and Sciences in 1977, Lowi is recipient of honorary doctoral degrees from Oakland University, the State University of New York–Stony Brook, the Fondation Nationale des Sciences Politiques of the University of Paris, and the University of Pavia, Italy. He is the only political scientist to have been elected president of the American Political Science Association, the Policy Studies Organization, and the International Political Science Association. In 2006 he was awarded the Stephen H. Weiss Presidential Fellowship for effective, inspiring, and distinguished teaching of undergraduate students.

Other than the completion of this volume—which has evolved over forty-five years—his recent work is a decade-long collaboration with his Cornell colleague Isaac Kramnick, *American Political Thought—A Norton Anthology* (2008). Another ten-year collaboration, with Mauro Calise, University of Naples, will be published in 2009: *Hyperpolitics—An Interactive Dictionary of Political Science.*

Leisure time is devoted to family and, in collaboration with coauthors, to keeping two American government textbooks up-to-date and ahead of the competition.

About the Editor

Norman K. Nicholson received his PhD from Cornell University, where he also did postdoctoral work in agricultural economics. He has taught at Northern Illinois University, Cornell University, and George Mason University. He is currently coordinator for bilateral and multilateral relations at the United States Agency for International Development (USAID). (The views expressed in this volume should in no way be interpreted as representing the views of USAID.) He has published on a variety of topics related to development, including political economy, agricultural development and food policy, and development administration. He has had extensive experience in development policy analysis, program and project design, and associated field research in Central America and the Caribbean, Africa, the Middle East, and South and East Asia.